D0341129

FEDERATION CANADIENNE DES SCIENCES SOCIALES
SOCIAL SCIENCE FEDERATION OF CANADA
151 Slater Street
Ottawa, Ontario
K1P 5H3

TIME OF FEAR AND HOPE

The North Atlantic Treaty was born out of fear and frustration: fear of the aggressive and subversive policies of Communism and the effect of those policies on our own peace and security and well-being; frustration over the obstinate obstruction by Communist states of our efforts to make the United Nations function effectively as a universal security system. This treaty, though born of fear and frustration, must, however, lead to positive social, economic, and political achievements if it is to live – achievements which will extend beyond the time of emergency which gave it birth, or the geographical area which it now includes.

LESTER B. PEARSON

At the signing of the
North Atlantic Treaty
April 4, 1949

Escott Reid

TIME OF FEAR AND HOPE

The Making of the
North Atlantic Treaty
1947-1949

McClelland and Stewart

Copyright ©1977 by Escott Reid

All rights reserved

0-7710-7440-9

The Canadian Publishers
McClelland and Stewart Limited
25 Hollinger Road
Toronto, Ontario

Printed and bound in Canada

Canadian Cataloguing in Publication Data

Reid, Escott, 1905-
Time of fear and hope

Bibliography: p.
Includes index.
ISBN 0-7710-7440-9

1. North Atlantic Treaty, 1949.
2. North Atlantic Treaty Organization.
I. Title.

D845.R43   355.03'1   C77-000115-7

The book has been published
with the help of a grant from the
Social Science Research Council
of Canada, using funds provided
by the Canada Council.

CONTENTS

Acknowledgements

I am most grateful to Arthur Blanchette and other members of the Historical Division of the Department of External Affairs of Canada for helping me to locate documents in the archives of the Department and to John A. Munro and Alex I. Inglis, the editors of the second volume of Lester Pearson's memoirs, for lending to me the documents on the North Atlantic treaty which they had assembled for Mr. Pearson, when he was writing his memoirs.

I am grateful to the Canada Council for a grant toward my expenses in writing this book. I am also grateful to Queen's University in Kingston, Ontario; I began working on the book when I was Skelton-Clark fellow there. My thanks are due to the Rockefeller Foundation for its hospitality at the Villa Serbelloni, Bellagio.

J. D. Hickerson and T. C. Achilles have been most generous in the encouragement and help which they have given me. They both read the entire manuscript in draft and made extensive comments. Lord Inchyra (formerly F. Hoyer Millar) also read the entire manuscript and made constructive suggestions. I consulted many others during the writing of this book. The list of persons to whom I am indebted includes but is not limited to: William P. Bundy, Michael G. Fry, Lord Gladwyn (formerly Gladwyn Jebb), and John W. Holmes.

Anne Evans, working under the direction of Professor Fry, checked the quotations and prepared the list of works cited and the references. Audrey McQuarrie typed and retyped the manuscript with extraordinary speed and accuracy. I am indebted to John Roberts of McClelland and Stewart for his help and encouragement.

Some of the material in the book appeared in my essay, "The Birth of the North Atlantic Alliance", *(International Journal,* Vol. XXII, No. 3, Summer, 1967), and some in my essay, "Canada and the Creation of the North Atlantic Alliance, 1948-1949", in *Freedom and Change: Essays in Honour of Lester B. Pearson,* edited by Michael G. Fry (Toronto, McClelland and Stewart) 1975.

PREFACE

The North Atlantic treaty of 1949 created the first multilateral military alliance to span the North Atlantic Ocean in time of peace. The alliance possessed in 1949 preponderant power over any potential adversary or combination of adversaries; not power to defend but power to defeat and thus to deter. The last time a comparable grand alliance had been created in peacetime was in 1815 after Waterloo when Britain, Austria, Prussia and Russia formed the quadruple alliance to keep Napoleon and his family off the throne of France and to defend the territorial settlement of the Congress of Vienna. That alliance lasted only seven years.

The North Atlantic treaty was a cover for a world-wide alliance against the Soviet Union of what were in 1949 the three great powers of the western world, the United States, Britain and France. The treaty committed them to come to each other's assistance only if one of them were attacked in the North Atlantic treaty area but, from the opening of the intergovernmental discussions in March, 1948, it was, as the Canadian Ambassador in Washington reported at the time, recognized that if a war between the Soviet Union and one of these powers "were to start anywhere in the world (e.g. by a Soviet attack on the U.S. forces in Korea), the North Atlantic agreement would be certain to come into operation, as attacks in the North Atlantic area would inevitably take place."[1] Less than four years after the ending of hostilities in the Second World War, the principal allies of the Soviet Union in that war entered into a military alliance directed against it.

The entry of the United States into the North Atlantic alliance was "one of the most far-reaching commitments the United States had ever made . . . ".[2] It constituted a revolutionary change in American foreign policy. During the century and a half since the termination in 1800 of the Franco-American alliance, the United States had never in time of peace made a military alliance with a European power. After the First World War, it had refused to ratify the treaty of alliance with France which Woodrow Wilson had signed in June, 1919. What the United States refused to do after the First World War, it did after the Second.

9

It was not only the United States which made a revolutionary change in its foreign policy when it joined the North Atlantic alliance. Canada had consistently refused to pledge itself in peacetime to defend any other country, even Britain or the United States, and since the Napoleonic wars Norway, Denmark and Iceland had never been involved in military alliances in peacetime.

The signing of the North Atlantic treaty, as Arnold Toynbee pointed out three years later,

> put an end to a debate about the policy which the western European states should adopt in the face of American-Russian rivalry. The ten European states that signed the treaty were thereby committing themselves outright to an alliance with the United States; and this positive act was politically and psychologically important, even though there had been a certain unreality about earlier suggestions that a 'neutral bloc' or a 'third force' might be fashioned out of a western Europe which, since the overthrow of the Nazi domination, had been dependent on American economic aid for its recovery and indeed for its survival.[3]

The Canadian government was the first government to suggest (in September, 1947) that "democratic and peace-loving states" might have to establish a collective defence association. The British government initiated in March, 1948, the multilateral intergovernmental discussions which resulted in the North Atlantic treaty. A British assessment of the dangers of the international situation, not a United States assessment, provided the background against which the Canadian government decided to participate in those discussions. During the first four months of the discussions, when there was powerful opposition within the United States administration to the idea of a North Atlantic treaty, Britain and Canada pressed hard in private in Washington for a treaty and Canada also conducted a public crusade for the treaty.

C. R. Attlee, the British Prime Minister at the time, took great pride in his share of responsibility for the creation of the treaty, but he gave much the larger share of the credit to his Foreign Minister, Ernest Bevin. In his memoirs, Attlee referred to the "making of the Brussels treaty and the Atlantic Pact" as "the work of Bevin" and in his broadcast on the death of Bevin, he said,

> It was largely due to his initiative that the Brussels Treaty and the Atlantic Treaty came into being. He rightly regarded the establishment of the Atlantic Treaty as one of his greatest achievements, and history will confirm that judgment.[4]

"The British government," Alastair Buchan has written, "felt that half a century of diplomatic effort had been successfully crowned by the permanent commitment of American power to the defence of Western Europe."[5] The creation of the North Atlantic alliance was the swan-song of Britain as a major power. Henceforth Britain became more and more the junior partner of the United States.

The North Atlantic treaty of 1949 was not the result of American cold war policies; it is not an example of the United States persuading other countries to support its cold war politices; but after the outbreak of the Korean War in the summer of 1950, the alliance became the principal instrument of the cold war policies of the United States.

The United States, Britain and Canada constituted an inner group in the intergovernmental discussions which resulted in the North Atlantic treaty. They drafted the general outlines of the treaty in very secret three-power talks at the end of March, 1948. When France and Belgium were being hesitant in the six-power discussions in Washington in the summer of 1948 and the Netherlands seemed lukewarm, each of the inner three used its persuasive powers in Paris, Brussels and The Hague.

This was not the first time that Canada had been a member, along with the United States and Britain, of an inner group of three drafting an important new international agreement. It had happened in the formation of the Food and Agriculture Organization, the United Nations Relief and Rehabilitation Agency, the International Monetary Fund, the World Bank and the International Civil Aviation Organization. It was, however, the last time that Canada played such a role. After 1949 countries such as France, Italy, Germany and Japan, which, because of defeat or occupation, had lost their normal influence, quickly began to get it back.

Lester Pearson was one of the half-dozen principal architects of the North Atlantic treaty. I was his second-in-command in the Department of External Affairs in Ottawa from April, 1947, to March, 1949. It was during these two years that the North Atlantic treaty was conceived and brought to birth. Pearson's two chief advisers in the negotiation of the treaty were Hume Wrong, the Canadian Ambassador in Washington, who represented Canada in the intergovernmental talks in Washington, and I who drafted in Ottawa most of the memoranda, speeches and telegrams on North Atlantic treaty matters. Wrong died in 1954. Wrong's assistant in the negotiations was T.A. Stone who died in 1965. During the first three months of the intergovernmental discussions (March to June, 1948) only seven cabinet ministers and officials in Ottawa were permitted to see the telegrams on the discussions.* Of these I am the only survivor.

*W.L. Mackenzie King (Prime Minister), Louis S. St. Laurent (Secretary of State for External Affairs), L.B. Pearson (Under-Secretary of State for External Affairs), Brooke Claxton (Minister of National Defence), General Charles Foulkes (Chairman of the Chiefs of Staff Committee), Arnold Heeney (Secretary of Cabinet), and Escott Reid.

This is a book on the *making* of the North Atlantic treaty. It is not a history of the North Atlantic alliance, nor an assessment of its accomplishments and failures. For this a separate volume would be required and a different author. Almost immediately after the treaty was signed I ceased to have direct responsibility in the Department of External Affairs for matters relating to the North Atlantic alliance and in 1952 I left Ottawa to be High Commissioner to India and subsequently Ambassador to Germany.

I look back with pride on the part which I played in the making of the North Atlantic treaty. But when I look back on the experience, I also find myself echoing what Dean Acheson said of his years in the State Department: "Yet an account of the experience, despite its successes, inevitably leaves a sense of disappointment and frustration, for the achievements fell short of both hope and need."[6]

I have tried in this book not to confuse what I now think about events in 1947, 1948 and 1949 with what I then thought, what other participants then thought and what they thought later. This means that, wherever possible, I have used contemporary accounts, not recollections. Memory is errant. I have tried to be objective but I know that my objectivity is flawed by my belief – natural to one who worked hard for the success of the negotiations on the treaty – that my efforts were worthwhile, and that the world would be worse off today if there had been no North Atlantic treaty. We who took part in the struggle for the treaty know that there was nothing inevitable about the treaty. There might have been no treaty. There might have been a better treaty or a worse treaty. We know that what we felt and thought and did at the time, that our insights and our errors, are reflected in the text of the treaty. I try in this book to explain why there was a treaty and why the treaty took the shape it did.

Ste. Cécile de Masham,
Québec, October, 1976

PART ONE

THE CONCEPTION
OF THE TREATY

CHAPTER ONE

FEAR

Je suis, quant à moi, à peu pres convaincu que les Soviets ne nous atta-
queront pas. Mais ce n'est pas comme si je disais – 'Je crois qu'il fera
beau, je ne prendrai pas mon parapluie!' Il s'agit d'eviter à la France le
malheur d'une nouvelle occupation tellement plus terrible que la
précédente et peut-être de sauver des millions de vies humaines. C'est
une responsabilité qu'on ne peut prendre à la légère. Or, nos
renseignements ne nous permettent pas de conclure à l'impossibilité
absolue d'une invasion soviétique. Nous devons donc essayer de parer
à ce risque.

Georges Bidault
Foreign Minister of France
July 18, 1948[1]

The governments of the three principal western powers, the United
States, Britain and France, believed in the spring of 1948, when the intergovernmental discussions on the North Atlantic treaty began, that the
Soviet government did "not want war at this time",[2] that it did not intend
to push "things to the extreme of war"[3] and that there was "no clear indication that the U.S.S.R. is now prepared to make war."[4] The first quotation is from the United States Secretary of State, General George
Marshall, the second from the British Foreign Secretary, Ernest Bevin,
and the third from the French Foreign Minister, Georges Bidault. The
statements were made in May, April and June of 1948 respectively. They
were made in private communications between the three governments.

In July, Field Marshal Montgomery, who was about to be appointed
chairman of the commanders-in-chief committee of the Brussels treaty
powers, told the British and Canadian Ambassadors in Paris that he "did
not think there existed an immediate danger of war. The Russians could

not make war now. Many of their industrial centres were destroyed . . . . The critical time might well be in four or five years during the 1952 United States presidential elections. If the U.S.S.R. wished to fight that would appear to be a danger period."[5]

This does not mean that the governments which took part in the negotiations on the North Atlantic treaty in 1948, the governments of the United States, Britain and France, the Benelux countries and Canada, ruled out the possibility of war with the Soviet Union breaking out in 1948 or shortly thereafter. In September, 1948, the negotiating group in Washington, composed of representatives of these governments, stated in a top-secret report to their governments that the Soviet Union was strategically capable of dominating the continent of Europe by force and that its armed forces could take the initiative at short notice. This supported "the Kremlin program of intimidation designed to attain the domination of Europe." The report went on to say,

> While there is no evidence to suggest that the Soviet government is planning armed aggression as an act of policy, there is always the danger that, in the tense situation existing at the present time, some incident might occur which would lead to war. War might also come about by a miscalculation of western intentions on the part of the Soviet government. Alternatively, a sudden decision by the Kremlin leaders to precipitate war might result from fear: (1) that their own personal power was being undermined, or (2) that Soviet strength in relation to that of the western nations was declining, or (3) that these nations had aggressive intentions toward the Soviet Union.[6]

This paragraph in the report may well have been written by one or both of the two chief experts on the Soviet Union in the State Department, George Kennan and Charles Bohlen, since it reflects accurately what Kennan said in July to the negotiating group on behalf of Bohlen and himself.

> Kennan expressed disbelief that the Soviet leaders contemplated launching world conflict by armed force . . . . [The Kremlin] believed it could win ideologically more easily than militarily. It was not operating on any fixed timetable, and parallels between Stalinism and Hitlerism were dangerous. The lack of a Soviet plan did not mean that the Russians might not be brought to take military action. The greatest danger would be in an abrupt weakening of their power in eastern Europe, which in their view might leave no choice other than military action.[7]

In an off-the-record speech six weeks before, Kennan had said, "It would be frivolous to say that there is no danger of war with Russia . . . . Had we failed to provide aid for Europe and had the Communists won the Italian

14

election [in April, 1948] . . . . the chances of war would have been greatly increased."[8]

Kennan was at the time director of the policy planning staff of the State Department. At the end of November, 1948, he submitted to the Secretary of State a paper from his staff which dealt with the tense situation created by the Soviet blockade of Berlin and the western airlift:[9]

A military danger, arising from possible incidents or from the prestige engagement of the Russians and the western powers in the Berlin situation, does exist, and is probably increasing rather than otherwise. But basic Russian intent still runs to the conquest of western Europe by political means. In this program, military force plays a major role only as a means of intimidation. The danger of political conquest is still greater than the military danger. If war comes in the foreseeable future, it will probably be one which Moscow did not desire but did not know how to avoid.

According to a note in the margin of this paper "there was no disagreement anywhere", (presumably in the State Department) with this statement.

Arthur Vandenberg, the influential Republican Chairman of the Senate Foreign Relations Committee, put the point succinctly in a letter on December 11, 1948: "Soviet aggression depends upon many other devices than war. Indeed 'war' is the last implement they want to invoke."[10]

The report of September, 1948, of the six-power negotiating group in Washington stated that a sudden decision of the Kremlin leaders to precipitate war might result from fear that the western nations had aggressive intentions toward the Soviet Union. By "western nations" the negotiating group presumably meant the United States with its monopoly of the atomic bomb, a monopoly which it was then expected might last for three or four years.[11] This monopoly was bound to give rise to apprehensions, which were not confined to the Soviet government, that the United States might precipitate war with the Soviet Union while it still had that monopoly. Thus John W. Holmes, the Canadian chargé d'affaires in Moscow, in a report to Ottawa at the beginning of April, 1948, said, "It is frequently said here among westerners that the real danger of war in the near future comes from the trigger-happy U.S. military, who argue that the best way to prevent the next war is to drop an atom bomb on the Kremlin", meaning, of course, by this not just bombs on Moscow but on other centres of Soviet production and distribution. Holmes did not himself believe that there was any real danger that the United States would launch a preventive war. What he feared was that the western powers might draw the Russians on to ground from which they could not retire "without a loss of face they could not contemplate."

He concluded his report to Ottawa as follows: "It seems to me . . . of desperate importance that we use our considerable influence in the coming months to prevent the United States from taking heady action without calculating the consequences."[12]

Ernest Bevin, a couple of weeks later, brought his influence to bear on Washington. In a message to Marshall he said that the United States and Britain must avoid two dangers: they must not allow themselves to be provoked into any ill-considered action which might land them in an impossible position from which it would be difficult for them to retreat; and they must likewise be careful, while remaining firm, not to provoke the Russians into ill-considered actions from which it would be difficult for them to retreat. The motto of the United States and Britain must be moderation, patience and prudence combined with firmness and toughness.[13]

Four months later the French used more forthright language in warning the United States against what Bevin had called "ill-considered action". At the beginning of August Armand Bérard, the second-in-command at the French embassy in Washington, speaking under instructions from Paris, said to Charles Bohlen, the Counsellor of the State Department, that the French government felt that "the developments in regard to Germany and in particular [the United States'] attitude thereto might well bring matters to a head in Europe" before the western European countries had been strengthened by United States support and especially military supplies. What his government had in mind were the "very strong statements from Berlin about armed convoys and not getting out of Berlin short of war," which General Lucius Clay, the Commander-in-Chief of the United States forces in Europe, had been making.[14]

On March 15, 1948, George Kennan had made a recommendation to Marshall which, like Clay's, might have brought matters to a head in Europe if adopted. Kennan's recommendation was that because a Communist victory in the general elections in Italy on April 18 would probably undermine "our whole position in [the] Mediterranean and possibly in Western Europe", the Italian government should outlaw the Communist party and take strong action against it before the election.

> Communists would presumably reply with civil war, which would give
> us grounds for reoccupation [of] Foggia fields or any other facilities we
> might wish. This would result in much violence and probably a mili-
> tary division of Italy . . . .[15]

The rejection by the United States government of both these risky proposals indicated that its motto was, indeed, that which Bevin had recommended, "moderation, patience and prudence combined with firmness and toughness."

All the conclusions of responsible western governments in 1948 about

Soviet intentions and capabilities and the risk of war had to be very tentative. There were too many unknowns. Georges Bidault, the Foreign Minister of France, put this point well in July, 1948, when he said to the Canadian Ambassador to the Netherlands,

> I am almost convinced that the Soviet Union will not attack us. But that's not the same thing as saying 'I believe it's going to be a fine day and I'm not taking my umbrella' . . .. Our information does not permit us to conclude in the absolute impossibility of a Soviet invasion. [16]

When Bidault warned that it was not possible to be absolutely certain that the Soviet Union would not make an overt military attack on western Europe he was expressing a scepticism which the Canadian chargé d'affaires in Moscow put in his report from Moscow on April 9, 1948. After summarizing the April 1 report of the United States embassy in Moscow on Soviet intentions and capabilities which had concluded that the "Soviet Union will not deliberately resort to military action in the immediate future but will continue to attempt to secure its objectives by other means",[†17] he warned that it would be unwise to attach too much weight to opinions from embassies in Moscow. Contact between western diplomats and Soviet officials had completely ceased.

> [N]ot even the most distinguished western ambassadors have any way of finding out what Soviet officials are thinking. It is no longer possible even to establish contact with the satellite ambassadors. In this respect, I think, the U.S. embassy report is deceptive. It is an extremely competent and lucid statement, but it is too categorical and perhaps too lucid. I have grave doubts if the embassy officers, although they are undoubtedly all very able, can know as much as they appear to know about the state of this country.[18]

Scepticism about the possibility of being certain about Soviet intentions meant that, in spite of all the agreed appreciations that there was no evidence that the Soviet Union was contemplating making an armed attack on western Europe, a fear persisted that the Soviet Union might do just that. Pearson put this apprehension about the immediate future in a letter to a cabinet colleague on May 3, 1948:

> Until the western world has forces in being rather than merely potential forces, there is little that the western world can now do to prevent a Soviet occupation of the whole of western Europe. The immediate danger now, it seems to me, is that the Soviet leaders may decide to occupy western Europe before the United States and the other western countries have been able to build up their forces to a sufficient extent to give them some reasonable chance of holding western Europe. This danger may last for two years or longer, depending on how long it

17

takes the United States and the other western countries to build up their forces in western Europe.[19]

On the whole, the government in Ottawa was more pessimistic about the possibility of war than the governments in London, Washington and Paris. Mackenzie King states in his diary that on March 15, 1948, a few days after receiving the messages from the British government proposing talks in Washington between the United States, Britain and Canada on a North Atlantic treaty, he told the leaders of the three opposition parties, "We might see fire around the world before very long. . . . It was not possible to say that war was certain; equally it was not possible to say that with the horizon as we saw it, there was not immediate danger of war".[20] Pearson in September, 1948, in his first public speech as Foreign Minister of Canada, said that "though war is by no means inevitable, there is a risk that war may break out at any time. The extent of this risk is incalculable, but its existence cannot be denied. It is greater today probably than at any time since the war ended a short three years ago."[21]

While the Canadian government was, in 1948, more pessimistic than the governments of the United States, Britain and France, the governments of Norway and Denmark were alarmist. They both feared, in the spring of 1948, an armed invasion by the Soviet Union. Norway was a neighbour of the Soviet Union. Denmark was only thirty miles from the Soviet Zone of Germany. Both were acutely conscious of how weak and exposed they were. On March 8 the Norwegian Foreign Minister asked Britain (and presumably the United States) "what help they might expect to receive if attacked".[22] Two weeks later, the Danish Foreign Minister sent for the United States Ambassador and disclosed the acute nervousness of the Danish government. He listed the numerous precautionary measures the government was taking to guard against internal attempts of the communists and to prepare against a possible Soviet invasion, and he emphasized that Denmark was determined to resist to the last any Soviet aggression.[23]

The policies of the United States, British and French governments in 1948 were thus based on belief that the Soviet government did not want war. The governments did not dismiss the possibility of war with the Soviet Union breaking out in 1948 or shortly thereafter but they believed that the clear and present danger was not a Soviet invasion of western Europe, but that unless the western powers changed their policies the Soviet Union would continue to expand its power and influence in western Europe by infiltration and by undermining one western European government after another until finally it had secured control of the whole of western Europe.

The first formal step which led to the North Atlantic treaty was taken by the British government in its messages to Marshall and Mackenzie

King in the middle of January, 1948, summarizing the proposals on western European union which the government intended to place before Parliament. There is no mention in these messages of a danger of war; what is imminent is a "Communist peril"; the danger is a "further encroachment of the Soviet tide" resulting from "a constantly increasing pressure" from the Russians "which threatens the whole fabric of the west"; the alternative to the west mobilizing force to defend western Europe is "to acquiesce in continued Russian infiltration and helplessly to witness the piecemeal collapse of one western bastion after another."[24]

Two months later much the same line was taken by J.D. Hickerson, director of the office of European affairs in the State Department, in a memorandum which he sent to Marshall. The memorandum was written twelve days after the Communist *coup* in Czechoslovakia:

Assuming that the Soviet government has no present desire for war, it appears to be counting on the slowness and uncertainty of American reaction, particularly during an election year, to extend its area of control as far and perhaps as fast as possible before meeting serious resistance. The greatest present danger lies in the Soviet government mistakenly believing that it could safely take some particular action which in fact this country would not stand . . . . The easy success of the Communists in Czechoslovakia and the probable outcome of the Finnish crisis . . . have created widespread fear and a certain bandwagon psychology, particularly in the crucial non-Communist left [especially in Italy, France and Austria]. . . . The problem at present is less one of defense against overt foreign aggression than against internal fifth-column aggression supported by the threat of external force, on the Czech model. An essential element in combatting it is to convince non-Communist elements that friendly external force comparable to the threatening external force is available.[25]

George Kennan believed that a bloodless victory by the Italian Communists in the Italian elections would not only give the Communists control over Italy, but would "send waves of panic to all surrounding areas. Our whole position in Mediterranean, and possibly in Western Europe as well, would probably be undermined."[26] At the end of May, two months after the Italian Communists had been defeated in the elections, Kennan said that if they had won, the Communists would have swept "through the territories lying along the western Mediterranean [and] a strategic situation would have been created in the long run intolerable to the interests of [the United States] . . . and the chances of war would have been greatly increased."[27] This Communist 'sweep' would have been accomplished without the use of armed force by the Soviet Union.

Kennan's analysis of the effect of a Communist victory in the Italian general elections was similar to the British government's analysis at the time of the effect of a "defection" by Norway to the Soviet Union. In the British message of March 11, 1948, to the United States and Canada proposing tripartite talks in Washington on a North Atlantic treaty, Bevin mentioned the Norwegian government's fears of an armed attack by the Soviet Union but he did not indicate that he, himself, believed that Norway might be attacked. Rather, he was concerned with what would happen if Norway did not hold out against Soviet demands. He believed that a defection by Norway

> would involve the appearance of Russia on the Atlantic and the collapse of the whole Scandinavian system. This would in turn prejudice the chance of calling any halt to the relentless advance of Russia into western Europe. Two serious threats may thus arise shortly: the strategic threat involved in the extension of the Russian sphere of influence to the Atlantic; and the political threat to destroy all efforts to build up a Western Union .... [An Atlantic security system should be established] so that, if the threat to Norway should develop, we could at once inspire the necessary confidence to consolidate the west against Soviet infiltration and at the same time inspire the Soviet government with enough respect for the west to remove temptation from them and so ensure a long period of peace. The alternative is to repeat our experience with Hitler and to witness helplessly the slow deterioration of our position, until we are forced in much less favourable circumstances to resort to war in order to defend our lives and liberty.[28]

Neither Kennan or Bevin believed that Soviet control over Italy or Norway would be accomplished by overt military action by the Soviet Union or that it would result immediately in war. Rather it would result in a strategic situation which would in the long run be intolerable to the interests of the United States and which would greatly increase the chances of war (Kennan) or which would result in a slow deterioration of the western position until the western powers were forced to resort to war (Bevin).

Western governments believed at the time that the Soviet government would try to follow the same sort of methods in gradually taking over western Europe as it had followed successfully in eastern and central Europe. In 1944 and 1945 the western powers had not had high hopes of co-operation with the Soviet Union in dealing with the problems of the postwar world. They had not, however, assumed that the borderline in Europe between the Soviet troops advancing from the east and the western troops advancing through France and Italy would become a borderline between a Soviet empire and the western world. They had believed that a buffer zone would be created between the two spheres consisting of Poland, Czechoslovakia, Hungary, Roumania and Bulgaria. These states

20

would be friendly to the Soviet Union but they would not be dominated by it. In 1946 and 1947 the ability of the Soviet government to control the governments of these states, an ability already strong in 1945, had rapidly increased according to a pattern which became frighteningly clear: first, a government of national unity; then a popular front government; then a Communist government; and finally a purge of Communists who were not considered reliable by the Soviet government, which usually meant liquidating those who had not spent the war years in the Soviet Union. During this process the leaders of the agrarian parties and of the social-democratic parties had been arrested, tortured, killed.

The State Department set forth its view of how these methods would be used in a western European country in a report to the National Security Council on March 8, 1948, seven weeks before the Italian general elections. The argument went as follows. The Italian Communists had formed a People's Bloc in association with the Nenni socialists and minor leftist parties. In order to achieve an electoral victory for the People's Bloc they were

> vigorously exploiting legitimate economic grievances, social unrest, and the pervading fear of vengeance in the event of Communist domination, most recently stimulated by the Communist coup in Czechoslovakia ... [If the People's Bloc won the elections, the Communists,] operating behind the facade of the People's Bloc ... would seek absolute control of Italy, first through the control of key ministries such as those of the Interior, Justice, Communications and Defense, then through a discreet but rapid infiltration of the armed forces, the police and the national administration. The end of the process would be a totalitarian police state. [This state would be] subservient to Moscow.[29]

Totalitarian police states in western Europe subservient to Moscow would, it was generally assumed at the time, become similar to the Stalinist state. John Holmes, the Canadian chargé d'affaires in Moscow, drew a horrifying picture of that state in a report to Ottawa in April, 1948. The picture he drew presumably did not differ greatly from the picture drawn for other western governments by their observers of the Soviet Union. The thought that the nations of western Europe might become similar to that state was repugnant to the leaders of the western world; this helps to explain why they were so determined that western Europe should not come under Soviet domination. In his report Holmes said:

> The Communists have created the most omnipotent and pervasive state in history. They took over the worst feature of the czarist tyranny, the secret police, and expanded it .... [The] security forces of the MVD have multiplied to such proportions that they virtually form a state within the state with their own private army .... The men who

set out to elevate the working man are now depending to an increasing extent on forced labour to achieve their economic goals . . . . It is the [eight to twenty million] political prisoners living like cattle in forced labour camps who have built the White Sea-Baltic canal and some of the other achievements attributed to Soviet labour . . . . The ideals of equality which inspired the early communists have been abandoned . . . . The officials of the Soviet Union form a caste with extraordinary privileges, and with complete control over every aspect of Soviet life . . . . The paths which the unhappy people of Russia and of the satellite states have been forced to follow by their masters in the Kremlin . . . lead to the establishment by force, and fraud and violence of a state ruled by a power-corrupted dictatorship; a dictatorship which protects itself by hordes of police, by informers, by arbitrary arrests, by mass deportations; a state which is so afraid of any other possible centre of competing loyalty that it persecutes all churches which refuse to become its instruments; a state which is so afraid of free inquiry that it seeks through its control of schools, newspapers and radio to create subjects who are incapable of thinking freely.[30]

The North Atlantic treaty was considered by its architects as a warning from the governments of the North Atlantic countries to Joseph Stalin and the other leading members of the government of the Soviet Union. On the day the treaty was made public, Louis St. Laurent, the Prime Minister of Canada, said,

The purpose of this treaty is to preserve the peace of the world by making it clear to any potential aggressor that if he were so unwise as to embark on war, he would be apt to finish up as the Kaiser did as a result of the first great war and as Hitler and Mussolini did in consequence of the last one. Those misguided leaders did not find out until after they got started what was going to be lined up against them. I think it will be fairer to future potential aggressors to let them know in advance.[31]

When, in the early months of 1949, the group in Washington which was negotiating the treaty was discussing the preamble, the Netherlands Ambassador, Dr. E. Van Kleffens, suggested that it should consist of only two words: "Dear Joe".[32]

The assessment in 1948 of Soviet intentions by the three great powers which formed the core of the North Atlantic community, the United States, Britain and France, differed markedly from the widespread belief at the time of many well informed ordinary men and women in the western world that the danger of war was imminent. This belief was reflected in articles written in March, 1948, by three influential and responsible

Washington columnists, Marquis Childs, James Reston and Walter Lippmann. Childs wrote at the beginning of March:

> Until the disaster to Czechoslovakia, there was a comfortable feeling here in Washington that the danger of war was something fairly remote – a matter of five to seven years. This was based largely on the assurance, which one heard over and over again from those in authority, that Russia did not want a shooting war. The comfortable assurance has vanished. It is not that the Soviet Union has come to want a war. But the attitude of the rulers in the Kremlin is now seen to make the possibility – yes, even the likelihood – of the war far more imminent.[33]

Reston wrote in the middle of March:

> The mood of the capital this week-end is exceedingly somber . . . . Responsible citizens are yelling, 'Quiet, quiet!' at the top of their voices, and even the President has mentioned that awful three-letter word, war.[34]

At the end of March, Lippmann wrote that Truman's message to Congress on March 17, the speeches, testimony, and press conferences of Marshall, of Forrestal (the Secretary of Defense), and of other senior officials in the Defense Department "have put this country in the position of preparing slowly and with half measures for a war of undefined objectives." Lippmann advocated

> a settlement [with the Soviet Union] induced by power and facilitated by compromise, which results in the withdrawal of the Red Army from the Stettin-Trieste line to the frontiers of the Soviet Union. Such a settlement may be impossible to achieve without war.[35]

The general public's fear of imminent war in March, 1948, was not confined to the United States. Anne O'Hare McCormick, who was at the time considered to be one of the ablest interpreters of what people in western Europe were thinking and feeling, wrote in the *New York Times* on March 24, 1948, immediately after returning from Europe, "The atmosphere of Europe is so tense that the agitated air of the United States seems normal by comparison . . . . [P]ressure on the west is increasing, and from Norway to Sicily the sense of danger is ever present. No one doubts that the western nations are the object of a new technique of aggression, or that this is the year that will decide whether it will succeed."[36] The Canadian embassy in Paris at the beginning of April, 1948, after describing certain improvements in the political and economic situation in France, went on to say, "All these hopeful symptoms are, however, jeopardized by the fear of war which more and more with every week is becoming an obsession with the peoples of Europe."

Richard M. Freeland, in his book *The Truman Doctrine and the Origins of McCarthyism,* contends that the United States administration in March, 1948, though it did not believe that war was imminent, deliberately generated a war scare in order to persuade Congress to approve the European Recovery Program. He holds the Defense Department mainly responsible; it was interested not just in getting the European Recovery Program through Congress but also in persuading Congress to approve of Truman's recommendations to it to enact a programme of universal military training and to renew selective service temporarily. A war scare would reduce opposition to these measures. [37] Reston, in his article in the *New York Times* in mid-March, 1948, had said much the same thing: "The Executive Branch of the government, in an effort to gain Congressional support of its policies, has been talking a good deal about war lately."

The talk about war in Washington in March, 1948, by spokesmen for the United States administration would not have had so much effect on public opinion if it had not been preceded by a Soviet war-scare campaign, what Halvard Lange, the Foreign Minister of Norway, called "a Soviet war of nerves." [38] The American embassy in Moscow stated at the end of December, 1948, that the campaign had been carefully planned and developed over the preceding two years "in order to frighten western peoples and impede west recovery efforts, facilitate the maintenance of internal controls on the Soviet population; and hide Soviet weaknesses." The embassy went on to say that the Soviet "war scare" had not been without advantage to the United States for it had been a factor in evoking public support for necessary defence and aid measures. But the danger was that this strong public opinion might recoil in the opposite direction if it became apparent that war was not an immediate prospect. Our leaders, therefore, should try "to base public sentiment on more solid foundation, to replace the present fever heat by a calm, informed determination to see the thing through on a long-range basis". Similarly, the acute war fever now sapping political courage and impeding recovery in western Europe should be alleviated and the non-communist world should be made confident that "its steadfast exertions and increasing strength can in fact ensure peace indefinitely".[39] The State Department was in general agreement with these views.[40]

The Soviet war-scare campaign had considerable effect on the public in the western world. It had little direct effect on the governments of the countries which made the North Atlantic treaty because the governments were in a better position than the public to distinguish between Soviet moves which only menaced and Soviet moves which mattered.[41] Their fear of the Soviet Union, based on Soviet moves which, they believed, mattered, led them to support in 1948 the idea of a North Atlantic treaty.

CHAPTER TWO

HOPE

It was not only fear of the Soviet Union which moved the hearts and minds of those who made the North Atlantic treaty, it was also hope; and fear and hope were linked. We knew that a common fear was a potent begetter of union; we hoped that countries which were afraid of the same external enemy might be persuaded to unite against that enemy. As we became more aware of the evils of the society which had been created in the Soviet Union and imposed by the Soviet Union on the people of eastern Europe, we also became more conscious of the virtues and values of our own civilization descended from the civilization of western Christendom. We realized that the things which divided us in the western world were as nothing compared with the gulf which separated us from the Soviet Union. Our common fear of the Soviet Union, our increasing consciousness of the unity of the western world and our increasing pride in its civilization, compared with that of the Soviet Union, gave us hope that a movement towards union which would have been impossible in normal times might now be possible. We believed that a North Atlantic treaty would help to defend the civilization to which we belonged. We hoped that behind the defensive barrier which that treaty would create, our civilization would purge itself of many of its faults and grow in unity and strength, in wisdom and compassion.

We believed that the governments and peoples of western countries which were moving towards greater political, economic and cultural union would have more confidence and more hope for the future. The greater the hope for the future, the less would be the fear of the Soviet Union. Those who made the North Atlantic treaty had nightmares of a Soviet occupation of Europe, but they also had visions of supranational unions of the western countries.

We had other hopes at the time of the making of the North Atlantic treaty. Thus most of us shared the hope which George Kennan had expressed in his famous article under the *nom de plume* of X in *Foreign Affairs* for July, 1947, that the pursuit by the western powers of wise foreign and domestic policies would "promote tendencies which must eventually find their outlet in either the break-up or the gradual mellowing of Soviet power."

Our fears of the Soviet Union would not have been so profound nor our hopes so high if our generation which made the North Atlantic treaty had not endured the terrors and horrors of the two apocalyptic decades which followed the crash of 1929. We had learned that civilization was fragile; we believed that the war had made international relations malleable. We believed that the times demanded and made possible revolutionary changes in the relations between nations. This, it seems to me, explains why my generation made proposals for changes in the international system which would probably be dismissed by our successors a quarter of a century later with such pejoratives as unrealistic, idealistic, doctrinaire, grandiose, and rhetorical. The following are some examples drawn only from the United States, Britain and Canada.

An official British report of 1943 recommended that all international airlines be owned and operated by an international agency. An official Canadian report of 1944 recommended the establishment of an international air transport board which alone would be competent to grant licenses to international airlines.

Dean Acheson, then Under-Secretary of State, proposed in 1946, in association with D. E. Lilienthal, "a plan under which no nation would make atomic bombs or the material for them. All dangerous activities would be carried on – not merely inspected – by a live, functioning international Authority . . . ."[1]

At the beginning of February, 1948, more than a month before the British proposed tripartite discussions on a North Atlantic treaty, Hume Wrong, the Canadian Ambassador in Washington, had a talk with J. D. Hickerson, director of the office of European affairs in the State Department and one of the principal architects of the North Atlantic treaty, about Ernest Bevin's proposals of the previous month which finally resulted in the Brussels treaty. Wrong reported that "some in the State Department have visions of a much more extensive union (than that proposed by Bevin which led to the Brussels treaty) based not only on a defensive alliance, but also on a customs union, perhaps with common citizenship. . . . [T]he United States and Canada might be included in such a union."[2] On April 6, 1949, three days after the signature of the North Atlantic treaty, Hickerson told me that he was in favour of the proposals made by Owen J. Roberts, formerly a justice of the Supreme Court; William L. Clayton, former Assistant Secretary of State for Economic Affairs; and others for the immediate formation of a federation of the North Atlantic countries.[3]

At about the same time George Kennan, director of the policy planning staff of the State Department, "had visions of a world-trading, maritime bloc, to include not only the British, the Canadians, and our-

selves but certain of the Commonwealth nations and possibly some entities of the Scandinavian and Iberian peninsulas as well, to be based on a
single currency, to develop eventually into a federal union with a common sovereignty, and to flank in this capacity a similar grouping on the
continent."[4]

T. C. Achilles, chief of the division of western European affairs in the
State Department, another of the principal architects of the North
Atlantic treaty, wrote in a departmental memorandum at the beginning
of August, 1948, that whether we liked it or not, the only ultimate answer
to the problem of establishing any kind of comfortable security must be
the creation of authorities, both political and military, to which countries
of western Europe and the North Atlantic would have to surrender some
degree of their national sovereignty.[5]

In January, 1948, Gladwyn Jebb, under-secretary at the British Foreign Office who probably sold the idea of a North Atlantic treaty to
Ernest Bevin, hoped that it might be possible "to construct a 'Middle
Power' consisting of western Europe plus the bulk of Africa which, while
remaining friendly with the U.S.A., would no longer be economically
dependent on that country and hence capable of pursuing an independent foreign policy."[6]

In March and April, 1948, St. Laurent, the Foreign Minister of
Canada, said:

> It may not be only Western Europe which will be forced into a spir-
> itual, cultural, economic and political union to offset the union of the
> totalitarian states. . . . The creation and maintenance [by the North
> Atlantic countries] of the necessary overwhelming preponderance of
> force and of the necessary degree of unity may require the establish-
> ment of new international political institutions which will appear to
> trench much more upon old-fashioned concepts of national sover-
> eignty than any of the international institutions which have been
> established in the past.[7]

In August, 1948, Lester Pearson, who was to become Foreign Minister
of Canada the following month, said,

> A North Atlantic treaty . . . will create a new living international insti-
> tution which will have within itself possibilities of growth and of adap-
> tation to changing conditions. The North Atlantic Community is a real
> commonwealth of nations which share the same democratic and
> cultural traditions. If a movement towards its political and economic
> unification can be started this year, none of us can forecast the extent
> of the unity which may exist five, ten or fifteen years from now.[8]

These people all thought in terms of building new international institutions – an international air transport board, an international atomic

authority, a North Atlantic federation, a federation of maritime countries, a western European federation. It was natural for them at that time to think in these terms because this was an era of institution-building. In the last years of the Second World War and the first years of the peace one international institution after another had been created: the United Nations Relief and Rehabilitation Agency; the International Refugee Organization; the Food and Agriculture Organization; the World Bank; the International Monetary Fund; the International Civil Aviation Organization; the United Nations Educational, Scientific and Cultural Organization; the World Health Organization; the United Nations itself.

Hickerson, Kennan, Achilles, Jebb, St. Laurent and Pearson all hoped that a supranational institution – North Atlantic, maritime or European – would emerge in the 1950s, and 1960s. They believed that the formation of a North Atlantic alliance would make more likely the emergence of the supranational institution on which their hopes were fixed.

CHAPTER THREE

THE CONCEPTION OF THE TREATY

It was clear before the San Francisco Conference of 1945 that the United Nations would be precluded by its charter from imposing sanctions against a great power which committed aggression. In a memorandum which I wrote in the winter of 1944-45 and which was published anonymously just before the conference opened, I said:

> If, in the unhappy event that a great power should in future act in such a way as to convince the other great powers that it is determined to dominate the world by force, the only way to prevent a world war from breaking out will be for the other great powers to form immediately an alliance against that power and to declare that the moment it commits aggression they will wage total war against it .... That declaration may bring the state which is planning aggression to its senses and so prevent the war from breaking out ....The alliance ... will not be an alliance growing out of the undertakings of member states under the [Charter]. Its effectiveness will depend not on legal obligations contracted in 1945 but on the will for peace of the peoples of the world when the threat of another world war arises.[1]

Four years later the three great western powers (the United States, Britain and France), supported by a number of middle-sized and small powers, created such an alliance against the Soviet Union.

The first proposal for an alliance to contain the Soviet Union was made by Winston Churchill less than a year after the opening of the San Francisco Conference. He proposed not a great power alliance but an alliance of the English-speaking peoples. He didn't call it an alliance, presumably because he knew that this would intensify opposition in the United States. He called it "a fraternal association of the English-speaking peoples". But what he described in his Fulton speech of March, 1946, was in fact an alliance, for in the association which he proposed there would be "joint use of all naval and air forces bases" and eventually "common citizenship", and the association would create "an overwhelming assurance of security" which would remove from the Soviet Union temptation "to ambition or adventure".

Churchill insisted that what he proposed was not contrary to the U.N. Charter:

> 'In my Father's house are many mansions' – Special associations between members of the United Nations which have no aggressive point against any other country, which harbour no design incompatible with the Charter of the United Nations, far from being harmful, are beneficial and, as I believe, indispensable.[2]

Some of the arguments put forward by Churchill in this speech were to become conventional wisdom in the intergovernmental discussions on the North Atlantic treaty which began two years later: that there were no limits to the desire of the Soviet Union to expand its power and doctrine; that to hold back Soviet expansion there must be created an overwhelming preponderance of power against the Soviet Union; and that collective defence agreements between members of the United Nations were compatible with the U.N. Charter. But what Churchill proposed was an alliance between the United States and Britain imbedded not in a North Atlantic Alliance but in an alliance of the English-speaking peoples. He did not realize that to be acceptable to the United States the alliance with Britain had to be imbedded in an alliance with western Europe and Canada.

C. R. Attlee was Prime Minister of Britain when the Fulton speech was given. Francis Williams, in his book on Attlee, which was based on documents and conversations with him, writes that at the time Churchill gave his Fulton speech, "American public opinion was unwilling to support any policy that seemed to be pulling British chestnuts out of the fire or entangling the United States in a British alliance. Attlee and Bevin had to play for time – although time was running out – and be very careful not to frighten America into a new isolationism by precipitate action."[3] Two years were to go by before Attlee and Bevin decided that it would be safe to ask the United States to enter into a military alliance with Britain and other North Atlantic countries.

My own feeling when I read Churchill's Fulton speech was that he had been led into extreme anti-Soviet statements by his latent anti-Sovietism which went back to the end of the First World War. It was not until the summer of 1947 that I concluded that it was necessary to form an alliance against the Soviet Union, not a Churchillian alliance of English-speaking peoples, but rather an alliance of the western world. I put my proposals forward in a speech on August 13, 1947, to the annual conference of the Canadian Institute of Public Affairs. I was then second-in-command to Lester Pearson in the Department of External Affairs in Ottawa, and, before giving the speech, I secured his permission. (I did not know at the time that before giving me permission he had secured the concurrence of Louis St. Laurent, who was then Foreign Minister.)[4]

In my speech I pointed out that nothing in the U.N. Charter precluded the existence of regional political arrangements or agencies provided that they were consistent with the purposes and principles of the U.N. and that these regional agencies were entitled to take measures of collective self-defence against armed attack until the Security Council had acted. Since I was a civil servant putting forward in public ideas not yet adopted by the government I used guarded language when I went on to say,

> The world is now so small that the whole of the western world is in itself a mere region. If the peoples of the western world want an international security organization with teeth, even though the Soviet Union is at present unwilling to be a member of such an organization, they do not need to amend the United Nations charter in order to create such an organization; they can create it consistently with the United Nations charter. They can create a regional security organization to which any state willing to accept the obligations of membership could belong. In such an organization there need be no veto right possessed by any great power. In such an organization each member state could accept a binding obligation to pool the whole of its economic and military resources with those of the other members if *any* power should be found to have committed aggression against any one of the members.

This may be the first public statement advocating a collective defence organization of the western world.

I was not content with suggesting a defence union of the western world. I also suggested that this union might include federal economic, social and cultural agencies just as later I was to urge in the negotiations on the North Atlantic treaty that the treaty should include undertakings to co-operate on economic, social and cultural matters. The Soviet Union, I pointed out, was not a member of the World Bank, the International Monetary Fund, the Food and Agriculture Organization, the International Civil Aviation Organization, UNESCO, and the International Refugee Organization.

> Most of these agencies have today very little executive power. . . . If the peoples of the western world feel that there should be a greater transfer of effective power from national governments to these international organizations the international agreements constituting these organizations can be amended. . . . [T]he states of the western world are not debarred by a Soviet veto or by Soviet membership in the United Nations from the creation of international federal institutions to deal with international economic and social questions if they decide that such institutions are required. [5]

31

When I put this idea a few weeks later in a confidential departmental memorandum I used less inhibited language. I said that the specialized agencies "should" be changed "into international federal institutions to deal with international economic and social questions ... in order to strengthen the western world in its struggle with the Soviet Union. ... The veto on these changes is not a Soviet veto; it is usually a United States veto."[6] I found that I was too far ahead of government policy. In commenting on this memorandum, St. Laurent said, "I would not care to state, as a matter of policy, ... that the specialized agencies should be transformed into international federal institutions."[7]

(In my departmental memorandum, my list of the actions which the western powers should take to create and maintain an overwhelming preponderance of force relative to that of the Soviet Union included: economic assistance to western Europe; the prevention or mitigation of an economic depression in the western world; rapid progress in granting self-government to colonies and in removing racial discriminations; the maintenance of the armed forces of the western world "at a level which is reasonable in relation to the armed forces of the Soviet world"; and a "guarantee [to] the states of western Europe against the establishment by force of pro-Soviet governments".)

I was greatly encouraged when I read in the *New York Times* a month after I had delivered my speech an article by the influential editor of *Foreign Affairs,* Hamilton Fish Armstrong, making much the same proposal as I had made for a collective defence organization, but in greater detail. He proposed a protocol supplementing the U.N. Charter. This protocol would establish a new international organization. The obligation of each member of the new organization to come to the defence of other members would come into effect if two-thirds of the members were to decide that collective action had become necessary under the Charter of the U.N. and if the Security Council of the U.N. had failed to act. Before signing the protocol the member nations would agree on the armed forces which each would put at the disposal of the new organization. This "international force actually in being" might have the atomic bomb at its disposal.[8]

When the time came to draft a speech for St. Laurent to deliver to the U.N. General Assembly in the autumn of 1947, I found that Pearson wanted to maintain in St. Laurent's speech an ambiguity between whether Canada was proposing a radical revision of the U.N. Charter, even at the cost of driving the Soviet Union out of the United Nations, or a collective security pact to supplement the U.N. Charter, whereas I wanted St. Laurent to come down unequivocally in favour of a supplementary agreement. Pearson won but the speech was heavily weighted on the side of a supplementary agreement and once the Canadian government had agreed six months later to support a supplementary agreement or agreements, it was this part of the speech which was emphasized to the exclusion of the other part.

The other part consisted of the following statements:

> This veto privilege ... if it continues to be abused, may well destroy the United Nations. ... Our peoples cannot be expected to accept indefinitely and without alteration, voting procedures and practices which ... reduce agreement to a lowest common denominator of action that in practice often means inaction. ... [These] procedures and practices ... must be changed. This can be done by the voluntary abandonment of these practices; by agreed conventions or understandings which will regulate them; or, if necessary, by amendments to the Charter. We hope that no member of the Security Council will flout clearly-expressed world opinion by obstinately preventing change, and thus become responsible for prejudicing, and possibly destroying, the organization which is now man's greatest hope for the future.

Immediately following this passage came the proposal for a security pact supplementing the U.N. Charter:

> Nations in their search for peace and co-operation will not, and cannot accept indefinitely an unaltered [Security] Council ... which, so many feel has become frozen in futility and divided by dissension. If forced they may seek greater safety in an association of democratic and peace-loving states willing to accept more specific international obligations in return for a greater measure of national security. Such associations ... if consistent with the principles and purposes of the Charter, can be formed within the United Nations. It is to be hoped that such a development will not be necessary. ... If, however, it is made necessary, it will have to take place. Let us not forget that the provisions of the Charter are a floor under, rather than a ceiling over, the responsibilities of member states.[9]

This statement in St. Laurent's speech of September 18, 1947, was the first public suggestion by a member of a western government that it might be necessary for "democratic and peace-loving states" to establish a security association within the United Nations which would not be subject to a Soviet veto over the imposition of sanctions. The significance of this statement was not appreciated at the time by the newspapermen who were covering the Assembly and it received little publicity. It seems likely that it also did not, immediately at least, make much impression on foreign offices.

Armstrong's article of September 14 did, however, make an impression on at least two of the principal architects of the North Atlantic treaty, J. D. Hickerson of the State Department and Gladwyn Jebb of the British Foreign Office. It is possible that it also influenced Senator Vandenberg, who played an important part in the negotiation of the treaty, because five days after the article appeared he wrote to a Michigan friend in terms which suggest this:

> I can fully understand the pessimism about the United Nations which has taken possession of many of our people. It would be both silly and dangerous to ignore the worsening relationships between Moscow and Washington. But there is a way to circumvent the deadly "veto" – as we demonstrated at Rio [the agreement on collective self-defence among the American nations].[10]

In the middle of October Hickerson said to Hume Wrong, the Canadian Ambassador in Washington, that he was almost convinced that the time had come to seek to give effect to Armstrong's suggestion for a grouping of the more or less like-minded countries inside the United Nations, making use of Article 51 of the Charter.*[11] Since Hickerson had not mentioned St. Laurent's statement in the General Assembly, I reminded Wrong of the statement and of my own statement.[12] This evidence of Canadian support for a security pact would, I thought, encourage Hickerson to press forward with his ideas. Wrong reported at the end of October that he had reminded Hickerson of St. Laurent's statement. Hickerson then went further than he had in his previous conversation with Wrong. Instead of talking of his own views, he now expressed an opinion about the probable attitude of the United States government. He said he thought it quite likely that the United States government would in time come out in support of the Armstrong suggestion but that the time had not yet arrived. "If, however, the Council of Foreign Ministers failed to reach any agreement on the German settlement – and he expected failure – the matter might possibly be raised in the so-called 'Little Assembly' before the next regular session of the General Assembly, presumably after some preliminary sounding out of the governments principally concerned."[13]

I wrote back to Wrong that, since there was a possibility that the United States might take the initiative within the next 12 months, it might be useful if we in Canada were to try to clear our own minds a little on some of the problems. As a first step in trying to clear my own mind I had prepared a draft of a "treaty for greater national security to supplement the Charter of the United Nations". This I sent him for his comments. I also sent it to Pearson, to Norman Robertson (Canadian High Com-

*The text of Article 51 of the U.N. Charter is given in Appendix 4.

missioner in London) and to five of the senior officers of the Department.

The treaty was based on the Anglo-Polish treaty of mutual assistance of August, 1939, and included provisions from the Rio treaty and the abortive Geneva Protocol of 1924. It was a treaty open to all members of the U.N. In order not to exclude countries whose admittance to the U.N. had been vetoed by the Soviet Union it was also open to any country whose application for membership in the United Nations had been supported in the General Assembly by a two-thirds majority of the members present and voting. The treaty was to come into force when ratified by three of the five permanent members of the Security Council (meaning the United States, Britain and France), and by a majority of the other members of the U.N.[14]

Armstrong, St. Laurent, Pearson, Hickerson and I were all at this time talking in terms of an agreement open to all members of the U.N. I, in my speech in August, had equated this with a regional security pact for the "western world", since I had assumed that it was only western countries, using western in a broad sense as virtually equivalent to non-Communist, which would join the pact. Similarly Wrong had "for purposes of brevity" called the Armstrong proposal "a western mutual assistance pact inside the United Nations".[15]

The first we in Ottawa heard of the possibility of one or more regional pacts as an alternative to a security pact open for signature by all members of the U.N. or as the first step to such a pact, came in a talk in New York on November 21 between Gladwyn Jebb of the British Foreign Office and George Ignatieff, a member of the Canadian Department of External Affairs. Jebb had been talking to Armstrong who had mentioned to him the statements which St. Laurent and I had made.

Jebb indicated that the British Foreign Office was giving thought to various possible approaches. One was the Armstrong plan under Article 51 of the Charter; another was one or more avowedly regional pacts under Chapter VIII of the Charter;* that is, pacts similar to the Rio treaty. The difficulty, Jebb said, was

> of defining the region in such a way as to constitute a sufficiently strong group of states which would be capable of taking enforcement action. . . . [I]f a regional group of this kind were constituted in Europe for the purposes of resisting Soviet aggression which excluded the United States, such a grouping would be regarded by countries likely to invoke guarantees, such as Turkey and Greece, as being too weak. Indeed a regional grouping on such a limited basis might lead countries like Turkey and Greece to make terms with the Soviet Union rather than associate themselves with such a regional group. . . . There-

*The text of Chapter VIII of the U.N. Charter is given in Appendix 4.

fore a regional arrangement providing for collective self-defence would have necessarily to include the United States if it is to be effective in containing Soviet expansion.[16]

(Within three months the British were proposing a regional pact for western Europe – the Brussels treaty – which would not include the United States. The British were gambling that the conclusion of such a treaty would increase the chances of the United States entering into a military alliance with western Europe against Soviet aggression. Their gamble paid off.)

At the beginning of December we received a report from the Canadian embassy in Washington of a conversation between Gerald Riddell of the Department of External Affairs and Dean Rusk of the State Department.* Riddell reported Rusk as saying that the State Department people concerned believed "that the plan as presented by Armstrong had an anti-Russian flavour which they implied was absent in their concept." Their concept appeared to be a number of mutual defence treaties, which would be implemented when the Security Council had failed to act, and which would be aimed at the prevention of aggression by a major power.[17] How this was less anti-Russian than the Armstrong proposal was not clear from Riddell's report.

Hickerson had predicted at the end of October that the Council of Foreign Ministers would fail to reach agreement on the German settlement and that this failure might be the catalyst which would precipitate intergovernmental discussions on a security pact or pacts. He was right in both his predictions. The Council began its sessions in London on November 25. It broke up in complete disagreement on December 15. That evening, Ernest Bevin, the British Foreign Secretary, invited Marshall, the Secretary of State, to have dinner alone with him. The next day Marshall gave John Foster Dulles and Hickerson an account of the talk. (Dulles was representing Vandenberg on the United States delegation, Vandenberg then being the Republican Chairman of the Senate Foreign Relations Committee.) Marshall said that after the dinner Bevin had said,

> There is no chance that the Soviet Union will deal with the west on any reasonable terms in the foreseeable future. The salvation of the west depends on the formation of some form of union, formal or informal in character, in western Europe backed by the United States and the Dominions – such a mobilization of moral and material force as will inspire confidence and energy within and respect elsewhere.[18]

According to Bevin, Marshall agreed that the time had come to call a halt to Russian aggression.[19]

* Dean Rusk was at this time director of the office of United Nations affairs in the State Department.

At Marshall's request Hickerson went to the Foreign Office the next day to try to secure an elucidation of Bevin's ideas. The official he talked to (presumably Gladwyn Jebb) said that Bevin envisioned "two security arrangements, one a small tight circle including a treaty engagement between the U.K., the Benelux countries and France. Surrounding that, a larger circle with somewhat lesser commitments but still commitments in treaty form bringing in the U.S. and Canada also."[20]

Marshall told Hickerson that he was impressed by Bevin's proposals but that he believed that the "union" must be solely European; United States participation in a military guarantee was not possible. United States participation would have to be confined to supplying material assistance to the members of a western European security pact. Moreover his 'Marshall Plan' speech was only six months old, the Europeans were still arguing over who was to get how much United States aid and Congress had still to authorize, let alone appropriate, any aid at all. In speaking about this conversation 22 years later Hickerson said that the congressional problem was a considerable one and that Marshall understandably did not want to complicate it any more than absolutely necessary.[21]

The only official document published so far which relates to these talks in London between Bevin and Marshall is a British memorandum of a discussion between them at the Foreign Office on December 17. This reports Bevin as saying:

> His own idea was that we must devise some western democratic system comprising the Americans, ourselves, France, Italy, etc. and of course the Dominions. This would not be a formal alliance, but an understanding backed by power, money and resolute action. It would be a sort of spiritual federation of the west. . . . If such a powerful consolidation of the west could be achieved it would then be clear to the Soviet Union that having gone so far they could not advance any further. . . . The essential task was to create confidence in western Europe that further communist inroads would be stopped.

A United States footnote to this document states that "Marshall indicated [to Bevin] that he had not definitely approved any particular course of action and he hoped to receive specific British proposals before making a final commitment."[22]

When he returned to the United States, Marshall found that his Under-Secretary, Robert Lovett, agreed with him in rejecting as at least premature any idea of a military alliance between the United States and Britain and other western European countries. Hickerson, on the other hand, believed that a military alliance was essential. He put the arguments for this to Dulles when they came back together by sea after the London meetings and he felt he had made some progress in convincing

Dulles. Dulles undertook to speak to Vandenberg.[23]

Marshall's cautious reaction to Bevin's sounding out of him in mid-December must have convinced Bevin that he would have to move with great caution if he were not to provoke opposition in the Senate of the United States or a rebuff from the State Department.

On January 13 and 14, 1948, the British government sent messages to the United States and Canadian governments giving advance notice of the proposals which Bevin would shortly be putting forward in the House of Commons at Westminster. The messages were similar but not identical. The following was the argument put forward in the messages: The British government had considered the situation in Europe resulting from the deadlock over Germany in the Council of Foreign Ministers. They had decided that the time had come to give a moral lead to the friendly countries of western Europe and to take a more active line against communism. Progress in the economic field was essential and the British would do all they could to bring the Marshall Plan to fruition. But economic progress would not in itself suffice to stem the tide of Soviet encroachment. We must organize and consolidate the ethical and spiritual forces of western Europe backed by the power and resources of the Commonwealth and the Americas in order to create confidence and energy in our friends and to inspire respect and caution in others. The British government had therefore concluded that they should seek to form a western democratic system, a Western Union, comprising at any rate France, the Low Countries and Scandinavia, Portugal, Italy and Greece. When circumstances permitted it could be extended to Spain and Germany. There need not be any formal alliance. As a first step to Western Union, the British government was suggesting to the French government that the two governments should make a joint offer of a treaty to Belgium, the Netherlands and Luxembourg along the lines of the Dunkirk treaty of March, 1947, between Britain and France.[24]

This was substantially what Bevin said eight days later when he spoke in the House of Commons. In this speech, as Jebb has put it in his memoirs, Bevin did not positively suggest any wider grouping than that of western Europe since this "might at that stage have disturbed the Senate of the United States," though he did say that "the 'resources' of America would be needed .... Altogether, it was a very clever speech. The Secretary of State [Bevin] knew perfectly well what he was after, but he had to achieve his end by stages, gaining as many allies as he could in the process."[25] Bevin contented himself at this stage with informing Marshall that he trusted that the policy he had outlined and the initial steps which he proposed to take would commend themselves to him.[26]

Two questions now had to be considered by the United States administration. The first was what comment would they make on Bevin's proposal that the first stage towards western European union should be treaties on the Dunkirk model. The second was what, if any, indication should they give of the eventual willingness of the United States to associate itself with a western European security pact.

On the first point there was no difference of opinion in the State Department. The State Department considered that bilateral treaties on the Dunkirk model directed against German aggression were clearly irrelevant, and that the appropriate model was the multilateral Rio treaty which was directed against any aggressor. Hickerson made this point when he spoke to the British Ambassador on January 21.[27] The State Department, ten days before this, had drawn the Rio treaty to the attention of Spaak, the Prime Minister and Foreign Minister of Belgium.[28] It may well have been as a result of this that the Netherlands and Belgian governments informed the British government early in February that they rejected the Dunkirk model and asked for a wider regional instrument.[29]

Later in February, the Benelux countries gave the British and French a formal note confirming that they favoured a regional organization of western Europe under Articles 51, 52 and 53 of the U.N. Charter, that this political agreement should be supplemented not only by military but also by economic agreements and that the ultimate goal should be "full economic and customs union".[30]

The French, however, were at first reluctant to depart from the Dunkirk model: they had refused to negotiate with Poland and Czechoslovakia on the basis of the possibility of an attack from any power other than Germany; domestic instability in France made a direct affront to the communists, impolitic. The Communist *coup d' etat* in Czechoslovakia on February 25 changed this: the French government decided that it was no longer restricted by considerations of Polish and Czech sensibilities; and the Czech *coup* made it possible for the French government to take a stronger line from the domestic political point of view.[31] The result was that the British and the French agreed to abandon the Dunkirk model in favour of a multilateral treaty against any aggressor. They also agreed to include economic provisions in the treaty. The British insisted that the provisions for collective self-defence be based on Article 51 of the Charter rather than on Article 52, which is the first article in the chapter on regional arrangements. Thus as a result of a British initiative, advice from the State Department and the Benelux countries, and the Communist *coup* in Czechoslovakia, the Brussels treaty agreed to on March 17 became a model for the North Atlantic treaty.

The first question which had confronted the United States administration in mid-January was whether they would suggest to the British a treaty on the Rio model. That was resolved, and resolved satisfactorily, with little difficulty. The second was much more difficult: what, if any, indication should be given the British of the eventual willingness of the

United States to associate itself with a western European security pact. George Kennan advised Marshall on January 20 that he should welcome Bevin's project of a union among the western European nations under combined French-British auspices "just as warmly as Mr. Bevin welcomed your Harvard speech". Kennan added, however, that he was afraid of a tendency among Bevin's subordinates to view his proposals too much as just another framework of military alliances:

> Military union should not be the starting point. It should flow from the political, economic and spiritual union – not vice versa. . . . If there is to be a 'union', it must have some reality in economic and technical and administrative arrangements; and there must be some real federal authority. . . . People in Europe should not bother themselves too much in the initial stage about our relationship to this concept; if they develop it and make it work, there will be no real question as to our long term relationship to it, even with respect to the military guarantee. This will flow logically from the consequences.

Hickerson disagreed. He bluntly advised Marshall on January 19 that for a European pact modelled after the Rio treaty "to be really effective, the United States would have to adhere. I believe that this country could and should adhere to such a treaty if it were clearly linked up with the U.N."[32]

Here was the first indication of the difference of opinion between Kennan, supported by Charles Bohlen, on one side and Hickerson, supported by Achilles, on the other side.* Bohlen and Kennan argued during the next few months for a unilateral declaration by the United States in support of western Europe. Hickerson and Achilles argued for membership by the United States in a collective defence agreement.

According to the British Ambassador, Marshall told him on January 19 "that he was already turning over in his mind the question of the participation of the United States in the defence of Europe."[33] The formal reply which Marshall sent the next day to the British Ambassador for transmission to Ernest Bevin did not go this far. Marshall praised Bevin's proposal as being of "fundamental importance to the future of western civilization"; and went on to say "his proposal has deeply interested and moved me and . . . I wish to see the United States do everything which it properly can in assisting the European Nations in bringing a project along this line to fruition. I hope [Bevin] will feel free to consult with me from time to time when he thinks I can be of assistance."

Hickerson, who was disappointed that the reply was not warmer, received permission to supplement the reply with an "oral statement"

*George Kennan was director of the policy planning staff of the State Department. Charles Bohlen was counsellor of the Department. J. D. Hickerson was director of the office of European affairs. T. C. Achilles was chief of the division of western European affairs.

expressing "ideas which were being considered on the pick and shovel level in the department". He gave the British Ambassador a copy of this statement. It went a good deal further than Marshall since it said "if it should be felt in western Europe that the direct participation of the United States in a defense arrangement, established in full harmony with the Charter of the United Nations, would be necessary to its success, the United States government would be no doubt prepared very carefully to consider this question." This indication of a willingness to consider immediately United States participation in a defence arrangement was, however, balanced by the next sentence drawn from Kennan's memorandum, "If the peoples of Europe are prepared to develop a concept of spiritual and material unity and to make this work, there will be no real question as to the long-term relationship of the United States with it."

But again this talk about a long-term relationship in an oral statement committed to writing was balanced by oral remarks not transmitted in writing to the British but put in writing in a memorandum for internal circulation in the State Department. In this memorandum, Hickerson stated that he had said to the British Ambassador:

> [S]hould . . . European nations decide that no regional defense organization could be completed without the United States and that this would give . . . more assurance to the smaller nations, we felt that this country would be sympathetically disposed and would at least give it very careful consideration. If it were closely associated with the Charter of the United Nations, it might receive a favorable reception.[34]

The warmth of these comments must have greatly encouraged Bevin, for a week later he proposed to the State Department that the United States "enter with Great Britain into a general commitment to go to war with an aggressor". This would reinforce the western European defence project. Lovett immediately said that "[W]hat Mr. Bevin was now suggesting would in fact mean consideration of a military alliance between the United States and Great Britain."[35] A little less than two years after Churchill's Fulton speech proposing a union of the English-speaking countries, Attlee and Bevin were proposing a military alliance between the two greatest of the English-speaking countries.

The British soon learned that they had moved too quickly. Lovett told them on February 7 that to pursue the British suggestion would endanger the European Recovery Program which was "at a crucial stage in the discussions in Congress. . . . If it became known in Congress that in addition to the economic commitments involved in the European Recovery Program the United States is asked to assume new and extensive military and political commitments it might well adversely affect the prospects for the approval by Congress of the European Recovery Program." This was one objection to the British proposal. The second objection was that it was premature. Before the United States could consider the part it might appropriately play in support of the Western European Union proposed by Bevin, there would have to be evidence of western European unity with a firm determination to effect an arrangement under which the various European countries were prepared to act in concert to defend themselves. Moreover the United States government did not have any very clear picture of exactly what Bevin's proposals for a Western Union really were, certainly not enough information to enable it to determine how it could best be helpful. "You are in effect asking us to pour concrete before we see the blueprints."[36]

Bevin complained that "without assurance of security, which can only be given with some degree of American participation, the British government is unlikely to be successful in making the Western Union a going concern. . . . But . . . until this is done, the United States government . . . does not feel able to discuss participation."[37] The British considered that the United States had set them an impossible task. The United States considered that the British were making "a slanting effort to entangle" them "in European quasi-military alliances or agreements."[38] Here was what Bevin in his message of February 6 called a vicious circle.

The argument about how to get out of this vicious circle might have gone on interminably, and the result might have been no treaty of Brussels and no North Atlantic treaty. Indeed sometime in February, 1948, before the Soviet *coup* in Czechoslovakia, the British government had sent Gladwyn Jebb to Washington to sound out the United States on how far it might be prepared to go to support a western European defensive pact and had recalled him before he spoke to the Americans "since the moment was deemed unpropitious".[39] Then came the shock of the *coup* in Czechoslovakia and the death of Masaryk, the opening of the formal discussions on March 7 on the Brussels treaty, and the message from the Norwegian government on March 8 that it feared that Norway might soon face Soviet demands for a pact which would reduce Norway to the level of a satellite. What had been unpropitious became urgent. On March 11 the British proposed to the United States and Canada that officials of the three countries should meet in Washington without delay to explore the possibility of establishing a regional Atlantic approaches pact of mutual assistance under Article 51 of the U. N. Charter. All the countries directly threatened by a Soviet move on the Atlantic could participate: Norway, Denmark, Iceland, Ireland, France, Portugal, Great Britain, the United States, Canada and Spain, once it had a democratic regime.[40]

I remember the mixture of hope and fear which gripped me when I read this message. Hope because I had become impatient with the slow progress to the objective I had set the previous August of a western security pact, fear because the news from Norway indicated that the Soviet Union intended to expand its power more rapidly and recklessly than I had anticipated.

On March 11 Canada accepted Bevin's proposal; the next day the United States accepted it. Marshall demonstrated his sense of the urgency of action by proposing that the discussions begin early the next week, that is about March 16 or 17.[41] (They began on March 22.)

The signature of the Brussels treaty on March 17 provided an opportunity for the governments of the United States and Canada to indicate publicly, though in guarded language, their willingness to consider ways by which they might associate themselves with the Brussels treaty powers. The statements made on March 17 by the President of the United States and the Prime Minister of Canada were in form blessings on the Brussels treaty. In fact, they were also blessings on the tripartite talks on a North Atlantic security pact which were about to begin. Truman said,

> This development [the signature of the Brussels treaty] deserves our full support. I am confident that the United States will, by appropriate means, extend to the free nations the support which the situation requires. I am sure that the determination of the free countries of Europe to protect themselves will be matched by an equal determination on our part to help them to do so. The recent developments in Europe present this nation with fundamental issues of vital importance. I believe that we have reached a point at which the position of the United States should be made unmistakeably clear.[42]

Mackenzie King went further. He went, indeed, just about as far as the United States Senate was to go three months later when it adopted the Vandenberg resolution. King pledged actual Canadian participation in regional pacts to complement the Brussels pact. He said,

> This [Brussels] pact is far more than an alliance of the old kind. It is a partial realization of the idea of collective security by an arrangement made under the Charter of the United Nations. As such, it is a step towards peace, which may well be followed by other similar steps until there is built up an association of all free states which are willing to accept responsibilities of mutual assistance to prevent aggression and preserve peace... The peoples of all free countries may be assured that Canada will play her full part in every movement to give substance to the conception of an effective system of collective security by the development of regional pacts under the Charter of the United Nations.[43]

By the middle of March 1948, the North Atlantic treaty had been conceived. Its parents were fear and hope. Its ancestors included the Geneva protocol of 1924, Churchill's speech at Fulton in 1946, the Rio treaty and the Brussels treaty. The next 12 months was the period of gestation. During this period there were possibilities of miscarriage. There were possibilities that the alliance would be still-born or that the infant would be puny or malformed.

PART TWO

THE ORGANIZATION OF THE DISCUSSIONS

CHAPTER FOUR

THE INTERGOVERNMENTAL DISCUSSIONS

The making of the North Atlantic treaty was a lengthy and difficult task. It was much more lengthy and much more difficult than any of us who were concerned with the first stage of the negotiations thought it would be. Before the first stage opened on March 22, 1948, we in Ottawa thought that the treaty might be signed by about April 11. When the first stage ended on April 1, the representatives of the United States, Britain and Canada who had been taking part in the talks believed that the treaty might be signed in May. It was not signed until April of the following year.

The representatives of the countries which made the treaty held over 60 meetings† in Washington before their governments were able to reach agreement on the text of the treaty, on interpretations of it and on the countries which should be members of the alliance. The meetings covered almost exactly a year, from March 22, 1948, to March 28, 1949. One reason the talks were so prolonged was that 1948 was an election year in the United States, and right up to the election in November it was generally assumed that the Republican candidate for the presidency would defeat Truman and that the Republicans would increase their majorities in the Senate and the House of Representatives. Another reason the task of reaching agreement was more difficult than it otherwise would have been was that during 1948, differences of opinion over Palestine strained relations between the governments of the United States and Britain.

There were four stages in the intergovernmental meetings. Only three governments (those of the United States, Britain and Canada) took part in the first stage which lasted from March 22, to April 1, 1948. The meetings were held in the Pentagon, and the resulting paper was called the

Pentagon paper. It contained an outline of the provisions of a "collective defense agreement for the North Atlantic Area." The paper was couched in the form of a report from the policy planning staff of the State Department.[1] One reason for this was, as Pearson put it at the time, that if it should leak out, it would not appear to other governments as having already been discussed with Britain and Canada.[2] The tripartite meeting did not approve of an actual draft of a treaty but by the time it ended, Achilles of the State Department had prepared a draft in the light of the discussions. According to Achilles, the eventual North Atlantic treaty, agreed to a year later, had the general form and a good bit of the language of this draft but with a number of important differences.[3] (The Achilles draft treaty was not circulated to the British and Canadian participants in the discussions and it cannot be found in the State Department records.)

There was a three-months' gap between the first stage and the second stage of the intergovernmental discussions. In the second stage, France, Belgium and the Netherlands were represented as well as the United States, Britain and Canada. This six-power stage lasted from July 6 to September 10 and produced the "Washington paper" which was dated September 9.[4] This paper took the form of a report from the participants to their governments and set forth in greater detail than the Pentagon paper the possible content of the articles of a "North Atlantic Pact."

There was another three-months' gap between the second stage and the third stage. The third stage lasted from December 10 to 24 and produced a draft treaty for submission to the participating governments.[5] Luxembourg had been represented by Belgium in the second stage but participated directly in the third stage, which thus became a seven-power meeting.

The recess between the third and fourth stages lasted for only two weeks. The fourth and final stage lasted from January 10 to March 28, 1949, and produced the final text of the North Atlantic treaty and agreed interpretations of it.* At the end of December and the beginning of January, the governments of Denmark, Iceland, Ireland, Norway and Portugal were sounded out on their willingness to participate as original signatories of the treaty. All agreed except Ireland. Norway's affirmative reply arrived in time for it to participate in the meetings beginning on March 4.

The treaty was made public on March 18, 1949. The agreed interpretations were kept secret; they were not published until 1975, when they were included in one of the volumes in the *Foreign Relations of the United States* published that year.[6] The treaty was signed in Washington on April 4 by Denmark, Iceland, Italy and Portugal as well as by the coun-

*The text of the North Atlantic treaty as signed on April 4, 1949, is given in Appendix 2, and the agreed interpretations in Appendix 3.

TABLE I
INTERGOVERNMENTAL MEETINGS

	Participants	Dates	Product
First Stage	Three powers United States Britain Canada	March 22-April 1, 1948	Pentagon paper
Second Stage	Six Powers The above plus France Belgium Netherlands	July 6-September 10, 1948	Washington paper
Third Stage	Seven powers The above plus Luxembourg	December 10-24, 1948	Draft treaty
Fourth Stage	Seven to Eight powers The above plus Norway (from March 4, 1949)	January 10-March 28, 1949	Treaty and agreed interpretations

tries which had participated in the discussions: Belgium, Britain, Canada, France, Luxembourg, the Netherlands, Norway and the United States. The Foreign Relations Committee of the United States Senate unanimously approved the treaty on June 6, 1949, and the Senate approved it on July 21, 1949. The treaty came into force on August 24, 1949.

The first stage of the discussions was called "the United States – United Kingdom – Canada security conversations".[7] The second stage was called "the Washington exploratory talks on security".[8] In between the second stage and the third stage all the governments concerned (other than the United States) agreed in principle to negotiate a North Atlantic pact between the Brussels treaty powers and the United States and Canada.[†] From then on the Ambassadors' Committee was no longer merely exploring – the members were negotiating under increasingly precise and firm instructions from their governments. It was thus appropriate for the Ambassadors' Committee to agree, when the third stage opened on December 10, 1948, that it was time to stop calling the talks exploratory and this word was deleted from the press release which was issued that day.[9]

Hickerson insisted that the first stage of the discussions was on what he called "the pick and shovel level" and he criticized the British representatives for seeking instructions from their Foreign Minister on issues arising in the discussions.[10] Perhaps Hickerson, in Lovett's absence from Washington, was not reporting daily to his superiors on the discussions. The British and the Canadians certainly were. Pearson consulted the Prime Minister and the Foreign Minister by telegram and telephone and when he returned to Ottawa in the middle of the first stage he had talks with them and sent a telegram of instruction to Wrong, the Canadian Ambassador in Washington, based on these talks.

In the first and second stages of the intergovernmental discussions, even when representatives were acting under instructions, they sometimes pretended that they were expressing only their personal views. In the third stage they started quoting from their instructions. Thus at the meeting of the Working Group on December 20, 1948, the British representative said that his instructions required him to say that he thought that Africa north of 30° north should be included in the area covered by the pledge in the treaty where the territory was owned or occupied by forces of a member of the alliance, and the French representative said that the instructions from his government were to the effect that France could not accept the treaty unless French North Africa was included.[11]

In the fourth stage of the intergovernmental discussions, as governments saw the end of the talks approaching, they became more alive to the domestic political problems they might confront when the treaty was published. Thus St. Laurent, just before the fourth stage opened, told Pearson and Wrong that he had read the draft treaty of December 24 with great care and that there "were three points which struck him as *being important for the public acceptance of the treaty in Canada"*: the treaty should not cover Algeria or any colonial territory; Italy should not be a full partner; he would prefer that the treaty be for a firm term of only 12 years. He had previously agreed that Canada could support 20 or 25 years.[12]

At one time it looked as if there was going to be a fifth stage in the intergovernmental discussions: a formal conference of foreign ministers which would hammer out the final text of the treaty. Wrong said at the beginning of February, 1949, that such a conference might open on a Monday and conclude by the end of the week.[13] A month later he was arguing (on instructions from Ottawa) that the text of the treaty could not be considered to be unalterable when the foreign ministers met to sign it. He said that governments must have an opportunity to revise the treaty after it had been published and before it was signed. They could not, he went on, be committed to every word and comma of the text which was about to be published.[14] He kept pressing on this, only to find what he called "a curious reluctance on the part of Acheson and others to commit themselves definitely on the arrangements immediately preceding [the] signature [of the treaty]."[15] But as soon as the treaty was published on March 18, even though it was called a draft treaty, it froze hard.† We in Ottawa tried to have some drafting improvements made in the English and French texts but our suggestions were brushed aside by the Working Group.†

In his memoirs Acheson says: "On March 18 ... we succeeded in releasing a treaty text for public discussion before final acceptance of it by governments (but, in reality, to force it)."[16] Acheson was successful; he did secure agreement on the text which had been made public. The reason for his reluctance to commit himself on the arrangements preceding the signature was clear. If he had agreed to a two-day or three-day session of foreign ministers preceding the signature of the treaty, he would have found it difficult to prevent them from considering amendments to the draft treaty. If he had announced that there would be no opportunity to revise the text, he would have stirred up a controversy. By his refusal to commit himself he succeeded in having only one meeting of the foreign ministers before the signing ceremony and they did not discuss the text of the treaty but confined themselves to discussing the organization to be created under the treaty, agreeing on a joint statement replying to the protest of the Soviet government against the treaty, and listening to a confused statement by Portugal on its treaty with Spain.[17]

The sense of urgency fluctuated during the discussions. The fear of Soviet expansionism had grown throughout 1947. The communist takeover in

Czechoslovakia in February, 1948, the threat to Norway in the second week of March, apprehensions about the Italian elections to take place on April 18 – all these brought an acute sense of urgency to the first stage of the discussions in March, 1948. On March 15, before leaving for the first talks in Washington, Pearson informed the Prime Minister that "if the communists are to be held in check in Italy, it may be essential to have the pact concluded and published a week or more before the Italian elections which are to take place on April 18."[18] By the end of the first stage of discussions this hope was given up, but the timetable then contemplated was still ambitious; it was expected that the United States would meet with the Brussels powers on April 12 and that a conference to negotiate the treaty would be held in May.[19]

Almost immediately after the first stage of discussions, however, the sense of urgency began to diminish in Washington, and whenever the sense of urgency diminished, the United States administration's apprehensions about getting in front of public opinion and especially senatorial opinion became more acute. Moreover, at this time, whenever there was a lull, George Kennan and Charles Bohlen, the principal opponents of a treaty within the administration in Washington, would counter-attack.

Part of the lull from the middle of April on resulted from the defeat of the Communists in the Italian elections on April 18. Part arose from what seemed to be a change in Soviet tactics. Lovett, in a talk with the Norwegian Ambassador and Wrong on May 8, referred to "the quiescence of the French Communist party faced with an internal split if the pace was forced by the extremists, the mildness of the terms imposed [by the Soviet Union] on Finland in comparison with the taking over of Czechoslovakia, the abrupt removal of the roadblocks on the road from the airport in Vienna and the failure to follow up vigorously the impediments put in the way of the movement of the western allies to and from Berlin."[20] We learned that the British government had told the United States government that it had heard that "Moscow has ordered the Communists in France and Italy to drop direct action, for fear that this might involve them in war."[21] Bevin on June 1 referred to "the recent Soviet peace offensive".[22]

When I read Wrong's account of his talk with Lovett I was concerned that Lovett might be putting too optimistic an interpretation on the change in Soviet tactics. I put my concern to Wrong in a letter of May 21 which Pearson signed. I said that from past experience in dealing with the Russians one could argue "that a period of relative calm is a danger signal that can precede a storm. My impression is that their practice has been to press hard and be tough for some months or a year or so, then relax the pressure, only to renew it later when conditions are better for them. Haven't we been told that this is the kind of technique which they use in the examination of political prisoners – periods of kindness, alternating with periods of toughness? They are pretty adept in this carrot and whip technique and we shouldn't be fooled by it."[23]

The three-months' gap between the end of the first stage of intergovernmental discussions on April 1 and the opening of the second stage on July 6 was caused only in part by a diminishing sense of urgency. Another cause was the desire of the administration in Washington to secure, before the opening of the second stage, a resolution of the Senate or of both houses of Congress supporting the idea of a North Atlantic treaty. The two causes were, of course, related since if the sense of urgency had been greater, the resolution might have been dispensed with or put through more expeditiously. As it was it took the State Department two months to sell the idea of the resolution to Senator Vandenberg, draft it in consultation with him, and get it through the Senate Foreign Relations Committee and the Senate. Lovett suggested the idea to Vandenberg on April 11; the resolution was adopted by the Senate on June 11. Twelve days later the United States informed the Brussels powers and Canada that it would be ready to begin top secret exploratory talks with them on June 29 pursuant to the resolution.[24] (The talks opened on July 6.)

The storm in relations between the western powers and the Soviet Union which followed the lull of April and May, broke in June in Germany. The three western occupying powers introduced their reform of the German currency on June 18. That same day the Soviet blockade of Berlin began. By June 24 the blockade was complete. The western powers countered with the airlift. The fear that some incident might precipitate war gave renewed impetus to the intergovernmental discussions on the North Atlantic treaty when they were resumed on July 6. The Berlin airlift also resulted in increased public support in the United States for the idea of a North Atlantic treaty. Twelve years later when Attlee was recalling this period, he said, "And although Greece and the Soviet *coup* in Czechoslovakia opened the eyes of Congress quite a lot, it wasn't, I think, until the Berlin airlift that American public opinion really wakened up to the facts of life. Their own troops were involved in that you see."[25]

But the renewed impetus to the discussions resulting from the crisis in Berlin was not sufficient to offset the influence of what was generally assumed to be the impending defeat of the Truman administration in the elections in November. The intergovernmental discussions in the summer of 1948 proceeded at what seemed to us in Ottawa an extraordinarily slow pace. Wrong reported a few days after the opening of the six-power talks in July: "I am sure that the State Department will not wish to get as far as a draft treaty until after the presidential elections. Once that convulsion is over it will be easier and safer to arrange for close cooperation between the [Democratic and Republican] parties."[26] Two weeks later he reported that it was not just a matter of postponing consideration of a draft treaty but that, according to Hickerson, the administration would not be able even to commit itself to any scheme for an agreement until mid-November, since after the elections it would have to have time to count heads in the Senate to ensure that there would be a safe two-thirds majority.[27] Thus the impending presidential elections resulted not only in the slow pace of discussions from July 6 to September 10 but also in the three-months gap between the ending of the second stage of the discussions on September 10 and the beginning of the third stage on December 10.

In the first three months of 1949, the negotiations were slowed down by Acheson taking over from Lovett and by his having to familiarize himself with the previous discussions and by his negotiations with the Senate. There were only two periods when the intergovernmental talks moved quickly: during the first stage, from March 22 to April 1, 1948, and during the third stage, from December 10 to 24. No senator was consulted during the first stage, and it seems probable that no senator was consulted during the third stage.

While the discussions on the North Atlantic treaty were taking place, the Palestine issue was straining relations between the British and United States governments. The U.N. General Assembly had voted in November, 1947, in favour of the partition of Palestine. The United States pressed this resolution through; the British abstained. Fighting broke out in Palestine between Arabs and Jews and continued throughout the whole of 1948. Truman considered Ernest Bevin to be prejudiced in favour of the Arabs and against the Jews. Bevin considered that Truman supported Zionism because of his need for Jewish votes, money and influence in the presidential elections in November. This made negotiations on the North Atlantic treaty more difficult. Thus Wrong reported at the end of May, 1948, that the two main difficulties in the way of negotiating the treaty were domestic party issues in the United States "plus the tense strain between London and Washington which had developed over Palestine". Wrong went on to say, "When Lovett appeared before the Senate Foreign Relations Committee in closed session to support the Vandenberg resolution, the Palestine issue was injected. Rusk the other day mentioned the personal message which he had sent to you by me a few weeks ago to the effect that an understanding over Palestine was necessary if the security pact was to be concluded, and asked me to tell you that he was still strongly of that opinion."[28]

It can be assumed that the United States administration gave this warning direct to the British government and that it hoped that the Canadian government might back the United States up in talking to the British. I am not aware that the Canadian government said anything to the British about this. Nor do I know whether the warning had any effect on British policy on the Palestine issue.

(If differences of opinion between the United States and Britain over Palestine might have endangered the success of the negotiations on the North Atlantic treaty, a failure of the British to grant independence to India in 1947 would probably have made the conclusion of the treaty impossible. Alastair Buchan's opinion is that "if Clement Attlee had not unilaterally defused the Indian issue by granting independence in 1947, it would have been difficult to sustain any intimate Anglo-American relationship in the postwar era.")[29]

The first stage in the intergovernmental discussions, the tripartite stage, was initiated by the British government's messages of March 11 to the United States and Canadian governments. In form, the second stage was initiated by the message of March 17 which Bevin and Bidault, the Foreign Ministers of Britain and France, sent to Marshall on behalf of the five Brussels treaty powers and by the passage of the Vandenberg resolution by the Senate on June 11. In fact, the second stage resulted from recommendations made in the first stage.

The communist *coup* in Czechoslovakia in February, 1948, had two somewhat contradictory results in France. On the one hand, it enabled the French government to support proposals for a multilateral security pact of Britain, France and the Benelux countries against an aggressor. On the other hand, it increased fears in France of further Soviet expansion and doubts about the wisdom of concluding a western European security pact which was not supported by the United States. Bidault at the time said that such a pact without the support of the United States might appear to be provocative without having sufficient backing to be effective.[30] Bidault therefore sent an urgent plea to Marshall on March 4 for some new action by the United States to underwrite western European security; he proposed a meeting between Marshall, Bevin and himself. [31] Before Marshall had replied to this he received Bevin's message[32] which led to the tripartite talks. Marshall, after consulting Truman, accepted the British proposal but stalled on the French proposal. He told Bidault on March 12 that as soon as the United States government had had an opportunity to study the treaty which was about to be concluded in Brussels, he would be ready to discuss with Bidault and Bevin what further steps might be desirable. Marshall added that it might be wise to have a Benelux representative included in the conversations.[33] On March 17, the very day the Brussels treaty was signed, the five signatories requested a meeting with the United States.[34]

On March 15 there seemed to be a possibility that France would be invited to participate from the beginning with the United States, Britain and Canada in the first stage of the multilateral intergovernmental talks. Then, on March 18, the United States proposed that the first question to be considered in these talks should be that of French participation. Both Hickerson and Jebb at this time seemed to be in favour of the French being asked to join the talks and Pearson told Jebb that Canada would welcome French participation from the beginning if this could be arranged satisfactorily to the United States and Britain.[35] However, at the first of the tripartite meetings the decision was against inviting the French. Pearson in his report on this meeting said that it was agreed that the French would not sit in on the discussions which would also be held without reference to the expected meeting between Bevin, Marshall and Bidault. "I expressed the hope," Pearson said, "that the French could be brought in at the earliest possible date and there was general agreement on this." [36]

If the French had been present at the March meetings, the task of reaching agreement at these meetings would have been more difficult. The French, no doubt, would have pressed their argument that what was urgent was not so much a North Atlantic treaty as a decision by the United States to transfer large military supplies to western European countries, especially France, and to agree that if war broke out, it would be fought as far east from France as possible. But the exclusion of France meant that the French put these arguments in the talks during the summer and probably put them more intransigently at that time than they would have put them in March. In March, because of the atmosphere of crisis, they would have been under more pressure to agree. In August they could explain their coolness to the idea of a North Atlantic treaty by saying that the idea had come to them as a surprise for they had not been informed prior to the opening of the conversations on July 6 that a pact of this nature was under contemplation.* The great advantage of including France in the March meetings would have been that if the French had been in the talks on the North Atlantic treaty from the beginning there would have been a better chance of their feeling that the North Atlantic alliance was, in large part, their creation.

The recommendation agreed to in the March tripartite talks was that the next move would be a meeting between the United States and the Brussels powers in response to the message of March 17 from the Brussels powers to Marshall. The expectation was that the meeting would take place about April 12. [37] This meeting would be followed by diplomatic approaches to Norway, Sweden, Denmark, Iceland, Ireland, Italy and Portugal. The President would make a statement late in April announcing the calling of a conference to conclude a collective defence agreement for the North Atlantic area. The conference would be held in May. Canada would not be a participant in the meeting between the United States and the Brussels powers but it would participate in the subsequent conference.

*See pages 117 to 118.

The meeting with the Brussels powers kept being put off. In mid-May the State Department sounded Canada out on whether it would wish to participate in the meeting with the Brussels powers.[38] Bevin in a message to Marshall of June 1 (which was not delivered until June 14) said that the British would be delighted if Canada were present.[39] George Kennan supported the inclusion of Canada. On June 23, the State Department extended an invitation to Canada and the Brussels powers.[40] France subsequently agreed "in view of the role played by Canada in the late war that it is justifiable and desirable that Canada" be included.[41]

The United States, in the intergovernmental discussions in the summer of 1948, insisted that since it was the Brussels powers which had requested these discussions, it was up to the Brussels powers, not the United States, to make proposals. Thus, at the meeting of the Ambassadors' Committee on September 3, Lovett said it was the Brussels powers which were "responsible for these conversations being held".[42] In a letter of August 24 to Caffery, the United States Ambassador in Paris, he instructed Caffery to make clear to the French government "that it is the French government, not ours, which insisted on holding these conversations and which is seeking commitments and material assistance."[43] Because the United States took this line, it refused to submit the revision it had made of the Pentagon paper as a basis for discussion in the talks in the summer of 1948. The fact that no paper was put before the participants in these talks resulted in diffuse discussions, confusion – and a slow rate of progress which was probably what the United States wanted. At one time Stone, the Canadian representative on the Working Committee, even suggested to Ottawa that he might submit a revision of the Pentagon paper as his own product.[44]

The nature of the discussions in the Ambassadors' Committee was greatly influenced by the nature of the agreed minutes which were kept and sent to the participating governments. At the second meeting in July it was decided that the agreed minutes would "consist only of a summary as brief as possible of the principal points brought out at each meeting".[45] Little attention was paid to this decision even at the next two meetings, and from the fifth meeting on, stenotypists kept a verbatim record which was circulated to the participants; and the agreed minutes, which were based on this record, became full accounts of the discussions. The minutes of the fifth meeting ran to over five thousand words. Toward the end of the negotiations it was even suggested "that instead of making minutes we might merely revise the verbatim texts of the remarks made at the meetings to avoid the extra secretarial work in producing the minutes."[46]

The advantage to foreign offices of verbatim records or of full agreed minutes is that a foreign office can check what its representative in the discussions said against what it expected him to say or had instructed him to say. If he has been told to oppose a certain proposal vigorously the foreign office will expect that the minutes will record him as having opposed it vigorously. If there is a wide gap between the expectations of the foreign office and the content of the minutes, the foreign office will expect an explanation. Full agreed minutes thus inhibit the freedom of action of the government representatives. Discussions will be frank if representatives have been told to be frank but they will not be free. The Belgian Ambassador in August, 1948, at an informal meeting of the Ambassadors' Committee of which no agreed minutes were kept, said that "he feared that we might not be coming to grips with the basic question since, in the formal meetings, each ambassador felt it necessary to state a position for the record or for the benefit of his Foreign Minister."[47]

Two informal meetings of the Ambassadors' Committee were held in order to permit of greater freedom of discussion. The meeting on August 20 discussed the French hesitations about the North Atlantic treaty. The meeting on February 19, 1949, discussed the objections of the Senate Foreign Relations Committee to the proposed wording of the pledge. Canada had two representatives at the first of these meetings but, apart from this exception, countries were represented at these informal meetings by only one person. There were no stenographers present and no junior diplomats present to draft the telegrams to the foreign offices reporting on the talks. The first meeting was held in Lovett's house, the second in Acheson's house.

Lovett, in his memorandum on the first meeting, said, "It was stated at the outset that this meeting was completely informal and unofficial, that there would be no minutes or records taken of it and that the results would not be reported to the respective governments since the purpose was to permit the members of the group to consider the problem as individuals apart from their official capacity and to express their personal difficulties or doubts as to various aspects of the program so far developed."[48]

When Lovett said that there would be no minutes or records taken of the meeting he must have meant that there would be no agreed minutes or records. In his own three-thousand-word-long memorandum, Lovett gave a blow-by-blow account of the discussions. Lovett said it had been agreed that the results of the meeting would not be reported to the respective governments. Lovett, nevertheless, reported the results of the meeting to his government. Presumably all the other participants did likewise. They were able, however, to use their own discretion in making these reports. That is the essential feature of an informal meeting of government representatives.

"Action summaries" of three meetings of the Working Group were maintained in December, 1948,[49] but no agreed records were kept of any of the other 30 or so meetings of the Working Group. Each representative presumably informed his government of what had happened. Because of the absence of agreed records the meetings of the Working Group were more informal and more free than they otherwise would have been. A representative who had under instructions put forward a proposal which his colleagues then rejected could more easily participate in working out a compromise. Achilles in his recollections of the meetings of the Working Group in the summer of 1948 says,

> The NATO spirit was born in that Working Group. Derick Hoyer Millar started it. One day he made a proposal which was obviously nonsense. Several of us told him so in no uncertain terms and a much better formulation emerged from the discussion. Derick said: "Those were my instructions. All right. I'll tell the Foreign Office I made my pitch and was shot down, and try to get them changed." He did. From then on we all followed the same system. If our instructions were sound and agreement could be reached, fine. If not, we'd work out something we all, or most of us, considered sound, and whoever had the instructions undertook to get them changed. It always worked, though sometimes it took time. [50]

The verbatim record and the minutes of the meetings of the Ambassadors' Committee provide a fascinating revelation of how intelligent, experienced diplomats conduct secret intergovernmental discussions on important issues.

The participants, other than the French, seldom used blunt language or veiled or open threats in the multilateral talks; they normally restricted their use of these devices to bilateral talks. Thus when Wrong was making his last-minute fight for Article 2 of the treaty, he did not state at a meeting of the Ambassadors' Committee that if the treaty did not contain an article along the lines Canada wanted, "the Canadian government would have to review its position towards the whole project". He said this to Hickerson when the two of them were alone together.[51] At the Ambassadors' Committee he said "that it would cause great political difficulty in Canada if there were no article in the treaty of a non-military nature. There was need for something which reflected the ideological unity of the North Atlantic powers."[52] When Oliver Franks, the British Ambassador, differed from the French Ambassador, he said "that he was not sure whether the analysis given by the French Ambassador was shared by the British representative."[53] When Pearson was stating Canada's opposition to including Italy in the North Atlantic pact, he emphasized "the difficulty of including, certainly at the beginning, borderline geographical communities which lead from one to another until the original geographic area had no longer any meaning".[54] Silvercruys, the Belgian Ambassador, said at a meeting in December, "Should Italy's participation lead to the inclusion in the area covered by the treaty of territories not situated in the North American, North Atlantic and western European regions he would have to reserve the position of his government."[55]

Bonnet, the French Ambassador, on the other hand, often departed from the diplomatic language of understatement. His government had firm views and he obviously had firm instructions. He put his arguments bluntly, so bluntly that at a meeting of the Ambassadors' Committee, Franks once rebuked him for his language:

> I think that the way in which the English put their views and the way in which the French put their views sometimes has something to do with our apparent disagreement, rather than the substance of the question . . . . When the [French Ambassador] talks about conditions, I am not happy because it is not the way we have done our business around this table . . . . I would, therefore, very much prefer if the French position could be put to us not in the language of conditions but in the language of views strongly held by the French government.

Franks added that when the French Ambassador spoke of conditions he felt as if a pistol had been put at his head, and this made it much more difficult for him to settle down and reach an agreed solution. Bonnet retorted that he had the same reaction when in negotiations he found himself talking to a wall.[56]

The year-long discussions on the North Atlantic treaty threw light on the methods governments use in efforts to strengthen their hands in intergovernmental discussions. There is the tough guy waiting in the back room; and this "person" can be the Senate, Cabinet, Parliament, etcetera. Here, one says, "Yours seems to me a very reasonable proposal but I doubt that I can sell it to the Senate committee (or to my minister or cabinet, etcetera)." When one uses this technique it is essential never to agree immediately to a compromise that is put forward but to say no more than, "I'm not certain I can get my principals to accept this compromise but I'll try my best." This was Acheson's technique on Articles 2 and 5 of the treaty, the articles on economic and social co-operation and on the pledge of assistance in the event of armed attack. If the other participants have been so unwise as to agree to the compromise without using a similar formula, it may be possible to get them to agree to a further compromise even farther from what they originally proposed. Thus if Acheson had been unsuccessful in selling a compromise on one of the articles to the Senators he might have said, "I'm sorry to have to report that the Senators won't accept the compromise we worked out at our last meeting.

They insist on deleting the phrase. . . ." If the other participants have been careful to reserve the position of their principals, they can reply, "I have consulted my government. They have instructed me to say that it is only with the greatest reluctance that they will accept the compromise and they will certainly not accept any further watering down of this provision."

During the intergovernmental discussions on the treaty, governments would make public statements or give speeches intended not only to rally support at home – and this might have the advantage of toughening the tough guys in the back room – but also to strengthen the will of their potential allies or to influence their thinking. These speeches thus constituted part of the negotiating process. To those in the know, the public statements made by the United States and Canadian governments on the signature of the Brussels treaty on March 17, 1948, were public affirmations of support in principle for the British initiative of March 11, 1948. St. Laurent's speech in the Canadian House of Commons on April 29, 1948, constituted support for the British initiative and an appeal to those in the State Department (such as Kennan and Bohlen) who were opposed to a treaty and wanted instead a sort of extension of the Monroe Doctrine to western Europe to reconsider their position.

Governments would try to strengthen their position at the negotiating table in Washington by arguing their case not only in Washington but also in the other capitals concerned. In August, 1948, the United States and Canadian Ambassadors in France, Belgium and the Netherlands pleaded with these three governments to be more forthcoming in the Washington talks. In January, 1949, Chauvel, the Secretary-General of the French Foreign Office, instructed the French Ambassadors in the capitals of all the countries participating in the Washington talks to make the French position on Algeria clear to the government to which they were accredited.[57] The five Brussels treaty powers (Britain, France, Belgium, the Netherlands and Luxembourg) tried to work out in their Consultative Council a common line in the negotiations.

Sometimes the intergovernmental talks about the proposed treaty held in capitals other than Washington would mean that governments believed that one or more of the ambassadors in Washington was acting without instructions or misinterpreting his instructions. More often it meant a desire to get the instructions changed. When the United States and Canada urged the arguments for a treaty in Paris in the summer of 1948, they knew that the French government was being difficult, and they thought that Bonnet, the French Ambassador, might be being even more difficult than his instructions called for. Lovett said at the time in a letter to the United States Ambassador in Paris, "How much of Bonnet's position is personal and how much is due to his instructions we do not know. . . ."[58] When Canada, in February, 1949, pressed the governments of the

Brussels treaty powers to support the Canadian proposals on Article 2, Canada was asking those governments to reverse the instructions which they had jointly given to their ambassadors. Similarly when Canada asked its Ambassador in Paris to try to persuade the French government not to press for the extension of the treaty to Italy and North Africa, Canada was asking the French government to change the instructions it had given to its ambassador.

There was not, so far as I know, any explicit bargaining on the provisions of the treaty in the sense of a trade of support for one provision against support of (or opposition to) another provision. Tacit bargains may well have been struck, however. Perhaps this happened in November, 1948, when the French went along with the British in their desire to delete Article 2 from the treaty and the British went along with the French in their desire to include North Africa in the area covered by the pledge in the treaty. Undoubtedly in the negotiations on the treaty the willingness of one party to change its policy in order to accommodate another party helped to create an atmosphere in which a return favour might more easily be granted. Canada gave in to the French on Algeria and on Italian membership in the alliance. This must have made it easier for Canada to persuade France in February, 1949, to support it on Article 2. If this is so, France may have been reimbursed once for supporting the deletion of Article 2 and once for supporting the strengthening of Article 2. Britain did not make its support for Canada on Article 2 conditional on a *quid pro quo*, but in February, 1949, Gladwyn Jebb wrote to the Canadian High Commissioner in London, stating that in return for United Kingdom support on Article 2, the United Kingdom government hoped that the Canadian government would give sympathetic consideration to their desire that the signatories of the North Atlantic treaty should agree on a declaration concerning the position of Greece and Turkey (and Italy if it did not come into the North Atlantic treaty).[59] The issue did not arise since no declaration was made on Greece and Turkey, and Italy became a signatory of the treaty.

In a negotiation such as that on the North Atlantic treaty, each participating country, no matter how small, has bargaining strength if there is a possibility that it will refuse to join the alliance should its views be disregarded and if its membership in the alliance is important to the other participating countries. For this reason the participants in such a negotiation will seek to reach unanimity. But on issues which are not fundamental, majority opinion will prevail, and in determining what constitutes a majority the views of the participating countries are weighed, not counted. There was an illuminating example of this at the final meeting of the Ambassadors' Committee on March 15, 1949. The Committee was discussing whether "armed attack" should be substituted for "aggression" at the end of Article 3. Canada, the Netherlands, Belgium and Norway were opposed to this change. Britain and France were in favour. "The United States was prepared to accept 'aggression' if it was agreed to mean 'armed attack'." If there had been a vote (there were, of course, no votes in the negotiations), the count would presumably have been four in favour of 'aggression', two in favour of 'armed attack', and the United States possibly abstaining. But the minutes of the meeting state, "As the majority preferred 'armed attack', the change was made."[60] The majority of countries did not prefer 'armed attack'; a minority of countries preferred 'armed attack' but the minority, being more important than the majority, constituted a majority. This sort of practice is normal at serious intergovernmental meetings which are attempting to make new international law.

CHAPTER FIVE

THE ARCHITECTS OF THE TREATY

The senior participants in the intergovernmental discussions in Washington on the treaty were the ambassadors in Washington meeting under the chairmanship first of Robert A. Lovett and then of Dean Acheson. This group was called the Ambassadors' Committee. It was assisted by a Working Group composed of the seconds-in-command of the embassies with a senior officer of the State Department, usually J. D. Hickerson, as chairman. There was also a drafting group of the Working Group. The members of these groups were able to devote only a small part of their time to the discussions on the treaty; they had many other problems to deal with. The same was true of the members of their foreign offices to whom they reported.

Lovett was the senior United States participant in the discussions on the treaty from March 11, 1948, when he advised Marshall on the reply which he should make to the British proposal for tripartite talks, until January 20, 1949, with the exception of the first stage of the discussions in March. He was away from Washington on holiday then and Lewis Douglas, the American Ambassador in London, was chairman of the tripartite meetings. Dean Rusk said in 1976 that Lovett was Marshall's alter ego and that the "combination of Marshall and Lovett at the leadership of the Department of State has never been equalled in our history and is not likely to be again."[1] When Truman formed his second administration on January 20, 1949, Marshall and Lovett resigned and Acheson became Secretary of State, and responsible for the negotiations on the treaty until they were concluded on March 28.

Lovett was thus in charge for about 10 months, Acheson for only about two months. Lovett chaired 12 meetings of the Ambassadors' Committee, Acheson eight. The draft treaty approved by the Ambassadors' Committee on December 24 under Lovett's chairmanship was close to the final text. One of Lovett's greatest contributions to the success of the negotiations was to persuade Vandenberg to support the idea of a treaty and to put the Vandenberg resolution through the Senate.

Where Acheson's task was more demanding than Lovett's was that in the last stage, when he was in charge, the Ambassadors' Committee was attempting to reach agreement on the final text of the treaty. This meant that decisions could no longer be put off. Governments had to decide how far they were prepared to give in to the demands of others in order to reach agreement. In efforts to strengthen their bargaining positions, governments uttered veiled or open threats and counter-threats. Tempers became frayed. And while Acheson was conducting these difficult negotiations with governments, he was also conducting equally difficult negotiations with the Senate Foreign Relations Committee. Acheson was not present at the creation of the North Atlantic treaty. He was present only on the sixth, the last day of the creation, but that was a particularly busy day.

In the first stage of the discussions Gladwyn Jebb (later Lord Gladwyn) was the principal British representative. He was then Under-Secretary at the British Foreign Office. Afterwards the British representative on the Ambassadors' Committee was Oliver Franks (later Lord Franks), the British Ambassador in Washington. Lester Pearson was the Canadian representative during the first half of the first stage and at a number of meetings in subsequent stages. At all the other meetings of the Ambassadors' Committee, Hume Wrong, the Canadian Ambassador in Washington, was the Canadian representative. Pearson was Under-Secretary of State for External Affairs during the first and second stages and Secretary of State for External Affairs during the third and fourth stages. The representatives of France, Belgium, the Netherlands, and Norway were their Ambassadors in Washington, Henri Bonnet, Baron Robert Silvercruys, Dr. E. Van Kleffens, and Wilhelm Morgenstierne. The Luxembourg representative was their Minister in Washington, Hugues Le Gallais.

Hickerson, director of the office of European Affairs, was the most influential officer of the State Department in the negotiations from the beginning to the end. He tells the story that when he was riding back to the State Department with Acheson from the ceremony at which the treaty had been signed, Acheson said,

> Well, Jack, I think this treaty is going to work. If it works, for generations there will be arguments in the United States as to who more than anybody else is responsible for it, but if it doesn't work, there will be no damn doubt, you did it.[2]

The second most influential officer of the State Department concerned with the negotiations was T. C. Achilles, the chief of the division of western European affairs.

Hickerson was the main spokesman for the United States at almost all the meetings of the Working Group. (He was also the main spokesman at the tripartite meetings in March.) Charles Bohlen and George Kennan were the main spokesmen at a few meetings of the Working Group.[†] Other leading members of the Working Group were F. Hoyer Millar (later Lord Inchyra) of the British embassy, Thomas A. Stone of the Canadian embassy, and Armand Bérard of the French embassy.[†]

There was the usual friendly rivalry between the Working Group and the Ambassadors' Committee. Achilles, presumably repeating a remark made at the time in the Working Group, wrote later that the treaty was negotiated by the Working Group despite the ambassadors.[3]

For the British the discussions in Washington were a prolific progenitor of peers. All three of the principal British representatives were later created peers: Jebb, Franks and Hoyer Millar. The junior member of the British group, after Donald Maclean's departure, was Nicholas Henderson, now (1976) Ambassador to Paris. It looks as if he too may end his diplomatic career as a peer.

The participants in the discussions in Washington were not, of course, free agents. They were subject to guidance, suggestions and instructions from their governments. Lovett reported to Marshall. Marshall and Acheson reported to Truman. Marshall and Lovett consulted Senator Arthur Vandenberg and his adviser, John Foster Dulles. Acheson consulted Senators Vandenberg, Tom Connally and Walter George, and later the whole Senate Foreign Relations Committee. Oliver Franks reported to Ernest Bevin, the Foreign Secretary. Bevin cleared important questions with the Prime Minister, Clement Attlee. Bonnet reported to Jean Chauvel, the Secretary-General of the French Foreign Office, and Chauvel reported to his minister, first Georges Bidault and later Robert Schuman. Paul-Henri Spaak, Foreign Minister and Prime Minister of Belgium, took an active interest in the discussions in Washington. D. U. Stikker was Foreign Minister of the Netherlands at the time but he was so preoccupied with events in Indonesia that he was not able to devote much attention to the discussions.[4] Hume Wrong reported to Pearson and to Brooke Claxton, when Claxton was Acting Foreign Minister, and sometimes to me as Acting Under-Secretary of State for External Affairs. Pearson and I cleared important questions with Louis St. Laurent and with Mackenzie King until St. Laurent succeeded him as Prime Minister in November, 1948.

The chief British architects of the treaty were Bevin, Jebb, Franks and Hoyer Millar; the chief United States architects, Lovett, Acheson, Hickerson, Achilles and Vandenberg; the Canadians, St. Laurent, Pearson, Claxton, Wrong, Stone and I.[†] Since Britain, the United States and Canada were especially influential in the making of the North Atlantic treaty these fifteen British, Americans and Canadians constituted a sort of inner group in the international negotiations.

Jebb, Hickerson and Pearson were especially influential. During the first half of the negotiations all three were career civil servants. During

TABLE 2

PARTICIPANTS IN THE INTERGOVERNMENTAL DISCUSSIONS

	POLITICS	FOREIGN OFFICE	EMBASSY IN WASHINGTON
Belgium	P.-H. Spaak (Prime Minister and Foreign Minister)		R. Silvercruys R. Taymans R. Vaes
Britain	C.R. Attlee (Prime Minister) Ernest Bevin (Foreign Minister)	Gladwyn Jebb	Oliver Franks Donald Maclean F. Hoyer Millar J. N. Henderson
Canada	W.L.M. King (Prime Minister) L.S. St. Laurent (Foreign Minister and later Prime Minister) B. Claxton (Defence Minister and Acting Foreign Minister) L.B. Pearson (Foreign Minister)	E. Reid	H.H. Wrong T.A. Stone R.L. Rogers
France	Georges Bidault (Foreign Minister) Robert Schuman (Foreign Minister)	Jean Chauvel	Henri Bonnet Armand Bérard Arnaud Walper

65

TABLE 2

PARTICIPANTS IN THE INTERGOVERNMENTAL DISCUSSIONS

	POLITICS	FOREIGN OFFICE	EMBASSY IN WASHINGTON
Luxembourg			H. Le Gallais
Netherlands	D. U. Stikker (Foreign Minister)		E. Van Kleffens Otto Reuchlin Caes Vreede
Norway	H. Lange (Foreign Minister)		W. Morgenstierne
United States	Harry S. Truman (President) Arthur Vandenberg (Chairman, Senate Foreign Relations Committee) Tom Connally (Chairman, Senate Foreign Relations Committee)	G.C. Marshall (Secretary of State) R.A. Lovett (Under-Secretary and Acting Secretary) Dean Acheson (Secretary of State) Charles E. Bohlen George F. Kennan J.D. Hickerson T.C. Achilles	

the second half, Pearson was a cabinet minister. The other politicians in the inner group of 15 were Bevin, Vandenberg, St. Laurent and Claxton.

Apart from St. Laurent whose father was French-Canadian (and whose mother was Irish), Vandenberg who had some Dutch ancestors, and Achilles, who had a little German blood, it seems as if the inner group of 15 may have been entirely of British and Irish origin. All had been brought up as Protestants, except St. Laurent who was a Roman Catholic. In 1948, twelve of the fifteen, including all the officials, were between 43 years of age (Franks and I) and 55 (Acheson). The others (Bevin, St. Laurent and Vandenberg) were in their mid-sixties. Of the 11 North Americans, nine were born and brought up in the eastern United States or in southern Ontario or southern Quebec. The other two (Lovett and Hickerson) were born in Texas but Lovett went to school and university in the eastern United States. Seven of the 10 principal British and Canadian architects of the treaty had been to Oxford; the exceptions were Bevin, St. Laurent and Claxton. Three of the five Americans (Lovett, Acheson and Achilles) had been to Yale. Thus 10 of the 15 had been either to Oxford or to Yale. The only one of the 15 who had not been to university was Bevin. All 15 had much in common; they shared political values.

Fourteen of the 15 (all except St. Laurent) were by origin, upbringing and careers members of the group of Protestant British and Protestant Irish origin which at that time dominated national political activities in the United States, Britain and Canada. It was thus natural for them to become advocates of a North Atlantic alliance of which these three countries would be the core.

Many of the members of the inner group from the United States, Britain and Canada had known members of the groups from the other two countries for many years and had had experience in working together. They knew each other's cast of thought. Hickerson had known Wrong and Stone since 1927 and Pearson since 1928. He had been the principal expert on Canadian affairs in the State Department for 20 years. He had participated in many intergovernmental discussions, formal and informal, with Pearson, Wrong, Stone and me. He had worked with Jebb at the Dumbarton Oaks conference in 1944. Wrong had known Acheson ever since the Canadian legation was opened in Washington in 1927. They quickly became close friends. Pearson, Wrong and I had worked with Jebb on United Nations affairs from 1945 on in San Francisco, London and New York.

Personal relations between the three national groups were not, of course, always harmonious. Jebb, a product of Eton and Oxford, with first class honours from Oxford in history, had intellectual distinction; he sometimes gave Americans who did not know him well the impression that he was rather arrogant and aloof.[5] Acheson, a product of Groton,

Yale and Harvard, was likewise intellectually distinguished and apt to appear arrogant. He got on well with Wrong and Franks. He and Pearson never developed really friendly relations but it was only from about 1951 on, mainly as the result of differences of opinion during the Korean War, that they began to dislike each other.

Within each of the British, Canadian and American groups close and friendly personal relations were the rule and this helped each group to reach agreement quickly on issues arising in the negotiations. Pearson and Wrong had been friends and colleagues for over 20 years. Lovett was a devoted friend and admirer of Vandenberg. Hickerson and Achilles were friends and thought alike on virtually all aspects of the negotiations. The only clash of personalities within the inner United States group was between Acheson and Vandenberg; they did not get on well together.

In all three countries relations between the principal negotiators and their political masters were excellent. Jebb was a favourite of Ernest Bevin and Bevin had the full confidence of Attlee. St. Laurent trusted Pearson's judgement and was, indeed, grooming him as a possible successor as leader of the Liberal party and Prime Minister. Marshall had confidence in Lovett and both Marshall and Acheson had the confidence and respect of Truman.

There was no division of opinion within the Canadian government on the necessity of a North Atlantic treaty and of Canadian membership in it though St. Laurent and Pearson were constantly apprehensive that Mackenzie King might switch from support of the treaty to his prewar isolationism. I am not aware of any division of opinion within the British government. There was a profound difference of opinion within the State Department between Hickerson and Achilles on one side and George Kennan and Charles Bohlen on the other side. At the beginning of the intergovernmental discussions Kennan and Bohlen opposed the idea of a treaty.

Civil servants were extremely influential in the making of the North Atlantic treaty. Gladwyn Jebb produced and sold to Ernest Bevin the original idea, the spark, which resulted first in the conclusion of the Brussels treaty and then of the North Atlantic treaty. Hickerson sold the idea of a North Atlantic treaty to Marshall and Lovett. Pearson sold the idea to Mackenzie King and St. Laurent. If it had not been for Hickerson, Italy would not have been an original member of the alliance and might, indeed, never have been admitted to the alliance. Pearson, when still a civil servant, persuaded the Canadian government that the treaty must create something more than a military alliance and without Canada's commitment to this proposition there would have been no Article 2.

Caution and conservatism are sometimes thought of as marking the civil servant's approach. These civil servants were neither cautious nor conservative. They were zealous and creative. Indeed, in their zeal for their creative ideas they may sometimes have given the impression in the negotiations that their ideas had more support from their political masters than they in fact had. This seems to have been true of some of the statements about Italian membership in the alliance which Hickerson made on behalf of the State Department.* It likewise seems to have been true of Jebb's statements about the British government's views on the movements toward European and North Atlantic unity. Thus Jebb told the Working Group in Washington at the beginning of September, 1948, that Ernest Bevin was opposed to the inclusion of Article 2 in the treaty because this would "slow up the present progress of the European nations toward that union which they all believed is so essential."[6] In November he said that the British government was "actively pursuing the idea of European unity, with gathering support behind them, and it would make difficulties for them at home if this idea were given a different direction by a merging of the western European nations in a larger political entity including the United States."[7] Eighteen years later, however, he wrote that at the time of the negotiation of the North Atlantic treaty Ernest Bevin "did not really believe in any kind of European idea. If anything he was against it. Some form of Atlantic union based on Anglo-American leadership he could understand. It made sense to him. . . . "[8]

For the first seven and a half months of the intergovernmental discussions on the North Atlantic treaty, President Truman had to deal with a Senate and House of Representatives which were dominated by the Republican Party. He did not have the political strength which is derived from having been elected as President. He was in the eyes of most people a lame-duck president since it was generally assumed that he would be defeated in the elections in November. Until shortly before the Republican convention it was also assumed that the next president would probably be Arthur Vandenberg, the Chairman of the Foreign Relations Committee of the Senate. Had Truman been a smaller man he might have used the international discussions on the North Atlantic treaty as an opportunity to portray himself as a far-sighted international statesman who was taking a bold initiative in foreign affairs. Instead, in April, 1948, he allowed his rival, Vandenberg, to get the credit for launching the six-power discussions. Had Truman been less courageous and far-sighted he would have capitulated in February, 1949, to demands from powerful senators that the central core of the treaty, the pledge to take joint action to halt aggression, should be gravely weakened. Instead, he insisted that a stout fight be made against these demands. He gave Marshall, Lovett and Acheson his confidence, support and his wise counsel.

* See pages 205 to 206.

CHAPTER SIX

SECRET DIPLOMACY

In the making of the North Atlantic treaty, a highly-secret diplomacy was used. The fact that the incident which precipitated the talks on the treaty was a Soviet threat to Norway seems to have been kept secret for ten years or more. The fact that discussions were held in March, 1948, between the United States, Britain and Canada was kept as a secret at the time and for perhaps 20 years afterwards – not only from the public but from friendly governments. As late at 1976, the official NATO account of the origins of the alliance did not mention these talks.[1] There were no leaks to the press about the divisions of opinion in the State Department in the spring of 1948 on whether there should be a treaty. There were no leaks about the two most bitterly divisive issues, whether Italy should be a member of the alliance and whether the area covered by the pledge should include Algeria. There were no leaks about the conflicts over the article on democracy and economic and social co-operation. Above all, there were no leaks about the impatience of the United States administration in the summer of 1948 over France's apparent lack of interest in the proposed North Atlantic alliance. The only major leak which occurred about a divisive issue – and that not until February, 1949 – was over the wording of the pledge in the treaty under which each participant promised to come to the assistance of the other participants if they were attacked. The preservation of secrecy about the tripartite talks in March enabled the United States administration to pretend to Congress that the second stage of discussions grew out of the Vandenberg resolution adopted by the Senate on June 11 whereas in fact the State Department, when Hickerson and Achilles helped Vandenberg to draft his resolution, was securing an *ex post facto* legitimation of the results of the first stage of the discussions. Secrecy about the first stage of discussions also enabled the United States, Britain and Canada to pretend to France and the Benelux countries that they had participated in the discussions from the outset. The negotiation of the North Atlantic treaty must constitute one of the rare instances in modern diplomacy of an important international agreement being negotiated with almost no publicity about the main differences of opinion between the parties to the negotiations.

The paradox is that, while knowledge of the tripartite talks of March, 1948, was kept from the public and from friendly governments, it was not kept from the Soviet government. The third officer at the British embassy in Washington who participated in the tripartite talks along with the Ambassador and the Minister was Donald Maclean, First Secretary and Soviet agent. Maclean also took part in discussions on the proposed treaty with senior officials of the State Department between the first and second stages of the discussions, and he attended the first meeting, and possibly subsequent meetings, of the second stage. He had access to the documents relating to the discussions until he left Washington on September 1, 1948, to take up his appointment to the British embassy in Cairo. Maclean was thus in a position to send the Soviet government a play-by-play account of the discussions up to the end of August, 1948.

Extraordinary precautions were taken to ensure secrecy about the tripartite talks in Washington in March, 1948. Jebb's cover story to explain his presence in Washington was that he had come to the United States to discuss with the British representative to the U.N. some of the issues before the Security Council.[2] He said at the first meeting of the tripartite talks that he would "probably visit New York to appear at the Security Council from time to time as a deception measure."[3] Pearson's cover story for his absence from Ottawa was that he was going to New York for a few days to help out General McNaughton, the Canadian representative on the Security Council, because he was under the weather.[4] General Charles Foulkes, the Chairman of the Canadian Chiefs of Staff Committee, came in civilian clothes for the ostensible purpose of calling on the new United States chief of staff.[5] Wrong, the Canadian Ambassador, considered that it would be unwise for him to attend the first two meetings because he had, before the talks were agreed to, made engagements in Toronto which he said he could not get out of "without giving an awkward explanation."[6] It was feared that some enterprising newspaperman might pick up a clue to a good story if he learned that Jebb, Pearson, the British Ambassador and the Canadian chargé d'affaires had all come to the State Department for a meeting. The meetings were therefore held in the "war room" of the United States Joint Chiefs of Staff in the "bowels" of the Pentagon, and the Joint Chiefs of Staff sent staff cars to pick up the participants and to deliver them directly to a secret entrance in the basement of the Pentagon. The entrance was so secret that one Pentagon chauffeur got lost trying to find it.[7] As part of the pretence that the first three-power stage of the discussions had never taken place, the agreement reached on April 1, 1948, was cast in the form of a "working paper" setting forth tentative proposals which might be put forward by the United States administration.[8] A revised version of this paper was shown to Senator Vandenberg by Lovett in mid-April but Vandenberg was not

told of the three-power talks.[9] One of the reasons advanced for not inviting France to participate in the first stage of the talks in March was that
the French government could not be depended on to maintain the secrecy
of the discussions. Pearson, in his report on the first meeting of the tripartite talks, said, "The United States representatives were reluctant to
include the French in talks during the opening stages, mainly for fear of
premature disclosures." (It was believed at the time that the Soviet
authorities had broken the French cypher, and that the Soviet government had agents or informants at high levels in the French administration.) Pearson went on to say that the United States representatives
"emphasized the necessity of absolute secrecy at this stage."[10] Each of the
three governments participating in the tripartite talks agreed to keep to a
minimum the number of people who knew about them. Pearson reported
to the Prime Minister on March 29, 1948, that only seven or eight ministers and officials in London and about the same number in the administration in Washington knew anything about the discussions.[11] In the
embassies concerned in Washington only two, or at most three, officers
were supposed to be allowed to know of the discussions. Bevin did not tell
the British Cabinet about the discussions; he consulted, he said, "in the
greatest secrecy" only "the Prime Minister and a few of my closest colleagues."[12]

As the discussions went on the number of those in the inner circles in
Washington, London and Ottawa increased – but very gradually. At the
beginning of July, 1948, almost four months after the British telegram of
March 11, information about the discussions had been given to only two
officers of the Department of External Affairs in Ottawa in addition to
Pearson and me.[13]

When the six-power discussions opened in Washington on July 6,
1948, Lovett "emphasized the need for absolute security. A leak, particularly during the political campaign in the United States, might throw the
whole enterprise into jeopardy. Political heat in this country will increase
up to election day, and scars will be left afterwards. Any leak as to the
subjects of discussion in these meetings, therefore, might cast a cloud over
the whole plan. The State Department for its part was, therefore, limiting
the number of people involved in these discussions to an absolute minimum."[14] (The State Department's idea of an absolute minimum would be
considered generous by most other foreign offices. In July, 1948, the
United States working group on the discussions had 14 members[15] and
papers relating to the negotiations were being submitted to the National
Security Council.)

At the second meeting of the six-power talks the participants agreed to
special procedures to prevent leaks. These were modelled on the measures which had been taken by the Brussels treaty powers. This procedure
known as "metric", precluded the transmission of documents from Wash-

ington to Europe except by accompanied diplomatic bag to the metric registry of the Foreign Office in London which would send them, likewise by accompanied diplomatic bag, to Paris, Brussels and The Hague. Governments agreed not to refer to the discussions in telegrams or over the telephone and to restrict drastically the number of persons permitted access to the documents.[16]

Lovett's plea that there should be no leak as to the subjects of discussion at the six-power meetings meant that none of the participants should say anything to the press. This was not what leading newspapermen such as James Reston of the *New York Times* were accustomed to. According to Hickerson, Reston descended on him after the first meeting of the six-power group and asked what had happened at the meeting. Hickerson said "We're not talking." Reston badgered him a bit and then said, "It's a hell of a note when the correspondent of the *New York Times* can't get a story from American sources. I'll just have to go to the British." Hickerson said, "I guess that's right, Scotty. You'll have to go there." Reston went to the British and got nothing. Hickerson, in his usual vivid language, says that Reston "nearly went nuts; he couldn't believe it; he couldn't believe it".[17]

(Reston may not have been able to learn much about the negotiations in the summer of 1948 but from about November on he became increasingly well-informed, so much so that in November and again in February, 1949, he made proposals privately to the participants for the incorporation in the treaty of a provision on special military agreements and, in January, after talking to Vandenberg and Dulles, he warned the Canadian Ambassador that the language of the draft treaty should be kept fluid until Congress had been consulted).

It had been possible to keep secret the mere existence of the three-power talks in March. It was agreed that it would be impossible to keep secret the existence of the six-power talks which opened in July, but that as little as possible should be said about these talks. The agreed press release issued after the first meeting of the second stage on July 6 said, "The Under-Secretary of State this morning received the Ambassadors of the United Kingdom, France, Canada and the Benelux countries for an informal and exploratory exchange of views concerning problems of common interest in relation to the Senate resolution of June 11, 1948 (S. Res. 239) [The Vandenberg resolution]. These conversations are expected to continue for some time. Since they are purely exploratory, no information concerning the substance of the conversations will be made public until such time as decisions may be reached."[18] The Canadian press release of the same date said not only that the conversations were purely exploratory but also that they were "on the diplomatic, not the governmental level".[19]

The main purpose of this emphasis on the informal and exploratory character of the intergovernmental discussions was to head off pressure from cabinets, legislators and the press for information about them. During the twelve-month-long intergovernmental discussions on the treaty, officials who were participating in the discussions kept assuring governments that they were not being committed by the discussions and governments kept assuring parliaments and voters that they were not being committed by their governments. Thus on March 15, 1948, before Pearson went to Washington for the three-power talks he told the Prime Minister that the "talks are purely exploratory and on the official level only".[20] When he returned from these talks he emphasized this point again: the recommendations agreed upon by officials "have not received approval of any of the governments concerned. They remain non-committal and official only."[21] The paper agreed to by the Ambassadors' Committee on September 10, 1948, for reference to their governments was headed "The Washington Exploratory Conversations on Security Problems of Common Interest."

Up to December, 1948, the governments participating in the intergovernmental discussions on the North Atlantic treaty had told the public the truth about the discussions and nothing but the truth – though not the whole truth. In December of 1948 the Ambassadors' Committee agreed to mislead the public. They decided that the draft treaty and commentary prepared by the Permanent Commission of the Brussels powers should not be presented to the Ambassadors' Committee in any form, and that it should be given to the Working Group not "as a complete document" but as "proposals item by item without having a consolidated document. . . ."[22] This would make it possible for the participants in the discussions to say that they had not received a draft treaty. For much the same reason the Canadian commentary of December 6, 1948, was not presented to the Ambassadors' Committee but was circulated informally.[23]

This was part of an effort to blur the gradual change, from the summer of 1948 to December, 1948, in the nature of the intergovernmental discussions. They were exploratory in July, but by December the representatives in Washington were negotiating a treaty. In this process governments were becoming more and more deeply committed to membership in a more and more precisely defined alliance. They could, of course, refuse at the last moment to sign the treaty, just as they could after signature refuse to ratify it, but as every week passed, the process of extrication became more difficult as the treaty took shape and embodied agreed-upon compromises and reconciliations. The reason governments wanted to blur the change from exploratory talks to negotiation was that this made it easier for the cabinet ministers directly concerned to fend off questions from their cabinet colleagues and from legislators and the press. It made it easier for governments to preserve secrecy about the discussions; if leaks to the press did occur they could be played down.

On February 10, 1949, Reston published an accurate story of the differences of opinion between the negotiating governments over the wording of the pledge; he said that the State Department was trying to get the pledge weakened. I told Wrong that Pearson was impatient and disturbed: "As you know he has not been bringing before Cabinet these difficulties [over the pledge] which you have been having in Washington. However, now that the precise differences have been made public in the press he feels that the time may have come when he will have to discuss these difficulties with his colleagues in Cabinet."[24]

The rules which were adopted to ensure secrecy were not adhered to strictly by the Canadian and United States governments and presumably not by other governments. Governments had agreed in July not to refer to the discussions in telegrams or over the telephone. Yet there was a voluminous exchange of telegrams between the Canadian embassy in Washington and the Department of External Affairs in Ottawa about the discussions; and Pearson and Wrong had many talks about them over the telephone. We assumed that our cyphers were unbreakable and that only the United States was likely to intercept our telephone calls and we were accustomed to take this into account when speaking over the telephone. Moreover, if we didn't break the rules, we in Ottawa would not be able, when discussions in Washington were proceeding at a fast pace, to give effective guidance and instructions to our representatives. In order to give guidance and instructions in time we had to receive reports by teletype and reply by teletype. Perhaps in July and the first half of August of 1948, when the discussions in Washington were leisurely, the British, French, Belgians and Dutch did not refer to the discussions in telegrams or over the telephone. By the end of August, however, they were probably all using telegrams to give instructions to their delegations.

From the end of February, 1949, the arrangements for promptly circulating minutes of the meetings to the participating governments had broken down; thus the minutes of the meetings of the Ambassadors' Committee of February 25 and March 1 were not available until about March 15.[25] If governments had had to depend on diplomatic bags for reports and had had to send instructions by diplomatic bags, the discussions in Washington would have dragged on for weeks or months longer than they actually did.

There is a dilemma here. If governments participating in an international negotiation all send and receive reports and instructions by cypher telegram, the security of the discussions depends on the weakest link – the country which uses a cypher which is the easiest to break. If governments don't use telegrams but depend on accompanied diplomatic bags, the host government and governments with quick air connections for their couriers to the capital where the negotiations are taking place are at an advantage over the other governments.

The preservation of secrecy about differences of opinion over divisive issues did not mean that governments kept the public of their countries in the dark about the kind of alliance they were hoping to forge. It would have been unsafe for democratic governments which were contemplating a major departure from traditional foreign policy to do this. In a democracy, secret international negotiations which may result in a substantial change in foreign policy need to be accompanied by measures by which the government brings parliamentary and public opinion along by giving parliament and the public a clear idea of the kind of departure from traditional foreign policy which it is contemplating and the reasons for it. This can be called democratic leadership, public education, the sounding out of the public or government propaganda. It is a delicate and difficult task. The government cannot give parliament or the public all the facts which it took into account in coming to its own decisions. Some secrets are not its but are the secrets of other governments. Thus none of the governments referred in public to the information they had received from the Norwegian government early in March, 1948, about its fears of Soviet threats. None of the governments referred explicitly in public to differences of opinion between them.

Very different methods were followed in Washington and in Ottawa in 1948 to bring parliamentary and public opinion along. In Washington a middle-level official in the State Department (Achilles) fed carefully selected background information to two carefully selected newspapermen. In Ottawa senior Cabinet ministers gave speeches inside and outside Parliament advocating a North Atlantic treaty.

In the summer of 1948 the State Department was covered by John Hightower for the Associated Press and by Frank Shackford and later Don Gonzalez for the United Press International. Achilles told them in the summer of 1948 that he would be available to them every week or two to talk about mutual defence on four conditions: that the A.P. and U.P.I. representatives came together; that he would tell them nothing about current discussions or negotiations; that whatever he told them was solely background and not for any kind of attribution, whether United States, State Department or informed sources; and that he would say nothing about any differences of opinion between the countries concerned. Achilles' recollection 28 years later was that the three newspapermen concerned "never pried on controversies in the discussions and such points as they did raise I would answer by referring to a provision of the Rio or Brussels treaties or the Vandenberg resolution. It sounds banal but well before the treaty was made public its general nature was fully known to anyone who read the daily press carefully and many who read it only occasionally."[26]

In Ottawa the first step in bringing along parliamentary and public opinion was taken by the Prime Minister, Mackenzie King. The succeeding steps were taken by the Foreign Minister (St. Laurent), the Defence Minister (Claxton) and by Lester Pearson. King first made sure on March 11, 1948, that the two Cabinet ministers most concerned (St. Laurent and Claxton) and Pearson, whom he was grooming to become foreign minister and then prime minister, approved of his agreeing to the British proposal for top-secret tripartite talks in Washington; on March 15 he told the full Cabinet and the leaders of the three opposition parties of the deeply disturbing appreciation of the dangers of the international situation which the British government had sent him; and on March 17 he secured the agreement of the Cabinet to Canada being prepared to join an Atlantic security pact. This enabled him later in the day to make a statement in Parliament blessing the Brussels treaty and also, to those in the know, blessing the tripartite discussions which were about to open in Washington. That night he wrote in his diary, "[I had] more or less prepare[d] the House [of Commons] as I had the Cabinet for a Security Pact and, to all intents and purposes secure[d] their tacit assent to Canada becoming a party thereto."[27]

The task of public education was then taken on by St. Laurent and Claxton and by Pearson after he became Foreign Minister on September 10, 1948. During the 12 months of negotiations, they gave a steady stream of speeches inside and outside Parliament about the kind of treaty they were hoping for and working for, and they set out the reasons why Canada should support that kind of treaty. St. Laurent, as Secretary of State for External Affairs, was the principal spokesman in the critical months from the middle of March to the middle of June, 1948. During those months he put the arguments for the kind of North Atlantic treaty that Canada wanted in five public speeches and two speeches in the House of Commons. At the end of that period, in a statement in the House of Commons, he agreed that what he had been doing could justly be described "as a crusade by Canada for the completion of a western Union or North Atlantic regional pact".[28] Pearson in September, 1948, in his first public speech as Secretary of State for External Affairs, presented at some length the arguments for a treaty, and the kind of treaty Canada wanted.[29]

The arguments advanced in these speeches were directed not only at the Canadian Parliament and public. They had other targets. Thus one of St. Laurent's targets in his April 29 speech in the House of Commons was the opponents in the State Department to the idea of a North Atlantic treaty, notably George Kennan and Charles Bohlen.* One of the targets in his June 19 speech in the House of Commons was his own Prime Minister, Mackenzie King, whose support for the North Atlantic treaty he

*See page 106.

always felt was undependable. After agreeing that he had been crusading for the treaty, he went on to say, "We feel that, should war break out that affected the United Kingdom and the United States, we would inevitably be involved and that there might be great value in having consummated a regional pact ... whereby these western European democracies [France, Belgium, the Netherlands and Luxembourg], the United Kingdom, the United States and ourselves agreed to stand together, to pool for defence purposes our respective potentials and co-ordinate right away our forces so that it would appear to any possible aggressor that he would have to be prepared to overcome us all if he attempted any aggression." That was strong medicine for June, 1948. It went beyond anything which had been said in public by the United States government, the British government or any western European government. But, St. Laurent went even further. He said that if the United States were willing to join in an alliance with Great Britain, France, and the three Benelux countries, "we think the people of Canada would wish that we also be associated with it." This was the first unambiguous public statement by any government of its willingness to enter a North Atlantic military alliance.

This speech was given during the annual debate in the House of Commons on the estimates of the Department of External Affairs. In accordance with custom I, as the acting head of the department, sat on the floor of the House in front of St. Laurent's desk. After making this declaration of government policy St. Laurent sat down, leaned across to me and said, "I wonder how that will go down." I said, "I think it will go down very well in the country." St. Laurent said, "I wasn't thinking of the country. I was thinking of Laurier House" [King's residence in Ottawa].

The arguments which St. Laurent, Pearson and Claxton used in public in 1948 about the proposed North Atlantic treaty were the same as those they used in memoranda to the Prime Minister and to Cabinet, in private communications to other governments and in instructions to Wrong. Indeed the public statements in 1948 borrowed passages from the private communications, and the private communications used language which had already been used in public. The public statements did not, however, touch on such issues as the membership of Portugal or Italy or the possible application of the guarantee article to French North Africa.

In a sense, there is a parallel between the sounding out of the Senate by the United States administration and the sounding out of the public by the Canadian administration. And just as the United States administration could strengthen its hand in negotiations by citing what was necessary to get Senate support, so the Canadian administration could strengthen its hand by citing what was necessary to get the support of Canadian political parties and the Canadian public. In their public speeches, the Canadian Cabinet ministers emphasized the importance of the North Atlantic treaty containing a strong guarantee article and a strong article on democracy and economic and social co-operation. They were then able to counter the efforts which some senators made in the final stages of negotiation to have a weak guarantee article and no article on democracy and economic and social co-operation by saying that if the views of those senators were accepted they would have such great difficulty in securing parliamentary and public support for the treaty that the Canadian government might have to consider not being a party to the treaty.*

There were three main arguments for secrecy about the intergovernmental discussions on the North Atlantic treaty: it was consided essential that the Soviet government should know as little as possible about what was going on; the governments participating in the discussions would find it more difficult to give up some of their proposals and to accept compromises on others if their differences of opinion became public; and the more the details of the discussions became known, the greater would be the demand in the Senate of the United States that its advice be sought constantly throughout the negotiations.

When the tripartite discussions began in March, 1948, it could not be assumed that they would be successful. If they failed, it would be best if the Soviet government did not know that they had taken place, for the Soviet government would conclude from failure that it could press ahead even more vigorously with its efforts to secure greater control over western Europe. It would be in the interest of the Soviet government to broadcast throughout western Europe the story of the failure and this would encourage defeatism among the opponents of Soviet control in western Europe; more and more members of the élite would try to make their peace with leaders of the local Communist party. The wave of the future would gather force.

When the six-power talks began in July, 1948, the agreed press release did not state that the purpose of the talks was to try to reach agreement on a North Atlantic security pact; instead it spoke merely of an exchange of views concerning problems of common interest in relation to the Vandenberg resolution. Nevertheless it would not have been difficult for the Soviet government to have concluded, if only from what St. Laurent had been saying in public, that the meeting was going to discuss a North Atlantic security pact. The participating governments could not, therefore, at this stage, avoid the risk that failure would encourage pro-Soviet forces in western Europe and discourage anti-Soviet forces. By keeping the content of their discussions secret from the Soviet government, however, they could deprive the Soviet government of opportunities to make

*See pages 153 to 154 and 175 to 176.

mischief by playing up differences between the governments. When in February, 1949, an extempore debate in the Senate of the United States uncovered the arguments over the guarantee article, Soviet propaganda immediately told western Europe that the United States was proposing a pledge in the treaty which was meaningless.[30]

The fact that, because of the activities of Donald Maclean, nothing about developments up to the end of August, 1948, was secret from the Soviet government does not affect whatever validity these arguments possess. The participating governments at the time could not have based their reasoning on an assumption that among the relatively few people who knew about the discussions there was an agent of the Soviet government.

If the tripartite talks had failed, Donald Maclean's presence would have resulted in a considerable setback for the western powers. Since the talks succeeded his presence may well have been advantageous for the west. In his reports to Moscow, he presumably informed the Soviet government that no one in the top-secret discussions evinced any desire to embark on a preventive strike against the Soviet Union while the United States still had a monopoly of the atomic bomb, but that the governments of all three countries were desperately afraid that the Soviet government would run risks which would precipitate war and that they believed that the formation of an Atlantic security pact would deter the Soviet government from running these risks. Such a message could have had two contradictory effects in discussions in the Kremlin: it could have been used to support proposals that the Soviet government press ahead with expansionist policies before the west had succeeded in creating an alliance; on the other hand, opponents in the Kremlin of expansionist policies could have argued that this would precipitate a world war. On the assumption that the motive of Soviet expansionist policies in western Europe was defensive, to protect the Soviet Union from aggression by the west, an assurance from Maclean that he could see no indications of such contemplated aggression would make it less likely that the Soviet government would run risks which might precipitate war.

One possibility, of course, is that Maclean's reports to Moscow had no or little influence on Soviet policy. Governments have an uncanny ability to disregard important information from secret sources. This, however, seems unlikely. In April and May of 1948, after receiving Maclean's reports, the Soviet government went in for what some at the time called a "peace offensive".* It is possible that Maclean's reports of the opposition of Bohlen and Kennan to the proposed alliance constituted one of the reasons for the peace offensive; by relaxing the pressure in western Europe the Soviet government may have hoped to strengthen the hands

*See page 50.

of those in the United States administration who were opposed to the creation of an alliance.

Perhaps the moral to be drawn from the Maclean episode is that governments conducting secret negotiations should either try to arrange for controlled leaks to the governments against which the negotiations are directed, or should inform those governments of certain aspects of the secret negotiations either officially or by statements to the press by "a senior official", the technique which Henry Kissinger used in 1974 in his middle-eastern shuttle diplomacy. Governments will, of course, discount information which they receive in this way, since they know they are not getting the whole truth and they are well aware that half truths can be deceptive.

The Soviet government would make a great contribution to an understanding of the cold war if it were to publish Donald Maclean's reports to them on the making of the North Atlantic treaty.

The second main argument for secrecy about the intergovernmental discussions on the North Atlantic treaty was that the governments participating in the discussions would find it more difficult to give up some of their proposals and to accept compromises on others if their differences of opinion became public. There is, Pearson has said, "nothing more difficult for a democratic government to abandon than a headline."[31] The headlines could have been startling: "State Department divided on proposed North Atlantic treaty; Kennan and Bohlen oppose it"; "No treaty without massive arms shipments: French demand"; " 'The French are getting into our hair': Lovett"; "France isolated in its demands for Italian membership"; "Reduce proposed North Atlantic treaty to level of Kellogg-Briand peace pact: Canada's attack on Senator Connally"; "Canada isolated in support of article on economic collaboration"; "United States only country to oppose article on economic collaboration"; "France demands that North Atlantic allies defend Algeria": "North Atlantic treaty for 50 years or for ten".

Undoubtedly the absence of publicity did make it easier for governments to accept defeats or compromises. If there had been a public debate in February, 1949, about the French demand that the alliance be committed to defend Algeria against armed attack, great public opposition would have been evinced to the proposal, especially in the United States, the Netherlands and Canada. Anti-colonialists would have mounted strong and politically powerful protests. The governments of the United States, the Netherlands and Canada would have been under pressure from their parliaments and from the electorate not to give in to French demands. If, after great publicity in France for the dispute, the governments had not given in, the French government might have found it impossible to sign a treaty which protected the Canadian Arctic but did not protect the Algerian departments of France.

81

It is, of course, possible to argue that publicity in France for the dispute would have had the opposite effect, that the French public and parliament, when they realized the extent of the opposition in other possible members of the alliance to the French demand over Algeria, might have pressed the government to withdraw the demand. This, however, seems unlikely. Publicity for the dispute over Algeria might therefore have resulted in no treaty or a treaty without France.

Publicity for some of the disputes in the intergovernmental discussions on the North Atlantic treaty might have made impossible the necessary give-and-take, the necessary compromises. Publicity for other disputes might merely have meant a somewhat different compromise. This was probably the result in February of 1949 of the publicity about the guarantee article in the treaty. The press had reported correctly in January, 1949, as the result of guidance from Achilles, that the allies would promise that if one of them were attacked, each of the others would assist it by taking "such military or other action . . . as may be necessary." When in February senators urged that no reference should be made to military action, the other participants were able to argue that, while they could have accepted this, although reluctantly, if it had been proposed earlier, they could not now accept it after newspapers had stated that there would be a specific reference to military action. This argument was successful; the pledge in its final form spoke of "the use of armed force." Publicity for the dispute over the pledge resulted in the pledge being stronger than it otherwise would have been.

In February, 1949, Canada was pressing for a strong article on economic and social collaboration and on the promotion of democracy. Lovett, the chief representative of the United States in the discussions from March, 1948, to the middle of January, 1949, had supported such an article. So had the four principal officers in the State Department who had been concerned with the negotiations in 1948, Bohlen, Kennan, Hickerson and Achilles. Canada had lined up all the five Brussels treaty powers behind its proposal. Acheson opposed the article and said that leading senators also opposed it. Perhaps if Canada had at that point leaked the story to the press Acheson and the senators might have discovered that they were out of touch with American opinion and the result would have been a stronger Article 2 than that which emerged from a controversy carried on behind closed doors. When Wrong on February 19, 1949, was arguing with Acheson about this article Bohlen intervened to say that "Eichelberger and others in the United Nations Association might take a different line from the senators and welcome a general undertaking for economic, social and cultural collaboration."[32] Alternatively, of course, publicity for Canada's demands might have resulted in Acheson and the senators finding that majority opinion in the United States was strongly opposed to the kind of article that Canada wanted, and the senators would have found it difficult to agree to the compromise which appears in the treaty.

There is a connection between the degree of secrecy in intergovernmental discussions and the frankness of the language used in the discussions. The greater the secrecy the less inhibited will the participants be from using forthright language rather than the guarded diplomatic language of understatement which, because it is not always clear, can lead to misunderstandings. If the newspapers had been publishing accurate reports of the meetings from "authoritative sources," the French representative might well not have said, as he did at the meeting of the Ambassadors' Committee on March, 1, 1949, that if the treaty included Norway but not Italy, the French government "would have to reconsider its position as far as its own participation was concerned". He might have used the language which Oliver Franks suggested to him that he should have used, that his government held strong views on the very great importance of the treaty including Italy and Algeria.[33]

There is also a connection between the degree of secrecy which it is assumed can be maintained about intergovernmental discussions and decisions on such matters as which governments shall be invited to participate in the discussions. If the United States, Britain and Canada had been less sure of their ability to keep their talks in March, 1948, secret from the French government, they would have been more willing to invite France to participate from the beginning in these talks. French participation in those talks might well have been in the general interest.*

The third argument for secrecy in the negotiations on the North Atlantic treaty was that the more the details of the discussions became known, the greater would be the demand in the Senate of the United States that its advice be sought constantly throughout the negotiations, and this would have made the task of the United States administration in negotiating the treaty much more difficult. This argument is not conclusive; the job of foreign offices is to tackle difficult tasks. But the main effect of the participation of senators in the international discussions would probably have been that there would have been leaks to the press about the discussions. Vandenberg's relations with James Reston were close: he gave Reston news and Reston gave him advice. Vandenberg was accustomed to keep Reston informed and Reston was accustomed to decide how much of what he was told was appropriate for him to make public. Vandenberg gave Reston so accurate an account of his discussion with Lovett on April 11, 1948, that a State Department official said that Reston's account in the *New York Times* was a better account than the memorandum which Lovett had dictated.[34] After Vandenberg's first meeting with Acheson at the beginning of February, 1949, he may have given Reston

*See page 54.

an account which was reflected in Reston's story in the *New York Times* on February 10 that the State Department was trying to get the pledge in the North Atlantic treaty weakened.[35] On the other hand, Vandenberg, a serious and highly responsible senior statesman, might, if he had been included in the United States delegation to the Ambassadors' Committee, have been persuaded that it was essential to keep the differences of opinion between the participating governments secret.

But, since the inclusion of senators in the discussions would have increased the possibility of leaks about the discussions, the greater the real necessity for secrecy the stronger the arguments against including the senators. Thus the arguments against including the senators in the tripartite talks in March, 1948, were stronger than the arguments against including them in the negotiations from January, 1949, on. Here again it must be kept in mind that the presence of the senators would have affected the nature of the discussions. In February and March, 1949, the ambassadors would have used different language and possibly different arguments if they had been speaking directly to the senators and not indirectly to them through Dean Acheson.

Even though it is clear that secrecy about the intergovernmental discussions on the North Atlantic treaty made it easier for governments to reach agreement, it is not possible to argue from this that secrecy in negotiations on international agreements is always in the public interest. The greater the secrecy, the easier it is to negotiate a bad agreement as well as a good agreement. What it does indicate is that the public interest may well be served if an agreement, the main lines of which are clearly favoured by parliamentary and public opinion, is negotiated in secret. This is what William Clark has called "negotiation carried out in considerable secrecy as to detail but with broad public understanding and sympathy".[36]

In their book *Secrecy and Foreign Policy*, from which this quotation is taken, Frank and Weisbank state that one reason for secrecy in diplomatic negotiations is to "prevent criticism for failures".[37] France and Canada proposed that the North Atlantic treaty should include an undertaking by the parties to refer to the International Court of Justice all disputes between them over their existing legal rights.* They failed. Because the negotiations were secret the French and Canadian governments were not criticized for this failure. The knowledge that they were not going to be criticized for their failure made it easier for them to withdraw their proposal when they could not get general support for it. There is thus a close relationship between two of the four reasons for secrecy in international negotiations which Frank and Weisbank list: to "encourage flexibility by making it easier to change positions without loss of face" and "to prevent criticism for failures".

*See pages 223 to 224.

The two other reasons they list are to "prevent interference by interest groups" and to "prevent grandstanding by participants." In 1948 members of United Nations Associations and opponents of the cold war could be considered as interest groups concerned with the outcome of the negotiations on the North Atlantic treaty. From the summer of 1948 on these two groups knew that the governments of the principal North Atlantic countries were contemplating an alliance directed against the Soviet Union. The kind of secrecy preserved about the actual negotiations could not therefore prevent them from "interfering" by putting pressure on these governments. As for grandstanding, a participant in negotiations grandstands in order, by hitting the headlines, to get either publicity for himself, if he is a politician or hopes to become one, or increased support for his government's views in his own and in other countries. Secrecy in the negotiations on the North Atlantic treaty prevented this.

Frank and Weisbank state that one "cost" of government secrecy is the threat to the internal balance of power within the executive as well as between the executive and the legislature and between the government and the people. Certainly the effect in Ottawa of the kind of secrecy imposed by the Canadian government during the negotiations on the North Atlantic treaty was a temporary change in the balance of power within the government. There was an increase in the influence of the Department of External Affairs relative to that of other departments of government. There was an increase in the influence which Pearson and I had within the Department of External Affairs relative to other members of the Department. This flowed from the fact that the only Cabinet ministers who were kept fully informed of the progress of the negotiations were the Prime Minister and the Ministers of External Affairs and of Defence; no Cabinet committee or interdepartmental committee of civil servants was established to make recommendations on Canadian policy in the negotiations; within the Department of External Affairs, Pearson and I were the only officers who had knowledge of the first stage of the negotiations and only two others had knowledge of the beginning of the second stage.

Whether this temporary change in the balance of power in Ottawa was a "cost" or a benefit involves weighing longer-run against shorter-run factors. Canada would not have played so active a role in the negotiations if telegrams of instructions to the Canadian embassy in Washington had had to be cleared with a working group of senior officers of the Department of External Affairs, or by an interdepartmental committee of officials, or by a Cabinet committee, or by all three. The delays would have been too great. The messages would have been too muted.

But there was a "cost" which had to be paid after the negotiations on the treaty were concluded and normal procedures were used for arriving at decisions by the government on the implementation of the treaty.

These procedures were: consultation within the Department of External Affairs between all the officials concerned; the establishment of interdepartmental committees of officials; and efforts to reach agreement on joint recommendations to Cabinet from the Cabinet ministers concerned with a particular aspect of the problem of implementation. Now officials and ministers became involved in the decision-making process who knew little or nothing of the policies which Canada had pursued in the negotiations or the reasons for the policies. This was one reason why, after the treaty was signed, the Canadian government was half-hearted over implementing those non-military provisions of the treaty for which it had fought so hard during the negotiations.

A week before the treaty was signed Pearson praised in the House of Commons in Ottawa the methods used in making it. These methods, he said, had "admirably combined the virtues of classical and confidential diplomacy with free and open discussions of the general principles under consideration." The result would be "an open covenant privately negotiated but publicly debated and decided."

The preparation of this treaty, I think, is an admirable demonstration of the way in which foreign affairs should be conducted amongst democratic countries. While the discussions in Washington have been confidential, their general purpose and the principles behind them have been well known to the public in all the countries concerned. Each participating government has been able to test public opinion in its own country as the agreement was being formulated. . . . [The Canadian government has] given a clear indication of the purposes of the treaty and of the nature of the commitments which would be involved, as the work was going on. At the same time, however, the men who actually participated in the discussions and the governments who instructed these men, have been free from day-to-day public comment on the specific details as opposed to the principles under consideration. In the result it has been possible to reach a conclusion generally satisfactory to all parties in the give and take of private discussion, without the difficulties which often arise when the early stages of delicate, detailed international negotiations are conducted in public. Honest differences of opinion, when they occurred in the afternoon, did not become sensational world headlines in the six o'clock editions, and, of course, there is nothing more difficult for a democratic government to abandon than a headline. . . .[38]

CHAPTER SEVEN

THE ADVICE AND CONSENT OF THE SENATE

The North Atlantic treaty was made not only with the consent of the Senate of the United States, expressed in its vote on ratification, but on the advice of the Senate. This advice was given from the beginning of April, 1948, shortly after the conclusion of the tripartite discussions, until the treaty was made public in mid-March, 1949. In the final six weeks or so of the negotiations, Dean Acheson, as Secretary of State, was conducting two sets of negotiations, one with the other governments concerned and the other with the Senate Foreign Relations Committee. Achilles, writing 15 years later, said that the advice of the Senate was

> sought constantly throughout the negotiations through frequent attendance by the Secretary [of State] and other officials at closed sessions of the Foreign Relations Committee and months of daily working cooperation between officials of the [State] Department and the Committee staff. Numerous suggestions made by members of the Committee were accepted, not only by our negotiators but by the others, and were incorporated in the text of the Treaty.[1]

In 1945 Truman had become President on the death of Roosevelt. In the mid-term elections in 1946, the Democrats were soundly defeated. For the first time in 18 years the Republicans secured a majority in both houses of Congress. Gallup reported in March, 1948, that if the presidential election were taking place then Truman would lose to Dewey, Stassen, MacArthur or Vandenberg. Right up to the eve of the election on November 2 it was assumed that the Republican candidate would be elected and that the Republicans would increase their majorities in the Senate and the House of Representatives. An indication of how general this assumption was is that the Canadian Ambassador in Washington reported on November 1 that Hickerson of the State Department had referred to an "interregnum" between a Dewey victory and his assumption of power in January as being "probable".[2]

It was also thought almost up to June 21, when Dewey was chosen as the Republican candidate for the presidency, that Senator Arthur Vandenberg would probably be the Republican candidate. Vandenberg was, in the first half of 1948, "at the apex of his power. He was the acknowledged Republican foreign policy spokesman in Congress, Chairman of the Senate Foreign Relations Committee, and, as Senate President *pro tem,* in a strong tactical position with respect to legislative matters."[3] Vandenberg was therefore consulted by the State Department in April, May and June, 1948, in two capacities, as the Chairman of the Senate Foreign Relations Committee and as a possible president. (John Foster Dulles was likewise consulted in two capacities, first, as adviser on foreign affairs to Vandenberg and, when Dewey had been chosen as the Republican candidate for the presidency, also as the probable Secretary of State if Dewey won.) Even if the United States Constitution had not required that treaties be made with the advice and consent of the Senate, it would have been wise, because of the likelihood of a Republican victory in November, for the Democratic United States administration to consult Republican leaders.

The necesssity of consultations between the United States administration and congressional leaders slowed down the pace of the intergovernmental discussions. When the other governments evinced impatience with the delays resulting from the negotiations with the Senate or with the suggestions emanating from senators to water down the treaty, the United States negotiators would point out how essential these negotiations were. Thus Hickerson made "a solemn and serious statement" on this subject at a meeting of the Working Group on August 12, 1948:

> Hickerson said that the fact that these talks were taking place in Washington was indicative of the most radical change in United States foreign policy which had ever taken place and he wanted the representatives of the countries present to appreciate this fully. With a thorough appreciation, Hickerson said, he thought that other countries would be able to understand that, in so far as the State Department was concerned, its officials were unwilling to risk failure in implementing this new United States foreign policy. It would be disastrous if they were to put forward to the Senate an unacceptable pact or treaty. It would be almost equally disastrous if a pact or treaty were to be ratified with a series of hampering reservations after protracted debate. During negotiations, therefore, it was the intention of the State Department to maintain the closest possible contact with political leaders in both Houses and to take their advice and counsel as to the phraseology and the content of a pact or treaty which would be acceptable to the Congress.[4]

Direct congressional soundings began a few days after the first stage of the intergovernmental discussions ended on April 1, 1948. By April 21, Lovett had had at least three talks with Vandenberg and Vandenberg had also had a talk with Dean Rusk. Then, on April 27, Marshall and Lovett met with Vandenberg and John Foster Dulles.[5]

At his first meeting with Vandenberg, Lovett sounded him out on the main proposals in the Pentagon paper of April 1 which had emerged from the tripartite talks. These were that the President should announce publicly that the United States was inviting Britain, western European countries and Canada to a conference to discuss the conclusion of a collective defence agreement for the North Atlantic area and that, if an armed attack on a signatory of the Brussels treaty occurred while the negotiations were in progress, the United States would regard it as an armed attack against itself. According to Achilles, Vandenberg said, "Oh no. Why should Truman get all the credit? Wouldn't it be better to have the Senate advise the administration to negotiate such an arrangement?"[6] Vandenberg at his next meeting with Lovett on Sunday, April 11, a meeting which lasted for three hours, said that he and his Foreign Relations Committee had been considering the possibility of a resolution on strengthening the United Nations. Lovett immediately suggested that the resolution "would fall far short of its maximum effectiveness unless it included some reference to the determination of [the United States] to take such steps as might be necessary to bring about the international peace for which the U.N. was presumably designed".[7] The office of United Nations affairs in the State Department drafted a resolution for use by its director, Dean Rusk, in his discussion with Vandenberg on April 13.[8] At this meeting Vandenberg said to Rusk "somewhat jokingly, that he thought the boys in the State Department were pushing him a little hard – that having just finished a battle to put across the European Recovery Program using as one of his big guns the fact that it was a substitute for military action, they were now pressing him to put across a pact giving a military guarantee of everybody's security."[9]

The State Department then, in consultation with the Chief of Staff of the Senate Foreign Relations Committee, revised the resolution which Dean Rusk's office had drafted.[10] Vandenberg, who was known as "one-page Vandenberg", considered that this resolution was too long and when he, accompanied by John Foster Dulles, met with Marshall and Lovett on April 27, he produced a one-page draft of his own "as proof that the main points could be stated briefly and clearly".[11] It was agreed at this meeting that the State Department should produce a one-page resolution and also a further revision of the revised Pentagon paper which Lovett had shown to Vandenberg. Achilles now became the principal draftsman of the Vandenberg resolution.[12]

On May 11 Vandenberg presented the resolution to the Senate Foreign Relations Committee, saying that it "had been developed with the co-operation of the State Department after a considerable period of study". The report of the Committee stated that the Committee "then proceeded to consider the resolution in executive session with the benefit of full information from the Department of State concerning its experience in carrying out United States foreign policy through the United Nations and concerning recent political developments in the international situation". On May 19 the Committee unanimously approved of the resolution. On June 11, the Senate passed the resolution by a vote of 64 to 4.

The resolution "advised" the President that it was the "sense of the Senate" that the United States government, by constitutional process, should pursue six objectives. The three most directly related to the North Atlantic treaty were:

> Progressive development of regional and other collective arrangements for individual and collective self-defence in accordance with the purposes, principles, and provisions of the Charter; association of the United States, by constitutional process, with such regional and other collective arrangements as are based on continuous and effective self-help and mutual aid, and as affect its national security; and contributing to the maintenance of peace by making clear its determination to exercise the right of individual or collective self-defence under Article 51 should any armed attack occur affecting its national security.[13]

In the report which accompanied the resolution the Committee said:

> The Committee believes that association of the United States with such regional or other collective arrangements as affect its national security will help protect this country and help prevent war. The great power and influence of the United States must be thrown into the scales on the side of peace. . . . The Committee is convinced that the horrors of another world war can be avoided with certainty only by preventing war from starting. The experience of World War I and World War II suggest that the best deterrent to aggression is the certainty that immediate and effective countermeasures will be taken against those who violate the peace.[14]

Achilles wrote a commentary on the resolution a month or so after it had been passed by the Senate. He said that the resolution laid down four conditions for United States support for the Brussels treaty powers, "(1) U.S. association must be within the framework of U.N. Charter; (2) It must be by constitutional process, i.e. treaty obligations must be clearly defined and approved by two-thirds of Senate and material assistance will require legislation and appropriations; (3) Arrangements must be based on continuous and effective self-help and mutual aid, i.e. U.S. assistance must supplement rather than replace efforts of others and must be two-way with Europeans contributing maximum to U.S. security; and

(4) Arrangements must affect (i.e. increase) U.S. national security."[15]

The adoption of the Vandenberg resolution by the Senate put the advice of the Senate behind the United States administration when it went ahead in July with the six-power intergovernmental discussions on the North Atlantic treaty. The administration also had the agreement of Vandenberg and Dulles to the revised Pentagon paper which served as the instruction to the United States representatives.

By constantly asserting that these six-power consultations were taking place pursuant to the Vandenberg resolution, the United States administration gave Vandenberg and the Senate undeserved credit for initiating the intergovernmental negotiations which led to the North Atlantic treaty, whereas, in fact, the intergovernmental negotiations had been initiated by the British government in March. This wise act eased greatly the task of the administration in securing the consent of the Senate to the treaty. Indeed it is possible, if not probable, that if Truman had not performed this act of self-abnegation, he would not have been able to secure the ratification of the treaty by the Senate.

The passage of the Vandenberg resolution by the Senate did not, Wrong warned us, clear away all the obstacles to United States participation in a North Atlantic treaty. Wrong said, "Whether this vote records in fact a momentous change in United States foreign policy will depend on how the policies approved by the resolution are developed. . . . I have doubts whether the discussion of the resolution in the Senate and the press has been explicit enough to make people realize that it blesses the participation of the United States in entangling alliances in Europe. As usual, the pathway from the general to the particular is likely to be steep and devious."[16]

From the passage of the Vandenberg resolution in mid-June, 1948, until the beginning of February, 1949, there appears to have been little consultation between the United States administration and the Senate on the proposed North Atlantic treaty. Wrong reported just before the November elections that after the elections the State Department intended to get in touch with Vandenberg and Tom Connally (the senior Democratic member of the Senate Foreign Relations Committee), and, if Dewey won the election, with Dewey directly or indirectly through Dulles and Vandenberg.[17] The election took place on November 2: by November 9, Lovett had given Vandenberg a copy of the September 9 paper and was about to give one to Connally.[18] Wrong reported that no other congressional soundings were contemplated pending the receipt of further European views in renewed exploratory talks.[19] Lovett did, however, explain the project late in November or early in December not only to Connally, who had become Chairman of the Senate Foreign Relations Committee, but also to Representative Sol Bloom, who had become the Democratic Chairman of the Committee on Foreign Affairs of the House of Representatives.[20] The renewed exploratory talks in the Ambassadors' Committee took place between December 10 and 24. On January 5 Wrong reported that Lovett had not been able to see a number of members of Congress he wished to sound out.[21] A week later Wrong said that James Reston of the *New York Times*, who was a confidant of Vandenberg's and who had been seeing both Vandenberg and John Foster Dulles, had in speaking to him insisted on the importance of keeping the language of the draft treaty sufficiently fluid to allow suggestions from them and from other congressional quarters to be discussed and possibly adopted.[22] Reston's warning proved to be well-founded.

Marshall had been ill in the last months of 1948 and in January, 1949, and Lovett had had to take over as Acting Secretary of State. He must have been extremely busy and he apparently failed to keep in close touch with congressional leaders in his last two months in office. He did not, for example, show Connally and Vandenberg the draft treaty which had been agreed to by the Ambassadors' Committee on December 24 for submission to governments: he did not tell them of the difficulties created by the French demands over Algeria and Italy; and he did not discuss the principles of the treaty with the Senate Foreign Relations Committee. The result, according to Acheson, was that when he first talked to Connally and Vandenberg at the beginning of February, he found that Lovett's discussions with them had not gone as far as he had thought [23] and when he first talked with the Senate Committee, he found that the Committee was less well-informed than he had expected.[24]

Acheson took office as Secretary of State on January 20. He was not able to look at the papers on the North Atlantic treaty negotiations until January 29. Five days later, accompanied by Bohlen, he had his first discussion with Connally and Vandenberg. They went over the latest draft of the treaty article by article. The senators made a number of suggestions for revision; their suggestions for revising the pledge article (Article 5) were of considerable importance; but most of the other suggestions were inconsequential. Acheson and Bohlen had a second meeting with Connally and Vandenberg on February 5. At this meeting, the discussion was almost entirely concerned with Article 5.[25]

Nine days later, a storm suddenly burst on the floor of the Senate; in an unexpected and impromptu debate, there was a demand, supported by Connally and Vandenberg, that Article 5 of the North Atlantic treaty should be so worded as to give rise to no obligation, moral or otherwise, on the part of the United States to go to war if a member of the North Atlantic alliance were attacked.* Acheson and Bohlen immediately had a talk with Connally and Vandenberg.[26] Three days later Acheson con-

*See pages 151 to 152.

sulted Truman. Truman insisted that a stout fight be made against weakening the pledge to the extent proposed by Connally and Vandenberg
and he said that he would talk to Connally.[27] On February 18 Acheson
had the first of a number of meetings with the Senate Foreign Relations
Committee to discuss the treaty; he circulated to them copies of the draft
treaty (but in the interests of security had them collected at the end of the
meeting).[28] In between meetings with the full Senate Committee he had
discussions with its principal members (Connally, Vandenberg and Walter F. George),[29] with the President,[30] and with the Ambassadors' Committee. The three principal senators and the Senate Committee as a whole
gave much advice and made clear that they would not give their consent
to the treaty unless they received satisfaction. They were consulted
particularly on the pledge, on Article 2, on the membership of Italy and
on Algeria.

Finally, on March 8, Acheson was able to report to the President on
the success of his shuttle diplomacy between the Ambassadors' Committee and the Senate Foreign Relations Committee. He told Truman that
on the previous day, the Ambassadors' Committee had completed a draft
of the treaty which was being sent to the governments for "their review,
and we hope approval," and that that afternoon he had gone over this
draft treaty with the Senate Committee. "The meeting was most successful. They approved the draft making only three minor requests for language changes – although for a few minutes they hesitated on the verge of
causing real trouble." Acheson added that on the previous day, Ernest
Gross, Assistant Secretary of State, "spent several hours before the House
Committee on Foreign Affairs discussing the broad purposes of the treaty
and the nations which might be invited to sign, [and] . . . this discussion
was very favorably received by the committee. . . ."[31]

Thus, as Achilles later put it, "by the time [the treaty] was signed every
member of the [Senate Foreign Relations] Committee knew it by heart
and had a vested interest in it. . . . Lessons for negotiating any such treaty:
agree with key senators as to who takes the initiative; keep it absolutely
bipartisan; and seek the 'advice' of the Senate long before you seek its
eventual 'consent'."[32]

The task of the United States administration in carrying the Senate
along with it in the final stages of the negotiations was made especially
difficult by Lovett's departure from the State Department on January 20,
1949, by Acheson's appointment as Secretary of State and by Connally
succeeding Vandenberg as Chairman of the Senate Foreign Relations
Committee. Lovett had got on very well with Vandenberg; Acheson and
Vandenberg did not get on well together. Connally was jealous of Vandenberg because Marshall and Lovett had, up to the November elections,
treated Vandenberg as if he were the sole ambassador of the Senate with
virtual plenipotentiary powers. Connally considered that he and not Van-

denberg was the elder statesman on the Senate Foreign Relations Committee. He had been Chairman of the Committee for six years, from 1941 to 1947. Vandenberg had been Chairman only since the beginning of 1948.

Shortly after Acheson had had his first discussions with Connally and Vandenberg, Wrong reported that Oliver Franks (the British Ambassador) and he agreed "that so far as we can judge Connally and Vandenberg have no objection to a North Atlantic treaty. Both, however, appear to be ready to delay proceedings, make difficulties, and assert their prerogatives. Connally is woolly, and may not like Acheson's incisive style of discussion. Vandenberg is in a sulky mood which started on November 3 [the day after the Republican defeat in the elections] and still endures."[33]

Vandenberg's sulkiness is not surprising. He had given invaluable support to Truman over the Truman doctrine, the Marshall plan, the Berlin airlift and the commencement of the talks on the North Atlantic treaty. Truman in his "Give 'em hell" presidential campaign had lashed out at the Republican-dominated do-nothing Congress, making no exceptions for such members as Vandenberg or for the fruitful co-operation between the administration and Congress on foreign policy. Vandenberg was also deeply disappointed by the to him totally unexpected Republican defeats in the elections.

Vandenberg's official biographer states that Stewart Alsop, the columnist, appeared to have "been reasonably accurate" when he wrote (presumably in January, 1949, after the Senate had confirmed Acheson's appointment) that "the bipartisan basis of foreign policy has been most gravely weakened. One reason is simply the ... departure of Marshall and Lovett, with whom the Republican foreign policy leaders and especially Senator Vandenberg have developed an intimate understanding. By contrast, the relationship between Vandenberg and Acheson, who have had serious policy differences in the past, is one of mutual, but distinctly chilly, respect."[34]

Acheson, after the Senate had confirmed his appointment by a vote of 83 to 6, "sent Vandenberg a handwritten note thanking him for his support when the going was rough and adding that he would need and ask Vandenberg's advice and help". But, Vandenberg's biographer adds, "the Senator's papers show no immediate follow-up on this letter by Acheson in an effort to ensure the continuation of the close, personal collaboration that had existed during the Eightieth [the preceding] Congress."[35] Vandenberg recognized that one reason Acheson did not consult him frequently was, as Joseph Alsop put it in an article published on July 31, 1949, that Connally had "openly resented" Vandenberg's pre-eminence in the past when the Republicans controlled the Senate and that he would "grow very touchy now" if Vandenberg and other Republicans were still consulted.[36]

Hickerson of the State Department confirmed this when I had a long talk with him in Washington on April 4, 1949, two days after the treaty was signed. He told me that Acheson's difficulties with Connally were caused by the fact that Lovett had been so certain of a Republican victory in November, 1948, that, while before the elections he had cleared the proposals with Vandenberg, he had never bothered to clear them with Connally. Connally was naturally angry at the pre-eminence which Lovett had given to Vandenberg. Connally happened to be out of the Senate when the impromptu debate on Article 5 of the treaty burst out on February 14, 1949; he arrived back in the Senate to find that Vandenberg was answering a question which a senator had asked about this article; this angered him and precipitated his bad-tempered speech.[37]

Vandenberg wrote to his wife that he was amused by Joe Alsop's story about Connally's resentment at Vandenberg's pre-eminence before the November elections:

> This will make old Tawm [Connally] fairly burn in his boots. But I don't object to having it down on record that Lovett and I spent an 'hour a day' together during the bipartisan days when we were getting invincible results. I feel rather sorry for Acheson. I think he would like to carry on the old pattern. But it just isn't possible under the new set-up. Alsop has identified one of the major reasons.[38]

Acheson in his memoirs describes the special relationship of intimacy, secrecy and complete confidence which existed between himself as Secretary of State and Oliver Franks, the British Ambassador. They met regularly, alone, at each other's houses, before or after dinner. "No one was informed even of the fact of the meeting." "Neither would report or quote the other unless, thinking that it would be useful in promoting action, he got the other's consent and agreement on the terms of a reporting memorandum or cable ... setting out the problem and suggested approaches." "We discussed situations already emerging or likely to do so, the attitudes that various people in both countries would be likely to take, what courses of action were possible and their merits, the chief problems that could arise."[39]

Acheson and Franks were able to work out this sort of relationship because they became friends and they recognized each other as intellectual equals. Lovett and Vandenberg appear to have been able to establish somewhat the same kind of relationship. They had a "usual Sunday rendezvous" in Vandenberg's apartment. At the time of the crisis over the Berlin blockade Lovett went to Vandenberg's apartment five times so that they could work out together a note to the Soviet government. When Lovett left the State Department in January, 1949, he wrote to Vandenberg, "If a man is very lucky he has an opportunity once in his life to serve a good cause with men of singleness of purpose, integrity and complete understanding, and with friends whom he both admires and loves. I have had that experience with you and the General [Marshall] . . . ."[40]

But it is not often that a secretary of state or under-secretary of state and a chairman of the Senate Foreign Relations Committee will turn out to be the kind of people who are so personally sympathetic that this kind of partnership is possible.

A standard technique in negotiations of all kinds, a technique which has been referred to above in the chapter on the intergovernmental discussions, is to attempt to strengthen one's bargaining position by referring to a tough person in a back room whom one has to consult. Sometimes a United States representative in the intergovernmental discussions on the North Atlantic treaty would use the alleged views of the Senate as a device to strengthen his bargaining position. He would say, about a proposal of which he disapproved, "We would like to do this but the Senate would not agree." This device was used in the arguments over the non-military provisions in the treaty. It is an argument which, even if flimsy, is difficult for a foreigner to question since, if he does, he puts himself in the position of asserting more knowledge of senatorial opinion than the United States administration.

Charles Ritchie reported from the Canadian embassy in Paris at the end of February, 1949, on a talk about the negotiations on the North Atlantic treaty which James Bonbright of the United States embassy in Paris had had with de Margerie of the French Foreign Office. In this talk, de Margerie said that the French government was much concerned about the difficulties which the North Atlantic pact might have in the National Assembly. "Bonbright replied to de Margerie that he had too high an opinion of the French Assembly to contemplate the possibility of their turning down the Atlantic pact."[41]

In sending this telegram on to Pearson I commented,"Next time we are told by the State Department that the Senate would not agree to something sensible let us give Bonbright's reply to de Margerie." Pearson, in a marginal comment, said "Hear, hear." Another possible reply is to say, "I should like an opportunity to discuss this proposal direct with representatives of the Senate."

George Kennan was, on occasion, the United States spokesman at meetings of the Working Group on the North Atlantic treaty. In his memoirs he speaks of his dislike at the time of

being placed in the position of spokesman for the views of unnamed figures in the legislative branch of our government – views which I could only relay in the most laconic form and the rationale of which I could neither explain nor, to tell the truth, myself accept. If senators were to constitute the final and unchallengeable arbiters of such proceedings, then, it seemed to me, they ought to conduct the negotiations themselves. I can recall an occasion, during one of the main plenary meetings, when some sort of suggestion made by one of the European representatives was crushed, properly and unavoidably, by Mr. Lovett, who said he could assure the gathering that anything in the nature of what had been suggested would be quite unacceptable to the Senate. The objection was final. It produced only a moment of glum silence. I could not help but wish, though, that one of our European friends had stood up at that point and said: 'Mr. Lovett, if you and your colleagues in the State Department cannot speak responsibly for American policy in this matter will you kindly introduce us to the people who can?'[42]

This is very much what the British and Canadian Ambassadors said to Dean Acheson in February, 1949. Acheson had had his first consultations with Connally and Vandenberg on February 3 and 5. He showed them the December 24 draft of the pledge article and they both objected that the pledge was too strong. On February 8 Acheson, at his first meeting with the Ambassadors' Committee, reported the amendments suggested by the two senators. Oliver Franks and Hume Wrong met two days later to discuss the situation. They agreed that it would be "disastrous" if the pledge were watered down to the extent suggested by the senators. Wrong said that they had found

> that we had independently been considering suggesting to Acheson that he should turn over in his mind inviting the two senators to attend future meetings with the ambassadors, so that we could impress directly on them, instead of indirectly through Acheson, our views on the need for speed and on the necessity of as clear a pledge as possible in Article 5. Franks is seeing Acheson late today, and will probably put this idea to him, saying that it had also occurred to me.[43]

Presumably Franks did make this suggestion to Acheson since Acheson, three days later, said to Wrong that he "had it in mind, if the president approved, to bring [Connally and Vandenberg] to a meeting with the ambassadors."[44] Nothing came of this. Whether Acheson spoke to Truman I do not know.

The political situation in the United States in 1948 before the November elections made it essential that there should be close consultation between the United States administration and the Senate in the making of the North Atlantic treaty. Since the treaty would involve a radical departure from traditional United States foreign policy, it was essential to ensure that the Senate would approve of the treaty without damaging reservations and by more than a bare two-thirds majority. What is not self-evident is that the administration had to make as many concessions to the Senate as it did make. When the vote on ratification took place 95 senators voted. A minimum two-thirds majority would have been 64 to 31; a safe two-thirds majority would have been something like 72 to 23. The actual vote was 82 to 13.

PART THREE

CONCEPTUAL ISSUES

CHAPTER EIGHT

ALTERNATIVES TO A NORTH ATLANTIC TREATY

The British proposal of March 11, 1948, was that very early steps should be taken "to conclude under Article 51 of the Charter of the United Nations a regional Atlantic Approaches Pact of Mutual Assistance, in which all the countries directly threatened by a Russian move to the Atlantic could participate." There would be two other systems: "The United Kingdom - France - Benelux system with United States backing" and "a Mediterranean security system, which would particularly affect Italy".[1] (The first of these two systems was created six days later by the signature of the Brussels treaty.)

The decision of the United States and Canadian governments to participate in tripartite meetings in Washington to explore the British proposal did not of itself mean that they had agreed that a North Atlantic security system should be established. There were other possibilities. Armstrong of *Foreign Affairs* had proposed a world-wide pact of collective defence based on Article 51 of the U.N. Charter. Dean Rusk's office of United Nations affairs in the State Department wanted a treaty "to be negotiated with selected countries, but not necessarily on a regional basis." Hickerson's office of European affairs wanted a North Atlantic-Mediterranean treaty.[2] Kennan's policy planning staff wanted a treaty which should include the Brussels treaty countries and "the other free nations of Europe and the Middle East who may wish to adhere".[3] I suggested that the treaty should include the Commonwealth countries as well as the North Atlantic countries. The United States and Canada might sign the Brussels treaty or accede to its military clauses. There might be no pact at all but instead the President of the United States might declare, borrowing language from the Monroe Doctrine of 1823, that the United

States would consider any attempt by the Soviet Union to extend its system to any portion of western Europe as dangerous to the peace and safety of the United States.* Such a presidential declaration might be accompanied by a congressional declaration in similar terms, and by the United States providing the western European countries with military equipment. Canada might make a declaration similar to the presidential declaration.

In March of 1948 the new Commonwealth had just been born. India and Pakistan had become fully independent member nations of the Commonwealth only seven months before, Ceylon only a month before. The Commonwealth now consisted of nine nations: three were Atlantic nations – Britain, Ireland and Canada; three were the other "old" members of the Commonwealth – Australia, New Zealand and South Africa; three were new members – India, Pakistan and Ceylon. The new nine-nation Commonwealth, as Alastair Buchan has written, "gained for a while a vitality which gave it many of the characteristics of alliance."[4] At that time both Stalin and Mao Tse-tung were highly critical of the Indian government and of Nehru personally. In 1948 Britain could consider the other members of the Commonwealth as part of its alliance potential.

It was this which moved me to suggest to Pearson on March 18, the day he left Ottawa for the tripartite talks, that all the nine nations of the Commonwealth should be invited to become original members of the security pact along with the United States and the western European countries.[5] When I recommended this I was echoing what the British government had said in their message to the United States and Canadian governments in mid-January, that what was required was the creation of "some form of union in western Europe, whether of a formal or informal character, backed by the Americas and the Dominions".[6] I did not, however, suggest that any American nation other than the United States and Canada should be a member of the security pact.

In putting this suggestion to Pearson I said that one argument for inviting Australia, New Zealand and South Africa to become members of the pact was that this "would help to preserve the unity of the [old] Commonwealth and would remove the possibility of criticism of the pact by the Commonwealth-minded people in Canada." It might, however, I went on to say, be invidious to invite these three countries and not to invite the remaining members of the Commonwealth, India, Pakistan and Ceylon. "I just don't know what the answer to this should be. Their inclusion in the pact would most certainly extend greatly the commit-

---

*President Monroe in his address to Congress on December 2, 1823, said, "We owe it therefore to candor, and to the amicable relations existing between the United States and those [European allied] powers, to declare that we should consider any attempt on their part to extend their system to any portion of this hemisphere as dangerous to our peace and safety."

ments of all the other signatories since India and Pakistan are exposed and weak states, but their very exposure and weakness is a source of weakness to the United States, the United Kingdom and ourselves. On balance I feel that they, too, should be invited."

At the three-power meeting the only person who is recorded as having mentioned India and Pakistan is Gladwyn Jebb. After suggesting that there might be a western mutual defence pact plus, later, a Middle Eastern pact, he went on to ask: "If so, however, what could be done with Afghanistan? With India and Pakistan? Would not even China want assurances?"[7]

In the view of the participants in the tripartite talks the answer to Jebb's questions was the creation of a series of regional security pacts "to the ultimate end that Article 51 security arrangements would be obtained for all free nations,"[8] and that this might lead to "a world-wide pact of self-defence based on Article 51".[9] Such a world-wide pact would not replace the U.N. Charter but would complement it.[10] "A world-wide Article 51 pact of the free nations was ... [however] abandoned as a possibility in meeting the urgencies of the present situation. It would be too cumbersome and too long in implementation. It was agreed that any approach adopted should not prejudice an ultimate development in this direction."[11] This ultimate development was referred to two weeks later by Ernest Bevin in a message to Marshall. Bevin said: "A real defence system worked out by the United States of America, Canada, the United Kingdom and the western European states would ... be the first great step towards what could ultimately become a real world collective security system, in accordance with the principles of the United Nations."[12]

At one time in the tripartite discussions there was a possibility that the conferees might give their blessing to Jebb's suggestion that the North Atlantic pact be followed by a Middle Eastern pact but later in the tripartite discussions it was agreed not to give an explicit blessing to a Middle Eastern security pact but to refer to "the possible negotiation of some general Middle Eastern security system".[13] Pearson explained that it was recognized that the negotiation of such a system "would be a complicated and difficult arrangement, and that too much encouragement should not be given to it at this time." "It would", Pearson said, "bring up the whole question of the Arab states and Palestine."[14]

(The North Atlantic treaty was followed by two regional pacts, one for the Middle East and one for southeast Asia, but these pacts were very different from the North Atlantic treaty. The Middle East pact included the two states in the area which border on the Soviet Union, Turkey and Iran, but it did not include what was probably then the most powerful non-communist state in the region, Egypt, and it did include Pakistan, which was more interested in arming against India than in arming against the Soviet Union or China. It was rather as if France had not been included in the North Atlantic alliance and if Norway had been more interested in arming against Sweden than against the Soviet Union. The only states in southeast Asia included in the South East Asia Treaty Organization were Pakistan, Thailand and the Philippines. India and Indonesia, the two principal states in the area, were not members. It was as if France and Belgium had not joined the North Atlantic alliance in 1949, and that the only members on the European continent were Norway, Denmark and the Netherlands.)

According to Pearson United States officials at the beginning of the tripartite talks "thought that possibly the best course would be merely the extension of the Brussels pact to include all the free countries of western Europe plus the United States and Canada. ... The accession of the United States and Canada would be the occasion for important pronouncements by the President and the Prime Minister explaining why the two North American countries were joining the Brussels system as a means of stopping the U.S.S.R. and combatting Communism. . . ."[15]

Pearson strongly objected to this suggestion. He said that there was neither more nor less reason for Canada acceding to the Brussels pact than for Brazil or Australia. "The accession of the United States would be an understandable action and would have a very important political effect; the accession of Canada could not, however, be considered in the same light." In his report to the Prime Minister he said that he himself doubted whether Canada should take action of this kind merely because the United States did.[16]

Hickerson brought forward another argument against the United States and Canada adhering to the Brussels pact. It was that the "U.S. hopes to see the eventual development of a United States of western Europe (possibly later of all Europe) and the Brussels pact offers the hard core for such a development. It would lose its utility for this purpose were the U.S. to join."[17]

Though the idea of the United States and Canada joining the Brussels pact was rejected on the second day of the tripartite talks, the necessity of giving some early assurance of support to the Brussels powers was recognized and it was agreed at the end of the talks that this would be met by a declaration by the President of the United States that he had called a conference to conclude a North Atlantic defence agreement and that, pending the conclusion of this agreement, the United States would "consider an armed attack in the North Atlantic area against a signatory of the five-power [Brussels] treaty as an armed attack against the United States in accordance with Article 51 of the United Nations Charter".[18]

The idea of a presidential declaration or a presidential-congressional declaration as a substitute for a North Atlantic pact was rejected mainly, as the United States minutes of the second meeting state, because, "while the U.S. might in an emergency situation extend assurances of armed support against aggression on the basis of a declaration of intent, sooner or later the U.S. would have to require reciprocal guarantees from others. Were reciprocal guarantees offered, the result would, in effect, be a mutual defense agreement. The objective therefore should from the out-set include a pact of mutual defense against aggression to which the U.S. (and Canada) would finally adhere."[19] Pearson said in his report to Ottawa that the idea of a unilateral declaration by the United States may have represented the view of the armed services of the United States.[20]

Once all the alternative possibilities had been eliminated the represen-tatives of the United States, Britain and Canada had little difficulty in reaching agreement on March 24 to recommend to their governments the creation of a security pact for the North Atlantic area; all the nations bor-dering the North Atlantic would be invited to be members (the United States, Canada, Iceland, Norway, Denmark, Britain, Ireland, the Nether-lands, Belgium, France and Portugal) plus Sweden, Luxembourg, Swit-zerland and Italy. At the end of the tripartite discussions Switzerland was dropped from the list.

The conferees in the tripartite talks had difficulty in finding the most appropriate name for the new security organization. The title suggested by the British in their message of March 11 was "Atlantic approaches pact of mutual assistance." Pearson suggested at the first meeting of the tripartite talks, "security pact of the free western nations."[21] At the second meeting it was agreed to use the term "western mutual defence pact" on the ground that to put the word 'Atlantic' in the title "would leave Italy out and would equally exclude Swiss and (possibly later) German or Western German participation." The use of the term "western" would permit inclusion of those states sharing western civilization. This would presumably exclude Greece, Turkey and Iran. ... "[22] Later, however, "North Atlantic" was substituted for "western" "to prevent efforts of Latin America, Australia, etc., to adhere, which would make the arrange-ment unwieldy, especially as none of these are now threatened by Soviet Communism. ... "[23] Finally the term "North Atlantic area" was agreed to in order to make the inclusion of Italy and Switzerland appear less illogical.

The idea of a unilateral declaration by the United States instead of a North Atlantic security pact was not going to be dismissed as easily as the participants in the tripartite discussions thought or hoped.

Lovett, the Under-Secretary of State, had been on holiday when the tripartite talks were held. On April 9, eight days after the conclusion of the talks, Hickerson told Wrong that Lovett was not completely convinced of the necessity of a pact in addition to a presidential declaration; and on that day, James Forrestal, the Secretary of Defense, noted in his diary that "the present American attitude is that the President should [give] his blessing to the five-nation [Brussels] alliance but without formulating it in the form of a treaty or even a protocol." He also noted the "curious fact" that "Canada is equally as strong as Britain for the formation of the [Atlantic] alliance."[24]

In speaking to Wrong on April 9, Hickerson had gone on to say that Lovett's hesitation about supporting the idea of an Atlantic treaty had been strengthened by Spaak, then Prime Minister and Foreign Minister of Belgium, who had just been visiting Washington and who had told Lovett that he was not particularly concerned about formal engagements provided that a United States promise of support to the Brussels Powers was publicly stated by the President.[25] The State Department memorandum of the talk with Spaak on April 5 reported him as saying, "If the United States were prepared to enter into formal guarantees of western Europe such commitments would be universally welcomed in western Europe, particularly in France, but formal commitments were not the essential need. The real need was for maximum military co-ordination at the earliest possible date. . . . A treaty by which the United States guaranteed the five [Brussels treaty] powers, who are not directly threatened by the Russians, would risk making other European countries which are threatened fear that the United States had written them off and might encourage the Russians to move against them."[26] Spaak did not, of course, know of the tripartite discussions.

As soon as the British learned of the emergence of support in the administration in Washington for a unilateral declaration in place of a treaty, Bevin urged on Marshall (in a message of April 9) the inadequacies of such a course of action: "One of my great anxieties in this business is whether, if trouble did come, we should be left waiting as in 1940 in a state of uncertainty. In view of our experience then it would be very difficult to be able to stand up to it again unless there was a definite worked-out arrangement for the western area, together with other assistance, on the basis of collective security to resist the aggressor."[27]

Pearson was likewise concerned when he learned of Lovett's attitude. In a memorandum to the Prime Minister on April 12 he warned of:

the possibility that no pact at all will be negotiated by the United States . . . [the argument being] that a unilateral guarantee of assistance to a selected group of states, if attacked, given after Congressional approval, will be adequate to provide the security required. It may be thought that some such statement will acquire the validity and authority in its field that the Monroe Doctrine, based also solely on a presidential statement, has acquired in its field. It is also hoped that, if such a declaration were made, it could be supplemented by one from Canada, though why we, any more than Brazil, Argentina or Australia, should give such a unilateral guarantee is not clear.

Pearson then went on to give six reasons for believing that "from almost every point of view, a multilateral security agreement is preferable to a unilateral guarantee." First, because a multilateral agreement would have to be ratified by the Senate, it would commit the United States much more firmly than a unilateral guarantee. Second, it would embody the element of mutual assistance. "Why," he asked, "should the United States and Canada come to the assistance of European countries if those countries are not willing to accept similar obligations to us?" Third, a unilateral guarantee, by underlining the satellite character of the relationship of the European countries to the United States, might unnecessarily offend their pride. His fourth objection to a unilateral guarantee was that it would increase the difficulties of making clear to the people of the United States and Canada that they needed the help of the western European democracies just as those democracies needed the help of the North American countries. (St. Laurent was to play up this argument in a speech in the House of Commons two weeks later.) Fifth, a multilateral agreement would be an important demonstration that security arrangements could be worked out under Article 51 of the U.N. Charter. "Eventually other arrangements could be negotiated for other areas until all free countries might be brought in." Sixth, and most important of all, a unilateral guarantee would be nothing more than a pledge of military assistance whereas a treaty could and should contain provisions for closer political, economic and cultural co-operation; it should set up new international institutions, and "it should set forth the principles of western society which we are trying not only to defend but to make the basis of an eventually united world."[28]

When Spaak visited Ottawa in mid-April, Pearson used some of these arguments in speaking to him. He reported Spaak as agreeing that a mere presidential declaration would not suffice and that a treaty commitment was required.[29] Pearson was over-optimistic. At the end of July, Spaak said to the United States Ambassador to Belgium that he believed that a North Atlantic pact would be premature.[30]

On April 15, Wrong reported, "Messrs. Hickerson and Rusk are, I think, both thoroughly convinced that the United States ought to enter into a formal international obligation and that a presidential declaration will not turn the trick. So, incidentally is Mr. Reston [of the *New York Times*], whose views on this point are important because he is a confidant of Senator Vandenberg."[31] Wrong's optimism about Vandenberg was justified. At his meeting with Lovett on April 18, Vandenberg agreed in principle to United States participation in a North Atlantic treaty. He also agreed to sponsor a resolution in the Senate which would endorse United States participation in regional security arrangements "as affect its national security".[32]

In Ottawa, we had decided towards the end of April that the time had come to present to Parliament and the people the arguments for Canadian participation in a collective security pact; and that we would take advantage of this opportunity to plead with those in the administration in Washington who thought that a unilateral declaration by the United States was sufficient. In his speech in the House of Commons on April 29, St. Laurent affirmed that he was sure that it was the desire of the people of Canada "that Canada should play its full part . . . with other free states in any appropriate collective security arrangements which may be worked out under Articles 51 or 52 of the Charter" which would "confront the forces of communist expansionism with an overwhelming preponderance of moral, economic and military force and with a sufficient degree of unity to ensure that this preponderance of force is so used that the free nations cannot be defeated one by one." Using language from Pearson's memorandum of April 12, St. Laurent went on to say,

> One thing we must constantly keep in mind as we approach this fateful decision is that the western European democracies are not beggars asking for our charity. They are allies whose assistance we need in order to be able successfully to defend ourselves and our beliefs. Canada and the United States need the assistance of the western European democracies just as they need ours. The spread of aggressive communist despotism over western Europe would ultimately almost certainly mean for us war, and war on most unfavourable terms. It is in our national interest to see to it that the flood of communist expansion is held back.[33]

No other government leader in any North Atlantic country had at that time gone as far as this in arguing in public for a North Atlantic security pact.

At the beginning of May, we learned from Wrong that the two chief opponents in the State Department of a North Atlantic treaty were Charles Bohlen and George Kennan; they favoured, instead, a unilateral United States declaration accompanied by the provision of military equipment by the United States. This was formidable opposition. They were two of the leading and most intelligent and influential members of the State Department; they were the principal experts in the State Department on the Soviet Union; and they were senior to the two chief proponents of the treaty in the State Department, J. D. Hickerson and T. C. Achilles. Bohlen was counsellor of the Department and responsible for relations with Congress; Kennan was director of the policy planning staff. They had both been absent from Washington when the tripartite talks had taken place, and when they returned, they made clear their opposition to the proposals which had emerged from those talks.

Bohlen was reported to us as having said that the proposals were too extensive because they proposed the membership of the Scandinavian states which, he thought, would be unwilling to participate, and not extensive enough because they did not envisage a United States treaty association with Greece, Turkey and Iran – countries as much threatened by the Soviet Union as those of western Europe. Insofar as the Benelux countries and France were concerned, the presence of United States troops in Germany ensured that the United States would automatically become involved as a belligerent if the Soviet Union were to make an aggressive thrust to the west. An Atlantic pact would cause undue provocation to the Soviet Union. He thought that Congress would be unwilling to undertake so far-reaching a commitment in an election year.

Kennan was reported as having said that he had discussed the matter at length with Bohlen and that they saw eye to eye. It was unthinkable that the United States would stand idly by if the Soviet Union were to make an aggressive move against any country of Europe. The Russians were fully aware of this state of affairs and the best deterrent to action by them was, not an Atlantic pact, but the provision of military supplies to western Europe by the United States accompanied by a resolution of the Senate.[34]

Kennan, in a memorandum to Marshall and Lovett on April 29, had given the following summary of the views of Bohlen and himself: "[T]he appeals from Bevin and Bidault spring primarily ... from their feeling that we do not have any agreed concept between ourselves and themselves as to ... what steps, if any, could be taken to save the continental members of the Brussels Union from the dual catastrophe of Russian invasion and subsequent military liberation. ... If this analysis is correct, what the western Europeans require from us is not so much a public political and military alliance (since the very presence of our troops between western Europe and the Russians is an adequate guarantee that we will be at war if they are attacked) but rather realistic staff talks to see what can be done about their defense ... to explore with them all serious suggestions as to how a Russian advance could be at least delayed and impeded in the early stages and possibly eventually halted at some point or another."[35]

The British embassy received at this time a message from Bevin to Marshall putting the arguments for a treaty, but it was so shaken by the opposition of Bohlen and Kennan to the idea of a treaty that it "was inclined not to present the message since it might merely produce a reply indicating United States unwillingness to conclude such a treaty." The embassy told Achilles this and found that he shared their fears and agreed that it would be wise to put off presenting Bevin's ideas on a treaty; there would, he said, be ample opportunity to present these ideas "as and when" the multilateral intergovernmental discussions started.[36]

When Bohlen wrote his memoirs 24 years later he had forgotten that he had opposed the idea of a North Atlantic treaty. He wrote

> NATO was simply a necessity. The developing situation with the Soviet Union demanded the participation of the United States in the defence of western Europe. Any other solution would have opened the area to Soviet domination. . . . Had the United States not inaugurated the Marshall Plan or something similar and had the United States not departed from its historical tradition and agreed to join NATO, the Communists might easily have assumed power in most of western Europe.[37]

Kennan, in his memoirs, stated that his reason in March, 1948, for opposing the conclusion of the North Atlantic treaty was that he did not

> see any reason why . . . the development of new relationships of alliance between [the United States] and European countries was required to meet . . . the Communist behavior – the strikes in France and Italy, the Czech *coup* and the Berlin blockade. . . . [These] were defensive reactions on the Soviet side to the initial success of the Marshall plan initiative and to the preparations now being undertaken on the western side to set up a separate German government in Western Germany.

He stated that the farthest he was prepared to go, and that with reluctance because he saw "no real necessity" for it, was that the United States, "in partnership with Canada, if Canada were willing", would give countries which joined the Brussels treaty a unilateral political and military guarantee plus a "readiness" to extend to these countries "whatever was necessary in the way of assistance in military supplies, forces, and joint strategic planning."[38]

Wrong had Kennan to lunch on May 19 to argue the case for a treaty. Wrong made two points. The first was that even if, as Kennan maintained, the countries of western Europe "were as much assured of U.S. support now as they would be under an alliance, plenty of people would not think this was the case, and would therefore refrain from running risks which it was in our interest that they should run." Wrong's second point related to the position of Canada:

> [I]t would be far more difficult for Canada to collaborate in planning defence against Soviet aggression on the basis of a unilateral U.S. assurance than it would be if both countries were parties to an Atlantic agreement. Furthermore, under such an agreement the joint planning of the defence of North America fell into place as part of a larger

whole and would diminish difficulties arising from fears of invasion of Canadian sovereignty by the U.S. It would be easier to advocate a policy of Canadian aloofness if the present state of affairs was maintained. An Atlantic pact would go a long way towards curing our split personality in defence matters by bringing the U.S., the U.K. and Canada into regular partnership.

Kennan said that he was much impressed by this second argument, which had not occurred to him before, and that he would think it over carefully.[39]

The day that Wrong had Kennan to lunch was the day on which the Senate Foreign Relations Committee unanimously approved of the Vandenberg resolution. The resolution was a victory for Hickerson and Achilles over Bohlen and Kennan. It spoke of the association of the United States with collective security arrangements; it would be difficult to contend that a unilateral declaration created an association. The collective security arrangements would have to increase the national security of the United States; a system of reciprocal guarantees embodied in a treaty would be more likely to increase the national security of the United States than a unilateral declaration.

The British embassy had waited for the passage of the Vandenberg resolution by the Senate Foreign Relations Committee before presenting to the State Department Bevin's message of May 14 countering the Kennan-Bohlen arguments against a treaty. They presented this message to Kennan and Bohlen on May 19 for transmission to Marshall and he read it to the National Security Council the next day. Bevin said:

> The presence of the American forces in Germany affords only indirect assurance to Italy and Scandinavia and the talks on Germany in London have shown that it does not suffice even to remove the perpetual uneasiness of the French as regards their own security. . . . [A] Treaty based on Article 51 [of the Charter] to which the United States would be a party would be far the best answer to those in our own two countries who are urging a revision of the [U.N.] Charter. . . . [T]he ultimate conclusion of some world-wide system based on Article 51 to which Mr. St. Laurent has recently drawn attention can only be rendered practicable if the way is prepared by a defence arrangement in the North Atlantic area. . . . [40]

Though we in Ottawa did not know it at the time, St. Laurent's statements in his speech of April 29 had changed Kennan's attitude to the proposal for a North Atlantic treaty. On May 24 he informed Marshall and Lovett that these statements added a "new and important element" to the problem of a North Atlantic security pact. In the light of these statements and of Bevin's message he said that he thought that "we must be very careful not to place ourselves in the position of being the obstacle to further progress toward the political union of the western democracies."[41] Four days later Wrong reported on the basis of information given him by Achilles that "Kennan is much more receptive now to the pact idea. Bohlen, I gather, remains to be converted."[42]

Kennan came to Ottawa at the beginning of June. To prepare for his visit we produced in the Department a memorandum of about 2,000 words setting out 19 reasons for believing that a multilateral treaty was preferable to a unilateral declaration by either the President or by Congress. This memorandum incorporated the arguments set forth by Pearson to the Prime Minister in mid-April, by Wrong to Kennan in mid-May, and by Bevin in his message which had been delivered on May 19. It also contained some additional arguments. One was that the existence of formal international bodies set up under a North Atlantic treaty "would help to ensure that, in the event of war, the occupied western European countries had a say in the making of the larger political and strategic decisions by the supreme war council and the combined chiefs of staff." In our opinion it was "in the general interest that these countries should have a say, because of their political experience, maturity and moderation." Another argument was that if United States military support was to be effective in western Europe, "the United States chiefs of staff must know where they can operate in the event of war or in an emergency. They must know the bases from which they can undertake a quick and effective offensive. They must be sure in advance of the territories which they can employ. They must, if necessary, establish bases immediately. All this will be much easier to do under a treaty."

There were three specifically Canadian considerations set forth in the departmental memorandum. The first was that a treaty commitment by the United States would lessen the danger that Canada would enter another world war long before the United States. In the first two world wars Canada had gone to war more than two years before the United States. We did not want this to happen again. A second consideration was one which we believed that Canada shared with Denmark, Iceland and Ireland. It was that it would be politically easier to grant defence facilities to a North Atlantic alliance than to the United States. The third consideration was that the military planning which would follow the conclusion of a treaty would tend to modify the rather unrealistic concentration of United States and Canadian defence planners on the passive defence of North America from outside attack. "If the North Atlantic is bridged by a defence alliance, the problems of North American defence would be seen as a small part of a larger plan, the purpose of which would be to defeat the enemy by offensive operations."[43]

The United States Ambassador in Ottawa gave a dinner for Kennan at the beginning of June. After dinner Pearson, Claxton, J. W. Pickersgill (then Special Assistant to the Prime Minister) and others launched at Kennan the reasoning set forth in the memorandum. When I sent Wrong a report on the discussion at this dinner I said that Kennan had said that he was impatient with the pressure from the United Kingdom and the western European states to make a formal treaty commitment. Those states did not seem to realize that if the United States gave this guarantee, it would be doing something which would be in the interests of western Europe but not necessarily in the interests of the United States itself, since it could at any time make a deal with the Soviet Union. "We naturally took him up on this and he withdrew from this exposed position. However it did give me a feeling that if you scratch almost any American long enough, you will find an isolationist. They suffer, and you can hardly blame them, from a homesickness for isolation."[44]

Towards the end of June, eleven days before the opening of the six-power talks on July 6, Wrong reported, "It is still uncertain whether the State Department is fully convinced that a treaty commitment is desirable. . . . I think that Lovett is inclined to be sympathetic but not fully satisfied on the treaty proposal. Bohlen still tends to oppose it, while Kennan appears to be converted. Hickerson is the staunchest advocate."[45]

It was not long, however, before the State Department committed itself to a treaty. According to the agreed minutes of the fifth meeting of the six-power talks held on July 9, "Mr. Pearson said that the Canadian government could not make any contribution to the collective security of the area by any unilateral guarantee of Western Union security. Mr. Lovett interjected that the United States government could not contemplate any such idea."[46]

These discussions were informal, exploratory and non-committal but it is scarcely likely that the Under-Secretary of State of the United States would have authorized the inclusion of this statement in the agreed minutes which were circulated to the participating governments if he had not been certain that he was stating correctly the views of the United States administration. This is confirmed by a telegram which Achilles drafted four weeks later to the foreign ministers of the Brussels powers in which he said, "We do not consider that the U.S. can effectively support Brussels Treaty arrangement as presently constituted except within framework of North Atlantic arrangement. . . . " Stone reported that Achilles had told him that the telegram had not been sent, but that the reason for this was not that his superiors disapproved of it, but that it was decided to use the arguments in it in Washington in the intergovernmental talks rather than to start arguing "all over the place."[47] The idea that a unilateral declaration by the United States could be a substitute for a North Atlantic treaty was squelched in July, 1948. At the end of August the United States pleaded the case for a North Atlantic treaty in Paris and Brussels with the zeal of a convert.* Opposition within the State Depart-

*See pages 121 to 122.

ment collapsed. Kennan had been converted to support of the treaty. Bohlen, who apparently still had doubts, was in September removed from Washington where he might be able to influence policy, by being sent to Paris as an adviser to the United States delegation to the U.N. General Assembly. He was absent from Washington from September 19 to December 14.[48] By the time he was back in Washington, it was too late for him to affect the course of events, even if he had wanted to, since only ten days after his return, the Ambassadors' Committee, under Lovett's chairmanship, agreed on the text of a North Atlantic treaty for submission to the governments.

CHAPTER NINE

HESITATIONS IN FRANCE AND BELGIUM

The French are in our hair.
Robert A. Lovett, August 24, 1948*

During the summer of 1948, while the second stage of the intergovernmental discussions was going on, we in Ottawa became increasingly concerned by the hesitant and negative attitude of the French and Belgian representatives in the discussions in Washington, and by indications that the Netherlands government might be lukewarm about a treaty. We feared that the trend towards increasing support for the treaty in the United States administration might be reversed if these three governments did not actively support the idea of a treaty.

Bidault had had doubts in early March about the wisdom of concluding the Brussels treaty because he feared that such a treaty without the support of the United States might increase the risk of attack by the Soviet Union, an attack which France would be powerless to meet.** "No Frenchman", wrote the Canadian Ambassador to Paris at the end of May, "deludes himself that the treaty of Brussels has any value as a weapon of defence against Soviet attack without the military backing of the United States". "There is no doubt", he went on to say,

> that the formal adherence of the U.S. to the Brussels treaty would be a valuable gesture of political and moral solidarity but the really important thing, from the point of view of the French, is that they should be furnished with the resources which would enable them to make a stand on their own frontiers and that they should know that the Americans will fight side by side with them in Europe to defend French soil from invasion.[1]

What the French considered in May to be the really important thing was exactly what Kennan and Bohlen were saying in Washington at the same time to be the really important thing.

*See page 121.
**See page 53.

It was assumed at the time virtually everywhere in the western world that, as the United States embassy in Moscow put it in a despatch at the beginning of April, 1948, "The Red Army and Soviet air forces are capable of taking continental Europe and key areas of Asia within a few months."[2] The French were naturally obsessed by this danger. Charles Ritchie, the second-in-command of the Canadian embassy in Paris, wrote on August 20, 1948,

> [The French] consider first that the occupation of France by Soviet armies would mean a knock-out blow from which France might never recover; secondly, that the elite of France (which usually includes, at any rate in his own estimation, any Frenchman who may be discussing the subject with you) would be liquidated by the invader.... [The prime concern of the French] was with two concrete and immediate questions. First, obtaining military equipment from the United States to re-arm their forces, and secondly, the development of an allied strategy which would ensure active United States co-operation in stemming the tide of Soviet invasion whether on the Rhine or further East. ... It may be ... that the French do think, however mistakenly, that instead of the concrete assistance for which they are asking, they are being put off with paper guarantees as to the future; that in the face of an immediate and pressing danger they are being asked to consider long-term and general propositions. Obviously if a man is threatened with armed robbery he might prefer a gun now to a promise of conditional assistance later. Although this is both a simplification and a falsification of the true situation, it is possible that the French see it in these terms.[3]

The allied strategy which France wanted had been set forth three months before by the Brussels treaty permanent commission in a statement prepared for the consideration of the United States administration:

> In the event of an attack by Russia, however soon it may come, the five [Brussels treaty] powers are determined to fight as far east in Germany as possible. If Russia overruns the countries of western Europe, irreparable harm will be done before they are liberated, owing to the Russian policy of deportation and pillage. Their preparations aimed at holding the Russians on the best position in Germany covering the territory of the five powers in such a way that sufficient time for American power to intervene decisively can be assured.[4]

Throughout the summer of 1948 the two representatives of France in the discussions in Washington, Henri Bonnet, the Ambassador, and Armand Bérard, the Minister, kept insisting on the two concrete and immediate questions referred to by Ritchie in his letter of August 20.

They did so at the risk of being tiresomely repetitious. Thus at the Ambassadors' Committee on August 20 Bonnet said that he wanted to stress a point which "he had already done more than once", that the French government wanted to have, if possible, an agreement on two points, "first, the question of assistance in re-arming the western European armies, and second, an understanding between the western powers and the United States on the manner in which an emergency would be met and where it would be met". Lovett's dry comment was that he "agreed that M. Bonnet had covered these points repreatedly".[5]

The French views on these questions were, we were told, shared by Spaak who was then both the Prime Minister and the Foreign Minister of Belgium. The Netherlands Foreign Minister told the Canadian Ambassador that at the meeting of the foreign ministers of the Brussels powers which had taken place at The Hague on July 19 and 20, the Belgian as well as the French delegates had said, with reference to the talks in Washington, "their governments were for the moment less interested in a long-term policy than in coping with any emergency in the near future."[6] Two weeks later, we learned that Spaak had said that he thought the North Atlantic security pact was premature and that the provocative effect on the Russians was not justifiable if one took into account the military potential of the North Atlantic countries.[7] It was, indeed, possible that Spaak, a future secretary-general of NATO, was at this time turning over in his mind whether an armed neutrality of western European countries might not be preferable to a North Atlantic treaty. The Belgian Ambassador to Canada sounded out Pearson on this in the middle of July. The Ambassador said that he was "speaking entirely personally and not necessarily reflecting in any way the views of his government," a formula customarily employed by an ambassador when he has received an instruction to sound out the government to which he is accredited without committing his own government. He expounded his "personal" ideas as follows. In two or three years a rearmed and united group of western European countries might well be able to maintain their neutrality against the Soviet Union in the event of war between the Soviet Union and the United States. In any such western European combination, it would be essential to include West Germany (and, if possible, the whole of Germany), for the Germans could provide the strongest military forces to be used against the Russians. Such an armed neutrality would serve the interests of the United States since, if a conflict between the Soviet Union and the United States automatically involved western European countries, the United States might have to come to the help of these countries on land and thereby weaken its air attack on Russia which was the only way at this time by which the Russians could be defeated. The Belgian Ambassador also, Pearson reported, "had . . . many fears that the United States would not be equal to the task of working out any great coalition which could defeat the Soviet. It had neither the wisdom nor the experience to bring about such a 'grand design'; [it] too often acted on impulse with only short-range objectives in mind."

Pearson said to the Belgian Ambassador that

> this thesis overlooked two things. One, the U.S.S.R. could not afford to allow western European countries to be neutral; they would, I assume, in case of war at once attempt to get control of the whole of continental Europe as essential for their survival against the United States and the United Kingdom. Secondly, it would be quite impossible for the United States to help the European countries build up their military strength without an assurance that this strength would be used with that of the United States to defeat any aggressive attack by Russia.[8]

Dr. van Roijen, the Netherlands Ambassador to Canada, told me a month later that a Dutch socialist leader had given him a possible explanation of Spaak's attitude. The Belgian socialist party, unlike the Dutch socialist party, was preoccupied with the problem of resisting United States imperialism as well as Soviet aggression, perhaps because they were more influenced by the French socialist party. The Belgian socialist party feared the possibility of continuing control by the United States over western Europe even after western Europe had been strengthened economically and militarily. Spaak had had to act counter to the wishes of the Belgian socialist party on a number of issues. He might therefore have a natural reluctance to act counter to their wishes or prejudices in the matter of a United States military guarantee.[9]

The attitude of the French and Belgian governments was, of course, reflected in the instructions or lack of instructions to their representatives in Washington. Stone, the Canadian member of the Working Group, reported at the end of July, after the seventh meeting of the Group, that "the contributions of the French and Belgian members of the Working Group to its discussions have so far been exactly zero. They have come forward with no positive or constructive ideas whatsoever, nor have they had anything to say about ideas that have been put forward by other people that contributed in any way to their development."[10]

By the time the next meeting of the Working Group took place, the French had received clear instructions, with the result that the situation worsened. Bérard, the second-in-command at the French embassy, stated that "his government had thought the present conversations were to be concerned with military aid to the Brussels powers rather than with the formation of a larger association. The French people, he said, were like a man who has been told that, if he will but climb 2000 feet up a mountain, he will secure a wonderful view. But, having made the ascent, he is told that the view cannot really be obtained from there after all: let him climb another 2000 feet and he will surely secure the view. He thought that overcoming the 'deception' that the French people would feel would present a major political problem. The French, having risked the Brussels pact, now want some security before they undertake further risks in a larger association."[11] (Bérard was presumably using the word deception in the French sense as meaning disappointment.)

Bonnet, the French Ambassador, went even further. Lovett told Pearson that Bonnet had called on Marshall in mid-August and "had had the effrontery to suggest that the French would only accept an Atlantic security pact on the following three conditions: unity of command at once; immediate movement of U.S. military supplies to France; immediate movement of U.S. military personnel to France." According to Lovett, this had had "such an irritating effect on General Marshall that . . . he felt like calling off the Atlantic pact negotiations at once."[12]

The use by Bérard of the word "déception" indicates that there had been a genuine misunderstanding in Paris about the nature of the intergovernmental discussions which had opened in Washington at the beginning of July. This misunderstanding was possible because France had not been included in the first stage of the intergovernmental discussions. We, who had taken part in the tripartite talks, knew that the purpose of the July talks was to carry on the discussions on the making of a North Atlantic treaty which had been launched in March. The French, on the basis of Lovett's message to Bidault in mid-May, had every right to believe that the July talks would, in Lovett's words, be concerned with "co-ordinated policy" and with "practical measures to increase western European security". The confusion was further confounded because Lovett in this message instructed the United States Ambassador in Paris to emphasize to Bidault "that we are not thinking and have never thought of guarantees." Bidault immediately replied that he too was not interested in "guarantees".[13] Six weeks later, just before the six-power discussions were about to begin, Bidault drafted an instruction to Bonnet, which he showed to the United States Ambassador, in which he said, "What the French government desires is not a spectacular system of guarantees, but an effective and concrete system of assistance."[14]

The use of the word "guarantees" in the discussions between the United States and France in May and June was unfortunate. When Lovett told the French that the United States was not thinking of guarantees he was making a point which the United States made constantly throughout the whole twelve months of negotiations: that the United States could not accept an automatic commitment to go to war in defence of another country since only Congress had the power under the constitution to declare war. Bidault, however, could well have interpreted Lovett's statement as meaning that the United States would not contemplate entering into a military alliance with the Brussels treaty powers. Certainly there is in the instructions which Bidault drafted for Bonnet at the end of June no mention of the possibility of such an alliance.[15]

The terms of the invitation to France to participate in the six-power talks which opened at the beginning of July did little to remove the misunderstanding in Paris. The invitation was to "top-secret exploratory talks pursuant to [the] Vandenberg Res[olution] at which there would be . . . an exchange of views on . . . nature of U.S. association under Vandenberg resolution with European security arrangements".[16]

That there was a genuine misunderstanding in Paris of the objective of the Washington discussions was confirmed by Gladwyn Jebb after he had spoken to Chauvel, the secretary-general of the French foreign office, on August 23. Jebb said that

> he thought that the reserve which the French had shown in this matter [of a North Atlantic security pact] might be explained, at any rate in part, by the fact that the idea had come to them as a surprise in Washington as they had not been informed prior to the conversations that a pact of this nature was under contemplation. They had viewed it with suspicion, perhaps thinking that instead of getting the concrete United States aid which they hoped for they were being put off with proposals of a vague and general character.[17]

By the middle of August the differences of opinion in the discussions in Washington had become so acute that it was decided to hold an informal off-the-record meeting in Lovett's house of representatives of the six countries participating in the Washington talks. This meeting was held on August 20. According to Pearson the idea of such a meeting had apparently been suggested by the Belgian Ambassador, Baron Silvercruys. Silvercruys said to him the night before the meeting took place that "he was very worried about the position that the French representative might have to take at a formal meeting." (He was presumably also worried about the position which he would have to take.) Silvercruys added that the Netherlands Ambassador, Van Kleffens, "also, it seems, had received instructions from his government which he hoped might be modified later in the light of views that could be expressed only at a very informal off-the-record gathering."[18]

Lovett in his memorandum on the meeting says that both Silvercruys and Van Kleffens felt that their governments did not fully understand the point of view of the United States and Canada, that they were trying to reorient the French Ambassador, Bonnet, and that they had doubts as to whether the French government "had really given much consideration to the basic approach, being much more fully occupied with the immediate rearmament problem in view of the nervousness which they felt arising from the tension in Europe".[19]

At the meeting of August 20 Pearson met head-on the French argument that a North Atlantic treaty might provoke the Russians into an immediate armed attack. He said that if the North Atlantic countries united in a pact and were growing stronger individually and collectively there was, of course,

> some risk of provocation while the process of strengthening was going on ... but the real act of provocation would not be the signing of a pact, but the increase of the military strengths of the members of that pact. Yet those [he meant the French] who are most worried about the provocative effect of a pact are most insistent on increasing their own military power. On this basis, the only way to avoid provocation would be to have everybody remain weak, which, however, is in fact the greatest provocation and which nobody wants.[20]

Lovett, according to Pearson, tried to drive home to the French Ambassador that

> while the long-term arrangements were being worked out, the United States was doing everything it possibly could to help meet the short-term emergency.... He talked about strategic planning of the commanders in Germany and the military discussions going on in London [between the Brussels treaty powers and the United States and Canada]. He mentioned the movement of aircraft and supplies across the Atlantic and the building up of an American air striking force in Europe. He asked M. Bonnet what more they could do in present circumstances.

As a result of this meeting and of talks with Lovett and later with the British, Pearson reported to Ottawa that "the attitude of the French is causing increasing impatience and irritation here and is incomprehensible to everybody."[21] Four days later he cabled the Canadian embassy in Paris: "These discussions demonstrated that the Americans are becoming profoundly impatient with the negative attitude of the French. There is, I think, a real danger of the whole project being wrecked."[22]

Before the meeting in Washington on August 20 we had sent to our embassies in Paris, Brussels and The Hague a comprehensive exposition of our reasons for believing that the national interests of France, Belgium and the Netherlands would be served by the conclusion of a North Atlantic pact at the earliest possible date.[23] Four days after the meeting, we instructed our ambassadors to speak along these lines to the government. Some of the arguments were the same as those we had put to George Kennan at the beginning of June. Others were tailored to meet the objections and fears of the western European countries.

Thus Pearson argued in his letter to Vanier, the Canadian Ambassador in Paris, that the wide differences between the right-wing Republicans who controlled the House of Representatives and the Republican supporters of a bi-partisan foreign policy emphasized the importance of a multilateral agreement binding the United States for not less than ten years. Such an agreement would commit the whole Republican Party and would considerably reduce the range within which the compass needle of United States policy could swing. (We shared the general assumption that Dewey would defeat Truman in the elections in November.)

The difficulty from the point of view of the United States is that a formal alliance would be a tremendous reversal of the traditional national policy of the United States. This very difficulty, however, is the reason why the alliance would be of great value to western Europe: it would be the outward and visible sign of a revolutionary change in United States foreign policy.

Pearson agreed with the French that there was danger that the United States might press the Soviet Union too hard and too fast and not leave the Soviet Union a way out to save its face.

To lessen this danger, the western European powers will have to exert a steady and constructive influence on Washington. The establishment of a North Atlantic union will give them additional channels through which to exert this moderating influence. Under a North Atlantic pact there would presumably be established a Consultative Council of Foreign Ministers, a Council of Defence Ministers and a combined Chiefs of Staff, as well as some permanent consultative committee. The pact will also contain undertakings among the members to consult. There will thus be established, at least in outline, a semi-constitutional structure of the North Atlantic powers.

He then cited a recent statement by Arnold Toynbee:

In an even semi-parliamentary international forum the political experience, maturity, and moderation of countries like these, [the western European and the Commonwealth countries] will weigh heavily in the balance alongside of the grosser weight of Brennus' sword. In a pure power-politics world, on the other hand, these highly civilized but materially less powerful states will count for nothing compared with the United States and the Soviet Union.[24]

Pearson went on to say that he realized that the French, particularly from their experience in the Second World War, must be worried by the possibility that, if another war should break out, they would have little or no say in the larger political and strategic decisions of the western countries. "The conclusion of a North Atlantic treaty would make it possible to set up formal international bodies, not only for making plans for preventing war, but also for making plans for the waging of war. The establishment in peacetime of these bodies would help to ensure that in the event of war France and other western European countries had a say in the making of the larger political and strategic decisions."

Hume Wrong showed this letter to the State Department and told them that we had sent it to our embassies in Brussels and The Hague to guide them in their discussions with the Belgian and Netherlands governments. Lovett, with our permission, enclosed our letter with the letter he sent on August 24 to Jefferson Caffery, the United States Ambassador in Paris, instructing him to speak forcefully to the French government about the line which their representatives had been taking in the Washington talks. This letter had been drafted by Achilles. The State Department also sent our letter to the United States Ambassadors to Belgium and the Netherlands.[25]

Lovett began his letter to Caffery, "Dear Jeff; The French are in our hair." He expressed his impatience with the four principal French demands: a guarantee which "approaches an automatic commitment to go immediately to war if France is attacked"; the "immediate re-equipment of French forces"; the exclusion of the Scandinavian countries and Portugal from the treaty; and an assurance from the United States "that in the event of war United States ground forces will immediately be sent to help in the defence of France." He rejected all these demands as impossible. He instructed Caffery to make clear to the French government that it was "fantastic" for France to attach conditions to joining a North Atlantic alliance since it was the United States and not France which was "doing the favors".[26]

Pearson was unhappy about some of the arguments in the letter to Caffery. They seemed to him to reflect that lack of sympathy with and understanding of France which had, it appeared to us in Ottawa, permeated the White House and the State Department ever since the fall of France in June, 1940. In his letter to the Canadian Ambassador in Paris transmitting Lovett's letter Pearson said that he did not like the impression Lovett gave that he was thinking of the western Europeans as clients, not as allies or partners. Nor did he like Lovett's "insistence that the United States military must keep a free hand on what United States strategy would be in the event of war in Europe." "If all the partners of the North Atlantic pact insist on keeping a free hand, there is not going to be any real joint planning or pooling of resources." He believed, however, and he obviously expected the Canadian Ambassador to tell the French this, that the establishment under the North Atlantic treaty of agencies for joint planning would "make it extremely difficult, if not impossible, for the United States to refuse to give an assurance that they will have certain ground forces available to send immediately to Europe to defend France in an emergency."[27] Pearson was soon to be proved right on this.

The first representative of the three active proponents of the treaty (Britain, the United States, and Canada) to speak at this time to the French government was Gladwyn Jebb. He made a special trip to Paris on August 22, and, accompanied by the British Ambassador, called on Chauvel, the Secretary-General of the French Foreign Office, and later on Robert Schuman, the Foreign Minister. Ritchie saw Dennery of the French Foreign Office on September 2; Caffery and Vanier saw Chauvel separately on September 4. There was a French government crisis at the time, so that ministers were not available for interviews until later. Similar talks by the representatives of the three powers took place in Brussels and The Hague.

The result of all this was that the French, Belgian and Netherlands Ambassadors in Washington received instructions during the first week of September to give full support to the idea of a treaty. The interventions of Britain, the United States and Canada, and second thoughts in Paris, Brussels and The Hague, removed a stumbling block to the conclusion of the treaty. On September 10, the Ambassadors' Committee unanimously adopted an agreed statement for submission to their governments which included a blessing on the idea of a North Atlantic treaty: "those nations having a primary interest in the security of the North Atlantic area should collaborate in the development of a regional or collective defence arrangement for that area."[28]

The French very soon received a reward from the United States for their decision to give full support to the idea of a treaty. On August 24, when the State Department had decided that it was necessary to twist the arms of the French, Lovett told Caffery:

To their demands for immediate reequipment of French forces we have patiently told them that the necessary equipment does not exist, that it will not be produced until someone is ready to pay for it, and that "lend-lease" is not a popular word in this country, that French inability to pay for it in dollars requires that it be paid for by appropriations from the United States Treasury, that such appropriations would require legislation which will not be enacted except on the basis of commitments on the part of recipients to exert their own maximum efforts to increase their own and each other's security and that of the United States.[29]

About a month later these obstacles to the immediate delivery of military equipment to France vanished; the State Department informed Schuman, the Foreign Minister of France, that the United States was ready to equip three French divisions from their present stock of weapons. The State Department had been doubtful whether Schuman would consider this adequate but he accepted the offer enthusiastically. In reporting this, Wrong said: "It is questionable whether existing legislation permits this delivery of arms to the French, but [the Administration] intend to find some way of going through with it." In the same message Wrong said that legislation authorizing military aid to western Europe was being drafted and it was hoped to secure soon after the elections in November a final decision on the presentation of this legislation to Congress.[30] (On July 25, 1949, Truman, within a few hours of signing the ratification of the North Atlantic treaty, sent to Congress a request for the transfer during the fiscal year 1950 of $1,130 million of military equipment and assistance to France, the Benelux countries, Denmark, Norway and Italy.)

At the same time as this was happening the United States was moving closer to the French position that the grand strategy of the alliance must be based on fighting the Soviet armed forces as far east of the Rhine as possible. Throughout the intergovernmental discussions on the treaty the United States had maintained that its military establishment wished to keep free from any commitment to defend any part of the territory of any ally. More than once the United States group stated that it would be necessary to take the broad view (what people in Washington liked to call "the over-all strategic plan") rather than to guarantee any specific territory against occupation by the enemy.[31] The day after the treaty was signed the opposing view was put forward publicly by one of the principal members of the United States military establishment, General Omar Bradley, Chief of Staff of the United States army. His statement made clear that the earlier view was the view not of the military establishment as a whole but of the air force:

> It must be perfectly apparent to the people of the United States that we cannot count on friends in western Europe if our strategy in the event of war dictates that we shall first abandon them to the enemy with a promise of later liberation. Yet that is the only strategy that can prevail if the military balance of power in Europe is to be carried on the wings of our bombers and deposited in reserves this side of the ocean. It is a strategy that would produce nothing better than impotent and disillusioned allies in the event of a war. Unless plans for common defense of the existing free world provide for the security of western Europe, these people cannot be expected to stake their lives on the common cause. As long as the helplessness of western Europe would invite military aggression, its increasing prosperity shall grow more tempting to the armies from the east. Not until we share our strength on a common defensive front, can we hope to replace this temptation with a real deterrent to war. Without western Europe, the New World would stand alone, an island of embattled freedom in a hostile and despotic world. Western Europe must count on us if it is to survive. And we must count on western Europe if we are to endure.[32]

Two months later, Louis Johnson, the Secretary of Defense of the United States, said in a speech before the National War College:

Because the United States could not – without grave distress to the civilized world – abandon western Europe to enemy occupation with the later promise of liberation, our long-term strategy – in the event of war – must rest in the containment and thereafter in the defeat of an aggressor's land-army strength.

At the beginning of July, 1949, Acheson in a message to Schuman quoted this passage from Louis Johnson's speech and referred to "various statements of a similar character" by Bradley.[33]

Thus three months after the treaty had been signed the United States had gone a long way to meeting the prime concern of the French government with the two concrete and immediate questions of obtaining military equipment from the United States to re-arm its forces, and of developing an allied strategy which would ensure active co-operation by the United States in stemming the tide of Soviet invasion whether on the Rhine or further east. If the United States had moved to this position in the summer of 1948 rather than in the spring of 1949 the intergovernmental negotiations would have gone more smoothly and more quickly, Franco-American relations would not have been strained, and perhaps France would not have insisted on the inclusion of Italy in the alliance and the bringing of Algeria under the protection of the pledge in the treaty. The long delay by the United States in giving the French some assurances on the two points on which they were legitimately deeply concerned must have been the result partly of the difficulty of making decisions on such matters before the elections in November and partly of a failure by high officials in the State Department to comprehend the feelings of the French. This failure is exemplified by the tone of Lovett's letter to Caffery. Another example is Hickerson's statement to me a few days after the treaty was signed that the French, in any discussions of "overall strategic planning" by the North Atlantic alliance, would insist on the primacy of the defence of the Rhine and would get "hysterical" if their views were not accepted.[34] Hickerson showed in this remark no comprehension of how understandable this hysteria was and of how much more hysterical the United States would be if the armed forces of the Soviet Union were as capable of launching a smashing attack on the United States from Mexico as they were of launching such an attack on France from Germany, and if the United States had only recently been subjected to defeat and occupation by Nazi Germany.

Twenty-seven years after the negotiations Hickerson and Achilles told me that they had been convinced at the time that the French wanted a North Atlantic treaty very badly and that their pretended lack of interest in the treaty and the difficulties they caused in the negotiations were purely tactical; if they had appeared during the negotiations to be insensitive to French fears this was perhaps an explanation.[35] I find this to be a partial explanation of their attitude. I do not, however, believe that their assessment of French opinion was accurate; it would certainly not have been concurred in by the Canadian embassy in Paris, and that embassy, under Georges Vanier and Charles Ritchie, was exceptionally well-informed and percipient.

CHAPTER TEN

THE TWO-PILLAR
CONCEPT OF THE TREATY

One recurrent theme in the history of the North Atlantic alliance from the intergovernmental discussions in 1948 and 1949 to the present day is advocacy by the United States of the two-pole or two-pillar or dumb-bell concept of the North Atlantic alliance, a concept which is sometimes called the Grand Design. One pole or pillar would consist of the United States and Canada, the other of the European members of the alliance, including Britain. This idea was put forward in various forms by spokesmen for the United States in the intergovernmental discussions in Washington in the spring and summer of 1948.

All the United States advocates of this idea were agreed that the national interest of the United States required a much greater degree of union among the European members of the proposed North Atlantic alliance. This, they believed, would not only be good in itself but would also make easier the ratification of the North Atlantic treaty by the Senate. The most extreme doctrine was that the United States would agree to a North Atlantic treaty only if the European members of the alliance created a union among themselves. The most extreme definition of the degree of unity ultimately required was "fusion", the term used by John Foster Dulles at the end of April, 1948, in his talk with Marshall and Lovett.[1] The term customarily used was "the United States of western Europe (possibly later of all Europe)". Hickerson said at the second meeting of the tripartite talks on March 23, 1948, that this was what the United States hoped would develop eventually.[2]

Progress towards European union would involve the removal of internal trade barriers, the establishment of freely convertible currency, the creation of a central bank and the free movement of persons.[3] Thus the United States advocates of a United States of western Europe wanted Britain and the other western European countries to transfer part of their sovereignty to the new federation. Some of these advocates also wanted the United States to transfer part of its sovereignty to a North Atlantic federation. Most of them, however, wanted federation for others but not for themselves – they had had their federation in the 1780s. "Support for

126

European unity," wrote Achilles in 1976, "enabled any United States senator, congressman or official to sound eloquently alive to the needs of growing interdependence without suggesting any new obligations for the United States."[4]

The roots of the belief in 1948 within the United States administration and the Senate that a condition precedent to United States entry into a North Atlantic alliance should be much greater unity in western Europe lay deep in United States emotions. Ever since the end of the First World War there had been a smouldering feeling of bitter resentment arising out of the belief that the United States had been dragged into the European civil war of 1914, because the western European nations had refused to learn how to live together and how to solve by themselves their own parochial western European disputes. One of the best expressions of this emotion had been given five months before the outbreak of the Second World War, not by a United States leader but by a Canadian, Mackenzie King, then Prime Minister. On March 30, 1939, he said in the House of Commons:

> The idea that every 20 years this country should automatically and as a matter of course take part in a war overseas for democracy or self-determination of other small nations, that a country which has all it can do to run itself should feel called upon to save, periodically, *a continent that cannot run itself,* and to these ends to risk the lives of its people, risk bankruptcy and political disunion, seems to many a nightmare and sheer madness. (Italics added)[5]

The contempt which many Americans had in the period between the two world wars for what seemed to them to be the inability of western Europeans to submerge their petty nationalities in a greater union remained in 1948, even though by then it had become clear that a third world war would not, like the first two, arise out of a civil war in Europe but rather out of a conflict between the Soviet Union on one side and western Europe and the United States on the other. Now the general feeling in the United States was that the danger of the Soviet Union extending its control over western Europe by direct or indirect aggression, and so endangering the security of the United States, would be substantially diminished if only western Europe would unite. A united western Europe would be stronger economically and militarily; it would be able to bear a larger share of the burden of the common defence against direct and indirect aggression by the Soviet Union; it would not need so much economic and military assistance from the United States; and it would not provide so great a temptation to Soviet expansionists. Western Europe would no longer be a fire trap. In October, 1948, the Canadian embassy in Washington stated, "It is scarcely an exaggeration to say that the strongest supporters of rapid progress towards the political and economic unification of western Europe are today to be found in the United States."[6]

At the first meeting of the six-power talks on the North Atlantic treaty, on July 6, 1948, Lovett said:

> The United States would endeavour in these talks to develop thoughts of closer military, political, economic and spiritual union between the countries of western Europe. Opinion in the United States favored the establishment of a permanent system of security in western Europe by modern and lasting methods. The countries party to the Brussels pact might provide the hard core. A phrase had been used in the Senate [in the debate on the Vandenberg resolution] that the United States could not afford 'to re-build a fire trap'. In other words, that European security must be re-built on a much sounder basis than in the past.[7]

Lovett liked this expression, firetrap. He used it again at the Ambassadors' Committee a few days later, "[U]nless the western European nations showed a high order of determination to solve their problems through some form of union based on self-help and mutual aid, the enterprise would not possess the degree of assurance for the future which the U.S. expected. . . . The U.S. could not 'rebuild a fire trap' "[8] Lovett kept referring to the argument that if the administration was to get a North Atlantic treaty through the Senate it had to be able to produce evidence that the western European countries were tending towards unity. The more compelling the evidence, the easier would be the selling job in the Senate.

Lovett tried to put his ideas in the form not of a United States prescription to western Europe but of United States support for an initiative taken in western Europe. Thus in his opening statement at the first meeting of the six-power talks he "recalled Mr. Bevin's approach to the United States government early this year in which he expressed the belief that the political, military, economic and spiritual forces of western Europe must be integrated into 'some form of union, formal or informal, backed by the United States'. For its part the United States government welcomed this approach."[9]

In the discussions in Washington in the summer of 1948, Kennan insisted that a union of western Europe was not enough. In the long run there must be a unification of the whole continent, (he meant up to the borders of the Soviet Union not up to the Urals):

> It was necessary that when the Marshall Plan period came to an end, or even earlier, there should emerge an economically self-supporting Europe which was on the road to greater political unity and which was militarily capable of taking care of itself. That could not be just part of Europe; eventually it would have to comprise the whole of the continent. The United States did not wish to see a return to the conditions existing before the war in eastern and central Europe where there were

either petty nationalisms or very small military alliances which could not stand the test when the strain came.[10]

It was not till the very end of the six-power discussions in the summer of 1948 that those in the State Department who wished to use the negotiations on the North Atlantic treaty to push the western European countries into federating showed their hand. At the meeting of the Working Group on September 2, the State Department presented a new draft of the paper on the territorial scope of the treaty which the group had been discussing. The new feature of this draft was "the requirement that full participation in the North Atlantic pact would be open only to those Western European countries which accepted all the obligations of the Brussels treaty."[11] (At that time the Working Group was considering three categories of relationship to the North Atlantic pact: full members, associate members, and other members of the Organization for European Economic Co-operation).

A month before, we had been warned that the thinking of the United States negotiators was moving in this direction. Wrong had reported that "there is so strong a sentiment in both the administration and Congress for an effective Western European Union, both political and economic, that it would be unwise to consider the conception [of establishing a link between a collective western European security system and North American defence arrangements] as having been rejected."[12] A few days later Stone reported that he thought the United States negotiators felt "that the ideal arrangement which they could put before the Senate would be a proposal for a security pact to which the three parties would be the United States of America, Canada and the United States of Western Europe. Since they cannot achieve this ideal situation they honestly feel that the more evidence that they have in hand that western Europe is tending towards unity the easier will be their selling job."[13] If all the European members of the North Atlantic alliance belonged to the Brussels pact this would be evidence that western Europe was tending towards unity.

Wrong, in his report to Ottawa on the meeting of the Working Group on September 2, said that the drafters of the proposal that all the European members of the North Atlantic alliance should belong to the Brussels pact included Kennan, Hickerson and Achilles, and that they were thinking not just in terms of making it easier to sell the North Atlantic treaty to the Senate. Wrong said that they had put the proposal forward

for reasons not mentioned at any of the meetings, but explained privately to me. They consider that it would increase the influence of the United States in promoting a closer political relationship among the western European countries leading to the establishment of a

129

European federation. They think that the United States would be able to employ the North Atlantic agreement to exercise pressure on the Brussels pact powers, collectively and individually, towards European federation, if the full advantages of the North Atlantic pact were restricted to those countries that assumed all the obligations of the Brussels pact. Kennan at the Working Group kept referring to their proposal as establishing group responsibility between the parties on each side of the Atlantic. He was, however, not at all clear on what this would involve.[14])

(It is difficult to believe that Kennan would have concurred in this explanation of why the proposal had been put forward since he states in his memoirs that he did not, at that time, want Britain and a number of other western European countries to enter a European federation; instead he wanted an eventual federal union of the United States, Britain, and Canada, plus "certain of the [other] Commonwealth nations and possibly some entities of the Scandinavian and Iberian peninsulas"; this federal union would "flank" a similar federal union on the European continent.[15])

On September 3 the Ambassadors' Committee discussed the wisdom of requiring that European countries could secure full membership in the North Atlantic alliance only by passing through the ante-room of the Brussels alliance. In his report Wrong said.

> It came out that Lovett had thought that this was not the effect of the paper, and when we examined the possible reluctance of Norway, Ireland, and eventually Spain, to accept the Brussels treaty, and their possible readiness, except for this, to join the North Atlantic group, Lovett expressed the view, to the discomfiture of his advisers, that it ought to be possible for such countries to become full members of the North Atlantic pact while not ratifying the Brussels treaty. It was therefore decided to resubmit the paper to the Working Group, and the State Department drafters this morning are scratching their heads over what to do.[16]

Three days later at a meeting of the Working Group it was agreed that the proposal should be dropped.[17] It does not, therefore, appear in the Washington paper of September 9, which was submitted on September 10 to the participating governments, and it was not resurrected during the later stages of the negotiations.

Gladwyn Jebb had been present at the Working Group meeting on September 2 and at the Ambassadors' Committee on September 3 when the Kennan-Hickerson-Achilles proposal was discussed and the British Ambassador, Oliver Franks, had questioned its wisdom. When Jebb wrote his memoirs 20 years later he had forgotten this episode, for he says that somebody in authority in 1948 should have advanced the theory of the "two-poles" in the western world and should have made an increasing advance towards real European unity an actual condition of the consent of the United States to enter a North Atlantic alliance. If this had happened, the Brussels treaty organization could have been enlarged and strengthened "(for instance, by arranging for a parliamentary body and an international secretariat with considerable powers)" and Britain and the other eight European members of the North Atlantic treaty would by the mid-1950s "most certainly have worked out a system for taking decisions in all spheres, military, political, economic and cultural".[18]

In its extreme form, the two-pillar theory would have meant that the North Atlantic treaty would have been "an arrangement between the Brussels pact powers and the North Atlantic group" consisting of the United States and Canada.[19] In a less extreme form, membership in the Brussels treaty would have been a condition of membership by a European country in the North Atlantic alliance. Both concepts of the two-pillar theory were still-born. But from 1948 to the present day, the advocates in Washington of a two-pillar concept of the North Atlantic alliance have remained powerful.

Pearson considered in the summer of 1948 that the tactics of the United States advocates of a two-pillar concept of the North Atlantic alliance were unwise. In a message to Wrong in mid-August he said that he sympathized entirely with the desire of the United States that western Europe should demonstrate its willingness to unite politically and economically; in his opinion the slow pace of the movement towards the unification of western Europe was disappointing. "However," he went on to say, "I think that it may well be true that the goal of the unification of western Europe can be reached more quickly by approaching it indirectly through the conclusion of a North Atlantic pact than by attempting to reach it more directly. Once the western European countries get a firm guarantee from the United States and machinery set up for the co-ordination of defence planning and for the pooling of resources, they will be given that renewed confidence and vigour which will make it easier for them to go ahead with plans for the unification of western Europe."[20]

Canadian opposition to a two-pillar concept of the North Atlantic alliance went much deeper than a mere difference in tactics. In a two-pillar alliance one pillar would be said to be the United States and Canada; in fact, because the United States was ten to 20 times as powerful as Canada, the pillar would be the United States; and Canada would be left with little influence on the policies of the alliance. If Canada was not to be left alone to deal with the United States on matters of concern to the alliance it needed to be able to form a common front with European members. The alliance had not been in existence for long when Canada found that on most important issues coming before the alliance, it was on the same side as Norway, Denmark and the Netherlands, and on many issues it was on the same side as those countries and Britain.

The most profound thinker in the Canadian foreign service at the time the North Atlantic treaty was negotiated was Norman Robertson, then High Commissioner in London. At the end of April, 1948, three weeks after the conclusion of the tripartite talks on the treaty, he set forth in a prescient despatch the reasons for Canada giving full support to the idea of a North Atlantic treaty. These were also, though he did not say so, reasons for Canada opposing a two-pillar concept of the treaty:

Ever since we have been in a position to shape our own policy abroad, we have had to wrestle with the antinomies created by our position as a North American country and as a member of the Commonwealth, by our special relationship with the United Kingdom and at the same time, although in less degree, with other countries in western Europe as well. A situation in which our special relationship with the United Kingdom can be identified with our special relationships with other countries in western Europe and in which the United States will be providing a firm basis, both economically and probably militarily, for this link across the North Atlantic, seems to me such a providential solution for so many of our problems that I feel we should go to great lengths and even incur considerable risks in order to consolidate our good fortune and ensure our proper place in this new partnership.[21]

Most advocates of the two-pillar concept of the North Atlantic alliance have failed to realize or to recognize openly that since the North American pillar would in fact be the United States and the other pillar western Europe, Canada would be odd-man-out in the alliance. Gladwyn Jebb, who has consistently from 1948 on advocated the two-pillar concept, has recognized this. In order to give Canada a part to play in a two-pillar alliance he has suggested that as much as possible of the North Atlantic institutions or machinery for co-ordinating policy between the two partners, and in particular the North Atlantic parliament, should be located in Montreal.[22] This gesture would, however, be unlikely to satisfy Canada. If ever the Atlantic alliance became a partnership between the United States of America and a United States of western Europe or of Europe, Canada might have to choose between applying for membership in one of the federations or withdrawing from the alliance. Those in the United States and Europe who believe strongly in the two-pillar concept of the North Atlantic Community might well consider that Canada's withdrawal from the alliance would, though regrettable, be a relatively small price to pay for the achievement of a partnership between a European federation and the United States.

CHAPTER ELEVEN

MORE THAN A MILITARY ALLIANCE

When agreement was finally reached on the text of the North Atlantic treaty, it contained, in addition to its military provisions, four undertakings on non-military matters, one on consultation, one on democracy, one on promoting conditions of stability and well-being, and one on economic collaboration. The first undertaking was set forth in Article 4 of the treaty, the other three in Article 2. There was never, during the twelve months of negotiation, any difference of opinion over the necessity of an article on consultation. There were many arguments about what other non-military provisions should be included in the treaty. Some of the negotiators at some point wanted none; some wanted extensive provisions – the result was a compromise.

The idea that the North Atlantic treaty should be more than a military alliance was supported at the beginning of the six-power talks in July not only by Pearson but also by Lovett and Kennan and by the Ambassadors of the Netherlands and Belgium. Thus at the third meeting of the Ambassadors' Committee on July 7, Kennan "emphasized that the community of interest of the participating governments was wider than military, it was traditional and historical and would continue. Association was necessary entirely aside from the troubles of the moment and might well go far beyond the military sphere." Lovett immediately observed that "the essential element was not the Soviet threat but the common western approach and that the western attachment to the worth of the individual would be the best cement." Van Kleffens, the Netherlands Ambassador, "saw advantages in presenting the matter in that light. If the arrangements appeared to be directed against Russia, public perspective would be unnecessarily unpleasant. It would have a better perspective and a more serene tone if based on the wider considerations." The Belgian Ambassador, Silvercruys, said, "Any effort of this sort would fall short of its purpose and lose its dynamic value if it were to assume a negative aspect instead of a positive one, namely the promotion of security and peace."[1] When Pearson at a meeting of the Ambassadors' Committee two days later said that "there should be as close a connection as possible with the United Nations, not only under Article 51 of the Charter, but also under Article 56,* which concerned co-operation for economic, cultural and spiritual purposes", Lovett interrupted to indicate his agreement. Van Kleffens, later in the meeting, picked up the reference to Article 56 and said that he "thought that the North Atlantic community was too good to be limited merely to material welfare and military security, in that it rested on a community of certain basic conceptions of the highest moral order."[2]

To some extent the argument over what non-military provisions should be included in the treaty was between Europeanists and Atlanticists. The Europeanists insisted that closer military union of the countries of western Europe was not enough; it must be accompanied by closer political, economic and cultural union; some of them believed that the ultimate goal should be a United States of western Europe or of Europe. The Atlanticists insisted that closer military union of the countries of the North Atlantic was not enough; it must be accompanied by closer political, economic and cultural union; some of them believed that the ultimate goal should be a federal union of the countries belonging to the North Atlantic community. Some of the Europeanists claimed at the time of the negotiation of the North Atlantic treaty and since that they were also partisans of North Atlantic unity. Similarly some of the Atlanticists claimed that they were also in favour of closer western European unity; they said their goal was an increasingly united western Europe within an increasingly united North Atlantic community. Some of those who said that they were in favour of both developments were sincere; others were not. Hickerson and Achilles, for example, confessed in 1976 that they had given lip service to the idea of European unity but that they had in fact believed that emphasis on European unity tended to delay or impede progress toward Atlantic unity.[3] Gladwyn Jebb, a fervent Europeanist, scarcely gave even lip service to the idea of Atlantic unity. In November, 1948, he said, in conversation with Charles Ritchie, that there was a danger that too great an elaboration of the functions of an "Atlantic community" would seriously interfere with the attempts which were being made to organize closer western European unity. There was a danger that the concept of European unity would be swamped in the wider idea of an Atlantic community. European nations, particularly France, whose recovery and prestige it was desired to encourage, would be completely overshadowed by the power of the United States. This, in turn, would give a handle to communist propaganda, which would not fail to point out that in an Atlantic community the European nations were merely satellites of the United States. He thought that there was a hopeful future

*The text of these articles is given in Appendix 4.

for the idea of a European community which might act as a balance between the two colossi of the United States and the U.S.S.R.[4]

Canada was the only country in the intergovernmental discussions in Washington which consistently advocated a North Atlantic approach. Without Canada there would have been no Article 2 in the North Atlantic treaty. But Canada's efforts would probably have failed if, within the State Department, two of the principal United States negotiators, Hickerson and Achilles, had not, as they themselves have said, strongly favoured the inclusion of Article 2 "as the basis upon which a true Atlantic Community, going far beyond the military field, could be built"; they were for Article 2, "almost to the point of crusading for it";[5] they, like the Canadian government, wanted a stronger Article 2 than that which finally emerged from the discussions.

On March 11, 1948, the Canadian government received and accepted the British proposal for tripartite talks in Washington on North Atlantic security. On March 13 we received the text of the draft of the Brussels treaty provisionally agreed to on March 12. The next day I sent Pearson a draft of a memorandum to the Prime Minister on the proposed Atlantic Pact of Mutual Assistance. In this I said that the two principal issues in the Washington talks were likely to be "what countries should be invited to become original signatories of the pact" and "what ground should the pact cover in addition to mutual guarantees of all-out aid against direct or indirect Soviet aggression." On the second point, I said, borrowing language from two British messages, that of January on western European union and that of three days before on the Washington talks, and from the draft of the Brussels treaty:

> Here it is essential to remember that the purpose of the pact is to rally the spiritual as well as the military and economic resources of western Christendom against Soviet totalitarianism; that it must therefore not be a merely negative anti-Soviet military alliance but must be the basis for a dynamic liberal counter-offensive. The pact may succeed in giving us a long period of peace if it results in creating an overwhelming preponderance of force against the Soviet Union, but the force to be overwhelming must not be only military and economic force; it must be the force that comes from ability to rally to our side all non-Communists in all countries, including our own, who are now apathetic, fearful or doubtful. A bold move is necessary to raise in the hearts and minds and spirits of all those in the world who love freedom that confidence and faith which will restore their vigour. The pact must set forth the gospel – the good news of our faith – for which we are willing to live and die. It must make as clear as possible the methods which the

peoples and governments of the Free World intend to follow to make good their faith in human rights and fundamental freedoms, in the worth and dignity of man and in the principles of parliamentary democracy, personal freedom and political liberty.[6]

Pearson changed "dynamic liberal counter-offensive" to "positive liberal and democratic counter-offensive". He substituted for the two sentences beginning "A bold move" a final sentence: "If it can do this it will underline that this pact is something far removed from alliances and arrangements of the old kind." The sentence was a characteristic Pearsonian touch: it expressed what he himself believed; and it was also calculated to allay Mackenzie King's deep-seated antipathy to military alliances. He then sent the memorandum to King and St. Laurent.[7] They both agreed with the line which Pearson proposed, and this became the foundation of the Canadian campaign for effective non-military provisions in the North Atlantic treaty.

A public indication that this would be the line which the Canadian government would take in the intergovernmental negotiations on the treaty came almost immediately in the wording of the blessing on the Brussels treaty which King gave in the House of Commons on March 17, the day the treaty was signed. This statement was drafted by Pearson and contained a sentence based on the sentence he had added to my memorandum. King said that "this [Brussels] pact is far more than an alliance of the old kind," and he cited in support of this statement the third article of the treaty: "The high contracting parties will make every effort in common to lead their people towards a better understanding of the principles which form the basis of their common civilization and to promote cultural exchanges by conventions between themselves or otherwise."[8]

The next day I sent Pearson a memorandum on the tripartite discussions in Washington which were to open in four days' time. I said that "in the present atmosphere of crises foreign offices may be tempted to have recourse to something which would be not much more than an old-fashioned military alliance and that clauses in the pact other than those providing for mutual guarantees would be merely window-dressing."[9] Though I did not know this at the time, I was in this memorandum arguing against the views of T. A. Stone, the second-in-command of the Canadian embassy in Washington, views which were shared by the Ambassador, Hume Wrong. When Pearson arrived in Washington, Stone, who was in charge of the embassy in the absence of Wrong, gave Pearson a memorandum in which he said that the secret of success in the impending tripartite talks "is to keep in mind the one immediate simple objective – military security – and to remember urgency.... The hour is now, it would seem, so very late that we must take a leaf out of [the Russians'] book ... devote ourselves to achieving what is obviously our common purpose by the simplest possible direct approach and to put what democratic trimmings on it as may be required later." [10]

I, on the contrary, recommended in my memorandum of March 18 to Pearson that the non-military provisions in the pact should be even more extensive than those in the Brussels treaty. In the Brussels pact the parties had maintained their reservations to the compulsory jurisdiction of the International Court over justiciable disputes between themselves; in the Atlantic pact the parties should accept the Court's jurisdiction over all justiciable disputes between them. The goals of economic co-operation should be set forth more precisely. The treaty should be based on the principle that the parties should make equal sacrifices in the struggle for a free world. The alliance should have revolutionary new political instruments, "not only a Board for Collective Self-Defence but a parliament, a president (Spaak?), a chancellor (yourself?), and a chief of staff (Eisenhower?)". (Instead of calling the central organ of the alliance the Board for Collective Self-Defence, it was called the North Atlantic Council. No North Atlantic parliament has yet (1976) been established.* Spaak became Secretary-General of the alliance in 1957. Eisenhower became Supreme Commander of the forces of the alliance in Europe in 1950.)

The contrary advice which Stone and I gave to Pearson in March of 1948, before the intergovernmental discussions opened, was the beginning of a duel between Wrong and Stone in Washington and me in Ottawa which lasted throughout the whole 12 months of the negotiations.

St. Laurent, then Secretary of State for External Affairs, was so convinced that the North Atlantic treaty must be much more than a military alliance that he pleaded for this in a series of public speeches given from the middle of March to the middle of June. His argument ran as follows. The best way of preventing a third world war is "to confront the forces of communist expansionism with an overwhelming preponderance of moral, economic and military force on the side of freedom." The Brussels treaty is "no mere military alliance directed against a possible aggressor from the east." "It seeks . . . to contain or restrain Soviet expansion, not by a Maginot line, but by building up in these liberal, democratic and Christian states a dynamic counter-attraction to the degrading tenets of totalitarian and materialistic communism." The purpose of a collective security league of some or all of the "free states" would, like that of the Brussels treaty, be to create

> the dynamic counter-attraction of a free, prosperous and progressive
> society as opposed to the totalitarian and reactionary society of the
> communist world. . . . To save democracy in Europe – or indeed any-
> where else – we must demonstrate by deeds and not merely by words
> that democracy is a more dynamic and humanitarian creed than com-
> munism. No regime in Europe or anywhere else has the right to

*See page 222.

assistance merely because it proclaims itself the only barrier against communism. . . . The Union of the Free World which is now rather painfully struggling to be born will possess the necessary overwhelming strength only if it is based on moral as well as material force; if its citizens are bound together not merely by their opposition to totalitarian communist aggression but by a positive love of democracy and of their fellow men, by a determination to make democracy work for the promotion of mutual welfare and the preservation of peace, for others as well as themselves.[11]

The main argument advanced by St. Laurent for effective provisions in the North Atlantic treaty on the promotion of democracy and on economic, social and cultural co-operation was thus psychological: the weakness of western Europe was not primarily a military weakness, it was a weakness of will; what was needed to combat this weakness was a bold imaginative leap forward. This was a common assumption at the time among those concerned with the negotiations on the North Atlantic treaty. Thus, according to Hickerson, Marshall considered in February, 1948, "that the fears and dissensions of the western European countries are unlikely to be overcome without a greater appeal to the imagination and hopes of the people."[12] Bohlen said in July, 1948, that "the first benefit which should derive [from the treaty] would probably be a psychological one, a certain confidence [in western Europe] in the future".[13] Kennan said in August that "he felt it would be a mistake, politically and psychologically, to put forward before the world at this time a pact or a regional arrangement which proved to be a strictly military alliance."[14] And in November he said that what value the treaty possessed was "insofar as it operates to stiffen the self-confidence of the western Europeans in the face of Soviet pressures."[15]

Our belief in Ottawa that the weakness in western Europe was primarily a weakness of will led us to conclude that the weakness could not be successfully combatted merely by increased co-operation between the western European countries or between the North Atlantic countries; increased co-operation was essential but it was not sufficient. The necessary leap forward had to be bolder and more imaginative. The goal should be a spiritual, cultural, economic and political union of the North Atlantic countries which would, in St. Laurent's words, trench much more upon old-fashioned concepts of national sovereignty than any of the international institutions which had been established in the past.* Our hope was that federal institutions for the North Atlantic community would emerge and gradually grow stronger.

One argument for the treaty containing effective provisions for consultation, co-operation and common action in the economic field which we

*See page 27.

put in the Canadian commentary of December, 1948, was that to strengthen the collective capacity of the North Atlantic alliance to resist aggression, it was essential that the combined production of goods and services by the members of the alliance should be as great as possible, particularly at a time when a large proportion of this production had unhappily to be devoted to preparations to resist aggression.[16] Effective collaboration in defence production was especially important; in a note which I wrote at the time, I said:

> Plans for the mobilization of the maximum military strength on the part of the [North Atlantic Treaty] Organization would not be fully effective without complementary plans for the pooling of essential resources and for the most economic combination of the production facilities of the signatory powers. Some countries are better suited than others for the production of certain types of [defence] material. Similarly, it would be more economical to have some countries specialize in certain branches of [defence] research and development.[17]

A second reason for our campaign for closer economic co-operation among the North Atlantic countries was that we believed that if the members of the North Atlantic alliance were constantly quarrelling over such matters as tariff and non-tariff barriers to trade, competitive currency devaluations, aviation rights, shipping cartels and access to raw materials, they would be less likely to be willing and able to co-operate in political and security matters to the extent necessary to make the military guarantees credible. Therefore pledges of military cooperation should be accompanied by pledges of economic cooperation.[†]

We also believed that the farther the North Atlantic community moved towards political and economic union the more the power of the United States would be restrained by the influence of its North Atlantic allies, especially Britain and France. The alliance would contain the United States as well as the Soviet Union. For Canada, next door to the United States, this consideration was especially important. The alliance would provide for Canada a countervailing force against the United States; the alliance would call in Britain and western Europe to restore the balance in North America.

We believed that the closer the union of the North Atlantic countries, the less the danger that in a third world war the United States and Britain would arrogate to themselves the sole right to make the big strategic and political decisions. The Big Two or the Big Three had done that in the Second World War and we did not want to be put in that degrading position again. We believed that in the North Atlantic alliance, the necessary sharing, in peace and in war, of risks, resources and obligations would, as Pearson put it in September, 1948, in his first speech as Foreign Minister, "be accompanied by, and flow from a share in the control of policy". We believed that France and the other western European countries would share our desire to establish a constitutional or semi-constitutional structure for the North Atlantic community which would ensure that all the members of the alliance would have a reasonable say in formulating and controlling the policies of the alliance in peace and in war.

Mackenzie King, at the outset of the discussions on the treaty, and Norman Robertson, then the Canadian High Commissioner in London, at the end of the discussions, put forward the consideration that an undertaking in the North Atlantic treaty to reduce or remove restrictions to trade within the North Atlantic area would assist Canada in its trade negotiations with the United States and Britain.

In the early months of 1948 secret discussions were taking place between officials of the United States and Canada on the possibilities of developing a treaty or agreement between the two countries for the elimination of tariff and other barriers to trade between them, the only exceptions being wheat and wheat flour and fresh fruits and vegetables. Canada would also make a similar offer of free trade to Britain.[18] Mackenzie King states in his diary that on March 22, 1948, the day the first stage of the discussions on the North Atlantic treaty opened in Washington, he informed the half-dozen Cabinet ministers and officials involved in the trade discussions that he

> felt trade proposals might be made to fit as it were into the larger Atlantic pact. That if, for example, the Atlantic security pact were agreed upon and were brought before Parliament and be passed as it certainly would be, we might immediately follow thereafter with a trade agreement as being something which still further helped to further the object of the pact, namely the removal of restrictions to trade within the area arranged by the pact.[19]

King thus assumed that the North Atlantic treaty would contain an undertaking by the parties to remove restrictions to trade between them.

When at the end of March, 1948, the Canadian government decided not to proceed immediately with the free trade project (and this in fact meant that it was aborted), the Canadian government told the United States government that the "trade discussions might begin again if and when a satisfactory North Atlantic security pact is signed." "It would be natural," the message said, "for the trade discussions to be related to the pact, since they are concerned with measures for economic defence against aggression." The message concluded with the statement that the opportunity for continuing the discussions on eliminating the barriers to trade "might be provided by the signature of the North Atlantic pact". In a discussion a few weeks later, C. D. Howe, the Canadian Minister of Trade and Commerce, and Lovett agreed that the elimination of barriers to trade between them would be a "natural extension . . . into the economic sphere" of United States and Canadian support for the Brussels treaty.[20]

In the middle of February, 1949, Norman Robertson reported that, in an effort to secure British support for an economic clause in the treaty, he had argued that an economic clause might acquire substantive importance as a basis for positive economic and financial co-operation between Britain and Canada, which would balance and complement the obligations assumed by Britain towards the European countries participating in the OEEC.

> The United States must share, in degree, our long-run worries of the effect on trans-Atlantic trade of methods now being employed to bring the [western] European economy into balance with the rest of the world. Inclusion of the clause we are advocating could provide a useful leverage for modifying policies required for European recovery so that their end result will permit resumption of multi-lateral clearings and achievement of non-discrimination. . . . It seems to me that the interest and position of the United States in relation to western Europe generally are substantially similar to our more concentrated interests in the solution of this problem as it affects the United Kingdom particularly.

Because of this, Robertson attached particular importance to the inclusion in Article 2 of the following sentence in the proposal which we had put forward: "The parties concerned agree to make every effort in common to eliminate conflict in their economic policies and to develop to the full the great possibilities of trade between them." He wisely suggested the addition of "international" before "economic".[21] He considered that "such a sentence in the treaty might not only prepare the way for another triangular attack [by the United States, Britain and Canada] on the trade and dollar problem but perhaps in the meantime make it easier for the United States to keep our interests in mind in determining E.C.A., and particularly off-shore, purchasing policies."[22] The possibility that E.C.A. (the United States agency charged with implementing the Marshall Plan) might refuse to finance the purchase of wheat in Canada for Britain provided added weight from the Canadian point of view to the need for including a strong economic clause in the North Atlantic treaty.[23]

There was another strong motive for the insistence by the Canadian government on "the paramount importance of the treaty providing a basis for positive economic co-operation among the signatories and for it not being a mere military alliance". That was the practical political consideration that unless the treaty provided such a basis the government might face "a definite weakening of support for the treaty in the House [of Commons] and in the country".[24] The weakening of support which the government feared would be in French-speaking Canada, where in the last months of 1948 the great majority of the French-language newspapers were severely criticizing the government for its advocacy of a

North Atlantic treaty,[25] and within the social democratic party, the C.C.F.

On February 8, 1949, at the height of the crisis over Article 2, when Dean Acheson was impressing on the Ambassadors' Committee his difficulties with the senators who, he said, "were fed up with treaties for the improvement of the general welfare" and wanted no Article 2, Wrong, speaking under instructions from Pearson, said that he wanted to tell Acheson about Pearson's political difficulties in Canada. It would, he said "be difficult to secure support in Quebec for a purely military pact and some article along the lines of Article 2 was important to get the support of that province and of other political elements".[26] He explained that what he meant by "other political elements" was the C.C.F.[27] A few days later, St. Laurent, on his first visit to Washington as Prime Minister, said to Truman and Acheson that "it was most important to him that the treaty should not be a military alliance only, but should hold out the prospect of close economic and social collaboration between the parties. An article to this effect would be of the greatest value to him politically in securing the full acceptance of the treaty by the Canadian people."[28]

From my knowledge of the thinking of St. Laurent and Pearson at the time, I believe that the domestic political argument for Article 2 did not even occur to them during the first six months or so of the discussions on the treaty. During those six months, they constantly emphasized, in all their public speeches, the importance of these non-military aspects because they believed in them for reasons not connected with the necessity of getting wide parliamentary and public support in Canada for the treaty. Only gradually did they come to realize that their emphasis on the non-military aspects was one of the reasons for the widespread support which they had succeeded in securing. In the crisis over Article 2 in February, 1949, the dominant motive of the Canadian government in pressing for the strongest possible Article 2 was that this was necessary in order to ensure wide parliamentary and public support for the treaty.

St. Laurent had become Prime Minister on November 15, 1948. He knew in February, 1949, that within a few months he would be facing a general election, and he hoped that a North Atlantic treaty with a strong Article 2 would help him in that election. It did. His close associate, J. W. Pickersgill, has written that in St. Laurent's election campaign in May and June, 1949, three things captured the public imagination. One was the successful conclusion of his efforts to bring Newfoundland into the Canadian confederation. Another was the North Atlantic treaty. The third was St. Laurent himself.[29]

PART FOUR

THE TERMS
OF THE TREATY

CHAPTER TWELVE

THE PLEDGE

The core of the North Atlantic treaty is the undertaking of each of the allies to come immediately to the assistance of another member of the alliance if it is subjected to an armed attack. Normally, this would be called the guarantee provision of a treaty of alliance, but the United States objected to the term, guarantee, and the provision was referred to in the negotiations as "the pledge."

The arguments over the language to be used in the pledge went on over the whole 12 months of negotiations. The basic considerations were simple: the firmer the pledge, the greater the effect the treaty might be expected to have in deterring the Soviet Union and in restoring in western Europe the confidence necessary for its recovery; the weaker the pledge, the less difficulty the United States administration would have in securing the necessary two-thirds vote in the Senate for ratification of the treaty. The European countries stressed the importance of the first consideration; the United States stressed the importance of the second; Canada usually supported the European position. The greater the importance attached to the first consideration, the closer the pledge in the North Atlantic treaty would be to that in the Brussels treaty of March, 1948. The greater the importance attached to the second consideration the closer the pledge would be to that in the Rio treaty (the Inter-American treaty of mutual assistance) of September, 1947, which the Senate had already ratified.

The first time Dean Acheson met the Ambassadors' Committee was on February 8, 1949. He came with the bad news that the two principal members of the Senate Foreign Relations Committee, Connally and Vandenberg, were insisting that the pledge be even weaker than that in the Rio treaty. This elicited from the British Ambassador, Oliver Franks, a classic statement of the arguments for a strong pledge. He began by conceding a point made by Acheson that, in a sense, the substance of the treaty was what mattered and the words were of secondary importance. But, he went on to say, it was not just a matter of what would in fact happen if one of the parties to the treaty were attacked. There was also the question of the effect which the articles of the treaty would produce in western Europe and in Russia. If the North Atlantic treaty came into being, it would be at once the foundation and the crown of what the United States had been able to do on the economic front in western Europe; it would establish a set of arrangements between the countries of North America and of the west of Europe which might ensure peace for a lifetime. One of the conditions of this was that the words of the treaty, while sober in tone, should make plain beyond misunderstanding what would happen if trouble occurred. The pledge should therefore include an undertaking by the parties to take military action if one of them were the object of an armed attack. From the point of view of people in western Europe, it was precisely the sober mention of that kind of possibility which would contribute toward making political, moral and economic recovery go all the way and make the western European countries into complete partners, rather than partial dependents. It was therefore necessary to balance what opinion in North America might be prepared to accept with what those on the eastern shores of the Atlantic would regard as necessary. Wording which erred on the side of understatement might make the treaty look weaker than it really was and thereby detract from its value in maintaining peace.[1]

Those who drafted the pledge in the Brussels treaty probably took as their starting point the pledge in the last of the treaties of mutual assistance concluded in the period between the two world wars, the Anglo-Polish treaty of August, 1939.

> Should one of the Contracting Parties become engaged in hostilities with a European power in consequence of aggression by the latter against that Contracting Party, the other Contracting Party will at once give the Contracting Party engaged in hostilities all the support and assistance in its power. . . . The methods of applying the undertakings of mutual assistance . . . are established between the competent naval, military and air authorities of the Contracting Parties.[†]

In the Brussels treaty this pledge was simplified. Instead of a separate sentence on methods of assistance, the military character of the assistance was mentioned in the pledge itself. The Brussels treaty formula was:

> If any of the High Contracting Parties should be the object of an armed attack in Europe, the other High Contracting Parties will, in accordance with the provisions of Article 51 of the Charter of the

United Nations, afford the party so attacked all the military and other aid and assistance in their power.*

The pledge in the Rio treaty was much weaker. It was only "to assist in meeting the attack." The Rio formula was:

The High Contracting Parties agree that an armed attack by any State against an American State shall be considered as an attack against all the American States and, consequently, each one of the said Contracting Parties undertakes to assist in meeting the attack in the exercise of the inherent right of individual or collective self-defense recognized by Article 51 of the Charter of the United Nations.

(The Rio treaty further provided that the "Organ of Consultation of the Inter-American System" consisting of one representative of each member country could, by a two-thirds vote of the members, decide that member states should impose diplomatic and economic sanctions and the "use of armed force". Decisions to apply diplomatic and economic sanctions were binding on all the member countries; decisions to use armed force were not binding; "no state shall be required to use armed force without its consent." It was never suggested by anyone in the negotiations on the North Atlantic treaty that the North Atlantic Council would be given the right to decide when sanctions, diplomatic, economic or military, would be imposed.)

It seemed to me in March, 1948, that the pledge in the North Atlantic treaty should begin with the first part of the Rio pledge and then use the language of the Brussels pledge adding a specific mention of economic aid and assistance. I therefore suggested to Pearson just before the opening on March 22, 1948, of the first stage of the intergovernmental discussions in Washington that the pledge in the North Atlantic treaty should read: "The Atlantic Nations agree that an armed attack by any state against any Atlantic Nation is an attack against all the Atlantic Nations. In accordance with Article 51 of the Charter, each Atlantic Nation undertakes to give immediately to any other Atlantic Nation which is attacked by any state all the military, economic and other aid and assistance in its power."[2] The policy planning staff of the State Department on March 23 made a similar recommendation; the only difference in substance was that the undertaking in their proposal was "to take armed action against the aggressor" rather than to give "all the military, economic and other aid and assistance in its power." The language I had suggested was agreed to on March 25, with "party" substituted for "Atlantic nation".[3] Pearson was delighted.[4]

His delight was short-lived, for there then occurred the first of a number of sudden sharp swings in United States policy on the pledge which

*The text of Article 51 is given in Appendix 4.

were to occur during the succeeding 12 months of international negotiation. On March 29 the United States representative in the tripartite
discussions announced that the pledge should, in terms of American
political realities, either be on the model of the Rio treaty (with definitions of armed attack) or should be explicit in indicating that each party
would determine for itself whether an armed attack had in fact occurred.
(The Rio treaty did not give member nations the right to decide for themselves whether an attack had occurred; that decision was made by a two-
thirds vote of the member nations.) Apparently the new view of
American political realities had come about as the result of indirect
soundings concerning the probable attitude of congressional leaders. The
new view also included a refusal to mention the possibility of military
assistance. The result was that the Pentagon paper of April 1 which
emerged from the tripartite talks proposed a pledge considerably weaker
than the Rio pledge. It would provide "that each party shall regard any
action in the area covered by the agreement, which *it considers* an armed
attack against any other party, as an armed attack against itself and that
each party accordingly undertakes to *assist in meeting the attack.* . . . "[5]
(Italics added.)

Thus in the first stage of the intergovernmental discussions on the
North Atlantic treaty, two key questions about the pledge came out into
the open. First, should the pledge mention explicitly that each ally had
the right to decide for itself whether an armed attack had occurred? Second, should the pledge mention the possible use of armed force in repelling the attack? The formula tentatively agreed to on March 25
represented the most which the participants other than the United States
could hope for; the formula of April 1 represented the least they could
settle for.

Pearson intensely disliked the explicit reference to the right of each
party to determine for itself whether an armed attack had occurred. This,
he said to Wrong on April 1, "will be interpreted as reducing to almost
nothing the obligatory character of the obligation. I realize that the determination of whether an armed attack has in fact taken place is the right of
the individual signatories but surely that can be left implicit rather than
be made explicit".[6†]

Pearson was also scornful of the United States insistence that the
pledge should refer merely to assistance in meeting an attack and should
not mention the use of armed force. In messages to Stone in mid-August,
1948, he said,

> The advantage of the Brussels formula [over the Rio formula] is that
> the parties promise to fight an all-out war if one of them is attacked.
> They obviously will have to fight an all-out war so why not say so
> instead of using the vague term 'assist in meeting the attack' which
> hostile critics could say means the kind of assistance Mexico gave in

the last war. . . . [7] 'Assist in meeting the attack' is certainly susceptible of the meaning 'all aid short of war'. . . . If this were the nature of the undertaking in the North Atlantic treaty, might it not mean that Canada would be fulfilling its obligation under the treaty in the event of a Soviet attack upon the United States, if its assistance to the United States went no further than United States assistance to Canada in the last war up to Pearl Harbor.[8]

By December 24, 1948, the United States had given in on both of the two key points: it withdrew its insistence that the pledge state explicitly that each ally had the right to decide for itself whether an armed attack had occurred; it agreed that the pledge should make an explicit reference to military assistance. The price of United States agreement on the second point was a change in the Brussels treaty formula so that the obligation was not to give military aid and assistance to an ally which had been attacked but to assist the ally which had been attacked by taking military or other action. The new formula made clear that military action need not take the form of sending armed forces to the territory of the ally which had been attacked. The Brussels formula could be interpreted as creating an obligation to do just that.

The change was made at the instance of the United States Chiefs of Staff. It was a return to the kind of language which the policy planning staff of the State Department had proposed at the beginning of the tripartite talks in March. The objection of the United States Chiefs of Staff to the Brussels treaty formula had been made clear in those tripartite meetings when General Gruenther,* obviously speaking on their behalf, had emphasized the "necessity for being entirely clear that no commitment to aid a state, victim of attack, should require that aid should be delivered locally. We should retain freedom to carry out action against the aggressor in accordance with strategic concepts."[9] Wrong explained what the Chiefs of Staff had in mind. "If, for example, Sweden became a party and was invaded by Russia, the agreement must not state or imply a commitment to send forces to Sweden. The commitment would be to defeat Russia according to the best strategic concept that could be devised. The offensive against Russia, however, should be undertaken anywhere and in any way that seemed best to the high command."[10] The United States Chiefs of Staff did not want to be committed to second, third and fourth fronts in the event of war.

In opposing on these grounds the language in the Brussels treaty about giving an ally which had been attacked "all the military and other aid and assistance in their power", the United States Chiefs of Staff were being scrupulous, perhaps excessively so. Britain had not regarded its commitment under the Anglo-Polish treaty of August, 1939, to give

---

*Maj. Gen. Alfred M. Gruenther, director of the joint staff, Joint Chiefs of Staff of the United States.

Poland "all the support and assistance in its power" as a commitment to send armed forces to Poland but as a commitment to go to war against Germany if Germany attacked Poland.

The other variation in the December 24 draft treaty from the language of the pledge in the Brussels treaty was that the action to be taken in the event of an armed attack was not to take "all the military and other aid and assistance *in their power*", it was to take "such military or other action . . . *as may be necessary to restore and assure the security of the North Atlantic area.*" (Italics added.) This language echoed the language of Article 42 of the U.N. Charter: "such action by air, sea, or land forces as may be necessary to maintain or restore international peace and security".

Thus after nine months of intergovernmental discussions and as the result of an intricate process of give-and-take, the Ambassadors' Committee agreed on December 24, 1948, to submit to their governments the following pledge:

> The Parties agree that an armed attack against one or more of them occurring within the area defined below shall be considered an attack against them all; and consequently that, if such an armed attack occurs, each of them, in exercise of the right of individual or collective self-defence recognized by Article 51 of the Charter of the United Nations, will assist the party or parties so attacked by taking forthwith such military or other action, individually and in concert with the other Parties, as may be necessary to restore and assure the security of the North Atlantic area.[11]

The language was in substance the same as that tentatively agreed to on March 25, 1948, in the middle of the tripartite discussions. The United States, under Lovett's leadership, had gone the whole way to meet the wishes of the Brussels treaty powers. The pledge was as strong or stronger than that in the Brussels treaty. Was it too strong for the Senate? The answer was not long in coming.

Acheson became Secretary of State on January 20, 1949; Lovett, who had been Acting Secretary, resigned; Acheson took over from Lovett the chairmanship of the Ambassadors' Committee. On February 3 and 5 he and Bohlen had their first talk with Connally and Vandenberg, the Democratic chairman and the senior Republican member of the Senate Foreign Relations Committee. Acheson showed them the draft of the pledge and they objected strenuously to it. We learned that they had proposed that the words "forthwith" and "military and other" be deleted. This would mean that all that an ally would undertake would be to take action; though the action would have to be such "as may be necessary to restore and assure the security of the North Atlantic area." The British

Ambassador, Oliver Franks, and Wrong, agreed that this watering down of the pledge would be "disastrous".[12]

Actually the demands of the senators for weakening the pledge had gone even further though we did not know this at the time. They wanted the words "as may be necessary" deleted as well as the words "forthwith" and "military and other". The wording of the pledge which Vandenberg proposed at the meeting with Acheson on February 3 was to take action "to restore and assure the security of the North Atlantic area. . . ." The watering down proposed by the senators was more disastrous than Franks and Wrong thought.

In the discussion on February 3 between Acheson, Bohlen, Connally and Vandenberg, Connally's principal concern, according to the record of the discussion drawn up by Bohlen and signed by Acheson, "related entirely to the automatic aspects which he found in Article 5 committing the United States to go to war in circumstances which might lie beyond its control". At the meeting on February 5, Connally "expressed the view that since we were giving so much to the countries involved and were considering taking the obligation inherent in the treaty that in negotiation we should insist upon certain safeguards in connection with the power of Congress to declare war". Vandenberg, according to the Bohlen-Acheson record of the discussion on February 3, "was apparently willing to go much farther than Senator Connally as to the extent of accepting the reality of the situation and making our willingness to act in the event of an attack in the North Atlantic area perfectly clear". Vandenberg, however, wanted the treaty to "make clear that it was up to each party to determine the nature and character of the assistance" which it would give if an ally were attacked.[13]

When Acheson met with the Ambassadors' Committee on February 8, he did not tell them of the deletions demanded by Connally and Vandenberg. He said instead that the senators thought that the adverbs and adjectives used at the end of the draft pledge gave an impression of a rising crescendo of rush and haste.[14]

> This language perhaps overstated the problem. It implied that the United States was rushing into some kind of automatic commitment. The Senators wanted the pact to avoid overstatement or rhetoric. There would be preliminary talks, there would be plans, but the ultimate action would depend upon the decision of each member country and would have to be in accordance with its international legal and moral obligations.

What was particularly disturbing was that Acheson did not, in his report to the Ambassadors' Committee, disassociate himself from the criticisms which Connally and Vandenberg had made of the language of the draft pledge. Rather, on the crucial point of whether the pledge should mention military action, he associated himself with their views. He told the ambassadors that the phrase "military or other action" was "an unnecessary embellishment". The phrase "merely meant 'action', i.e. of military, diplomatic, and any other kind of action . . . as may be necessary to restore security. That was what would actually happen."[15]

Wrong believed that the violence of the reaction of the two senators to the language of the draft pledge might have been caused in part by their dislike of Acheson's incisive style when he discussed the pledge with them.[16] Acheson was not at that time arrogant of heart and mind but he was sometimes arrogant of expression and it was an arrogance of expression which irritated the ambassadors when he discussed the pledge with them on February 8. The draft of the pledge on which Acheson was commenting had been agreed to unanimously on December 24 for submission to the governments. This agreement had come after long debate. The Ambassador of Canada had been working on the problem of the pledge for almost 11 months of intergovernmental discussions, and the Ambassadors of Britain, France, Belgium and the Netherlands for seven months. Every word in the draft had been weighed on delicate balances by the ambassadors and their governments. Acheson was the new boy at the negotiating table; this was his first appearance there, and it was only 10 days since he had been able to look at any of the papers on the intergovernmental discussions. Yet he spoke to the ambassadors not as a neophyte but as a teacher lecturing not very intelligent students.

Acheson may, of course, have decided that the more arrogant the language he used in presenting to the ambassadors the senators' demands for watering down the pledge, the more likely he was to break down the opposition of the ambassadors and their governments.

Bonnet, the French Ambassador, had to impress on Acheson at the meeting of the Ambassadors' Committee on February 8 what Acheson might wisely have prefaced his own remarks with, that "the draft text as it stood at present had been arrived at after much thought and negotiation . . . after protracted talks." The Belgian Ambassador, in speaking of the language of the pledge, drew attention to the many months which had elapsed since the start of the talks, and the thorough discussion in detail which had occurred in working groups and subcommittees. "He did not therefore think it could be said that there had been precipitation or an absence of thoroughness in dealing with the problem."[17]

Acheson also appears to have failed to take into account that it was one thing for the United States to propose weak language for the pledge at the end of March, 1948, during the tripartite meetings, but it was quite a different thing to propose such language ten months later after the press had reported that the pledge would contain a reference to military action. Leaks to the press about the wording of the pledge had begun some months before Acheson consulted the senators. These leaks had resulted from Achilles' briefing of the Associated Press and the United Press.[18] Wrong had referred to the leaks when the ambassadors resumed their meetings on December 10 after a three months' adjournment. He said that he had been considerably concerned by the publicity about "the differences between the Rio formula and the Brussels formula and possible compromises."[19] When at the meeting of the ambassadors on February 8 Acheson proposed the deletion of the reference to military action, Wrong said, "If the negotiations had been just starting it might have been possible to avoid such a reference. But such a change of wording after so much had appeared in the press about the present wording would cause difficulties and might be of considerable advantage to Soviet propaganda."[20] De Margerie of the French Foreign Office said much the same thing about 10 days later. He thought that a formula which did not mention military action might at one stage have been possible for the French, but was now impossible. Earlier draft texts of the article which included a reference to military action had been published in Washington, so that any text which did not include this phrase would now be widely regarded as a weakening of the original conception.[21]

On February 14, six days after Acheson had reported to the Ambassadors' Committee on his discussions with Connally and Vandenberg, the crisis over the pledge was greatly exacerbated by a storm which suddenly burst out on the floor of the Senate. The storm was precipitated by an article in the *Kansas City Times* of February 12 on the discussions about possible Norwegian membership in the North Atlantic alliance which Lange, the Foreign Minister of Norway, had had with Truman, Acheson and Vandenberg. Acheson was reported to have told Lange that the pledge in the treaty "would be interpreted as a moral commitment to fight" even though only Congress could declare war.

Senator Donnell of Missouri protested "against our country being made subject to any moral commitment which, in good conscience, would in the ultimate effect require Congress to go ahead and declare war sometime. . . ." He asked Connally and Vandenberg if he was correct in his understanding that "neither of the Senators desires to put into the North Atlantic pact anything which constitutes a moral commitment on the part of the United States of America to go to war". He said, "If I have misinterpreted their statements, I pause now for a statement to the contrary from either or both of them." They remained silent.

When Connally intervened in the debate he said that in the case of governments he did not know the difference between moral commitments and legal commitments. He did "not believe in giving carte blanche assurance to . . . [the nations of Europe], 'Do everything you want to do, you need not worry, as soon as anything happens we will come over and fight your quarrel for you'." We should not "blindfold ourselves and make a commitment now to enter every war that may occur in the next 10 years, and send our boys and resources to Europe to fight." "We cannot . . . be Sir Galahads, and every time we hear a gun fired plunge into war and take sides wihout knowing what we are doing, and without knowing the issues involved". "[T]here are many people, and we have found them in government and elsewhere, who would favor automatically going to war, which would mean letting European nations declare war and letting us fight." In this debate, the Democratic Chairman of the Senate Foreign Relations Committee thus echoed the isolationist speeches of the 1930s. It was the Republican minority leader, Vandenberg, who presented the case for internationalism. He pleaded that the treaty was necessary ta prevent a third world war; that the treaty was the "outcome and implementation" of the resolution which bore his name; and that there would be nothing, in his expectation, in the North Atlantic pact "which is not written within the four corners of the United Nations Charter".[22]

This impromptu debate depressed and discouraged the State Department, the Ambassadors' Committee and their governments. Wrong said,

> If the type of reservation is written into the treaty which Senator Connally's remarks would imply, it will, of course, seriously reduce the effectiveness of the treaty as a deterrent to aggression and will also assist Soviet propaganda in belittling the value of the pledge. . . .[23] The worst feature of the debate . . . was the denial by Connally and others that the signature of the treaty would create a moral obligation to go to war. I welcome attacks in the communist press in Europe, making out that the treaty would be worthless in view of the interpretation of the senators, because they should open some eyes to the folly of belittling the commitment.[24]

A few days later Schuman, the Foreign Minister of France, told the Canadian Ambassador that the language proposed by Connally for the pledge "was meaningless and unacceptable and as for himself he would not sign any treaty which was not 'sérieux et complet'." He said that it was deplorable that American senators should be bandying the North Atlantic pact about in public. "This was the worst possible thing that could happen."[25]

We in Ottawa did not know at the time that immediately after the impromptu debate in the Senate on February 14, Acheson and Bohlen had had a talk with Connally and Vandenberg. At this meeting, "both Senators were even more strongly than heretofore of the opinion that it must be made clear in Article 5 that there was no obligation, moral or otherwise, to go to war." Connally even questioned the advisability of using the Rio treaty language of an attack on one being considered to be an attack on all; he wanted to weaken this by saying that "an attack on one would be regarded as a threat to the peace of all," but Vandenberg did not support him on this. Both senators, however, agreed that Article 5 should not refer to the possibility of military assistance and both insisted that the article make plain that each of the allies would determine individually the type of action it should take to assist an ally that had been attacked. (They did not resurrect the provision in the Pentagon paper of April 1, 1948, that each ally would have the right to decide for itself whether an armed attack had occurred.)[26]

The principal officers in the State Department who were at that stage concerned with the negotiations were Bohlen, Rusk, Hickerson and Achilles. They were so impressed by the opposition of the two senators to a firm pledge that they were prepared to give in to their demands. They fortunately recommended, however, that Oliver Franks should first be asked if he believed that this would impair the objectives of the treaty. Acheson saw Franks, who urged that it was essential that the pledge refer to the possibility of military assistance. Acheson then discussed the matter with the President who agreed with Franks. Truman said that Acheson should propose to the Senate Foreign Relations Committee that the pledge contain the words "including the use of armed force"; he would talk to Connally over the telephone about this and, if possible, ask him to come in that evening for a talk in order to impress on him that on this matter Acheson was speaking for the President with his full knowledge and support; only if it were "absolutely necessary after a stout fight" should the administration agree to omit the reference to the possible use of armed force.[27]

The day before this talk took place, Wrong had requested us in Ottawa to send him a restatement of our views on the pledge, leaving him, as he put it, "wide discretion in employing the statement".[28] I immediately set to work to draft this restatement. Pearson revised my draft, secured St. Laurent's approval and we sent the long message off on February 17.

The message was a forthright statement of why we believed that the language of the treaty should make clear that "the signatories are determined to resist by all necessary means any further encroachments by the Soviet Union" in the North Atlantic treaty area. The

> purposes of the treaty are not going to be fulfilled by an undertaking which is so watered down that it does not create even a moral obligation to take effective action, but is put forward as a charitable donation from the United States. This is reducing the proposed North Atlantic treaty almost to the level of a Kellogg-Briand peace pact. If there is no satisfactory pledge in the treaty, and if the treaty is interpreted by the Senate merely as a mechanism for getting the European states out of difficulties which really don't concern the United States directly, then its value is greatly reduced and we might have to re-examine our whole position. It might be that in the light of such re-examination we will be compelled to decide that the Canadian national interest

involved in this kind of treaty interpreted in this way by United States opinion, is not sufficiently direct and immediate to warrant the government recommending to Parliament our adherence to it. We would do this, of course, with the greatest regret, but we might, in the circumstances, conclude that it is better to have no treaty at all than to have a treaty which is so weak and ambiguous as to be meaningless and therefore mischievous, especially since the conclusion of such a treaty might render less likely the conclusion of a really effective arrangement in the future.

In order to make it impossible for Vandenberg to oppose a firm pledge on constitutional grounds, we quoted the pledge in the draft treaties on the disarmament and demilitarization of Germany and Japan which the United States had publicly proposed in 1946 be entered into by the United States with the Soviet Union, Britain and France: "The high contracting parties will, by common agreement, take such prompt action – including action by air, sea or land forces – as may be necessary to assure the immediate cessation or prevention" [of a violation of the treaty.] This pledge, we said, had been based on Vandenberg's speeches in the Senate on January 10, 1945, and in Detroit on February 5, 1945. In the Detroit speech Vandenberg had proposed that the United States should "with all its major allies sign a hard and fast treaty. . .which pledges our constant armed co-operation, instantly and peremptorily available through the President of the United States without further reference to the Congress, to keep Germany and Japan out of piracy for keeps." Vandenberg had gone on to say, "Oh, but you ask, if 'only Congress can declare war' how can you give the President plenary power to use our armed forces to keep the Axis permanently demilitarized? The answer is that for 150 years the Constitution has permitted the President to use this plenary power for 'the national defence' – short of war – and it repeatedly has thus been used without question."

We said that the draft treaties on Germany and Japan had been public for almost three years and "so far as we know have not been attacked in responsible quarters in the United States as being unconstitutional. Hostile critics of the United States might interpret any marked inconsistency between the United States attitude to these treaties and to the proposed North Atlantic treaty as indicating that the United States was not acting in good faith when it put forward the draft four-power treaties, and that it puts strong pledges in treaties which it knows have no chance of coming into force." We insisted that the pledge in the North Atlantic treaty must be such as to involve the Congress of the United States in "a moral obligation to declare war if, in future, such a declaration is necessary to defeat an attack made against a co-signatory of the treaty".[29]

Before Acheson met the Foreign Relations Committee on February 18, Wrong brought to his attention, through Hickerson, that part of our telegram which referred to Vandenberg's position in 1945 and to the draft treaties on the demilitarization of Germany and Japan. How far Wrong used the other arguments in the telegram in speaking to Hickerson or Acheson on this or on a later occasion I do not know; he reported on February 21 merely that "the change in the situation here made it unnecessary for me to use a number of your arguments".[30]

The "change in the situation" was that Acheson had, at his meeting with the Senate Foreign Relations Committee on February 18, the day after Truman had talked to Connally, secured the tentative agreement of the Committee to the December 24 draft of the pledge with one change. The words "such action as it deems necessary, including the use of armed force" would be substituted for the words "such military or other action . . . as may be necessary". The agreement of the Committee to the mention of armed force was dependent on the use of the words, "as it deems necessary".[31] Acheson told the ambassadors at an informal meeting on February 19 that, while the senators were not committed to this language, he thought that they would be satisfied with it. The article with the revision would read as follows:

> The Parties agree that an armed attack against one or more of them in Europe or North America shall be considered an attack against them all; and consequently they agree that, if such an armed attack occurs, each of them, in exercise of the right of individual or collective self-defense recognized by Article 51 of the Charter of the United Nations, will assist the Party or Parties so attacked by taking forthwith, individually and in concert with the other Parties, such action as it deems necessary, including the use of armed force, to restore and maintain the security of the North Atlantic area.

Wrong reported Acheson as saying,

> Some senators had gone on a spree in the debate [on February 14] . . . and were now in a more sober mood. There was no disposition to question both the purposes of the treaty and the manner in which it ought to operate. Everyone [in the Senate Committee] . . . understood that what the parties proposed to do was to agree on a firm policy that each would assist the other in case of an armed attack. They also understood that the President possessed powers independent of Congress to act as Commander-in-Chief of the armed forces in a serious emergency. They were satisfied now that the treaty did not contain a provision for an automatic declaration of war.[32]

At a formal meeting with the ambassadors a week later (February 25), Acheson expanded on this. The use of the phrase "as it deems necessary" was essential in order to distinguish between the response to a minor incident and to a major attack:

In the event of a major attack such as the Treaty was designed to meet: the President would exercise his authority as Commander-in-Chief and the Congress would exercise its authority to declare war, appropriate funds and set the necessary machinery in action. It was necessary, however, to be able to point out that a minor incident [if, for example, some border guard began shooting] would not produce a reaction of this sort. There was always some suspicion that at some time in the future a President might use a minor incident as an excuse for declaring an emergency and acquiring all the power that accrued to him in those circumstances.[33]

Hickerson also explained at this meeting that the reference to constitutional processes in Article II ("This Treaty shall be ratified and its provisions carried out by the Parties in accordance with their respective constitutional processes") constituted an inconspicuous assertion of the right of Congress to declare war.[34]

The agreement of the other governments to the change to "as it deems necessary" was given with reluctance.[35] The governments could, however, congratulate themselves that the pledge in the North Atlantic treaty was, on balance, stronger than the pledge in the Rio treaty. After 12 months of negotiation, the British, the western European countries and Canada had won a partial victory. The members of the North Atlantic alliance undertook to consider an armed attack on one to be an attack on all. Each undertook to come forthwith to the assistance of an ally which was attacked. Each undertook that this assistance would consist of such action as it deemed necessary, including the use of armed force, to restore and maintain the security of the North Atlantic area.

CHAPTER THIRTEEN

INDIRECT AGGRESSION

The countries which negotiated the North Atlantic treaty were chiefly afraid of indirect aggression by the Soviet Union, not of direct aggression, yet the words, indirect aggression, do not appear in the treaty and the treaty does no more than call for consultation if a member country considers that it is threatened by indirect aggression. During the negotiations on the treaty efforts were made to put stronger provisions on indirect aggression in the treaty. They all came to nought.

I proposed to Pearson on March 18, 1948, just before the opening of the tripartite talks, the extreme solution of making no distinction in the treaty between direct aggression and indirect aggression.[1] The policy planning staff of the State Department proposed at the same time an even more extreme solution.

My proposal was that the treaty should provide that the member countries would come to each other's assistance if one of the allies were subjected either to an armed attack or to "attempts by any State to undermine [its] political or economic independence ... by intimidation or by subversive processes of political or economic penetration". This language was in part derived from the provision in the Anglo-Polish treaty of August, 1939: "Should a European power attempt to undermine the independence of one of the Contracting Parties by processes of economic penetration or in any other way, the Contracting Parties will support each other in resistance to such attempts. Should the European power concerned thereupon embark on hostilities against one of the Contracting Parties, the provisions of Article 1 will apply." Article 1 was the guarantee article. My argument at the time for this proposal was:

The whole game of the Russians is obviously to conquer without armed attack. So far they have been successful in playing that game and it is to be assumed that they will continue to play it. The new treaty will look pretty futile if it is a treaty to guarantee us against the kind of attacks on our independence which might have been made 30 years ago but not the kind of attacks which may be made during the next weeks and months.

I realized that it could be argued that the inclusion in the proposed North Atlantic treaty of the kind of provision I had suggested would not be in accord with the obligation which members of the United Nations had assumed under the Charter to "refrain in their international relations from the threat or use of force"; and in my memorandum to Pearson I contended that any state which committed the kind of indirect aggression I had referred to would have itself violated this undertaking and that this breach of the Charter would release all other members of the U.N. from any obligations which they might have incurred under the Charter not to resort to force against it unless it made an overt armed attack. Later I suggested that the North Atlantic treaty should contain a declaration to this effect.[2]

The policy planning staff of the State Department proposed on March 23, 1948,[†] that the North Atlantic treaty should

> provide that, in case of an indirect aggression against any one of them, the contracting parties will consult as to the necessary assistance to be given to preserve the territorial integrity and political independence of the threatened party and that, if any one of them be attacked in the course of extending such assistance, the several parties will regard such an attack as an attack against all of them. Indirect aggression should be defined as an internal *coup d'état* or political change favorable to an aggressor; or the use of force within the territory of a state against its government by any persons under direction or instigation of another government or external agency other than the United Nations.[3]

Pearson was told at the time that this definition of indirect aggression had been put forward by Molotov in the course of the abortive discussions in 1939 on an Anglo-Soviet treaty of mutual assistance.[4]

The definitions of indirect aggression which I and the policy planning staff of the State Department suggested in March, 1948, demonstrate the difficulty of finding a wise and workable definition. My definition was intended to cover attempts by the Soviet Union to undermine the independence of a member of the North Atlantic alliance by intimidation or by subversion. I was thinking of attempts launched directly by the Soviet government against the government of that ally or mounted on its territory by the local Communist party. But an ally's independence could be endangered by indirect aggression by the Soviet government against a neighbour. Should not the definition also cover this eventuality? The policy planning staff apparently thought it should and this led them to suggest a definition of indirect aggression which would, if it had been included in an Anglo-Soviet treaty in 1939, have authorized the Soviet Union "to rescue any Baltic state from Hitler, even if it did not want to be rescued";[5] and, if included in the North Atlantic treaty, could have been interpreted as authorizing any one of the allies to "rescue" almost any state in the world from Stalin, even if it did not want to be "rescued". The justification would have been that the Communist party in that state, under the direction or instigation of the Soviet Union, was using force against the government of that state and that this constituted indirect aggression against an ally because, if this use of force were successful, the territorial integrity and political independence of the ally would be threatened.

Each of the three participants in the tripartite talks of March, 1948, circulated on March 24 a brief paper of "suggestions". The Canadian draft said that "an effort should be made [in the treaty] to cover indirect aggression." The British paper contained nothing on indirect aggression. The United States paper put forward, word for word, the proposal of the policy planning staff of the State Department.[6] The Canadian and United States proposals were discussed by the tripartite meeting on March 24. The British knocked the proposals down with an argument so strong that there was never much chance from then on that the words "indirect aggression" would occur in the body of the North Atlantic treaty.

"The British", Pearson reported, "felt that indirect aggression could not and should not be defined, as this might suggest that the signatory powers were attempting to interfere in the internal affairs of other states. As such it would be attacked by the communists and some non-communists as the beginning of a new Holy Alliance." Jebb "pointed out that the subject had come up at the Brussels discussions and that the French had been adamant there in rejecting any guarantee against indirect aggression or any attempt to define it."[7]

As a result the drafting group of the tripartite talks, consisting of Jebb, Pearson and Achilles,[8] agreed to recommend that the proposed treaty should not contain explicit provisions on indirect aggression but that the treaty should merely provide for consultation in the event of an ally considering it was threatened by indirect aggression. They suggested that indirect aggression might, however, be mentioned in the presidential declaration which it was intended at that time would be issued pending the conclusion of the treaty: "This [presidential] declaration of support might include an expression of willingness to consider whether any specific case of indirect aggression should be deemed to be an armed attack."[9]

In the paper which emerged from the tripartite talks, the Pentagon paper, this sentence was omitted and the only reference in the Pentagon paper to indirect aggression is the statement that the proposed treaty should provide for consultation between the parties if one of them considered that its territorial integrity or political independence was threatened by indirect aggression as well as by direct aggression in any part of the world.[10] The reference to indirect aggression in any part of the world was dropped during the subsequent negotiations and the word "security" was added after "political independence," so that in its final form the article on consultation in the treaty (Article 4) read, "The Parties will consult together, whenever in the opinion of any of them, the territorial integrity, political independence or security of any of the Parties is threatened."

The failure to refer explicitly to indirect aggression in this article made no difference to its meaning. The article clearly meant that consultation would take place if any ally considered that either it or another member of the alliance were threatened by indirect aggression. When the Norwegian Ambassador at one of the last meetings of the Ambassadors' Committee sought an elucidation of the meaning of Article 4, he was told by the Netherlands Ambassador that the article, by using the word "security," covered "aggression by subversive action".[11]

Thus if Soviet aggression by subversive action took the form of support for one side in a civil war in, say, Portugal, any member country could call for consultation under Article 4, either on the ground that Soviet intervention in the civil war threatened the political independence of Portugal or that it threatened the security of the alliance as a whole.

Pearson at one time hoped that even though there would be no explicit reference to indirect aggression in the body of the treaty it might be mentioned in the preamble. He suggested this in a message to Stone in the middle of August, 1948. At that time it was proposed that the preamble should contain a "statement that the parties have concluded the treaty in order to ... provide for effective reciprocal assistance to meet armed attacks against any of them, and in order to deal with threats of aggression against any of them."[12] Pearson suggested that it would be better to say "to meeting armed and other forms of attack against any of them and in order to deal with threats of aggression, direct and indirect, against any of them".[13] Nothing came of this.

Though Pearson was not successful in getting a reference to indirect and direct aggression in the preamble, the word "aggression" did appear until the very end of the intergovernmental discussions in the article in the treaty dealing with mutual aid (Article 3). Thus the Washington paper of September 9, 1948, said that the treaty should contain an article providing "for individual and collective effort, on the basis of continuous and effective self-help and mutual aid, to strengthen the individual and collective capacity of the parties to resist *aggression*". (Italics added.)[14] Much the same language appeared in the December 24, 1948, draft of the treaty.[15] Pearson considered that the article as thus drafted was "designed to deal with indirect aggression, e.g. if the French government feared a *coup d'état* by the communists, they could consult and presumably seek assistance under this article."[16] In his opinion Article 3 "should cover preparations to resist both indirect aggression and direct aggression".[17] The Belgian Ambassador also urged that the treaty provide that the alliance should make preparations in advance to deal with indirect aggression. He along with the Canadian, Netherlands and Norwegian Ambassadors, pleaded at the final meeting of the Ambassadors' Committee that the words "armed attack" should not, as the British had proposed, be substituted for the word "aggression" in Article 3 which at that time read, "In order more effectively to achieve the objectives of this treaty, the Parties separately and jointly, by means of continuous and effective self-help and mutual aid, will maintain and develop their individual and collective capacity to resist aggression."

The argument of the Belgian Ambassador was that if the word "aggression" were maintained, measures could be concerted beforehand to deal with indirect aggression; if reliance were placed solely on Article 4, which dealt with consultation, plans could be made only after the indirect aggression had started.

In spite of these arguments, it was agreed at the last meeting of the Ambassadors' Committee that the words "armed attack" should be substituted for "aggression" in Article 3. The British said that their legal advisers thought that unless this were done, Article 54 of the U.N. Charter might apply. They were apparently worried not just because this would mean that the activities of the North Atlantic alliance would have to be reported to the Security Council, but that it would strengthen the case for arguing that the North Atlantic alliance was a regional arrangement within the meaning of Chapter VIII of the U.N. Charter, and that consequently the alliance could not take enforcement action without the authorization of the Security Council.[18]*

Thus the only part of the North Atlantic treaty which deals with indirect aggression is Article 4, the article on consultation, and it does not explicitly mention either indirect or direct aggression.

When Pearson presented the treaty to the House of Commons in Ottawa on March 28, 1949, he said that Czechoslovakia had not fallen to the Soviet Union in February, 1948, because of an armed attack:

No war was declared and no frontiers were crossed. No bombs were dropped, yet the fate of Czechoslovakia was as clear a case of aggression as one could find in history. Article 4 of this treaty provides that the members of the North Atlantic community shall consult together about this new and sinister kind of danger, indirect aggression. This does not mean that they propose to interfere in each other's internal affairs or hinder the healthy political growth of any member of the group. They will be able, however, to co-operate with a view to ensuring that no temporary difficulty in any state is exploited to impose by force a communist or, indeed, a fascist regime against the wishes of its people and with aid from outside.[19]

*The text of Chapter VIII, which includes Article 54, is given in Appendix 4.

CHAPTER FOURTEEN

CONSULTATION

In any military alliance the policy of one ally on issues which may increase the risks of war for the other allies is the concern of all the allies. Unless an alliance has effective methods by which the allies can influence each other's policies on such issues, it will be subjected to severe strains. The strains may become so severe that they will give rise to doubts about the likelihood of some of the members of the alliance being willing to carry out their obligations under the alliance if war should break out. If doubts of this kind arise the deterrent effect of the alliance on a potential aggressor will be lessened and the risks of war will be increased. It was because those who negotiated the North Atlantic treaty realized this that they attached such importance to including provisions on consultation in the treaty.

Pearson put the argument clearly in September, 1948, half-way through the negotiations on the treaty, in his first public speech as Foreign Minister. The "sharing of risks, resources and obligations" in the alliance must, he said, "be accompanied by, and flow from a share in the control of policy. If obligations and resources are to be shared, it is obvious that some sort of constitutional machinery must be established under which each participating country will have a fair share in determining the policies of all which affect all. Otherwise, without their consent, the policy of one or two or three may increase the risks and therefore the obligations of all." These one, two or three countries could not "make decisions which may have far-reaching consequences" for the allies and then ask them "to jump in and help in solving the problems which those decisions have raised". There were, he acknowledged, times "when the requirements for consultation and for co-operative decisions must be subordinated to the necessities of a grave emergency. But those occasions must be reduced to a minimum." "That is one reason why I hope that the North Atlantic regional system for security and progress will soon be formed so that within its framework the decisions which affect all will be taken by all. Only then will the common responsibility for carrying out these decisions be clear and unequivocal."[1]

Pearson was still arguing this in 1957 after he had had eight continuous years of dealing with the North Atlantic alliance as Canadian Foreign Minister. He wanted "the establishment of a programme of consultation [within the alliance] with an agreed list of current topics on which every effort will be made by the Permanent Council to come as close as possible to a common policy". He suggested that the list should include the turmoil in eastern Europe, the situation in Hungary, disarmament, relations between NATO and the Baghdad pact, and Middle East problems, including the new United States policy, the Suez Canal and the Palestine dispute.[2]

For Canada this objective of a common foreign policy within the alliance on issues of common concern meant a complete and deliberate break with the principles which had governed its approach in the period between the two world wars to issues which involved risks of war. Canada and Britain were not linked at that time in an alliance, but Canada's special relationship with Britain meant that, if Britain became involved in a first-class war, Canada would probably also become an active belligerent. In spite of this, the policy of Mackenzie King, Prime Minister of Canada for about two-thirds of the inter-war period, was: Beware of consultations with Britain on foreign policy; do not attempt to influence British policy by commenting on it; above all do not get involved in a common foreign policy for the British Empire; the less the Canadian government comments on British policy, the less Canada is committed to it; the more the Canadian government comments, the more Canada is committed, and if the policy leads to war Canada will be morally committed to take part in the war. Some people, stated Mackenzie King in May, 1938, in a speech in the House of Commons, said that Canada should "advise Great Britain as to what course she should follow [in foreign affairs], so that we will not be involved in the consequences of a policy we thought wrong. . . . [The British government] might be prepared to take advice which fell in with their own views; but otherwise they would find it difficult to do so unless the adviser could guarantee them against the consequences."[3]

The Pearson doctrine was: Since Canada is committed under the North Atlantic treaty to help defend the North Atlantic community if war breaks out, the Canadian government must do its best to ensure that war does not break out. This means, among other things, that the Canadian government should take advantage of every opportunity to comment on the foreign policies of its allies if it believed that those policies might increase the risks of war; the Canadian government must try within the alliance to work out a common North Atlantic foreign policy on matters of common concern.

One policy was "no comment" in order to avoid being drawn into war. The other policy was to comment in order to avoid war. One policy sought to avoid commitments to go to war. The other policy sought to avoid war since we were already committed to participate in it. The Mackenzie King policy had failed; we had made no comments but we were drawn into the Second World War in September, 1939. That was one reason why we believed nine years later that a Mackenzie King policy would not keep us out of a third world war. That was one reason why, when the North Atlantic treaty was negotiated, we attached such importance to its provisions on consultation.

All the allies considered at the time the North Atlantic treaty was negotiated that the provisions on consultation in the treaty under Articles 4 and 9 would have some effect in deterring the Soviet government from indirect aggression against an ally. The allies other than the United States believed that these provisions could also be used to restrain the United States from pressing the Soviet Union too hard and too fast and not leaving it a way out to save its face. Vandenberg, and presumably other Americans who helped to make the treaty, considered that the provisions on consultation could be used to restrain the allies of the United States. In the middle of April, 1948, Vandenberg told Dean Rusk that he was concerned with "the possibility that guarantees of security from the United States, whatever form they might take, might ... encourage [European countries] to act provocatively.... To meet ... [this] possibility he thought that the consultative body, if one were created, should have the authority to review actions of one signatory which might be considered provocative by another signatory."[4] Vandenberg's wish was fulfilled: any signatory which considered that action by another signatory was provocative and therefore threatened its security could demand that the allies consult together on this action. The other allies were under a treaty obligation to participate in this consultation.

Article 4 is the only article in the treaty which explicitly speaks of consultation: "The Parties will consult together whenever in the opinion of any of them, the territorial integrity, political independence or security of any of the Parties is threatened." But consultation on a wide range of subjects may also take place under Article 9: "The Parties hereby establish a council, on which each of them shall be represented, to consider matters concerning the implementation of this treaty. . . ."

Discussion at the Ambassadors' Committee on March 4, 1949, made clear the distinction between consultation under Article 4 and consultation under Article 9. Norway was represented on the committee for the first time. The Norwegian Ambassador, Morgenstierne, "asked whether consultation between members [under Article 4] had to be limited to instances where one of the parties felt threatened". "Could it not also," he asked, "take place in connection with political matters? He thought that under certain circumstances it might be useful to consult on other matters than those especially mentioned in Article 4." Wrong replied that the parties under Article 9 could consult on "any matters which they felt had a bearing on the execution of the treaty". He added that he "did not want to see the area of mandatory consultation expanded".[5]

The distinction was thus clear: Article 9 was permissive; Article 4 was mandatory. Under Article 9 the North Atlantic Council had the right to discuss any matter concerning the implementation of the treaty. Under Article 4 each of the allies undertook a treaty obligation to participate in consultation with all the other allies whenever any one of them considered that the territorial integrity, political independence or security of itself or of any other ally was threatened.

The area of possible discussion under Article 9 was as wide as the matters covered by the treaty. The Council could discuss the settlement of disputes between allies arising anywhere in the world or disputes between allies and non-member states arising anywhere in the world (Article 1). It could discuss how best to promote democracy within the alliance and conditions of stability and well-being in the world, how to eliminate conflict in the international economic policies of the allies occurring anywhere in the world, and how to encourage economic collaboration between any or all of them anywhere in the world (Article 2). It could discuss self-help and mutual aid in maintaining and developing the individual and collective capacity of the allies to resist armed attack (Article 3). The Council could discuss how best to implement the pledge which each of the allies had given to come to the assistance of an ally which was attacked (Article 5).

The area of mandatory consultation under Article 4 was likewise wide. The agreed interpretation of the article stated that it was "applicable in the event of a threat in any part of the world, to the security of any of the Parties, including a threat to the security of their overseas territories".* Thus the allies were obliged to consult at the request of any one of them on a threat real or apprehended to the territorial integrity, political independence or security of an ally in any part of the world. The threat did not have to arise from threats or acts by the Soviet Union or its allies; it could arise from threats or acts of a member of the North Atlantic alliance. The threat might arise from indirect aggression by the Soviet Union or by any other country anywhere in the world, or from the actions or inactions of any member of the alliance anywhere in the world.† If any member of the alliance believed in 1950 and 1951 that United States actions in the Korean War created unnecessary risks of precipitating a world war, as many of them did, it could have invoked Article 4 of the treaty. If any member of the alliance believed at any time from 1954 to

*See Appendix 3, "Agreed interpretations of the treaty".

1974 that United States actions in Vietnam threatened their own security, as many of them did, it could have invoked Article 4. Similarly the United States could have invoked Article 4 against Britain and France in 1956 when they invaded Egypt.

The universal extent of the provisions on consultation in the North Atlantic treaty reflected the fact that if the United States, Britain or France became involved in armed conflict with the Soviet Union anywhere in the world, the conflict would almost inevitably spread to the North Atlantic treaty area and thereby bring the pledge of assistance in the treaty into operation. All the members of the alliance had therefore a direct and immediate concern with the policies pursued by the United States, Britain and France anywhere in the world if these policies involved a risk of hostilities with the Soviet Union.

CHAPTER FIFTEEN

ARTICLE 2

The Parties will contribute toward the further development of peaceful and friendly international relations by strengthening their free institutions, by bringing about a better understanding of the principles upon which these institutions are founded, and by promoting conditions of stability and well-being. They will seek to eliminate conflict in their international economic policies and will encourage economic collaboration between any or all of them.

Article 2 of the treaty

Just as it is surprising that Italy became a member of the North Atlantic alliance when it is probable that at one time in the negotiations none of the negotiators wanted this except Hickerson and Achilles, so it is likewise surprising that there was such difficulty in getting Article 2 included in the treaty when at one time everybody concerned with the negotiations wanted this except the British. It is particularly surprising since, until Acheson became Secretary of State in January, 1949, the five American senior officers concerned with the negotiations (Lovett, Kennan, Bohlen, Hickerson and Achilles) were all strongly in favour of Article 2.

In the negotiations Article 2 was referred to as the Canadian proposal. Its most convinced advocate in Washington during the negotiations was not, however, a Canadian spokesman, but Achilles of the State Department. Indeed the two Canadian spokesmen in Washington, Wrong and Stone, were never convinced that the non-military aspects of the North Atlantic alliance were essential.[1] The strongest opponents of Article 2 were Jebb and Acheson. France, Belgium and the Netherlands could be persuaded by Britain in November, 1948, to oppose Article 2; they could be persuaded by Canada in February, 1949, to give strong support to it. The argument during the intergovernmental discussions was not, of course, just over whether there would be an Article 2; it was also over how much content the article would have if it were included in the treaty.

On March 18, 1948, just before the tripartite talks opened, I proposed to Pearson that the North Atlantic treaty should contain not just one article on economic, social and cultural co-operation but a chapter consisting of four articles. The first three of the articles which I proposed came from the Brussels treaty. The fourth put in treaty language the proposal which I had been putting forward since February, 1946, for strengthening the specialized agencies of the U.N. – and which I have been putting forward from time to time since 1948. I proposed that the provisions in the North Atlantic treaty on economic and cultural co-operation should read as follows:

(1) The Atlantic Nations agree so to organize their economic activities as to produce the greatest possible returns by the elimination of conflict in their economic policies, the co-ordination of production and the development of commercial exchanges.

(2) The Atlantic Nations undertake to make every effort in common, both by direct consultation and in the United Nations and the specialized agencies, to promote the attainment of a higher standard of living by their people and greater economic and social justice, and to develop on corresponding lines the social and other related services of their countries.

(3) The Atlantic Nations undertake to make every effort in common to lead their people towards a better understanding of the principles which form the basis of their common civilization and to promote cultural exchanges between themselves.

(4) In order to attain as rapidly as possible the objectives set forth in this Chapter, and thus to create in the Atlantic Community the economic and moral basis on which to build an overwhelming superiority of force on the side of peace, the Atlantic Nations undertake to use their best efforts to secure those amendments to the international instruments setting up the specialized agencies as are necessary to ensure that the agencies become the most effective possible instruments for the speedy attainment of the objectives set forth in this chapter.[2]

While Pearson did not put this proposal before the tripartite meeting, he stated "more than once" at the meeting that the treaty "should not be exclusively military in character and that there were economic and even spiritual defences against Communist attack which should not be overlooked . . . The Brussels arrangements had taken these important factors into consideration and it was even more important that the North Atlantic pact should do so. Otherwise, it would be considered as merely another old-fashioned military alliance."[3] There was no objection to this and the draft treaty prepared by the State Department at the end of the tripartite talks contained the following article: "The high contracting parties will make every effort, individually and collectively, to promote the economic well-being of their peoples and to achieve social justice, in order to create overwhelming moral and material superiority, as well as military superiority, in the cause of peace and progress." There was also a reference to economic co-operation in the State Department's draft of the preamble and, according to Wrong, this was almost verbatim what Pearson had proposed.[4]

In the discussions in July and August Achilles of the State Department pressed for a strengthening of the references in the treaty to economic and social co-operation with the result that by the first week in August the draft of the Washington paper which the Working Group was considering called not only for an Article 2 providing "for efforts to promote the general welfare through collaboration in the economic, social and cultural fields," but also for the article on the implementation of the treaty stipulating that the agencies to be set up to implement the treaty should be concerned, among other things, with "the progressive development of the objectives listed [in Article 2]". The draft paper went on to say that the inclusion of such an Article 2 in the treaty would "provide a basis for the long-range development of practical co-operation between the North Atlantic nations in other than the military fields".[5] Achilles attached particular importance to including the words "to promote the general welfare" in the article. Indeed, in a memorandum which he circulated at this time to his colleagues in the State Department, he suggested that all the six objectives of union stated in the preamble of the United States Constitution might be incorporated, with modifications, in the preamble and in articles of the North Atlantic treaty: "to form a more perfect union, establish justice, insure domestic tranquility, provide for the common defence, promote the general welfare and secure the blessings of liberty to ourselves and our posterity".[6]

Thus, in August of 1948, there appeared to be general agreement that the treaty should include an Article 2 and that the article on implementation (which became Article 9) would specifically mention Article 2. Then Gladwyn Jebb arrived in Washington from London and informed the Working Group the following day (September 2) that Ernest Bevin "had expressed considerable concern over the emphasis being placed in these talks on the establishment of machinery for the solution of common economic and cultural problems. In his view, this would not only duplicate much of the machinery now in existence, such as the OEEC, but might inject considerable confusion into the international picture and slow up the present progress of the European nations toward that union which they all believe is so essential".[7] Bevin was therefore opposed to an article in the treaty on co-operation in the economic, social and cultural fields but would agree to a reference to this in the preamble. The message which Jebb delivered from Bevin resulted in only relatively minor changes in the draft which the Working Group had been considering at the beginning of August. The main change was that the agencies set up to implement the treaty would not be required to implement Article 2 though they could do so.[†]

The British were not satisfied with this compromise and they succeeded at the end of November in persuading the Brussels treaty permanent commission to propose in their London paper that there should be no Article 2 in the North Atlantic treaty.[8] The French representative assented to this even though a few weeks previously de Margerie of the French Foreign Office had told the United States embassy in Paris that he was surprised "the the United Kingdom should be cool toward the Canadian proposal for the inclusion of economic and social clauses in the treaty, particularly as these clauses had been included in the Brussels pact. The French for their part would like to see them included in the Atlantic pact also."[9]

At this time France was trying to persuade the Brussels treaty powers to support its demand that Algeria be covered by the pledge in the treaty. It succeeded in getting British support though not the support of the Benelux countries. Perhaps French support for the British view on Article 2 was a tacit *quid pro quo* for British support for the French view on Algeria. The Benelux countries went along with the British and French on Article 2 but not on Algeria.

The support which the British had secured for the elimination of Article 2 soon dissolved. When the intergovernmental negotiations resumed in December, Lovett for the United States and Wrong for Canada strongly opposed the elimination[10] and on December 24, the Ambassadors' Committee unanimously recommended to their governments that the treaty should include:

Article 2 (General Welfare). The parties will encourage co-operative efforts between any or all of them to promote the general welfare through collaboration in the cultural, economic and social fields. Such efforts shall, to the greatest possible extent, be undertaken through and assist the work of existing international organizations.

The Committee's report stated that it was agreed that this text "would be generally acceptable as a compromise, since the Canadian representative would have preferred a more strongly worded provision" and the Brussels powers "doubted the necessity of including [any such] article".[11] This compromise, reached on December 24 at the end of the third stage of the intergovernmental discussions, was virtually the same as the compromise embodied in the report approved of at the end of the second stage of the discussions on September 10. The British attack on Article 2 had been repulsed. It had been repulsed because Canada was supported by the United States State Department under Lovett, who was then Acting Secretary of State. When at the beginning of February the State Department under Acheson switched to opposing Article 2, the Brussels treaty powers withdrew their support of the December 24 compromise.

I was not satisfied with the December 24 compromise, and as soon as I saw it, I urged Pearson that we should not give up the struggle for a more strongly worded provision and I suggested amendments to him.[12] Pearson agreed that the article "should go farther if possible but [he thought that it was] not likely to be possible". Wrong agreed with Pearson that there was not much chance of making the article stronger but said that he would see what he could do, possibly by including some such words as, "The parties agree to make every effort in common to eliminate conflict in their economic policies and to develop the great possibilities of trade between them." This was based on a proposal I had made to Pearson.[13] Wrong reported on January 5, however, that "we shall not be able to secure agreement on strengthening [the article's] language".[14]

I did not accept Wrong's judgment that it was impossible to strengthen Article 2, but it was not until February 7 that I succeeded in getting Pearson to instruct Wrong to do his best to get the article strengthened. What had happened was that St. Laurent and Pearson, with a general election impending, had become increasingly apprehensive that if the article were not strengthened the necessary degree of public support for the treaty in Canada would not be forthcoming. In his instruction of February 7 to Wrong, Pearson for the first time told Wrong to explain to his colleagues in the negotiations in Washington the practical domestic political considerations which lay behind the insistence by the Canadian government that Article 2 be strengthened: the existing draft of Article 2 could scarcely be much weaker; the Parliament and people of Canada would expect the government to secure something a good deal stronger; failure might result in the government facing "a definite weakening of support for the treaty in the House [of Commons] and in the country". Pearson therefore instructed Wrong to do his best to get the article strengthened by the addition, after the first sentence, of two sentences:

> The parties agree to make every effort in common to eliminate conflict in their economic policies and to develop to the full the great possibilities of trade between them. The parties also undertake to make every effort in common to promote the attainment of a higher standard of living by their people and greater economic and social justice, and to bring about a better understanding of the principles which form the basis of their common civilization.[15]

By this time the opposition of Acheson and leading senators to Article 2 must have become known to the ambassadors in Washington, even though Acheson had not yet met with them, for Wrong immediately wired back, "We are now the only party to the negotiation that really favours the inclusion of anything in the treaty about social and economic collaboration outside a general reference in the preamble. . . . I think that the most we may be able to do is to retain the existing language."[16]

Pearson did not accept this pessimistic conclusion. He telephoned Wrong just before the Ambassadors' Committee met with Acheson on February 8, with the result that Wrong told the Committee that "he had just received instructions from the Canadian government urging the strengthening of Article 2" and he proposed the addition of the two sentences which Pearson had sent him.[17] A good deal of the effect of this move on improving our bargaining position was lost, however, by Wrong stating, "I don't suggest it's feasible to put in all the suggested additions I just read."[18]

Acheson immediately said that there was growing opposition in the Senate Foreign Relations Committee to general commitments by the United States on economic, social and cultural matters. This must have come as a surprise to the ambassadors, for Lovett, only two months before, had told them that the treaty should cover a wider range than the military aspect alone "in order to make the treaty more acceptable to the American Congress".[19] (As it turned out Lovett's assessment was more accurate than Acheson's.)* Acheson explained to the ambassadors that one reason for the opposition of senators to general commitments on economic, social and cultural matters was that the Bogota treaty, which was just then being examined by the Senate, had "every worthy aspiration that ever occurred to any human being in it". The two examples which Acheson gave were: "Everyone was going to have a college education" and "Women were going to have the same rights as men."[20] Acheson apparently considered that the two propositions were equally preposterous; he would not have been a warm supporter of "women's lib."

Wrong, in his report to Ottawa explaining Acheson's views, said that when Acheson had appeared before the Senate Foreign Relations Committee to support ratification of the Bogota treaty, he "had expected to read only a prepared statement and leave in five minutes. Instead, he was subjected to a grilling examination and [he] has told me that he took a terrible beating."[21] Wrong reported that among the reasons for the opposition of senators to Article 2 were their distaste for some of the activities of UNESCO and of the Economic and Social Council of the U.N., and a desire to keep the North Atlantic treaty strictly limited to the organization of defence. Senator Lodge had taken a leading part in objecting to

*See pages 179 to 180.

Article 2, but there was an almost universal reluctance by the members of the committee to include any article of this nature in the treaty. Wrong also reported that Acheson did not like the existing draft of Article 2 on the ground that it meant next to nothing.[22] (This is always a problem in multilateral international negotiations. One government puts up a proposal, and some governments object that it goes too far; the proposal is watered down, and now those governments and possibly other governments object to it because it means next to nothing.)

In his report to Pearson on the meeting of the Ambassadors' Committee on February 8, Wrong said, "There was next to no discussion of our suggestions [for adding two sentences to the draft of Article 2]. I think we can at least maintain the present article, subject to finding some alternative to the phrase 'to promote the general welfare', which seems to rouse in senatorial minds a vision of endless hand-outs to the other parties. . . ."[23] Achilles recalls that Senator Connally said, "The reference to the general welfare in the United States Constitution has caused more litigation than any other provision in it. Get it the hell out of this treaty".[24]

On February 9, Wrong put up to Pearson a new proposal: If we could not, as he expected, get acceptance of the two additional sentences which we had proposed, we should propose a compromise between the existing text and our maximum demands. The compromise he proposed was:

> The parties agree to make every effort to bring about a better understanding of the principles which form the basis of their common civilization, and to develop to the full the possibilities of trade between them. To this end they will encourage collaboration between all or any of them in the cultural, economic and social fields. Wherever it may be appropriate, action to give effect to this article shall be undertaken through and shall assist the work of existing international organizations.[25]

The principal difference between this and the December 24 draft was the addition of the first sentence, which reproduced parts of the two sentences in the amendment proposed by Canada. It omitted, however, the provision in the first of these two sentences that the parties should make every effort to eliminate conflict in their economic policies. When Wrong drew up this compromise he did not know that Robertson, the Canadian High Commissioner in London, attached great importance to this provision. If he had known he would undoubtedly have included it in his compromise draft, because he had profound respect for Robertson's judgment.

Two days after Wrong submitted his compromise draft to Pearson, St. Laurent on his visit to Washington put to Truman and Acheson the practical domestic political reasons for Canada's insistence on Article 2. Wrong reported that Truman and Acheson had "listened sympathetically and I think we should have no difficulty with the administration in securing at least the maintenance of the present draft."[26]

Because of the difficulties which we were having in Washington we now decided to appeal over the heads of the ambassadors in Washington to their governments. We had on February 9 asked our High Commissioner in London to try to get British support for our position. On February 17 we instructed our ambassadors in Paris, Brussels and The Hague to try to persuade the governments to which they were accredited to support our proposals on Article 2. We told them that Wrong would do his best to get agreement on adding the two sentences and that if he failed, he would retreat to the compromise text.[27] We were informed of British, Dutch, French and Belgian support on February 11, 18, 19 and 24 respectively. The Belgians appear to have put off telling us their views until the Consultative Council of the Brussels treaty powers had, at its meeting on February 23, unanimously agreed to support the Canadian draft of Article 2. By this they meant our maximum demands, not our compromise or fall-back position.

The support from the British was, at least in response to our first message, reluctant. The British instructed their Ambassador in Washington to give full support to our desire to have an economic clause included in the treaty, but Robertson reported that he thought "it is clear that they decided to do so because they wanted to meet our wishes and not because they had any special interest themselves in having such a provision in the treaty."[28] The support from France was unexpectedly warm. Schuman told Vanier that "he would telegraph to the French representative in Washington instructing him to support the Canadian proposal "à fond", which means up to the hilt. . . . He said that this was not only his own policy but that of the government as a whole which was anxious to eliminate as far as possible the aggressive character of the treaty."[29] The support from the Netherlands government was also enthusiastic.[30] It must have been to this that Stikker, the Netherlands Foreign Minister, referred in his memoirs when he wrote that he had taken "an active part in the efforts, initiated by the Canadians, to broaden the scope of the alliance in the fields of politics and economics".[31]

Wrong discussed Article 2 with Acheson, Bohlen and Hickerson on February 19. (By this time, he knew that we had British and Dutch support; we had not, however, heard from the French and Belgian governments.) At the meeting, Wrong did not press for the acceptance of the additional two sentences we had proposed. He reported to Ottawa that since he believed that this "would only increase [Acheson's] difficulties with the senators" he had given Acheson, Bohlen and Hickerson his compromise proposal which they had promised to take under consideration.[32]

At this time we in Ottawa had not realized that Wrong had on February 8 formally put forward the additional two sentences at the

Ambassadors' Committee. Pearson therefore replied on February 21 that because of the support we were likely to get from all the Brussels powers for our maximum demands, Wrong should put them forward at the next meeting of the Ambassadors' Committee. "If you get substantial support for them from all the representatives other than the United States, Acheson could report this back to the Senate Committee and in the light of the reaction from the Senate Committee we can decide whether to press for these two sentences or to be content with your compromise."[33]

This crossed with a very pessimistic telegram from Wrong: "If strong objection continues to be taken [by the United States] to the inclusion of anything on the lines of Article 2, do you think it would be possible for us to get by with Article 3 and suitable language in the preamble? That may be the most that we can secure."[34] Article 3 was the article on mutual aid; at that time it read:

In order more effectively to achieve the objectives of this treaty, the parties will use every endeavour, separately and jointly, by means of continuous and effective self-help and mutual aid, to strengthen their individual and collective capacity to resist aggression.[35]

The suggestion from Wrong that there might be no Article 2 must have evoked a strong response from St. Laurent and Pearson. Since there is no record of this response, it must have been given in a telephone call. Pearson must have authorized Wrong to accept compromise language but to insist in the strongest terms that there must be an Article 2. Wrong therefore gave Hickerson, on February 22, a memorandum setting forth the arguments for Article 2[36] and accompanied this by an oral statement. In the memorandum, Wrong stated, "If the Canadian government were to agree to sign the treaty without a pledge of this nature, it would be essential to explain to the public that the pledge was dropped at the insistence of the government of the United States. The Canadian government has received assurances of support from the French and Netherlands governments for the inclusion of an article stronger than the present draft of Article 2 as well as a general promise of support from the British government. It is understood that the Belgian government is also favourable. It would be very difficult to explain satisfactorily why the United States government was unwilling to accept a general article of this nature in view of the many more specific engagements to which the United States is a party, including a number of inter-American treaties now in effect and the Lend-Lease and OEEC agreements."

In his oral statement to Hickerson, Wrong went much further. He said "that unless we could get an article on these lines in the treaty the Canadian government would have to review its position towards the whole project."[37] This diplomatic formula was the equivalent in ordinary language of a threat not to sign the treaty, and it would be interpreted by Hickerson as such. One must assume that Pearson not only gave firm instructions to Wrong to say this but that the language was Pearson's, and that on a matter of this importance Pearson would have secured St. Laurent's concurrence.

The result was that Wrong worked out with Hickerson, Achilles and W. J. Galloway a new compromise draft of Article 2, which Hickerson said they would try to sell to Acheson the next day before he met the senators. Hickerson went on to say that he had been told by Acheson to try to persuade Wrong to accept the general language in the preamble and no article at all, and now he was going back to Acheson with an article which was stronger than the one to which the senators had taken exception.[38] In reporting on this to Ottawa, Wrong said, "I think that this is as strong a text as we can secure because of the cantankerous attitude adopted by the Foreign Relations Committee towards any article at all. Indeed, I doubt that they will take this as it stands. Apart from other possible changes, we may have to re-insert the reference to working through existing international institutions whenever this is possible."[39]

The next day Hickerson and Wrong called on Acheson at his house in Georgetown where he was in bed with the flu. According to Hickerson, Wrong "on one side [of the bed] and I on the other side beat the poor sick man over the head",[40] until he accepted the draft with minor modifications.

After Acheson had given his approval, Ernest Gross, Assistant Secretary of State in charge of congressional relations, informed the Senate Foreign Relations Committee. The next day, February 25, Acheson submitted the new draft to the Ambassadors' Committee. By then all the ambassadors had been instructed by their governments to support the addition of the two sentences proposed by Wrong at the meeting of the Committee on February 8. All of them therefore supported the new draft and indicated that they would have been happy to support a stronger text. The Netherlands Ambassador said that his government considered that the proposal which Canada had put forward on February 8 covered the subject "admirably". The French Ambassador "was sure that Article 2 would be welcomed by his government as it would tend to show that the treaty was not purely military. He was strongly in favour of mentioning cultural co-operation." (The December 24 draft had called for collaboration in the cultural, economic and social fields. The new draft contained no reference to cultural collaboration.) The British Ambassador agreed that it would be a good thing to have something about cultural co-operation in the treaty and said that he "would have been pleased if the article had gone perhaps a little farther". The Belgian Ambassador wondered if the new draft "went far enough to be accepted by the Canadian government." He asked Wrong if the new draft gave satisfaction, at least personally to him. Wrong "replied that at the end of the second sentence of the present text he would like to add, 'to encourage economic collaboration between any or all of them with a view to developing the great possibilities of trade between them'. He would also like to add another sentence which would refer to the attainment of higher standards of living and greater economic and social justice as general objectives. He understood that these proposals would cause great difficulty with the senators. He considered them reasonable proposals coming within the general purpose of the treaty and that was why he could not, at the moment, say whether the present text would satisfy the Canadian government." "If it was the best article that could be had, he would try to get the Canadian government to support it." (Wrong had, the day before, asked Pearson over the telephone whether he would be satisfied with "the present text", and Pearson had said that he would be satisfied.)[41]

Acheson "said that he would not like to expand the wording of this draft. He had been surprised at Mr. Gross's success in getting this draft past the senators. The President also had been helpful after his conversations with Prime Minister St. Laurent. He thought the senators had been co-operative and reasonable. For domestic reasons the senators were wary of ideas concerning welfare and cultural development." The "insertion of a reference to cultural co-operation would be harmful. ... [T]he word 'cultural' had unfortunate connotations in the United States." "If the present draft could be accepted by the Canadian government it would make the task of the United States administration much easier."[42] (It is a pity that one of the ambassadors did not ask Acheson to elucidate his reference to the unfortunate connotations which the word "cultural" had in the United States. For most of the ambassadors, the connotation which was most likely to spring to mind was the statement attributed to Hermann Goering, "When I hear anyone talk of culture, I reach for my revolver.")

The question of Article 2 came up again at the meeting of ambassadors on March 4. The Netherlands Ambassador "said that his government regretted that this Article did not go as far as the Canadian proposal". The French Ambassador reiterated his plea "that there be some mention in the Article of intellectual or cultural co-operation". Wrong said that he had secured the agreement of Pearson to the article as it now stood, subject to a drafting change. "He recognized that it would cause great difficulty to the United States government if they had to try and secure the acceptance of an Article more in accordance with the original Canadian proposal, and did not wish to press for any further changes."[43] Article 2 therefore remained as it now is in the treaty.

Acheson's statement at the meeting with the ambassadors that he had been surprised at Gross's success in getting this text past the senators arouses suspicion that Gross might have been successful in persuading the senators to accept a stronger Article 2 and that Acheson, who as Hickerson said years later, "didn't like [Article 2] worth a damn,"[44] was indulging in wishful thinking when he stressed the strength of the opposition of the senators to Article 2.

Certainly there is nothing in Bohlen's memorandum on the meeting which Acheson and he had with Connally and Vandenberg on February 3, 1949, to indicate that the two senators were strongly opposed to Article 2. They were only, as Acheson reported to the ambassadors, "worried" about it.[45] Their worry was, as Vandenberg put it, that "there was strong opposition in the Senate towards the expansion of cultural, economic and social co-operation beyond the limits of the [U.N.] Charter and [Vandenberg] felt that anything which might be regarded as adding to the Charter obligations would be very undesirable". The senators asked no more than that the State Department "have another look" at the language of Article 2 to make sure that it did not exceed the requirements of the Charter, and that the State Department consider the possibility of merely making a reference to the Charter instead of having Article 2 in the treaty. The State Department did take another look and recommended to Acheson "that no change be made [in Article 2] and the senators be reassured that the Article as drafted does not involve this government in any commitment."[46] If Acheson had accepted this recommendation it seems likely that he could without much difficulty have reassured Connally and Vandenberg, and with them on his side the Senate Foreign Relations Committee would probably not have objected to Article 2. Acheson, because he disliked Article 2, exaggerated the opposition of the senators. Wrong, because he did not attach much importance to Article 2, allowed himself to be convinced by Acheson that he would have great difficulties in getting a strong Article 2 accepted by the Senate Foreign Relations Committee.

Two weeks before Acheson became Secretary of State, Wrong reported that "we shall not be able to secure agreement on strengthening" the December 24 draft of Article 2. Five weeks after Acheson took office, he agreed to the text in the treaty which is much stronger than the December 24 draft. Acheson believed that he "defused" the Canadian draft of Article 2,[47] but he was mistaken. Acheson did not defuse the Canadian draft of Article 2; rather by the vigour of his opposition he helped to infuse new life into it.

We could, I believe, have got an even stronger version of Article 2 if I had not committed an error in the negotiations and if Wrong had not compounded that error. The error I made was that I did not recommend to Pearson that we should make our appeal to the French, Belgian and Netherlands governments on February 9 (the day we appealed to the British government) instead of waiting until February 17. If we had made the appeal eight days earlier, Wrong would have been able to tell Acheson, Bohlen and Hickerson, when he saw them on February 19, that all the governments participating in the negotiations other than the United States were prepared at the next meeting of the Ambassadors' Committee to give full support to the amendment proposed by Canada. In that event Wrong might have considered that he could not withdraw the amendment and accept a compromise at least until the matter had been discussed in the Ambassadors' Committee.

Wrong made two errors. The first was on February 8 when he indicated that Canada would be prepared to compromise. The second was on February 19 when he tooksthe initiative in putting forward a compromise. Once he had retreated to a fall-back position it was difficult, if not impossible, for him to press vigorously for our maximum demands when he later learned that we had the full support of all five Brussels treaty powers for these demands. The probable explanation of his two errors was his consistent overestimation of the strength of the opposition to a strong Article 2 (as indicated by his pessimistic messages on January 5, February 7, 21 and 23). His overestimation was probably related to his own lack of enthusiasm for a strong Article 2. Even the most conscientious and able negotiator, and Wrong was extremely conscientious and able, is apt to see more difficulties in the way of a proposal that he is not keen on than he is of one that he is enthusiastic about.

The reason Wrong gave for not pressing our maximum demands on February 19 was that this would increase Acheson's difficulties with the senators. Wrong's task was to get the strongest possible language for Article 2 in order to diminish the difficulties of St. Laurent and Pearson in getting support for the treaty in the House of Commons of Canada and in the country. Whether this increased Acheson's difficulties in getting support for the treaty in the Senate of the United States was relevant only if the additional burden on Acheson would result in his not attempting the task of persuading the senators. Acheson could scarcely have refused to undertake the task if all the other participants in the negotiations had asked him to.

On March 25, a week after the treaty had been made public, Wrong reported that Vandenberg and Connally had "both made emphatic references to Article 2" as had Acheson. Hickerson, years later, dwelt with satisfaction on the statement about Article 2 which, he said, Vandenberg had made during the debate in the Senate on the North Atlantic treaty: "Unless this treaty becomes far more than a mere military alliance, it will be at the mercy of the first plausible Soviet peace offensive."[48]

In his message to Pearson on March 25, Wrong said:

You will I think be interested to know (as indeed you have probably already gathered) that I have yet to see any public statement in the United States about the Atlantic pact from which has been omitted reference to Article 2. Indeed, as we anticipated, Article 2 is being used constantly as one of the principal pillars supporting the view that the treaty is not a military alliance of the old kind and that it is designed to encourage activities on the part of its signatories which lead away from and not towards war. . . . Without Article 2, or with an Article 2 in the meaningless form which we struggled against, there certainly would have been a serious link missing from the chain of arguments now being used in the United States to justify the treaty.[49]

Wrong's message makes clear that Acheson should have been grateful to Canada for insisting on the inclusion of Article 2 in the treaty. He wasn't. Instead, in later years, he poured scorn on the Canadian efforts. Thus in 1966, he wrote,

The plain fact, of course, is that NATO is a military alliance. Its purpose was and is to deter and, if necessary, to meet the use of Russian military power or the fear of its use in Europe. This purpose is pretty old-fashioned. Perhaps to avoid this stigma, Canadian draftsmen had Article 2 inserted in the treaty.[50]

This is all the more surprising since he had, only two years after he had so vigorously opposed the inclusion of Article 2 in the treaty, been converted to the belief that the North Atlantic treaty "was more than a purely military treaty". When he briefed Eisenhower on his appointment as the first commander of North Atlantic forces in Europe, he told him this, and he went on to say that the treaty was "a means and a vehicle for closer political, economic and security co-operation with western Europe".[51]

A natural question to ask of those who pressed hard for the inclusion of Article 2 in the North Atlantic treaty is, what did they hope might be done to give effect to the undertakings in the Article? I can speak only for myself. I set forth my views in a series of confidential memoranda after the treaty was signed; and I summed them up and elaborated on them in a memorandum which I sent to Pearson in July, 1954.[52]

In this memorandum I dealt first with the undertaking in Article 2 to contribute to the further development of peaceful and friendly international relations by promoting conditions of stability and well-being. I knew it had been argued that this meant conditions of stability and well-being not in the world as a whole but only in the North Atlantic treaty area. I maintained that this interpretation was incorrect. The purpose of promoting conditions of stability and well-being was to contribute to the development of peaceful and friendly international relations; and this surely meant peaceful and friendly international relations in the whole world. "It is not only," I went on to say, "that the North Atlantic community cannot be an island of stability and well-being in a sea of tempest and misery. It is also that the more a group of nations such as the North

Atlantic nations co-operate in constructive tasks the more sense of community is likely to develop."

I suggested that the best way for the North Atlantic countries to carry out their undertaking to promote conditions of stability and well-being in the world would be by strengthening the specialized agencies of the United Nations and such other bodies as the International Court of Justice and the General Agreement on Tariffs and Trade. The specialized agencies were intended to be

> the instrument for a comprehensive and varied offensive against poverty, disease, unemployment, ignorance, racial discrimination and denial of freedom and justice. A re-examination of what can be done to make each agency more effective has been long overdue. The North Atlantic countries are an obvious group to undertake such a re-examination. They include most of the wealthier countries of the world. If the NATO countries were to act as a ginger group in each agency, they would demonstrate to the poor and underdeveloped countries their willingness to accept the responsibilities of greater wealth. This would not be a matter of ganging up against the underdeveloped countries but of taking the leadership in making the agencies more effective bodies for promoting the welfare of all countries – the developed and the underdeveloped.

I included in my memorandum some examples of the kind of programmes which the North Atlantic countries might agree to push for in the specialized agencies. They might see to it that the World Health Organization was given sufficient funds, equipment and staff to carry out a programme of virtually eliminating in five or 10 years such diseases as malaria, smallpox, cholera, trachoma and yaws and of making a frontal attack on leprosy, syphilis and tuberculosis. The North Atlantic countries might agree to provide the Food and Agriculture Organization with resources sufficient virtually to eliminate the plague of locusts. The volume of lending by the World Bank could be greatly increased. UNESCO might undertake a concerted programme virtually to eliminate illiteracy in 20 years or so and to establish facilities for basic technical training in countries where secondary education was still a luxury. The North Atlantic countries should also take a new look at proposals ranging from the Special United Nations Fund for Economic Development to commodity agreements. The costs of such programmes would be very high. "But it may well be that the Free World would be safer if all the members of NATO were to reduce their defence expenditures by 10 percent and devote the savings to making international organizations more effective and to helping in speeding up the economic development of underdeveloped countries." (In 1954 a 10 percent cut in the defence expenditures of the North Atlantic countries would have amounted to

$5.6 billion. Since United States dollars in 1954 were worth at least twice as much as dollars 22 years later, this would have been the equivalent in purchasing power of over $11 billion in 1976.)

I then in my memorandum dealt with the pledge by the allies in Article 2 of the treaty to seek to eliminate conflicts in their international economic policies and to encourage economic collaboration between any or all of them. Here my suggestions were numerous and far-reaching.

My first suggestion was that after the North Atlantic countries had completed their campaign to strengthen a specialized agency, they should examine how much farther they, and other like-minded countries, might be prepared to go among themselves in the direction of increased co-operation and pooling of resources in matters within the field of that agency. Perhaps, for example, the North Atlantic countries might be prepared to merge their national meteorological bureaus into a North Atlantic meteorological bureau. In the same way, they might set up a North Atlantic air transport board along the lines of the International Air Transport Board proposed by Canada at the International Civil Aviation Conference at Chicago in 1944; such a board would have the sole right to issue licences for flights from one member country to another and between other countries and member countries. They might set up a joint agency for pressing forward with developing the peaceful uses of atomic energy.

My second suggestion had to do with the international agencies which had been conceived or born whose membership was limited to some of the North Atlantic countries. I suggested that an examination should be made of each of these agencies, especially the European Defence Community, the Organization for European Economic Co-operation and the European Payments Union, to see whether it might not be wise to open membership in it to all the North Atlantic allies and, if so, what changes should be made in the agency either by making the obligations of membership more extensive or less extensive.

A North Atlantic payments union, for example, might have four functions. It might be a forum for reaching decisions on the effect of the domestic monetary and budgetary policies of member countries on their international balance of payments. It might determine either the rate at which the currencies of member countries should be temporarily pegged or the circumstances in which freely floating rates should be temporarily supported by official equalisation funds. It might arrange for the provision of the special funds required to raise the level of international reserves and to operate any international exchange equalisation fund. It might provide machinery for deciding in what exceptional circumstances, if any, a deficit country in the North Atlantic community could temporarily reimpose import restrictions or exchange controls over current payments in order to protect its reserves. (I stated that these suggestions on a

North Atlantic payments union had been made by a leading British economist, J. E. Meade, in a pamphlet, "The Atlantic Community and the Dollar Gap".[53])

Among the other proposals which I recommended was one which both Meade and Barbara Ward[54] had recently made. It was that the North Atlantic countries enter into a treaty under which they would agree to eliminate within a certain period all barriers to trade and current payments between them. This might be extended to the eventual elimination of barriers to migration and to capital movements. On this I said:

> If the North Atlantic nations should agree by treaty that at the end of, say, 15 years there would be complete freedom of movement within the North Atlantic community for capital, goods and people, the immediate effect might be profound. It would give concrete meaning to the goal of the 'political and economic commonwealth' [of the North Atlantic] which Mr. Pearson has referred to. It would also make it easier to secure agreement between the North Atlantic nations on the steps which should be taken to reach that goal. Once, for example, the more prosperous North Atlantic nations are faced with the prospect of eventual freedom of migration within the [North Atlantic] community they will be impressed with the urgent necessity of taking the steps required to raise the standards of living in the less prosperous North Atlantic nations in order to prevent their countries from being flooded by migrants from those countries.

Article 2 of the treaty stated that the allies would "encourage economic collaboration between any or all of them." This meant, I pointed out in my memorandum of July, 1954, that not every ally need participate in every new advance in international co-operation brought about under the auspices of the North Atlantic alliance:

> The North Atlantic nations will not be prepared to move at the same speed to the goal of a North Atlantic political and economic community. It is not desirable that the speed of all be held down to the speed of the most laggard. [Moreover, not every advance need be restricted to members of the alliance.] Ireland, Sweden, Switzerland, Germany, Austria, Australia and New Zealand could be invited to come in on many or most of them. Yugoslavia and Spain could be invited to come in on some. What is required is flexibility and imagination.

I went on to say that the building up of the North Atlantic community could be thought of as the creation of new rights for the citizens of North Atlantic countries – rights which they would possess as citizens of the North Atlantic community. "As time went on and the North Atlantic community matured, the rights which would flow in the NATO area from the status of a North Atlantic citizen would increase." Eventually the rights would include "a right to live and work and, after a short period of residence, to vote in any part of that community".

I ended my memorandum as follows:

> If the sort of programme sketched out above is realized, the North Atlantic nations and their associates will in another decade have become much more closely united not only by treaties and agreements and by the lowering of barriers to the movement of goods, money and people, but from having worked together in constructive causes such as putting new life into the specialized agencies. The time may then have come when a constitutional convention of these countries might usefully be held to examine whether some or all of them might wish to unite under some sort of federal constitution. . . . Up to date, NATO as a security organization has achieved reasonable success. As a body for securing co-ordination of foreign policies it has achieved much less success. NATO has become to most people outside the North Atlantic area a simple anti-Communist military alliance of white, wealthy countries dominated by the United States and pursuing a dangerously unimaginative militaristic policy. There is danger that an increasing number of people in the North Atlantic nations, other than the United States, may come to agree with this dominant outside view. If so the North Atlantic alliance will, before long, go the way of all other alliances. If the alliance is to be preserved it must become more than an alliance. This is the truth which Article 2 embodies.

CHAPTER SIXTEEN

THE UNITED NATIONS

One of the pressures which led to the North Atlantic treaty was the mounting demand in 1947 and 1948 by many leading supporters of the United Nations in the United States, Britain and Canada, that the United Nations be "strengthened" by drastically reducing or even eliminating the veto rights of the permanent members of the Security Council. This demand had resulted from what was considered by most western supporters of the U.N. to be the Soviet Union's abuse of the veto. Those who sought this change knew that the granting of their demand would mean the destruction of the United Nations as a bridge between the Soviet world and the western world. If the Soviet Union were to veto the proposed amendments to the Charter, the western countries could either secede from the U.N. or negotiate with the Soviet block the dissolution of the U.N. The other possibility was that the Soviet bloc would secede and leave the western countries in command of a rump U.N. which they would then convert into a grand alliance against the Soviet Union. In either event the result would probably be two rival international security organizations, one dominated by the western countries and the other by the Soviet Union. Statements by Marshall, Bevin and St. Laurent in the spring of 1948 make clear why their governments considered that such a schism was unwise and unnecessary.

Marshall told the Foreign Affairs Committee of the House of Representatives that if proposals for revising the Charter of the U.N. which would not be accepted by the Soviet Union and a number of other states were put through, the U.N. would probably be destroyed. "The result would be a dispersal of the community of nations, followed by the formation of rival military alliances and isolated groups of states. This result would weaken us and expose us to even greater dangers from those who seek domination of other states".[1]

A week later Bevin sent a message to Marshall saying that he had read this statement with the greatest admiration and that he entirely agreed with it. In his opinion "a treaty based on Article 51 [of the Charter] to which the United States would be a party, would be far the best answer to those in our two countries who are urging a revision of the Charter." "But," he went on to say, "in default of some positive and spectacular move by the [United States] administration it may be that Charter revisionism will endure and prove to be a real difficulty in the future. . . . [I]t is clear that the ultimate conclusion of some world-wide system based on Article 51 to which Mr. St. Laurent has recently drawn attention can only be rendered practicable if the way is prepared by a defence arrangement in the North Atlantic area. It is surely along the road indicated by Mr. St. Laurent that it would be wise if possible to lead our peoples and thus to canalise discontent with the United Nations in the right direction while preserving the centralizing and pacifying functions of a central international authority for reasons so excellently described in Marshall's statement to the Foreign Affairs Committee."[2]

These statements of the three foreign ministers were, it can be assumed, drafted by officials who were advising their ministers to press hard for an effective North Atlantic security pact. These officials had been behind the drive three and four years earlier for an effective United Nations and they still wanted an effective United Nations: Hickerson of the State Department; Gladwyn Jebb of the British Foreign Office; Pearson, Wrong and I in the Canadian External Affairs Service.

The governments which negotiated the North Atlantic treaty had to take account not only of those supporters of the U.N. who wanted to "strengthen" it even if this resulted in a schism in the U.N., but also of those supporters of the U.N. who feared that the North Atlantic treaty would weaken the U.N. by setting up a rival institution. In January, 1949, Wrong, at a meeting of the Ambassadors' Committee, referred to these fears. He spoke of criticisms which were being made in the United States that the result of the North Atlantic treaty "would be to create a second United Nations organization and to substitute its agencies for the present authority and responsibility of the Security Council."[3] Lovett agreed that there were in the United States "opposition groups who felt that a competitor to the United Nations was being set up."[4]

Lovett's worry that supporters of the United Nations in the United States might oppose the North Atlantic alliance because they feared it would be a competitor of the U.N. was reflected in the attitude of the United States representatives in the negotiations to the provisions on consultation in the treaty and on where the headquarters of the alliance should be located. At the Ambassadors' Committee on January 14, 1949, Lovett said that "some of the proponents and supporters of the United Nations feared that the consultative provision of the [North Atlantic] pact constituted a threat to the Security Council. It was important not to carry the provisions of the treaty to the point where it might appear to be a competitor of the United Nations."[5] Hickerson told me just after the treaty was signed that one reason some people in the State Department hoped that the North Atlantic Council would not sit in Washington was that the farther it sat from New York, the less it would look like a rival to the U.N. Security Council.[6]

At least some of the architects of the treaty, notably Pearson, believed that the North Atlantic alliance, as a security organization, was a temporary expedient. They looked forward to the time when the relations between the western world and the Soviet world had so improved that the United Nations Security Council, assisted by its Military Staff Committee, and with forces at its disposal provided under special military agreements, could become an effective security organization. Then the security aspects of the North Atlantic alliance would wither away. While the security aspects were withering away, the political, economic and cultural unity of the North Atlantic community would have been growing within the chrysalis of the North Atlantic alliance. The result would be a metamorphosis of alliance into community, a community which would increasingly acquire the characteristics of a federation.

Acheson never said anything like this but when he gave his support to a proposal that the treaty should be reviewed any time after 10 years he said that he "thought that this provision took away from the treaty the idea that it was a permanent military alliance and came back to the thought that it was an arrangement directed at the particularly unstable state of the world which might be reviewed in about 10 years. The Senators, he said, like this idea."[7]

These various considerations about the future of the United Nations and the relations between the U.N. and the North Atlantic alliance impinged on the discussions in the Ambassadors' Committee on the duration of the treaty. The Brussels treaty was "to remain in force for 50 years"; after 50 years any member could withdraw after giving one year's notice. The Rio treaty was "to remain in force indefinitely," but any member could withdraw at any time after giving two years' notice. The statement in the Rio treaty that it was to remain in force indefinitely is virtually meaningless. How long a treaty of alliance remains effective depends in fact on how many members and which members remain in the alliance. If the United States and other key members were to withdraw from the Rio treaty, it would for most practical purposes have ceased to exist, even though it would presumably remain in force between the remaining members as long as there were still at least two members. One can therefore say that the real duration of the Rio treaty was two years, compared with a real duration of 51 years for the Brussels treaty.

In the draft treaty of March 19, 1948, which I gave to Pearson, I suggested that the treaty have the same provisions on duration as the Brussels treaty subject to the provisions of an article which I had taken from the first article of the Geneva Protocol. This provided that the North Atlantic treaty would lapse once the U.N. Charter had been amended on the lines of the provisions in the treaty.[8] My hope was that the creation of a North Atlantic alliance would in time lead to a world-wide system of collective defence based on Article 51 of the Charter; to begin with this system would supplement the Charter; ultimately it might be incorporated in the Charter.

In the tripartite talks in Washington in March, 1948, Pearson did not put this proposal forward. His suggestion was that the treaty should last for five years and be renewable.[9] Perhaps what he had in mind was that the Charter would have been suitably amended within five years or that the treaty would have been replaced by a treaty of mutual assistance of all the "free states". It is interesting that John Foster Dulles also at one time wanted the treaty to have a term of only five years.[10] The British did not put forward any proposal on duration in the tripartite talks. The United States suggested that the treaty should remain in effect for 10 years and be automatically renewed unless denounced. The Pentagon paper, which resulted from the tripartite talks, spoke of a duration of 10 years, with automatic renewal for five-year periods unless denounced.[11]

No agreement was reached during 1948 on the duration of the treaty. The United States continued to think of a 10-year term, the maximum which the State Department thought that the Senate would accept.[12] The Brussels treaty powers wanted the North Atlantic treaty to have the same provisions on duration as the Brussels treaty. The Canadian commentary of December 6, 1948, stated, "Generally speaking, the longer the initial duration of the treaty the more effective it is likely to be as a deterrent to aggression and as an encouragement to self-help and mutual aid. The treaty might therefore remain in force for, say, 20 or 25 years."[13]

The Canadian government soon had second thoughts on this. The Prime Minister was apprehensive that so long a duration might reduce public support for the treaty in Canada. Pearson told St. Laurent on January 4 that he and Wrong felt that the duration of the treaty should be no longer than 20 years and might be even 16 or twelve.[14] St. Laurent said that he preferred 12 years "If a longer term was accepted, he thought that it would be well to include a provision which would permit the parties to hold a conference in eight or 10 years to discuss whether further continuation of the treaty was necessary to assure international security. . . . Obviously the treaty was now directed towards the Soviet Union, and while this state of affairs continued, it would be politically easy to defend Canadian participation. The world situation, however, may change drastically within a decade."[15]

Pearson modified St. Laurent's proposal by linking a mid-term review of the treaty with a possible strengthening of the United Nations. The review of the treaty at the half-way mark should, he instructed Wrong, be made "in the light of the progress made by the United Nations and its organs in the maintenance of international peace and security".[16] The St.

Laurent-Pearson proposal was accepted and became Article 12 of the treaty.

> After the treaty has been in force for 10 years, or at any time thereafter, the Parties shall, if any of them so requests, consult together for the purpose of reviewing the treaty, having regard for the factors then affecting peace and security in the North Atlantic area, including the development of universal as well as regional arrangements under the Charter of the United Nations for the maintenance of international peace and security.

Agreement on this provision of the treaty made it easier to reach agreement on the duration of the treaty.

In the middle of January, 1949, at the last meeting which Lovett had with the ambassadors, there was a discussion of the duration of the treaty. Lovett said that the soundings which he had so far taken (presumably of Senators Connally and Vandenberg) indicated that the term would have to be what he called moderate – ten or twelve or twenty years – but that the United States had no firm opinion. Wrong said that the period suggested by Lovett was about what the Canadian government had in mind. The Brussels powers had proposed 50 years, but the Ambassadors of the Brussels powers did not press for so long a duration and indicated that they were prepared to compromise. Thus Oliver Franks said that the Brussels powers had proposed 50 years "without too much deep thought. However, the U.K. would not like the term to be markedly shorter than a generation. It would fail in one of its most important aims if it were what people would call a short-term agreement. He would like to see it concluded for at least 25 or 30 years." The Netherlands Ambassador said that the "psychological influence of the pact would be stronger if a period of 20 years could be adopted than if it were for 12 years".[17]

The maximum period suggested by the United States and Canada and the minimum period suggested by the Netherlands was the same – twenty years – and this was not far from Britain's minimum of 25 years. It was not, therefore, difficult to reach agreement that the treaty should have a firm duration of 21 years. This was accomplished by providing that after the treaty had been in force for 20 years, any party to it might cease to be a party one year after it had given notice of denunciation. (Article 13). Since the treaty came in force in August, 1949, it would continue in force for all its members until August, 1970. After August, 1969, any member could leave after giving one year's notice.

One of the problems relating to the U.N. which faced the negotiators of the North Atlantic treaty was whether they should assert that the treaty came under Article 51 of the Charter of the U.N. or under Chapter VIII. Article 51 is the concluding article of Chapter VII, the chapter entitled "Action with respect to threats to the peace, breaches of the peace and acts of aggression"; this is the chapter on sanctions. Article 51 states:

> Nothing in the present Charter shall impair the inherent right of individual or collective self-defense if an armed attack occurs against a Member of the United Nations, until the Security Council has taken the measures necessary to maintain international peace and security.

Chapter VIII is the chapter on regional arrangements; it consists of three articles, 52, 53 and 54.* Article 53 states that "no enforcement action shall be taken under regional arrangements or by regional agencies without the authorization of the Security Council. . . ." The sole exception was measures against any state which, during the Second World War, had been an enemy of any signatory of the Charter.

The North Atlantic treaty was obviously, in important respects, a regional arrangement within the meaning of Chapter VIII. But to state this explicitly in the treaty would mean that Article 53 would apply. The Soviet government could then tell the European states contemplating membership in the alliance that the United States did not mean anything by its pledge of assistance, since the pledge would become effective only after the five permanent members of the Council had voted in favour of the North Atlantic alliance taking "enforcement action"; and the Soviet Union, against which the treaty was obviously directed, could scarcely be expected to vote in favour of enforcement action by the North Atlantic alliance against it. Alternatively the Soviet government could argue that the countries which were negotiating the North Atlantic treaty, while profuse in their declarations of devotion to the United Nations, were creating an alliance based on an intention to violate one of the central provisions of the Charter, namely the obligation of members of a regional arrangement or agency not to take enforcement action without the authorization of the Security Council. This argument was likely to impress many supporters of the United Nations in western countries.

To meet these arguments, Dean Acheson, at the Ambassadors' Committee on March 7, 1949, argued that "there were two concepts which would have to be mutually exclusive, although it would be difficult to draw the line between them. One was collective self-defence – something that could be engaged in at any time without anybody's approval in the event of armed attack. The other concept was enforcement action, which was something done to somebody else not in self-defence." The North Atlantic alliance, he went on to say, would not undertake enforcement action without the authority of the Security Council. The action it would take would be collective self-defence or collective defence.[18]

This was too subtle an argument to be persuasive to the ordinary well-informed citizen in western countries. A simpler and more persuasive

*The text of Chapter VIII is given in Appendix 4.

190

rebuttal of any assertion that the Security Council could veto measures of self-defence undertaken by the North Atlantic alliance or that the taking of such measures would constitute a violation of the U.N. Charter was put forward in the Canadian legal opinion which was circulated to the negotiating group in Washington. This legal opinion cited the statement made by Leo Pasvolsky of the State Department before the Senate Foreign Relations Committee on July 10, 1945, when he was being cross-examined on the interpretation of these provisions in the Charter. (Pasvolsky was the leading United States authority on these provisions.) He said of Article 51: "The word 'collective' relates in part to the regional arrangements. . . ." This meant that nothing in Chapter VIII on regional arrangements impaired the inherent right of collective self-defence undertaken by a regional arrangement. Article 51 was the governing article.[19]

The Ambassadors' Committee at its final meeting agreed to an "understanding" which, while not denying that the treaty created a regional arrangement, recorded the intention of the parties to stress in their public statements the primary purpose of the treaty, "to provide for the collective self-defence of the parties, as countries having common interests in the North Atlantic area", a primary purpose which was "recognized and preserved by Article 51, rather than any specific connection with Chapter VIII or other Articles of the United Nations Charter".*

The architects of the North Atlantic treaty owed a debt to the American republics. If it had not been for their stubborn insistence at the San Francisco conference there would have been no Article 51 in the Charter and it would have been a good deal more difficult to put up a persuasive argument that the North Atlantic treaty was consistent with the Charter.

At the beginning of March, 1949, the Canadian Ambassador reminded the Ambassadors' Committee that the Canadian government had proposed that the governments make a joint declaration when they signed the treaty,[20] and he circulated a draft of such a declaration. Though this declaration was not made, it seems likely that it represented the views of the negotiating governments on the relations between the North Atlantic treaty and the United Nations.

> We, the representatives of the North Atlantic nations, have today signed a North Atlantic treaty which we shall submit to our governments and legislatures for approval. In signing the treaty, we reaffirm our support of the United Nations as the only world organization established to maintain international peace and security and to promote the economic and social advancement of all peoples. We also reaffirm our adherence to the purposes and principles of the Charter of the United Nations.

*The text of this understanding is given in Appendix 3.

The first purpose of the United Nations is to maintain international peace and security, and to that end to take effective collective measures for the prevention and removal of threats to the peace and for the suppression of acts of aggression. It had been hoped at San Francisco that the United Nations might be able to achieve this purpose without delay through the Security Council, on which primary responsibility for the maintenance of international peace and security was conferred. Unfortunately, these hopes have not yet been realized. It is now clear that the Council cannot at present be relied on to take effective action to deal with serious threats to the peace, breaches of the peace or acts of aggression in such a manner as to guarantee the security of all members of the United Nations.

The Charter of the United Nations provides in Article 51 that nothing in the Charter 'shall impair the inherent right of individual or collective self-defence, if an armed attack occurs against a member of the United Nations, until the Security Council has taken the measures necessary to maintain international peace and security.' Recognizing the necessity of uniting our efforts to prevent aggression, it has seemed to us essential to make the present arrangements for our individual and collective security until the Security Council is able to take the measures necessary to maintain international peace and security.

The aim of this treaty is peace. Under its terms the North Atlantic nations will, on the basis of self-help and mutual aid, work together to strengthen their capacity to resist aggression and thus to prevent war.[21]

PART FIVE

THE DOMAIN OF
THE TREATY

CHAPTER SEVENTEEN

MEMBERSHIP

The 12 original members of the North Atlantic alliance were two North American countries (the United States and Canada), one country in the middle of the North Atlantic ocean (Iceland), two of the three Scandinavian countries (Denmark and Norway), the three Benelux countries (the Netherlands, Belgium and Luxembourg), three other western European countries (Britain, France and Portugal), and one Mediterranean country (Italy). The alliance thus included all the countries bordering on the North Atlantic except Ireland which refused an invitation to join. The only two of the original members which did not border on the North Atlantic were Luxembourg and Italy. All of them except Portugal and Iceland had been members of the coalition against Germany in the second world war. Portugal had, during the war, granted defence facilities to Britain in the Azores under the Anglo-Portuguese treaty of alliance of 1373. Iceland had been occupied during the war first by armed forces of Britain and Canada and then by those of the United States.

The original members of the alliance governed all but an insignificant part of the then extensive non-self-governing territories in the non-communist world. All the original members except Portugal were parliamentary democracies. All the original members except Italy and Portugal were wealthy; in 1949 only five countries in the whole world (Australia, New Zealand, Sweden, Switzerland and Venezuela) had as high an income per capita as these members of the alliance. In 1949 one-eighth of the people of the world lived in the 15 wealthiest countries of the world; nine out of 10 of the inhabitants of the wealthiest countries lived in North Atlantic treaty countries.[1] All these countries were inheritors of the civilization of western Christendom derived from Greece and Rome and

Palestine. The North Atlantic alliance of 1949 was an alliance of the white, wealthy, industrialized, western democratic world.

All 12 original members of the North Atlantic alliance were on the list of possible members agreed to by the representatives of the United States, Britain and Canada at their tripartite meetings in March, 1948. The list also included Ireland and Sweden. The memorandum approved on March 24, half-way through the tripartite talks, spoke of three eventual members: "When circumstances permit, Germany (or the three western Zones), Austria (or the three western Zones) and Spain should be invited to adhere to the Brussels treaty and to the security pact for the North Atlantic area. This objective, which should not be publicly disclosed, could be provided for by a suitable accession clause in the security pact."[2] (The British in their message proposing the tripartite talks had recommended that Spain could become a member "when it has a democratic regime.")

In the tripartite talks the representatives of all three governments had at first agreed that Switzerland should be invited to become a member[3] but Switzerland was dropped at the meeting on March 31. "Jebb presented the view of Mr. Bevin that *Switzerland should not be invited* to participate in a conference looking to preparation of an Atlantic security pact, since this would be certain to court a rebuff, but rather should be informally advised that it would be welcome to participate on its own initiative. Hickerson accepted this view."[4] The position with regard to Switzerland remained unchanged during the six-power discussions in the summer. Wrong at a meeting of the Ambassadors' Committee on July 9 "remarked that Switzerland was spiritually and economically a member of the North Atlantic community and that in spite of its traditional policy of neutrality this was worth mentioning." Hickerson "said that State Department thinking had taken this into account, and had proceeded on the assumption that Switzerland might not wish to join at the beginning but would be welcome if she did."[5]

Though the representatives of the United States, Britain and Canada had found it easy to reach agreement in March on the membership of the proposed alliance, it took 11 more months of negotiation before they and France and the Benelux countries were able to reach agreement. There was no difficulty over Portugal, though I hoped there would be; but there was difficulty over some of the other so-called "stepping-stone" countries (Norway, Denmark, Iceland and Ireland). The greatest difficulties were over Italy, and over whether Algeria should be covered by the pledge in the treaty.

Some of the arguments advanced in the discussions on the domain of the treaty were strategic such as the importance of the stepping-stone countries. Other arguments were geographical – the alliance should be strictly confined to the North Atlantic region; or ideological, the member states should be democracies. Other arguments were put in terms of parliamentary and public opinion which in most of the negotiating countries was opposed to the inclusion of non-self-governing territories within the domain of the treaty.

The Stepping-stone Countries

When Hickerson started talking in late 1947 and early 1948 with representatives of the United States Chiefs of Staff about the possibility of the United States giving military guarantees to western European countries, he found that they were insistent that if the United States assumed military obligations in regard to Europe, it had to have dependable lines of communication. It was for this reason that from the outset of the intergovernmental discussions the American representatives contended that it was essential that the alliance include the five stepping-stone countries: Norway (for Spitzbergen), Denmark (for Greenland), Portugal (for the Azores), Iceland and Ireland. Twenty-eight years later Hickerson said that perhaps the Joint Chiefs of Staff of the United States had been wrong in insisting that Portugal be a member of the alliance in order to ensure that the United States had landing rights in the Azores, "but at the time I don't think we could have prevailed against their insistence."[6]

Bohlen on August 9, at a meeting of the Ambassadors' Committee, pointed out that "without the Azores, Iceland and Greenland, help could not be got to Europe [from North America] in significant quantities at all. Furthermore . . . any pact which did not include these areas vital to the defences of North America would fail, at least in part, to meet one of the United States' desiderata [under the Vandenberg resolution] that it must contribute to the security [of the United States.]"[7] About two weeks later Lovett said that there "must not only be a bridge over which help might flow in both directions in case of need, but also a bridge in the sense of a series of land stepping-stones to permit aid to be given".[8] At a meeting on July 8 Lovett had said that "Greenland and Iceland were more important than some countries in western Europe to the security of the United States and Canada." Pearson had concurred.[9]

According to the United States Chiefs of Staff, Greenland was "a major bastion of United States air defense" and could "provide advance bases both for [United States] offensive operations and from which to conduct anti-submarine warfare". Its use had to be denied to any potential enemy of the United States. The Spitzbergen Archipelago of Norway was also of some strategic importance to the United States in the event of war, but it was of greater importance to the Soviet Union, since it could provide the Soviet Union with advance air and naval bases and a position from which to dominate the sea lanes to the Soviet ports in the Barents Sea. It was therefore greatly to the advantage of the United States to deny the Spitzbergen Archipelago to the Soviet Union for military purposes.[10]

In the intergovernmental discussions in July and August of 1948, the French objected "to the treaty including any country in the North Atlantic or western Europe other than the present parties to the Brussels Treaty." Lovett in his letter to the United States Ambassador in Paris at the end of August stated that the French say "they do not want to weaken the existing defense arrangements by commitments for the security of other countries at this time, but it is clear that they do not want others to share in the United States arms pie."[11]

By the end of the summer the French agreed that the formation of the kind of security arrangement contemplated by the six-power talks would be impossible unless the signatories included not only the Brussels powers, and the United States and Canada, but also the stepping-stone countries.[12] This made it possible for the representatives of all the powers to agree to the recommendation in the Washington paper of September 9 that "to be fully satisfactory" a North Atlantic security system would have to provide not only for the security of the United States, Canada and the Brussels treaty countries, but "also for that of the North Atlantic territories of Denmark (especially Greenland), Norway, Iceland, Portugal (especially the Azores) and Ireland which, should they fall into enemy hands, would jeopardize the security of both the European and the North American members and seriously impede the flow of reciprocal assistance between them".[13]

On November 26, the governments of the Brussels treaty powers accepted this recommendation and agreed that Denmark, Iceland, Ireland, Norway, Portugal, and, if possible, Sweden, be sounded out on whether they wanted to join the North Atlantic alliance.[14] On December 24, the Ambassadors' Committee concurred, except for Sweden, which was omitted from their list.[15] Norway was sounded out on December 31, 1948, and the other countries at the beginning of January. All of them except Ireland eventually accepted the invitation. Ireland stated that it could not consider becoming a signatory of the North Atlantic treaty until the partition of Ireland was ended by the union of Northern Ireland and the Irish Republic. In an *aide-memoire* of February 9, 1949, which was given to the State Department, the Irish government said:

Any military alliance with, or commitment involving military action jointly with, the state [Britain] that is responsible for the unnatural division of Ireland, which occupies a portion of our country with its armed forces, and which supports undemocratic institutions in the north-eastern corner of Ireland, would be entirely repugnant and unacceptable to the Irish people. No Irish government, whatever its political views, could participate with Britain in a military alliance while this situation continues, without running counter to the natural sentiment of the Irish people. If it did, it would run the risk of having to face, in the event of a crisis, the likelihood of civil conflict within its own jurisdiction.[16]

Thus Ireland became the only country bordering the North Atlantic which did not become a member of the North Atlantic alliance.

The Scandinavian countries

The countries which negotiated the North Atlantic treaty appear to have taken for granted during the discussions throughout 1948 that Norway and Denmark would wish to become original signatories of the treaty. This is not surprising since it was Norway's fear of the Soviet Union which precipitated the tripartite discussions in March, 1948, and Norway's fear of a Soviet armed attack was shared by Denmark.

They did not have the same feeling about the possibility of Swedish membership, though Sweden was included in the list of possible member countries recommended by the tripartite talks. Indeed, according to Oliver Franks, the British government had never expected that Sweden would be willing to join the North Atlantic pact.[17] The doubts about Swedish willingness to consider joining the pact were reflected in the report of December 24, 1948, which was agreed to by the Ambassador's Committee. This report said that "it was doubtful whether a direct approach should be made to Sweden at this time. It would nevertheless be appropriate for the Norwegian and Danish governments to be informed that, if Sweden wished to become a party, she would be welcome – the Norwegians and Danes being at liberty to pass this information on to the Swedes."[18]

In January and February, 1949, the question of the membership of the Scandinavian countries became complicated by the emergence of a proposal, intitiated by Sweden, for a Scandinavian defence pact composed of Sweden, Norway and Denmark. Membership in a Scandinavian defence pact need not have been incompatible with membership in a North Atlantic pact. Before the tripartite meetings started, the British proposal was for three pacts with overlapping membership: the Brussels pact, a North Atlantic pact and a Mediterranean pact. Britain and presumably France would have belonged to all three; the United States would have been a member of two. Thus it might have been possible to work out an arrangement under which Norway and Denmark would be members of both a Scandinavian pact and a North Atlantic pact. But the kind of Scandinavian pact which Sweden proposed in January and February of 1949 would apparently have precluded this; it would, the Ambassadors' Committee was informed, apply only to the metropolitan territory of an ally and not to overseas territories such as Greenland; Norway would have to stay neutral unless directly attacked.[19] Hickerson said that "what the Scandinavians had been considering was the possibility of a 10-year treaty providing that an attack on one would be an attack on all, with the tacit understanding that during the period of the treaty none of the members would join the North Atlantic pact." At this point in the discussions at the Ambassadors' Committee, Acheson "asked what would be the total effect, including that of propaganda, of having at one and the same time a North Atlantic pact which would include Iceland, a Scandinavian defence arrangement, and a treaty between Denmark and the Atlantic group as regards overseas Danish territories." The Netherlands Ambassador, Van Kleffens, immediately replied that he "was afraid that such a solution would, rightly or wrongly, be construed by Soviet propaganda as a great success for Soviet policy."[20]

If Sweden had been successful in its efforts to create a Scandinavian pact whose members could not join the North Atlantic pact, Iceland would apparently have refused to join the Atlantic pact. Hickerson told the Working Group on January 13 that Iceland had informed the State Department "that the adherence of Norway and Denmark to the [Atlantic] pact would be essential to make it politically acceptable in Iceland."[21]

A decisive factor in the decision of Norway and Denmark to join the North Atlantic alliance, even though this meant that there would be no Scandinavian pact, was their need for arms from the United States to help them build up their defences. At the beginning of January, Norway and Denmark told Sweden that their agreement in principle to a Scandinavian pact was conditional on the United States agreeing to furnish arms to the members of the pact. Sweden apparently said that it could supply arms but, according to the British, Sweden was not even in a position to manufacture fast enough to equip and modernize its own army.[22] The United States made it clear to the three Scandinavian countries that little or no military assistance would be forthcoming if they remained outside the Atlantic treaty.[†]

Portugal

It was with reluctance that Pearson had gone along with the decision reached at the tripartite meetings to invite Portugal to be an original member of the alliance. Just before the meetings took place he had said to Gladwyn Jebb that "if a pact were to be worked out which included declarations of belief in democracy, free institutions, etc., such as were included in the Brussels pact, it would be a little anomalous to have Portugal as an original signatory." Jebb replied that it would be even more difficult to exclude Portugal since bases in the Azores were so important.[23] Pearson had raised the matter again at the tripartite meetings; he "mentioned the disadvantage of including Portugal from the ideological point of view". It was felt, he reported, "that this disadvantage was more than neutralized by the strategic advantage of Portugal's membership in the pact."[24]

Pearson was not the only person involved in the negotiations who found the prospect of Portuguese membership distasteful. In the meeting at the end of April, 1948, between Marshall, Lovett, Dulles and Vanden-berg, "great doubt was expressed as to the desirability" of Portugal being invited to participate in intergovernmental discussions on the treaty.[25] Van Kleffens said at the Ambassadors' Committee on July 9 that he thought that the definition of the countries to be included in the alliance "should be kept somewhat flexible to allow for the application at the same time of the geographic test and a test in the realm of general ideas, some basic conception of society and the value of the individual."[26]

These doubts about the propriety of including Portugal in the alliance were not reflected in the Washington paper of September 9. That paper did suggest, however, that Portugal, and the other stepping-stone coun-tries, might not be prepared to accept the responsibilities of full member-ship and they might therefore be invited to accept a sort of associate membership which "would only involve limited commitments as, for example, to provide facilities for the common defense in return for com-mitments by the full members to defend their territories ..." There might, also, the Washington paper suggested, be a third category of coun-tries: "other nations, not members of the pact, a threat to whose political or territorial integrity would require action by the full members."[27] Lovett called these three categories, "resident members, non-resident members, and summer privileges".[28] Pearson's query at the time was, "Why should anyone take on the commitments [as full members] when they get all the benefits [by belonging to the second or third categor-ies]."[29] The suggestion was quietly suppressed.[30]

Before it had been suppressed I had, encouraged by the hope it held out that Portugal might not be asked to be a full member of the alliance, raised the question of Portuguese membership with Pearson. In a memo-randum at the end of October, I said, echoing language used by St. Laurent in a speech in June,* that the members of the North Atlantic alli-ance should be bound together "not merely by their common opposition to totalitarian communism but also by a common belief ... in the princi-ples of democracy, personal freedom and political liberty, the rule of law and constitutional tradition. These were the common heritage of all the possible members of the North Atlantic alliance except Portugal. "To invite Portugal to become an original member of the Alliance would seri-ously weaken its effectiveness as a basis for mobilizing an effective spir-itual counterforce against Soviet aggression."[31] I did not propose that Portugal should be a sort of "associate member" of the alliance as the Washington paper had suggested. I proposed that the treaty should pro-vide that the North Atlantic council could conclude an agreement with Portugal under which the North Atlantic alliance would receive defence facilities in the Azores. (A few weeks later I drafted this provision as fol-lows, "The North Atlantic Community may, on terms to be agreed

*see pages 137 to 138.

between the [North Atlantic] Council and the state concerned, extend some or all of the guarantees of this treaty to any state whose defence is considered by the Council to be vital to the defence of the North Atlantic community."[32]) Pearson noted in the margin of my memorandum to him, "Surely we cannot insist on the exclusion of Portugal against U.S. opposition."

The United States was able to secure military facilities in Spain even though Spain was not a member of the North Atlantic alliance. Perhaps Portugal would have been willing to grant military facilities in the Azores under a treaty with the United States or under an agreement with the North Atlantic alliance. It seemed to me at the time, and it still seems to me, that this possibility was not adequately explored. The price which the alliance has paid for Portuguese membership has been high; until the Portuguese dictatorship was overthrown, Portuguese membership alienated opinion in Africa and Asia.

Italy
Italy became an original member of the North Atlantic alliance even though the President of the United States didn't want it, the leading members of the Senate Foreign Relations Committee didn't want it, and Britain, the Benelux countries, Canada and Norway were strongly opposed. The main argument advanced against the inclusion of Italy was that Italy was not a North Atlantic country and if it became a member, it would be difficult later to keep Greece and Turkey out; their admission would weaken the alliance by making it less homogeneous; commitments under the treaty would become extended and diffused; and it would be more difficult to use the alliance as a chrysalis for a North Atlantic community. Some governments, including the Canadian, also believed that the admission of Italy would weaken public support for the treaty in their countries.[33] The British kept putting forward another argument, that Italy would demand as its price for entering the alliance far-reaching changes in the Italian peace treaty, in particular the return of some of its colonies.[34]

There are four main reasons why, in spite of this, Italy became an original member of the alliance: Hickerson wanted it; the French government believed that if it pressed for Italian membership it would strengthen its case for having the pledge in the treaty cover Algeria; the other governments did not give in early enough to the French insistence about Algeria; and Acheson succeeded Lovett as the principal United States negotiator. If the governments had capitulated earlier on Algeria the French might have accepted a compromise on Italy under which either the alliance would have made some kind of special arrangement with Italy or the allies would, on signing the treaty, have issued a declaration of their interest in the security of Italy.

I asked Hickerson, 28 years later, why he had pressed so hard for

Italy's admission to the alliance. He replied that he had felt at the time that Italy would probably go communist, despite the victory of the Christian Democrats in the election of April, 1948, if it were left out of a group to which historically and culturally it belonged.

> I think that an Atlantic Community that didn't include Italy would not only be incomplete but contrary to our heritage. . . . I felt that operating bases in Italy would be highly useful. I don't know what we would do with the Sixth Fleet if Italy hadn't been included.[35]

At the tripartite talks, which were concluded just three weeks before the Italian elections, it was agreed that "because Italy, more even than Norway, is now directly menaced", Italy should be invited to become an original member of the North Atlantic alliance if the Prime Minister of Italy "in terms of Italian domestic conditions desired such an invitation."[36] Jebb and Pearson gave their concurrence with some reluctance and after the Communists were soundly defeated in the Italian elections, Britain and Canada decided to oppose Italian membership. The United States also at this time came to the same decision. When Marshall, Lovett, Dulles and Vandenberg met two days after the Italian general election, they all "felt that the inclusion of Italy [in the North Atlantic alliance], unless it had theretofore become a member of the Brussels pact, would be a mistake since it would destroy the natural geographic basis of the North Atlantic area."[37] In the discussion on membership at the Ambassadors' Committee on July 9, Lovett omitted Italy from his list of countries which should be members of the alliance, and he said that if the North Atlantic community went beyond this group, it "would get out of the North Atlantic and begin to get into a mid-European, Near Eastern or Mediterranean group."[38]

France, in the summer of 1948, wanted the Atlantic alliance confined to the Brussels powers, the United States and Canada and it did not want Italy in the Brussels pact. When the French Foreign Minister sent instructions at the end of June to the French Ambassador in Washington on the French approach to the Washington discussions, he said that the French government believed that Italy should belong not to the Brussels pact, but "to another defensive system covering both shores of the Mediterranean and extending to [the] Persian Gulf and [the] northern Iran frontier".[39] When France reluctantly agreed at the beginning of September that the stepping-stone countries should be original members, it did not propose that Italy also be an original member. Rather it suggested that once the United States, Canada, the Brussels powers and the stepping-stone countries had formed a North Atlantic alliance "certain other states, which might be defined as not being 'natural members of the North Atlantic community' such as Sweden, Italy and perhaps western Germany and

Austria, might be admitted under certain prescribed conditions.[40]

While the French at this time held out the possibility of eventual Italian membership in the North Atlantic alliance, the general opinion among the representatives of the other countries in the six-power talks in the summer appears to have been against either immediate or eventual Italian membership. Thus Pearson reported that at the informal meeting of the ambassadors on August 20, the Netherlands Ambassador said "that his government feared that membership in the Atlantic pact might be so widened that certain countries, particularly Italy, would be included which were more of a liability than an asset." His emphasis on the disadvantages of Italian membership, Pearson said, "met with considerable support from others".[41]

At this point Kennan and Hickerson put to Lovett their opposing views on Italian membership: Kennan wanted the membership of the pact confined "strictly to the North Atlantic area"; Hickerson wanted Italy to be an original member of the alliance.[42] Since this difference of opinion could not be resolved, the United States took refuge in an imprecise formula. It said that it preferred that the Brussels treaty powers should take the initiative in solving the problem of Italian relationship to a North Atlantic arrangement; the solution would, however, have to be satisfactory to the United States.[43]

Hickerson was not prepared to leave the initiative to the Brussels powers and on November 22, he sent a message to them, through Spaak, that the United States was strongly in favour of Italy being an original member of the alliance. Since Hickerson knew that one reason the British and possibly other members of the Brussels pact opposed Italy was that they believed that Italy would attempt to make its acceptance of membership conditional on the return to Italy of certain of its former colonies and some revisions of the Italian peace treaty, the message said that the United States would oppose any such attempt by Italy.[44] (The United States had, indeed, already received assurances from Italy that it would not attach any such conditions.[45]) Robert Schuman, the Foreign Minister of France, was thus correct when he stated three months later that it was the United States which first suggested Italian participation in the North Atlantic treaty, laying down certain conditions which the Italians accepted.[46]

This attempt by Hickerson to persuade the Brussels powers to agree to Italian membership in the North Atlantic alliance was unsuccessful. The Permanent Commission of the Brussels powers examined the case of Italy "and when unanimous opinion could not be formed, it was decided the discussion of this country constituted a problem too delicate and complex which it did not seem possible to resolve before [the next intergovernmental discussions in Washington]".[47]

The United States message of support for Italy, sent on November 22,

1948, though it had no effect on the views of Britain and the Benelux countries (as became apparent when the intergovernmental discussions resumed in December), must have encouraged the French to use the Italian question as a means of strengthening their position on Algeria. The French now began pressing for the inclusion of Italy in the alliance and for the inclusion of North Africa in the area to be covered by the pledge in the treaty. The French saw that the inclusion of a purely Mediterranean country in the alliance would make it more difficult for the other countries to oppose extending the pledge in the treaty to cover the south shore of the Mediterranean opposite France and Italy. Wrong conceded this at a meeting of the ambassadors on December 22 when he said, "Canada did not think that Italy should be a full partner in the North Atlantic pact, but if that country should nevertheless become one, there would be a good case on geographical grounds for including the Mediterranean coast of North Africa."[48]

Three weeks later Jebb gave the same interpretation to French policy. He thought that some part of the French desire for the inclusion of Italy could be attributed to a feeling that this would make it easier to extend the pact to cover their North African possessions.[49] Perhaps also, even as early as the end of November, 1948, the French government had concluded that if it pressed hard on both Italy and Algeria it might be able to do a deal under which it would withdraw its demand for Italian membership in return for an acceptance of its demand about Algeria.

The Hickerson message of November 22 to Spaak had been a victory for Hickerson over Kennan but the victory was short-lived. Kennan immediately objected strongly and successfully to Italian membership in the North Atlantic alliance,[50] with the result that by December 24, the United States had retreated from advocating that Italy be an original member of the alliance to proposing a "simultaneous association [of Italy] in some mutually acceptable form with the Brussels and Atlantic Pacts" – association, not membership.[51] Thus by early January the French were alone in pressing for the membership of Italy in the North Atlantic alliance. Britain, the Benelux countries and Canada were strongly opposed. Norway, which was being sounded out on membership, was also strongly opposed.

We in Ottawa thought that the French might be open to argument and on Wrong's advice[52] we instructed Vanier to point out to the French our difficulties over the inclusion of Italy as a full partner in the treaty and to say that our inclination was to agree with the United States proposal that Italy should not be a full member but should be *associated* with the Brussels and Atlantic treaties.[53] (Italics added.) This message evoked from the French a broad hint that they would be prepared to abandon their support for Italy if they got their way on Algeria. Vanier saw Schuman on January 12 and discussed with him both the Algerian and the Italian

issues. On Algeria, Schuman was adamant. The question of Italy, however, was different and the French attitude would not be as intransigent;
the French believed that it was in the common interest that Italy should
be a contracting party; however, he quite realized the implications of this
extension, which might lead to requests from other countries farther
afield. Chauvel, the Secretary-General of the French Foreign Office,
whom Vanier saw immediately after his call on Schuman, complained of
the change in United States policy. He said, obviously referring to the
United States message to Spaak of November 22, that the United States
had been favourable to United States membership "until recent weeks".
He then referred to the statement in the report of December 24 that the
Canadian representatives in the Washington talks, while opposing the
inclusion of Italy as a full member, believed that measures of some kind
would have to be taken to assure Italy that, as part of the western world, it
was not being overlooked. He said that France, after exploring these
measures, might not insist on the inclusion of Italy. This was a matter
which could be settled on a basis of satisfactory guarantees or assurances
to Italy.[54] We repeated Vanier's telegram to Wrong and he presumably
passed the information on to the State Department.

(Two "measures" were at this time being considered by the Ambassadors' Committee. One was that the North Atlantic alliance might make

> agreements with countries situated outside the [North Atlantic]
> area . . . , which in matters of human rights, state and society hold
> views similar to theirs, and whose defence is considered vital to the
> defence of the Parties to this treaty.[55]

The other was that the signatories of the treaty would, at the signing
ceremony,

> solemnly declare that any armed attack on certain countries, the secu-
> rity of which is of direct importance to the countries in the North
> Atlantic area, and notably on Italy, Greece and Turkey (and Iran)
> would be a matter of grave concern to them necessitating immediate
> consultations with a view to deciding what action should be taken in
> the event of the Security Council not immediately taking adequate
> measures to repel the armed attack on any of the countries indi-
> cated.[56])

On the very day that Vanier saw Schuman and Chauvel, the Italian
government introduced a new element into the discussions by formally
requesting in writing that Italy be an original signatory of the treaty and a
participant in the negotiations. Hickerson said that when the Italian
Ambassador presented this request, the Ambassador had said that the
effect on Italy of excluding her from the pact would be very bad: it would
lead to political unrest and create a field day for the communists and left-

wing socialists.[57] It is highly unusual for a government to make a formal written request of this kind of other governments unless it has found out by preliminary informal soundings that the request will be granted. No government likes to have it known that it has been rebuffed, but the injurious effect on Italian opinion of a rebuff lessened the risk that it would be rebuffed. Moreover, Italy may have been assured in advance by officials in the State Department that the risks of being rebuffed were slight since once Italy had made the request for membership, the United States would be able to come out in favour of granting the request. This was our belief at the time.[58] Hickerson and Achilles, however, categorically deny that they suggested to the Italians that they apply for membership.[59]

When the Ambassadors' Committee met on January 14, two days after the presentation of the Italian memorandum, Lovett reiterated his objections to full Italian membership in the alliance; he said that "the opposition to the pact would be magnified if the area were expanded. It would be difficult enough to obtain acceptance for the idea of a tightly knit regional pact, but to expand the area would make the title 'North Atlantic pact' meaningless."[60] This was Lovett's last appearance at the Ambassadors' Committee. Six days later, Acheson took over as Secretary of State.

After what Lovett had said at the Ambassadors' Committee on January 14, it is surprising that four days after that meeting, Hickerson informed the Working Group that the United States was now in favour of the full participation of Italy in the alliance and that leaving Italy out would be politically difficult for the United States. This was the direct opposite of Lovett's statement. Hickerson qualified his announcement by adding that he did not know what Acheson thought about Italian participation and he would want to get his views before going any further.[61]

Hickerson did not wait for Acheson's views before going further. The very next day, January 19, the day before Lovett left the State Department, Hickerson sent a message to Spaak in Lovett's name, stating that the United States wanted full membership for Italy in the Atlantic treaty and explicitly rejecting the alternatives of some form of limited membership for Italy or a declaration by the signatories of the treaty that they would consider an armed attack on Italy as cause for a strong reaction.[62] To make Italian membership in the North Atlantic alliance less unpalatable to Britain and the Benelux countries which did not want Italy admitted to the Brussels pact,[63] the United States declared that it no longer insisted that Italy should simultaneously become a member of the Brussels and the Atlantic treaties; the United States would accept the inclusion of Italy in the Council of Europe as sufficient evidence of close Italian ties with the Brussels treaty countries as to warrant the inclusion of Italy in the Atlantic pact. Three days later the United States Ambassador to Belgium reported that Spaak "now clearly understands that we strongly favor Italy's entrance into [the Atlantic] pact", and that Spaak had said that if the United States feels "strongly that Italian inclusion is essential, he will certainly not oppose this".[64] When the foreign ministers of the Brussels treaty powers met a few days later in London as the Brussels Pact Consultative Council, they all, apart from the French Foreign Minister, took the same line as Spaak. Wrong reported that "even though all the members other than France said that they would prefer that Italy not be taken in as a full member, they would not object to Italian membership if the United States government felt strongly about it."[65]

By this time the Canadian government had reluctantly come to much the same conclusion. It had been in the forefront of opposition to Italian membership but on January 26 we informed the Italian Ambassador to Canada that we did not intend to press further the doubts about Italian membership which our representative in Washington had been expressing.[66]

From January 19 to 24, the United States had been making clear to the Brussels treaty powers that it strongly favoured Italian membership in the North Atlantic treaty. It is therefore difficult to understand why Oliver Franks said at the Ambassadors' Committee only a month later, that he "did not think there had been any clear statement of preference from the United States, ... [and the Benelux countries and Britain] wanted to know a little more definitely what the United States thought." Perhaps Acheson, whose relations with Franks were close, had asked Franks to make this request. In any event, Acheson immediately replied with the clear statement which Franks had asked for; and the statement was the opposite of the messages which the State Department had sent to the Brussels treaty powers in the last day of the Lovett regime and the first days of the Acheson regime. Acheson said, "From a practical point of view, he thought it would be well if the question of Italian membership could be deferred until the treaty had been ratified [since the] United States government would prefer not to have to carry the burden of Italy through the debates in the Senate on ratification." He gave as a reason for opposing Italian membership the very argument most of the ambassadors had been advancing for seven months, that "if Italy were brought in, Greece, Turkey, Iran and other countries might claim to be only slightly removed [from the area in western Europe covered by the treaty]", and he added the Kennan argument against the inclusion of Italy, that it would mean the commitment under the treaty "might become extended and diffused".[67]

The French government had by the time of this meeting on February 25, become so exasperated over the failure of its efforts to have Italy invited to be an original member of the alliance and to have Algeria protected by the pledge in the treaty that it had instructed Bonnet to refuse to agree to Norway being invited to participate in the intergovernmental discussions unless Italy were also invited. (The Norwegian government had asked whether it could be certain of being allowed to take part in the discussions at once if it should decide to ask for an invitation.) Bonnet's ultimatum angered the other participants. Acheson said that the North Atlantic treaty would be ruined if the parties began linking the admission of one country to the admission of another. To refuse an invitation to Norway to participate would be "a colossal blunder"; if the Norwegian Parliament voted in favour of participating and "were told that they could not, he could imagine nothing more catastrophic".[68]

Immediately after this meeting Wrong wired us to say that he believed that the issue was serious and, unless at once resolved by the issuance of an invitation to Norway, might "even affect the fate of the whole project". He therefore recommended that we should instruct Vanier to see Schuman "with a view to Bonnet receiving by February 28 instructions to agree unconditionally to an immediate invitation to Norway". The United States Ambassador in Paris was receiving strong instructions in this sense.[69] Acheson in his message to the Ambassador said that he had stated to Bonnet that he "appeared ready, in order to get Italy in, to run extreme risks over Norway, risks to which he was not entitled to subject all of us and that if the French government insisted on this position I would not take responsibility for the consequences."[70]

Vanier called on Schuman on February 26. Vanier said that while Canada would not oppose an invitation to Italy to become a signatory of the treaty, Pearson felt strongly that France should not demand a decision on the Italian question as a condition precedent to agreeing that an invitation be extended to Norway to participate in the Washington discussions. Schuman's reaction was one of great annoyance with the way the United States had handled the Italian request for membership. In the first place, it was the United States which had suggested Italian participation, laying down certain conditions which the Italians had accepted. That was the reason the Brussels powers had opened the door to Italy. He had not obligated himself in any way to Italy, but he believed that from a military and strategic point of view, it was necessary that Italy be a signatory of the treaty. It meant that the first line of defense would be the Brenner Pass instead of Ventimiglia (on the Italian Riviera, three miles from the French border). He would instruct Bonnet to agree to extending the invitation to Norway immediately without linking it with an invitation to Italy. All he asked was that before the signing of the treaty, a decision should be taken on whether Italy should or should not be invited to take part in the negotiations.[71]

At the Ambassadors' Committee three days later, Bonnet acquiesced in an invitation to Norway, and the Committee agreed that Algeria should be covered by the pledge in the treaty. Before these decisions were taken, Bonnet said exactly what Schuman had said he would be instructed to say, "that if it were decided to send an invitation to Norway immediately, he hoped that he could report to his government that the question of Italy would be discussed soon and that every effort would be made to meet the French position." But before saying this, Bonnet had made intransigent statements: "If [the French government] had to present to the public and the Parliament a pact including Norway and to which Italy would not be a party, not mentioning the question of the Algerian departments in addition, then the French government would have to reconsider its position as far as its own participation was concerned. He had received the clearest possible indications on this question and felt that it would be difficult for his government to secure ratification of a pact signed under such conditions. . . . [He] hoped that conclusions would not be reached which, by including Norway, would exclude France."[72]

The day before the meeting of the Ambassadors' Committee on March 1, Acheson discussed Italy with President Truman and with Senators Connally, Vandenberg and George. (According to Acheson, Marshall and Lovett had not consulted Truman on the question of Italian membership.) Truman said that "he had no final views on the matter; that he wished [Acheson] to talk with the senators, but that he was inclined to believe at present that it would be wiser not to have Italy one of the original signers and possibly not in the pact at all. He would like to consider at some time the possibility of a Mediterranean arrangement . . . [Acheson should] continue to hold the Italian matter open".[73] When Acheson and Hickerson saw the senators later on the same day they found that the senators were likewise not in favour of Italian participation in the North Atlantic alliance. Acheson, in his memorandum on this talk, said:

> The senators were unanimous in their view that the wisest course at present would be not to have Italy an original signatory. They expressed considerable doubt as to the wisdom of having Italy in the pact at all. However, they were maintaining an open mind upon this point. They thought that the presence of Italy in the pact would not be a help in putting it through the Senate, but would probably be a hindrance. The points that they raised were: First, the difficulty which this raised as to the pact's regional character; second, the problems which it raised in regard to Greece and Turkey; third, the problem that with Italy in, Tito might be forced to closer relations with Russia. . . .[74]

Thus, when the Ambassadors' Committee met on March 1, Britain and the Benelux countries were presumably of the same opinion as at the end of January: they would prefer that Italy not be a full member of the alliance, but they would not object to Italian membership if the United States government were strongly in favour of it. The United States was not strongly in favour; rather, the President and the three leading members of the Senate Foreign Relations Committee were inclined to believe that it would be wiser not to have Italy as one of the original signatories of the treaty and possibly not in the pact at all. Acheson, four days before, had taken very much the same line when speaking to the Ambassadors' Committee. The Foreign Minister of France, three days before the meeting of March 1, had stated that he believed that Italy should be an original signatory of the treaty but that all he asked at the moment was that before the treaty was signed, a decision should be taken on whether or not Italy would be invited to take part in the negotiations.

Wrong, believing that the United States favoured Italian accession to the treaty, had told the Italian Ambassador in Washington, just before the ambassadors met on March 1, that Canada had withdrawn its original objections to Italian participation, having come to the conclusion that, on balance, the arguments for were stronger than the arguments against. Wrong's statement could be interpreted to mean not support for Italy becoming an original member of the alliance but for Italy's later accession to the treaty. Wrong had not, so far as I know, received authority to go this far and in his report to Ottawa on his conversation with the Italian Ambassador he said, "I did not, of course, make any final commitment."[75]

At the meeting of the Ambassadors' Committee on March 1,[76] Acheson told the ambassadors that the President and the senators "were entirely open-minded [on the question of Italy] and prepared to discuss and decide the question on its merits and as to whether it was for the best interests of the pact. . . . [The senators] thought that explaining the North Atlantic pact would be more diffucult if a large Mediterranean factor was involved. . . . It was fair to say that at the present time [the President and the senators] did not favor Italy being an original signatory, but were thinking in terms of its accession later."

There is nothing in Acheson's own record of his discussions with the President and the senators to support his statement to the ambassadors that they "were thinking in terms of [Italy's] accession later." What the President had said was that "he was inclined to believe at present that it would be wiser not to have Italy one of the original signers *and possibly not in the pact at all.*" The senators had *"expressed considerable doubts as to the wisdom of having Italy in the pact at all."* (Italics added.)

Acheson told the President the next day that the Netherlands, Belgium and Luxembourg "were now positive rather than merely non-objecting." (What the Netherlands Ambassador had said was, "If there was a unanimous feeling around the table for admission of Italy he would not be found in opposition." The Belgian Ambassador, speaking on behalf of Belgium and Luxembourg, had said that "for political and psychological reasons Italy should not be ignored and its request for admission made some six or seven weeks previously should receive a reply soon". These views were surely closer to non-objecting than to positive.) Acheson told the President that the "British had stated that they would withdraw their objections if the other nations around the table were in favor of Italian inclusion and we thought that at the next meeting the British objection would be withdrawn". (This was correct: the British Ambassador had said that "the U.K. had always thought that on the whole it was better not to have Italy a member of the pact. However ... the strength of that preference had diminished during the progress of negotiations. The U.K. would not stand in the way of a general opinion and would not press its initial preference.") On France, Acheson said that she "was so emphatically in favor of Italian participation that she had stated, and we believed she meant it, that she would have to reconsider her whole position to the pact if Italy was not to be included". Acheson's summary of the situation was that the United States "would find itself in the position of either accepting the European judgment or rejecting it.[77] (There was surely no "European judgment" in favour of Italian membership in the alliance.)

After hearing this report, Truman agreed to the inclusion of Italy in the alliance though he "would have preferred, certainly at this time, a pact without Italy".[78] On March 4, the Ambassadors' Committee agreed to the inclusion of Italy.[79] On March 7, Ernest Gross, an Assistant Secretary of State, discussed the treaty with the Foreign Affairs Committee of the House of Representatives and, according to Acheson, found strong support there for the inclusion of Italy among the signatories. The next day Acheson secured the agreement of the Senate Foreign Relations Committee to the inclusion of Italy.[80]

Acheson was a man of integrity. Yet, on this occasion he appears to have succumbed to the temptation, always present to negotiators, of not being scrupulously careful to avoid misleading one party to a negotiation about the views of other parties. If he had been a fervent believer in Italian membership in the North Atlantic alliance, his giving in to the temptation would be comprehensible, but he was not. He was, no doubt, pressed hard by Hickerson yet he does not seem to have tried to balance this pressure by seeking Kennan's advice.[†] Kennan would, presumably, have advised him to do his best to keep Italy out of the alliance.

The grey eminence in the story is Hickerson. From the beginning, he wanted Italy in the alliance; and whenever he lost the argument within the State Department, he bided his time and returned to the attack. He was forced to agree to a compromise in September of 1948; he won in November, but then had once again to agree to a compromise in December. In the *de facto* interregnum between the Lovett regime in the State Department and the Acheson regime, he committed the United States to strong support of Italian membership. Acheson the next month withdrew this support. Then, presumably under pressure from Hickerson, Acheson managed to convince the President, the senators and the governments of

Britain and the Benelux countries to acquiesce in Italian membership. Twenty-eight years later Hickerson told me that if Acheson had not replaced Lovett, Italy would not have become an original member of the alliance.[81]

The admission of Italy to the alliance made it more difficult to keep Greece and Turkey out. Their admission made it more difficult to use the alliance as a chrysalis for the North Atlantic community. Hickerson wanted Italy in the North Atlantic alliance; and wanted the alliance to be the chrysalis of a North Atlantic community. By attaining his first objective he made more difficult the attainment of his second objective.

Expulsion and Suspension from Membership

John Foster Dulles appears to have been the first person concerned with the intergovernmental discussions on the North Atlantic treaty to suggest that there should be a provision in the treaty for expelling member states from the alliance. At the meeting which Vandenberg and he had at the end of April, 1948, with Marshall and Lovett, Dulles said that the United States should make clear that it was "talking about an association of free peoples" and that the "undertakings" should provide "some method whereby, if [member nations] become Communist, they are automatically stricken from the group".[82] He is not reported as being concerned with what should happen if one of the "free peoples" lost its freedom not by becoming communist but by the coming into power of some other variety of dictatorship. Nor is he reported as explaining how a country could "automatically" be expelled from membership.

No progress was made on this matter during the discussions in the summer of 1948. The agreed Washington paper of September 9 merely stated that the "question of including a provision [in the treaty] for disqualification under certain circumstances of any of the signatories from enjoying the benefits of the treaty requires further consideration".[83] Wrong commented that "the European representatives are now asking their governments to give special attention at the present time to the terms on which participants might be deprived of the benefits of the pact by reason of a fall from grace. Possibly this will not be so easy to settle as they now assume.[84] Wrong was correct in his forecast. The Brussels powers found the task so difficult that their Permanent Commission had to remain silent on the subject in their draft treaty and commentary circulated at the beginning of December.

Meanwhile Wrong and I were trying to work out a provision. I suggested that "a member could be expelled or suspended by a unanimous vote of all the other members."[85] Wrong played with the idea of "an experiment in weighted voting for expulsion of members ... [but] rejected it as complicating what should be a straightforward treaty of not more than 10 or 12 articles". He thought that we might accept a two-thirds vote of the parties for expulsion "in case any party goes too far left for our taste", but he added that one could not be sure about the suggestion of a two-thirds vote until we knew how many member states there would be in the alliance.[86] The commentary which we circulated to the negotiating group in Washington in December was a compromise; it said, "The treaty might provide for the expulsion or suspension of a member by a unanimous vote of the other members or by a vote of, say, two-thirds of all the members." We noted in the commentary that the circumstances under which a member might be expelled or suspended presumably "include the coming into power of a communist-dominated government". By using the word "include" we left open the possibility that there might be other grounds for the disqualification of a member.[87]

When the ambassadors met in December they decided to recommend to their governments that no article on disqualification be included in the treaty. Their Working Group had reported to them that it had discussed various forms of an article on disqualification but that this had proved "difficult to express".[88] In spite of this, Pearson hoped that the issue might be re-opened. In a memorandum to the Prime Minister on January 4, 1949, he said that he thought that on the whole it would be useful to include in the treaty a provision for suspension, to be followed in certain cases by expulsion.[89] Nothing more, however, was heard of the proposal.

The vestigal remnant of the discussion on expulsion and suspension from membership is the second half of Article 8 of the treaty in which the parties to the treaty undertake "not to enter into any international engagement in conflict with this treaty". At his meeting with Senators Connally and Vandenberg on February 3, 1949, Acheson explained why the United States wanted this provision in the treaty. He said

> that we had in mind the possibility that one of these countries might go Communist and some ground should be provided for disassociating them from the pact. ... It was probably a theoretical question since almost the first act of any country going Communist would be to pull out of the pact on Moscow's orders.[90]

At the meeting of the Ambassadors' Committee on February 25, Hickerson said that the provision was intended in a measure as an alternative to an expulsion clause.[91]

CHAPTER EIGHTEEN

ALGERIA

The pledge article in the treaty (Article 5) states that if an armed attack occurs against one or more of the allies in Europe or North America, each of the allies will forthwith give the ally or allies so attacked such assistance as it deems necessary, including the use of armed force, to restore and maintain the security of the North Atlantic area. This article has to be read along with Article 6 which states that for the purpose of Article 5 an armed attack includes not only an armed attack on the territory of any of the allies in Europe or North America but also an armed attack "on the Algerian departments of France. . . ." The words "on the Algerian departments of France" are a monument to a prolonged and bitter argument in the intergovernmental discussions. France insisted on the inclusion of these words to the point of threatening not to sign the treaty if Algeria were excluded from the area covered by the pledge. The other governments wanted to exclude all colonial possessions from the protection of the treaty and they were particularly insistent on not getting involved in any kind of obligation to help France suppress Arab uprisings in Algeria. (When Algeria became independent the reference to Algeria in the North Atlantic treaty became "inapplicable".)[†]

The argument about Algeria goes back to the discussions between Britain, France and the Benelux countries which led to the Brussels treaty. The British and French first proposed that the pledge in that treaty should refer to one or more of the allies being the object of an armed attack, with no limitation on where that armed attack might occur. The Netherlands government objected; it said that the Parliament of the Netherlands would not give its approval to a treaty which committed the signatories to give military aid to an ally whose troops or territories had been attacked anywhere in the world. As a result the pledge of military help in the Brussels treaty was limited to attacks in Europe; if attacks occurred outside Europe the parties would consult.[1]

In the tripartite discussions in Washington in March, 1948, Jebb, mindful of this, "pointed out that the smaller participating countries would probably object if the [Atlantic] pact were to become operative in the event of attacks delivered, for example, in the Near and Far East."[2] It was therefore agreed that "some territorial limitation had to be devised."[3] The formula tentatively agreed on was that the pledge would cover the "continental territory" of any Party in Europe or North America plus "the islands in the North Atlantic whether sovereign or belonging to any Party".[4] This excluded not only the Near and Far East but also Algeria and any other part of Africa. In the six-power talks in the summer, no agreement was reached on the area to be covered by the pledge in the treaty, but the general assumption seems to have been that since the Brussels treaty excluded North Africa from the scope of its pledge the North Atlantic treaty would likewise exclude North Africa.

Perhaps in the summer of 1948 the French government shared this assumption. By November, 1948, however, it had decided to insist on the inclusion of Algeria. It began, presumably as a bargaining device, by proposing that not only Algeria but the whole of North Africa, north of latitude 30° north, should be covered by the pledge. This area included the Mediterranean coast of Egypt, the Suez Canal, the whole of Tunisia, and the north of Libya, of Algeria and of Morocco. The French government succeeded in having this proposal incorporated in the draft treaty approved by the Permanent Commission of the Brussels powers on November 26. The success was only partial, however, since the accompanying commentary stated that "certain delegations" of the Brussels powers preferred not to include Africa in the area covered by the pledge.[5]

When the matter was discussed at the Ambassadors' Committee on December 22, it became clear that these "certain delegations" were the delegations of the Benelux countries. They had been consistent in taking the same line in respect of the North Atlantic treaty as they had taken nine months before in respect of the Brussels treaty. The only support which the French received in the Ambassadors' Committee was from the British – and even the British support was qualified. Oliver Franks said that "while the British government would probably not wish to continue to press for inclusion of all of Africa north of 30° it would want the part west of Libya included." Moreover the "British position was not rigid". This, being interpreted from Franks' language of diplomatic understatement, meant that the British were prepared to compromise on excluding all of Africa except Algeria. Wrong, who also habitually used understatement, said that he hoped that the European commitments could be limited to countries bordering on the North Atlantic. Lovett "thought that it would be a mistake to try to expand the area beyond the basic limit of the homelands."[6] A week before, in a telegram to the United States embassy in Brussels, Lovett had put the United States position more forcefully for the benefit of Spaak. He had said that the United States opposed the inclusion of any African territory.[7]

At the meeting on December 22, Bonnet did not withdraw the French proposal that the whole of North Africa be included in the treaty but his main argument was directed to the necessity of including Algeria. It would, he said, "be extremely difficult for France to leave a part of its metropolitan territory out of the area. Algeria was a part of France and in the same relation to France as Alaska or Florida to the United States." To Lovett's statement that the State Department would have difficulties with Congress if North Africa were included, he countered "that the State Department's difficulties with Congress would be paralleled by those of the French government if Algeria were left out and the North Pole were included."[8]

St. Laurent and Pearson were not impressed by the French argument. They were impressed by the weakening of public support in Canada for the North Atlantic treaty which they believed would result from giving in to the French by including any part of North Africa in the area covered by the treaty. Pearson, in a memorandum to St. Laurent on January 4, said that French North Africa should not be included "as this would give rise to possible colonial difficulties and introduce a new and complicating factor",[9] and after talking with St. Laurent, Pearson telephoned Wrong to instruct him to take a stiffer attitude against the French on this matter.[10] Wrong saw Bérard of the French embassy that night and presumably told him this. In return Bérard told him "that the French instructions were 'adamant' in insisting on the inclusion of Algeria in the area covered by the treaty." Wrong added, "The British, on the other hand, who had previously given mild support to the French position, have now been instructed to support the exclusion of African territory. I am sure that the Americans as well as the Belgians, Dutch and ourselves will continue to oppose the inclusion of North Africa, and there is, therefore, danger of a deadlock."

Wrong, therefore, suggested that we might instruct Vanier to see Schuman or Chauvel at once to urge that the French modify their instructions to their representative in Washington. The British Ambassador was making a similar recommendation to the British Foreign Office.[11]

Vanier saw Schuman on January 12. Schuman said that "it would be quite impossible for any French government to accept the idea of excluding Algeria which was part of metropolitan France, on political grounds of course because no French government could possibly propose this to Parliament, but also on purely strategic grounds because the general defence of France could not be envisaged without the inclusion of Algeria as a base for defensive action as well as for purposes of retreat". (He used the words *pour se replier.*) Vanier said that Schuman added that the Americans, by the interest they showed in North American bases, could appreciate the soundness of this reasoning. Schuman "considered that Algeria bore the same relation to France as Alaska to the United States. It would even be difficult for the government to accept the exclu-

215

sion of Tunisia and Morocco, but that of Algeria quite impossible."[12] The next day, when Schuman was in London, Bevin spoke to him about Algeria, but Schuman refused to budge.[13]

When the Canadian representatives in the Washington talks went to the Working Party meetings on January 11 and 12, they had not seen the telegrams from Paris and London reporting on Schuman's insistence on the inclusion of Algeria. They were therefore surprised by the vigour of the language used by the French representative in putting forward his government's demand. They reported him as having made "some rather rash statements about the complete unacceptability to the French of a pact which did not include at least the three departments of Algeria". They clearly did not believe that when he made these statements he was faithfully repeating the instructions which he had received from Paris. They also reported that the "United States representatives have brought out into the open their two principal objections [to the inclusion of Algeria] – (a) that the inclusion of Algeria would bring up the whole controversial problem of overseas territories, and (b) that their military people are fearful lest the pact might be called into operation in the event of native tribal troubles in these areas." ("Native tribal troubles" indicates an extraordinary failure to foresee the nature and extent of the struggle for independence which broke out in Algeria a few years later. In a subsequent message from Washington, Wrong, in reporting the views of the Pentagon, used the term "native uprisings".)[14]

The united front of the other governments against the French demand on Algeria was short-lived. On the very day, January 12, that Schuman had made known to Vanier the unyielding position of the French government on Algeria, Chauvel instructed the French ambassadors to the countries represented in the Washington talks to make the French position clear to the government to which they were accredited in the hope that the governments would issue new instructions to their ambassadors in Washington.[15] To ease the position of the other governments, the French government now formally withdrew from its maximum demand that Tunisia and Morocco also be included under the pledge, and insisted only on the inclusion of the three departments of France in Algeria. At the Ambassadors' Committee on January 14, the French Ambassador "emphasized the seriousness with which his government regarded the question of Algeria. France did not see how a pact could include part of the Arctic regions and the northern part of Canada without including the three departments of Algeria which were a part of France." The Netherlands and Belgian Ambassadors indicated their support for the inclusion of Algeria.[16] The British Ambassador said that his instructions were that if the United States were to accept the inclusion of Algeria, his government would be glad and would support its inclusion.[17] The opposition to the French demand on Algeria now consisted only of the United States and Canada.

Wrong, in reporting this to Ottawa, said that there seemed no doubt, when one examined all the information which we had from Washington, London and Paris, "that the French are not prepared to budge in this matter, even to the point of sacrificing the treaty . . . . In my judgment the inclusion of Algeria would make no real difference in the operation of the treaty, although it might add an undesirable ground for public criticism of its provisions."[18] We replied three days later that we would be prepared, although reluctantly, to accept the inclusion of the three departments of Algeria, but that we still hoped that the French would make some concessions on this point.[19] By January 24 the State Department had also moved to this position. Achilles told Stone on that day "for his own very private ear that the United States will swallow Algeria." In turn, Stone told Achilles – for his own very private ear – that Canada would also swallow Algeria, and asked him if he had any idea when the United States would make a move to take the French out of their misery. Achilles said that for various reasons they wanted to let this question hang in the balance for as long as possible.[20] The United States let the issue hang in the balance for another five weeks.[21]

Why the United States should want to let the question of Algeria hang in the balance as long as possible is not clear. At the end of January a deal might have been arranged with France under which France would have agreed that if the three departments of Algeria were included in the area covered by the treaty, France would not insist on Italian membership in the alliance. A deal consummated then would have made unnecessary five weeks of unpleasant debate between the United States and France. In the course of this debate, the French government became intransigent not just on Algeria but also on full membership for Italy.

There are a number of possible explanations of the gap between the decision which the State Department made some time before January 24 to agree to the French demand on Algeria and the announcement of that decision on March 1. Acheson, who took office on January 20 and was not able to read the papers on the negotiations until January 29, may not have agreed with the State Department's decision on Algeria. Perhaps he agreed with the decision but knew that it would be unpopular in the Senate and therefore decided not to commit the United States administration until he had secured the concurrence of the Senate Foreign Relations Committee or at least of Connally and Vandenberg. But since the inclusion of Italy was also unpopular in the Senate, he would have had less difficulty with the senators over Algeria if he had told them, as he probably could have at the beginning of February, that if they swallowed Algeria they might not have to swallow Italy. It may be that those officials in the State Department who wanted Italy in the alliance managed to arrange that France was not told about the State Department's decision on Algeria until it was too late to make a deal with France under which it would withdraw its support of Italy in return for getting its way on Algeria.

Gladwyn Jebb was of the opinion in mid-January, 1949, that the French wanted Algeria in the area covered by the pledge because they were "intent on getting support against some possible nationalistic uprising in North Africa."[22] France did not succeed in getting a pledge from its North Atlantic allies to come to its assistance if it faced an Arab rebellion within Algeria. It did succeed in getting a pledge of assistance if the Algerian departments of France were invaded by Arab armed forces. If such an invasion took place, each of the allies was pledged to take "such action as it deems necessary, including the use of armed force, to restore and maintain the security of the North Atlantic area." It was likely, however, that countries which had opposed the inclusion of Algeria in the area covered by the pledge would argue that the invasion of Algeria by Arab armed forces did not endanger, to any marked degree, the security of the North Atlantic area; and that consequently they would not deem it necessary to give France much, if any, assistance in its efforts to restore and maintain that security by repelling the invasion. By skilful diplomacy, France had won a victory on the Algerian issue but the victory did not have much substance.

PART SIX

CONCLUSION

CHAPTER NINETEEN

DISAPPOINTMENTS AND FRUSTRATIONS

In the preface to this book, I said that when I look back on the part which I played in the making of the North Atlantic treaty I find myself echoing what Dean Acheson said of his years in the State Department: "Yet an account of the experience, despite its successes, inevitably leaves a sense of disappointment and frustration, for the achievements fell short of both hope and need."

My chief disappointment about the results of the negotiations on the treaty was that the non-military provisions of the treaty were weaker than what I hoped for and what I believed were needed. I wanted comprehensive provisions on economic, social and cultural co-operation and the promotion of democracy within the member states. I did not want Portugal and Italy in the alliance or to have the pledge in the treaty cover Algeria. I wanted a North Atlantic parliament. I wanted the members of the alliance to agree to refer to the International Court of Justice all disputes between them over existing legal rights. I wanted the treaty to make clear that the military organs of the alliance, in peace and in war, were responsible to the North Atlantic Council. I wanted the treaty to be couched in the form of a constitution for the North Atlantic community – albeit a rudimentary constitution – and to be written in language capable of inspiring the citizens of the member states, just as the Declaration of Independence and the United States Constitution had been a constant source of inspiration for generations of Americans. This meant, in my opinion, that the treaty should be written in the name of the people of the North Atlantic community, and that the language should be forceful, simple and direct. I wanted the treaty to be a long first step in the direction of a close union of the North Atlantic countries.

The treaty included provisions on economic and social co-operation and on the promotion of democracy, though these provisions were not as far-reaching as I wanted them to be. The language of the treaty went some way to meet my wishes. For the rest, my efforts were abortive either because of opposition within the Canadian group which was directly concerned with the negotiations or because of lack of support or opposition from the other countries participating in the negotiations.

I have told the story of the controversies over Article 2, Portugal, Italy and Algeria. It remains to tell the story of what happened to proposals relating to a North Atlantic parliament, the International Court of Justice, the relationship between the military organs of the alliance and the North Atlantic Council and the language of the treaty.

North Atlantic Parliament

In my draft treaty of March 19, 1948, which I gave to Pearson, I proposed that the treaty establish an Atlantic parliament consisting of representatives of the member states. The Atlantic parliament would have the same sort of powers of discussion and recommendation in its field as the General Assembly of the U.N. had in its field. The article on this in my draft treaty stated, "The Parliament may discuss any questions or any matters within the scope of this treaty or relating to the powers and functions of any organs provided for in this treaty and may make recommendations to the Atlantic nations or to the [North Atlantic Council] or to both on any such questions or matters."

There might have been a good chance of my securing the immediate acceptance of this proposal by the Canadian government if I had not made the mistake of accompanying it with a proposal which was not only revolutionary but sounded even more revolutionary than it in fact was. I proposed that the parliament should have power by a two-thirds majority to adopt conventions on the questions or matters on which it could make recommendations and that these conventions would be binding on all the member states when ratified by two-thirds of them.[1] I suggested as a basis of discussion that in a parliament of a 100 members the United States would have 40 members, Britain 18, France 14, Canada six, the Netherlands and Belgium five each, Sweden four, Norway, Denmark and Ireland two each, and Luxembourg one.[2][†] The effect of requiring a two-thirds vote of both the members of the parliament and of the member states would be to make it difficult for legislation to become effective unless it had general support throughout the whole North Atlantic community. The United States, if 34 of its 40 members voted against a convention, could prevent its adoption. The representatives of Britain and France in the parliament would, if they voted as a bloc, need the support of only two representatives from other countries to prevent the adoption of a convention. If Britain and Canada were united, they would need only 10 more votes. The five smallest countries could block the coming into force of a convention. I said to Pearson that my suggestions on voting made "a clean break with the old issues of 'veto' and 'unanimity'. The United States would in fact have a veto but it would be a logical and defensible veto."[3]

I very soon gave up hope that it would be possible to secure agreement on giving an Atlantic assembly power beyond that of making recommendations. (Pearson had changed the term "parliament" to "assembly" since he felt that "parliament" might have too much of an Anglo-Saxon flavour for western Europeans.) But Hume Wrong in Washington and Norman Robertson in London still thought that this was going too far. In mid-November in a memorandum to the Prime Minister[4] I said,

> Mr. Wrong . . . fears that the State Department might interpret a suggestion from us that a 'North Atlantic Assembly' be established as indicating that we are thinking in terms of the new North Atlantic organization as a federation or quasi-federation and not simply as an alliance and this might frighten the Americans away from the whole project. (He and Mr. Robertson have much the same objection to the suggestion that the new organization be called the 'North Atlantic Community'.) Alternatively, Mr. Wrong fears that, if the United States administration accepted the proposal for a 'North Atlantic assembly', this might endanger ratification of the treaty by the United States Senate. Mr. Robertson feels that the creation of a North Atlantic assembly might give the impression that the powers signing the North Atlantic treaty are trying to sponsor an alternate world organization to the United Nations.

In reply to Wrong's argument that a proposal to establish a North Atlantic assembly might frighten the Americans away from the whole project, I said that "with public opinion in the United States moving as fast as it has been for the last eight years, we should not reject the possibility that large and influential sections of the United States public might welcome enthusiastically the inclusion in the North Atlantic treaty of a provision setting up a North Atlantic assembly, and that instead of criticizing their government for going too far they might criticize it for agreeing to a treaty under which the powers of the assembly were narrowly limited to the making of recommendations."

To meet Robertson's argument, I said that the Prime Minister had, in a number of speeches since September, 1947, expressed the hope that the creation of the North Atlantic alliance would be followed by the creation of other regional security organizations and ultimately of an organization of all the free states. It was surely inevitable that if the Soviet Union continued to paralyze the work of the U.N. these organizations would do much of the work which we had three years before hoped the U.N. would

221

do. We had, therefore, "been in effect sponsoring a world organization which, if not an 'alternate' to the U.N., is a supplement to it". This, I said, seemed to me to be indeed the core of the thesis which the Prime Minister had put forward at the U.N. General Assembly the previous year.

My arguments were unavailing. Wrong said, "I see no useful role for 'a deliberative body'. Surely the [North Atlantic] Council ought to deliberate as well as decide. We have too many international agencies already." [5] Pearson decided that to include in the North Atlantic treaty provisions for an Atlantic assembly "at this time might provoke unnecessary controversy and discussion though some development of this sort may ultimately be desirable".[6] The proposal was deleted from the Canadian commentary.

Twenty-seven years later, Elliot R. Goodman in his book, *The Fate of the Atlantic Community*, wrote,

> As time has demonstrated, there was an obvious need for a NATO parliamentary assembly, but when the NATO treaty was drafted in 1949 no one had the foresight to give it a 'parliamentary coiffure.' In retrospect, the sense of commitment generated by the founding of the Atlantic alliance would have easily allowed a clause providing for a parliamentary assembly to have been inserted in the Treaty of Washington. But the chance was missed. . . .[7]

Perhaps Elliot Goodman is right and Canada could easily have got an article in the North Atlantic treaty establishing a North Atlantic parliamentary assembly. I thought at the time that we could have got it in, though I did not assume that the task would necessarily be easy, but I failed to persuade the Canadian government to put the proposal forward.

A North Atlantic assembly was established in 1966. It grew out of a "NATO parliamentarians conference" which had been established eleven years before. But at present (1976) the assembly has few of the attributes of the kind of assembly which I had hoped in November, 1948, might be established by the North Atlantic treaty. Its committees discuss the problems of the alliance throughout the year and the assembly itself meets once a year and makes recommendations to the Secretary-General of NATO who, after consultation with the North Atlantic Council comments on them. But it has never received the formal consultative status which it has sometimes asked for and it is clear that the North Atlantic Council regards the assembly not so much as a body competent to make recommendations to it on the policy of the North Atlantic alliance but rather as "a link between member parliamentarians and the alliance." The Atlantic Declaration adopted at the meeting of the North Atlantic Council in Ottawa in June, 1974, declared that the governments of the member states of the North Atlantic alliance recognized "that the cohesion of the alliance has found expression not only in co-operation among their governments, but also in the free exchange of views among the elected representatives of the peoples of the alliance" and accordingly declared "their support for the strengthening of links among parliamentarians".[8]

The International Court of Justice

There are two types of disputes between states: a justiciable dispute is one between two or more states over what are their existing legal rights; a non-justiciable dispute is one over what changes, if any, should be made in their existing legal rights. France and Canada proposed that the North Atlantic treaty should include an undertaking by the parties to refer all justiciable disputes between them to the International Court of Justice. (The Brussels treaty made it possible for the parties to maintain whatever reservations they had already made to their acceptance of the optional jurisdiction of the Court.) France also proposed that the treaty should give the North Atlantic Council power to act as an agency for the conciliation and peaceful settlement of non-justiciable disputes between the parties to the treaty.

Drafts of the preamble of the treaty being considered in the negotiations referred to the determination of the parties to the treaty to "safeguard the freedom and the common heritage and civilization of their peoples, founded . . . [among other things], on the rule of law between nations."[9] In our commentary of December, 1948, we said that the acceptance of our proposal about the International Court "would be a useful demonstration of the belief of the signatory states in the rule of law among nations". It would also, we believed, contribute to the positive and moral content of the treaty.[10]

The inclusion in the treaty of an obligation to submit all justiciable disputes between the parties to the International Court would have been in accord with the then contemplated policy of the Canadian government on the International Court. In June, 1948, St. Laurent had informed the other Commonwealth governments that the Canadian government was proposing to make a new declaration accepting the optional clause of the Statute of the Court without reservations, and inviting their comments.[11] (The Canadian government did not, however, go through with this.)

The proposals on justiciable and non-justiciable disputes were rejected. Wrong explained why they would be in a message at the beginning of January, 1949. He said that the British had been instructed to oppose the addition of an article dealing with the peaceful settlement of disputes between the parties, and that the State Department was also strongly opposed. The State Department, he said, considered that such an article would only be window-dressing, since those who would participate in the treaty would, on their record, be sure to adopt means of peaceful settlement in any case. (Even for the original members of the North

Atlantic alliance this was an unrealistic assessment. Britain and Iceland have been slow to adopt peaceful means for settling their disputes over the cod fisheries. Two of the later members, Greece and Turkey, have likewise been slow to adopt peaceful means for settling their disputes over Cyprus and oil rights in the Aegean.) In his message Wrong went on to say that the State Department believed that it would get into interminable legal arguments on the drafting if it were agreed in principle to include an article dealing with the peaceful settlement of disputes between the parties.

> There is no possibility that the others will agree to drop their reservations to the jurisdiction of the International Court, not so much because they are wedded to the reservations as because the proposal raises difficult legal issues not germane to the central purposes of the treaty.

Wrong therefore asked for authority to discontinue our support for the proposal.[12]

Wrong received this authority and the French were likewise authorized to withdraw their support of the two proposals they had made. When the French announced this at a meeting of the Working Group in January, "Hickerson gave it as his view that the dropping of these two matters meant that the negotiations, in view of the difficulties which they anticipated with both their legal advisers in the State Department and the people in Congress, had been shortened by approximately one month."[13]

In the summer of 1956, when Pearson was chairman of the Committee of Three on non-military co-operation in NATO, he put the two abortive proposals of 1948 and 1949 before the Committee, the Franco-Canadian proposal on justiciable disputes, and the French proposal on non-justiciable disputes. The report of the Committee of Three was silent, however, on the reference of justiciable disputes to the International Court of Justice. On non-justiciable disputes it recommended that those of an economic character might first be referred to the appropriate specialized economic organization. All other non-justiciable disputes between members of the alliance which had not proved capable of settlement directly should be submitted "to good offices procedures within the NATO framework before resorting to any other international agency". The Secretary-General of NATO should be empowered "to offer his good offices informally at any time to the parties in dispute and with their consent to initiate or facilitate procedures of enquiry, mediation, conciliation or arbitration."[14] The North Atlantic Council approved of these recommendations.

The Military Organs of the Alliance

In my memorandum to the Prime Minister in mid-November, 1948, I recommended that in the commentary to be circulated to the negotiating group in Washington we should insist that

> The Supreme Commander, if another war should occur, must not be appointed, as in the last war, by the United States and the United Kingdom, but must be appointed by a council on which all the states concerned are represented. We have recently learned that top United States and United Kingdom military people assume that, in the event of war, the Supreme Allied Command and the various subsidiary commands would be responsible to the Anglo-American Chiefs of Staff and they in turn would be responsible to the United States and United Kingdom governments. It seems to me of the greatest importance that we should, as soon as possible, and as firmly as possible, make clear to the Governments of the United Kingdom and the United States that, while we accepted during the last war a similar arrogation of power by the Big Two or the Big Three, we are not prepared to accept it either now, in peacetime planning to prevent war, or, if war should break out, in the conduct of that war.[15]

The Canadian commentary of December 6 went some way to meet my wishes. It said:

> The treaty could be based on the principle of a pooling of risks, of resources, and of combined control over policy and establish a constitutional basis for the collective organization of defensive power in peace and for the devolution of power in war from the members of the alliance to its organs and agents.[16]

Our draft treaty of December 17 contained a provision that in "the event of hostilities arising in consequence of the application of this treaty, the [North Atlantic] Council shall perform the functions of the Supreme War Council of the North Atlantic Community."[17] Wrong does not appear to have submitted this proposal to his colleagues and the treaty, as adopted, did not establish a constitutional basis for devolving military power in peace and war from the members of the alliance to its organs and agents.

The Language of the Treaty
The Brussels treaty was written in traditional form and language. The preamble first listed the heads of state of the signatory countries. Then followed a list of the objectives of the treaty cast in the form: "Resolved to reaffirm ... ; to fortify ... ; to strengthen ... ;" etcetera. The preamble concluded with the names and titles of the plenipotentiaries who were signing the treaty. In the body of the treaty the member states were called "High Contracting Parties" and the treaty was called "the present Treaty". The alliance created by the treaty was not given any name.

From the beginning of the negotiations on the North Atlantic treaty I urged that the treaty should be written in modern form and in as simple language as possible, and I succeeded in getting into the Canadian commentary a plea "that the treaty should be easily understood", "that it should, if possible, be drawn up in such a way as to strike the imagination of the public and kindle their enthusiasm" and that every effort should be made "to draft the treaty in simple, clear and unambiguous language avoiding 'officialese' and pedantic terms which might create an unnecessary bar to understanding."[18]

We had some success in these efforts. The treaty contains no list of the heads of state of the signatories and no list of the names and titles of the plenipotentiaries. There is no statement that the plenipotentiaries had "exhibited their full powers found in good and due form" and that they had not only signed the treaty but had "affixed thereto their seals". The treaty was called "this treaty", not "the present treaty". Each article, apart from Article 5, consisted of only one paragraph.[†]

I proposed that the preamble consist of two parts as in the Charter of the U.N. The first part would be a declaration in the name of the people of the member states. The second part would be an undertaking by their governments. The draft of the preamble which I prepared before the first discussions in March, 1948, reads as follows:

We the people of the Atlantic Community reaffirm our faith in those human rights and fundamental freedoms which are a bulwark against both internal tyranny and external aggression. We believe in the worth and dignity of the individual man, woman and child. We are determined to preserve and strengthen the principles of parliamentary democracy, personal freedom, and political liberty which are our common heritage. With this aim in view, we intend to strengthen progressively the political, economic, social and cultural ties which already unite us. We shall work together loyally in order that we may by our joint and sustained efforts create in the Atlantic Community a firm basis for a free and united world, a world in which men may live out their lives free from fear and from want and with liberty of thought and of worship. We shall assist each other as good neighbours, in accordance with the Charter of the United Nations, to create and preserve peace and security for all nations and economic and social justice for all men. We know that divided we may fall, one by one, before the forces of totalitarian tyranny working within and without our borders. United we can preserve our freedom and our peace. Therefore we unite. With God's help we shall prevail. And our governments have agreed to this Treaty of the Atlantic and do hereby establish the Atlantic Community whose member states shall be known as the Atlantic Nations.[19]

When after 10 months of negotiations it became clear that the preamble would have to be briefer, Russell Hopkins, the legal adviser of the Department of External Affairs, and I with assistance from some of our colleagues in the Department, worked out a second draft of the preamble. This was shorter but along the same lines.[20] While this draft was not formally approved by the Canadian government, the government gave its blessing to this kind of preamble. The Canadian commentary stated that the preamble might set forth in a number of short sentences the

> common belief of the signatories in the values and virtues of their common civilization and their common determination to work for the promotion of their mutual welfare and the preservation of peace. The preamble could also make clear that the contracting states are uniting their strength not for the purpose of waging war but for the purpose of preventing war and that the aim of the treaty is peace. . . . The preamble might . . . be written in the name of the people of the North Atlantic nations and not in the name of the contracting states.

The preamble finally agreed to went only part way to meet our wishes. It did set forth the purposes of the treaty in a number of short sentences but it was written in the name of the contracting states, not of their people. It reads as follows:

> The Parties to this treaty reaffirm their faith in the purposes and principles of the Charter of the United Nations and their desire to live in peace with all peoples and all governments. They are determined to safeguard the freedom, common heritage and civilization of their peoples, founded on the principles of democracy, individual liberty and the rule of law. They seek to promote stability and well-being in the North Atlantic area. They are resolved to unite their efforts for collective defence and for the preservation of peace and security. They therefore agree to this North Atlantic treaty.[†]

What was especially disappointing to me was that the treaty did not in the preamble or elsewhere establish an organization to be known as the North Atlantic community. The North Atlantic community had existed for generations and I wanted the treaty to make clear that it was giving that community an organization and a constitution. I was not able to commit the Canadian government to this. I was able only to get into the Canadian commentary a suggestion that one of the possible names for the international security organization established by the treaty was North Atlantic community; the other possible names suggested in the commentary were the North Atlantic alliance or the North Atlantic union. The French titles which we suggested were "La Ligue de l'Atlantique Nord" or "L'Alliance de l'Atlantique Nord," or "L'Union de l'Atlantique Nord."

Our failure to get the words "North Atlantic community," into the treaty was all the more surprising since Acheson realized the relationship between the treaty and the community. In the national radio address which he gave the day the treaty was published, he said:

The really successful national and international institutions are those that recognize and express underlying realities. The North Atlantic community of nations is such a reality. . . . The North Atlantic treaty which now formally unites [the North Atlantic powers] is the product of at least 350 years of history, perhaps more. . . . North America and western Europe have formed the two halves of what is in reality one community. . . .[21]

The failure to give a name to the security organization established by the treaty has led to confusion. The treaty created an alliance, the North Atlantic alliance. After the outbreak of the Korean War the alliance created an integrated defence system which became known as the North Atlantic Treaty Organization or NATO. It is possible to leave NATO but to remain in the alliance – which is what France did in 1966. The distinction between the North Atlantic alliance and NATO would have been clearer if the treaty had said that it created a North Atlantic alliance, or community or union.

Looking back now on the intergovernmental discussions from a distance of 28 years I see that I would have suffered fewer disappointments and frustrations and accomplished more if I had played my cards better. I should not have disclosed that my ambitions for the North Atlantic alliance were so far-reaching. This aroused opposition. I should not, for example, have put forward a proposal that the North Atlantic parliament should have legislative power. I should have used less emotionally charged language in my communications. Pearson wrote many years later that I had striven "so long and with an almost feverish and single-minded intensity to bring into being the perfect North Atlantic treaty."[†] I would have been more effective if I had not given the impression that my intensity was almost feverish.

Hume Wrong and Norman Robertson took me to task for the language of the draft commentary and the draft treaty which I sent them in November, 1948, for their comments. Wrong said:

Put the ideology of the treaty in the preamble where it belongs (as is done in the Brussels treaty) and let the rest be put in as direct language as we can find, without frills or use of phrases such as North Atlantic Community, North Atlantic Assembly, or free world in capitals. Some of your phraseology seems designed to establish a semi-commitment to set up a super-state. Nothing would more surely bring about the rejection of the whole project by this country.[22] . . . "We are making an alliance, not a federation.[23] . . . I am most anxious that we should stick to the central purpose in these negotiations, which is, put bluntly, the creation of a military alliance encircling the North Atlantic. The numerous omissions I suggest [from the draft commentary] are designed to avoid confusion of the issue and to facilitate rapid negotiation. If we pushed hard for all the proposals in your draft, we would secure no support at all in many cases, and the greater the support we got for some of them the more protracted would the negotiation be. If we put forward a project like your draft treaty and it was seriously considered, the negotiation would last at least until midsummer.[24]

Many of Robertson's comments on my draft of the commentary were caustic.

In general, I think that your paper is written in larger language than is appropriate or required. I see no need for rhetoric in a secret working paper for circulation to governments which, when they meet together, will have already agreed on the main objectives of a North Atlantic regional defence pact. Specifically I would cut out all the three-decker phrases . . . most of the double-barrelled ones, and any remaining echoes from the Anglican prayer book. . . .[†] I can see no point in trying to work in sub-crusades for basic English and simplified spelling with the principal object of getting the countries around the North Atlantic to combine their strength for their security.[25]

(I had never recommended the use of basic English or simplified spelling in the treaty. Robertson's exaggeration was the product of exasperation, and of his recollection that I had succeeded in getting basic English into some of the articles in the convention establishing the International Civil Aviation Organization.)

The difference of opinion between Wrong and Robertson on one side and me on the other was, of course, not primarily a difference of opinion over whether or not to use emotionally-coloured words. It was a difference of opinion over the nature of the treaty. Robertson believed that when the governments met in the third stage of the negotiations in December they would already have agreed on the main objectives of the North Atlantic treaty. I did not believe this. I believed that they would have agreed on the main military objectives, but not on the main non-military objectives. Wrong believed that we were making an alliance not a federation. I believed that we were making an alliance which would be the foundation of a federation.

There would have been a better chance of my getting more of my views into firm instructions to Wrong in Washington if Pearson had been in Ottawa between the ending of the second stage of the intergovernmental discussions on September 10, 1948, and the opening of the third stage three months later, because Pearson and I shared the same general approach to the treaty as providing a rudimentary constitution for the North Atlantic community. Unfortunately Pearson was in Paris heading the Canadian delegation to the General Assembly of the U.N. for most of this period.

It was during this period that my colleagues and I in the Department of External Affairs were drafting four documents on the North Atlantic treaty. One was a memorandum to Cabinet setting forth the main lines of the instructions to the Canadian representative in the Washington talks. This was approved by Cabinet on December 1. The second was a commentary on the Washington paper of September 9; the final draft dated December 6 was circulated to the participants in the Washington talks on December 14. The third was a letter to be sent by Pearson to Wrong supplementing the views set forth in these two documents for his "information and guidance during the forthcoming discussions".[†] The fourth was a draft treay. In preparing these documents I was assisted by Russell Hopkins, George Ignatieff, and G. G. Crean.

During most of the time we were drafting these documents, Brooke Claxton, the Minister of National Defence, was Acting Secretary of State for External Affairs. I would go over drafts of these documents with Claxton, and I would send them to Pearson in Paris, Wrong in Washington and Robertson in London for their comments. When I received their comments, these would be circulated. I would also send copies of the more important documents to the Prime Minister for his information. The documents went through many drafts; for example, by November 14, the commentary was in its fifth draft.

This was an exhausting process for all concerned. It would have been less exhausting and more fruitful if Pearson had been in Ottawa, but he decided that it was important that he head the Canadian delegation to the General Assembly. His attendance there, following on his absence from Ottawa to fight a by-election, meant that in the ten critical weeks from October 7 to December 17, he was in Ottawa for only four days (October 16, 17, 27 and 28). If Pearson had been in Ottawa the memoranda would have been better. They would also have been ready in time for us to send the commentary and the draft treaty to the other governments well before the talks resumed, thus increasing the chances that Canada would influence their attitudes.

Pearson, like everyone else, liked doing what he did best. He enjoyed taking part in U.N. General Assemblies; he was good at it. He liked to get away from his desk in Ottawa.

I attached particular importance to our circulating a draft treaty to the other participants in the discussions. In my memorandum to the Prime Minister in mid-November, 1948, I said:

If you have a draft treaty prepared in advance and can get it accepted as the basis of discussion or as one of the bases of discussion, you are put in a strong position. This certainly was our experience at the Chicago International Civil Aviation Conference in 1944. At that conference, the United States, for the first three or four days, strenuously resisted every effort to have any other text than the United States draft taken as a basis of discussion in the committee dealing with the structure of the organization and with rules on international air transport. They finally had to give in to the point where they accepted the Canadian draft as a basis along with the United States draft. However, our draft was so much better than theirs that after about one meeting ours became the only basis of discussion with the result that we were able to get a much larger number of our proposals accepted than otherwise would have been possible.[26]

Acheson has put the point briefly, "Long experience had taught me the advantage that lies in preparing the paper for discussion: the burden of making changes is on dissenters."[27]

The draft treaty prepared in the Department of External Affairs was sent to Wrong on December 17 but it was not circulated to the participants in the Washington discussions. Nor did Wrong evince any interest in it. The frustration which my colleagues and I felt was only slightly mollified by the testimonial we received at the end of December from Brooke Claxton, who had been Acting Foreign Minister while the draft treaty was being prepared. He congratulated us on "the fine job" we had done, and went on to say, "While there are points on which there will be different views, the document as a whole is really a brilliant piece of work on which you and your staff deserve the warmest congratulations."[28]

The North Atlantic treaty might have been a slightly better treaty if I had not had to work so hard during the six months I was Acting Under-Secretary of State for External Affairs, following Pearson's appointment to the Cabinet on September 10, 1948, since overwork exacerbated my two chief weaknesses as a diplomat: I was a perfectionist and I displayed *trop de zèle*. There were a number of reasons for my being overworked. When Pearson became a cabinet minister he kept the office and the staff which he had had as Under-Secretary; I had to create a new under-secretary's office. Pearson was away from Ottawa for more than nine weeks of my first 14 weeks as head of the External Affairs Department. This meant that I had to deal with an acting foreign minister, who was also a busy Minister of National Defence, while at the same time keeping Pearson constantly informed and seeking his advice and decision. The problems before the Department of External Affairs during the period of Pearson's absence were numerous and difficult. There were the negotiations on the entry of Newfoundland into Confederation; financial relations with Britain; and Canadian policy with respect to the situations arising out of the

Berlin blockade, the establishment of the state of Israel, and the advance of communist power in China. The government was apprehensive about the declaration of human rights then under discussion at the U.N. General Assembly because the subject matter fell mainly under provincial not federal jurisdiction. There were problems relating to the newly-established nine-nation Commonwealth on which recommendations had to be made to Cabinet: the first meeting of Commonwealth prime ministers to be attended by the prime ministers of India, Pakistan and Ceylon; the recommendations on Commonwealth consultation which emerged from that meeting; the status of Commonwealth high commissioners; the attitude to be adopted to Ireland when it left the Commonwealth. All this in addition to the negotiations on the North Atlantic treaty and a host of minor matters.[29] To deal with these problems the Department of External Affairs had a small and mainly inexperienced staff. The number of foreign service officers in the Department in Ottawa in the autumn of 1948 was only 71, less than a quarter of what it was in 1975. There were only 27 officers with at least three years' experience; in 1975 there were nine times as many.[†]

This provides an excuse for my displaying, in an exaggerated form during the negotiations on the North Atlantic treaty, my two weaknesses of perfectionism and too much zeal. If I had not set my sights for the treaty so high, and if I had not displayed so much zeal in advocating my views I might have been able to convert Wrong to a less restrictive view of the treaty. If Wrong had been converted to a less restrictive view he would have been more receptive to suggestions for broadening the treaty; he would have been more willing to apply "his fertile and flexible mind",[30] and his great diplomatic skills, to the task of persuading his colleagues in the negotiations to support the suggestions; and, if that was not possible, to propose to Pearson modifications which would make the suggestions more palatable to his colleagues and their governments.

Unfortunately, as Pearson has stated in his memoirs, Wrong was "never personally convinced that the non-military aspects of the proposed alliance were essential" and he was "not much in sympathy with Reid's views on . . . [the nature and purpose of the North Atlantic treaty] or with the intensity of his expression thereof".[31] By perfectionism and zeal I probably confirmed Wrong in his belief that the non-military aspects of the proposed alliance were non-essential.

Pearson, as is clear from his memoirs, was convinced that the non-military aspects of the proposed alliance were essential; St. Laurent and Claxton were likewise convinced. All three believed that the more the treaty emphasized the non-military aspects of the alliance, the bigger the advance it would make to the goal they had in mind of an ever closer union of the North Atlantic countries. Also, as the discussions proceeded, they became more and more conscious of the domestic political necessity of emphasizing the non-military aspects of the treaty in order to rally support for it in Canada. Wrong, being away from Ottawa and not being a politician, was not as conscious as they of political necessities in Canada. Being ambassador in Washington, he was more conscious than we in Ottawa of political necessities in the United States.

CHAPTER TWENTY

EPILOGUE

From the outset of the intergovernmental discussions which led to the North Atlantic treaty, I had erroneously assumed that the signature of the treaty would be followed immediately by a substantial increase in the armaments of at least those signatories, such as Canada, which had gone farthest in reducing their defence expenditures after the end of the Second World War. Thus on March 12, 1948, in my first memorandum to Pearson on the proposed alliance, I said, "It would be dishonest for us to enter an Atlantic pact unless we are prepared to increase considerably our defence appropriations in order to have a striking force immediately available."[1] Pearson made no comment on this. In the summer of 1948 I said to Pearson that I assumed that the creation of the alliance would be followed by an increase in the defence expenditures of Canada and of the other North Atlantic countries. Pearson replied that he saw no reason for this; under the alliance, national armed forces would become part of a balanced collective force; there would be joint planning; all this would increase the efficiency of the allied forces – that, and not an increase in defence expenditures, was all that would be required.

The Department of National Defence of Canada did not believe like Pearson that there should be no increase in the defence expenditures of the North Atlantic countries. Rather, it contended that "by pooling resources, the effect of the pact should be to reduce the total expenditures which each of the twelve [member] countries would have found necessary for their security had there been no pact".[2]

Hickerson shared Pearson's views. He thought at the time that the mere commitment by the United States to the North Atlantic treaty would be enough to deter the Soviet Union from committing aggression and that it would therefore not be necessary for the United States to make any material increase in its defence expenditures. He felt even more strongly that the western European nations could ill afford a big increase in their defence expenditures.[3]

The Brussels treaty countries were not thinking, when the North Atlantic treaty was negotiated, of even a small increase in their defence expenditures. Paul Nitze of the State Department made a trip to London and Paris in January, 1949. On his return he reported that none of the defence programmes so far considered by any of the Brussels treaty countries contemplated any further increases in their current military budgets. All these countries, he said, felt "not only that economic recovery must have a clear priority over the military rearmament program, but that no additional military cost over their current military programs can be carried by them." Thus "the additional cost of the rearmament program would fall entirely on the U.S. taxpayer".[4]

The United States administration hoped at the time that there would be "some increase" in the defence expenditures of the Brussels treaty powers, but it also agreed that the economic recovery of these countries "must not be sacrificed to rearmament and must continue to be given a clear priority. . . . [I]n principle, rearmament expenditures and manpower diversion should not be permitted to bring about any serious reduction in the allotment of European resources to the recovery effort."[5]

This conclusion was in accord with the paper from the State Department's policy planning staff which George Kennan had submitted to Marshall and Lovett three months before. In this paper, Kennan contended that

> the best and most hopeful course of action [for the western Europeans] if they are to save themselves from communist pressures, remains the struggle for economic recovery and for political stability. Compared to this, intensive rearmament constitutes an uneconomic and regrettable diversion of effort. A certain amount of rearmament can be subjectively beneficial to western Europe. But if this rearmament proceeds at any appreciable cost to European recovery, it can do more harm than good.

Kennan noted on the file that "there was no disagreement anywhere" (presumably within the State Department) to the part of the paper in which this statement occurred.[6]

The belief that substantial rearmament was not necessary, apart from the provision of military supplies by the United States to the western European countries, may have been linked to the belief, as Marshall, the Secretary of State, put it at the end of November, 1948, that "the main deterrent to Soviet aggression has been the possession by the United States of the atomic bomb." Marshall went on to say that, until fairly recently, he had thought that the Soviet leaders had probably felt that the American people would never permit the use of the bomb but that in the light of developments of recent months, including Berlin, and of "developments here", he felt that the Soviet leaders must now realize that the use of this instrument would be possible; hence the deterrent effect now was perhaps greater than heretofore.[7]

The United States monopoly of the atomic bomb in 1948 was certainly a deterrent; but if it failed to deter the Soviet Union, it would not protect western Europe from occupation by Soviet armies. In the event of war the Soviet Union would, presumably, occupy western Europe and hold it as a hostage. My guess in October, 1948, was that the studies then being made by the military organs of the Brussels treaty powers would lead to the conclusion that if the western powers were to be in a position to hold the Soviet forces east of the Rhine, they would require something like three times the forces which they then had in western Europe.[8] The official estimate 18 months later was five times, not three times.

Even though there may well have been a link between the belief in the deterrent effect of the United States monopoly of the atomic bomb and belief that rearmament was unnecessary, the determination of the North Atlantic countries not to divert to defence resources that were needed for economic recovery was not affected by the explosion of an atomic bomb by the Soviet Union at the end of August, 1949, nor by the conclusion, reached six months later, that the Soviet Union might by July, 1954, be capable of launching a major atomic attack.

(There had been a close race, though we did not know it at the time, between the coming into force of the North Atlantic treaty and the explosion by the Soviet Union of its first atomic bomb. The treaty won by six days. It came into force on August 24, 1949; the bomb was exploded on August 30. A month later, on October 1, Mao Tse-tung proclaimed the People's Republic of China from the balcony of the Gate of Heavenly Peace in Peking.)

In April, 1950, a Canadian external affairs officer who had been at meetings of the alliance, which had discussed defence and which were aware of the conclusion that the Soviet Union might be capable of launching a major atomic attack in four years' time, reported that "neither the United States nor the United Kingdom have any intention of increasing their budgets for North Atlantic defence", and that "the total budgetary resources for defence of the North Atlantic countries are likely to remain at about the present level of $20.5 billion per annum."[9] (The actual level of expenditures in 1950 was $20 billion, an increase in real terms of only seven percent over the previous year.) The creation of the North Atlantic alliance did not result in rearmament. Rearmament was the result of the Korean War.

The outbreak of the Korean War in June, 1950, was followed by a sudden sharp increase in the defence expenditures of the North Atlantic allies. United States expenditures increased in real terms from $14 billion in 1950 to $31 billion in 1951 and to $43 billion in 1952, three times what they had been in 1950. The total for the whole alliance in 1951 was almost double what it had been in 1950; the next year there was a further increase of about 40 percent; the total expenditures in 1952 were $54 billion (in 1950 U.S. dollars) compared with $20 billion in 1950.

The Korean War established a new plateau for defence expenditures by the North Atlantic countries. In 1974 the total expenditures of the original members of the alliance were $59 billion (in 1950 U.S. dollars).[†]

Canada had withdrawn its armed forces from Europe after the end of hostilities in the Second World War. As a result of the Korean War it decided late in 1950 to send a brigade group to Germany (as well as one to Korea). This was the first time in its history that Canada had stationed armed forces abroad in peacetime. Canada's expenditures on defence increased (in terms of 1950 U.S. dollars) from less than $500 million in 1950 to $1,750 million in 1952.

The effect of the Korean War on Senator Vandenberg's attitude to expenditures on defence was typical of the effect on many other influential people in the North Atlantic countries. His official biographer says that before the outbreak of hostilities in Korea, Vandenberg was opposed to the alliance having forces in being sufficiently powerful to match Soviet strength; the alliance should have only an "efficient nucleus" of forces which could be expanded in an emergency. "Meanwhile, this efficient nucleus will build internal morale and assure control of internal subversion." There is evidence, writes his biographer, that Vandenberg sharply altered this position "after the Communists showed their readiness to use force to gain their ends in the attack on Korea."[10]

At the time, I stated as follows my reasons for believing that the attack of North Korea on South Korea demonstrated the necessity for a great rearmament by the North Atlantic countries: "Recent events in Korea have demonstrated that Russia and China are now prepared to run grave risks of precipitating a third world war. It is possible that these two countries have by now decided to precipitate that war during the next twelve months."[11] Eight years later, I expanded on this. I said that our belief in 1950 was that

> North Korea would not have made an open attack on South Korea without, at the very least, the acquiescence of the leaders of the Soviet and Communist Chinese governments. We believed that those leaders might well have thought, with good reason, that it was unlikely that the West would help South Korea to defend itself. But we also believed that they must have known that there was a considerable risk that the West would come to South Korea's defence. They must also, in our opinion, have known that if the West did come to South Korea's defence there was a contingent risk of a local conflagration spreading and developing into a general war. To Canadians, therefore, the attack on South Korea was an alarm bell. We considered that this bell warned us that the then leaders of the governments in Russia and China were prepared to run clear risks of precipitating a general war in order to extend the borders of their world. What was to be done? How,

we asked ourselves, could these leaders be deterred from running these risks, terrible for both them and us? To us it seemed, in the months that followed the invasion of South Korea, that the first step that had to be taken was to build up the military strength of the West so that the Russian-Chinese leaders would be encouraged in future to be more cautious. We believed that one reason for their lack of caution was their military preponderance. The primary purpose of our rearmament was to deter them from running risks which might land us all in the catastrophe of an atomic war.[12]

The Korean War led not only to the rearmament of the North Atlantic countries, it led also to United States insistence on the admission of Greece and Turkey to the alliance, on the rearmament of West Germany and its inclusion in the alliance, and on the creation of a military structure for the alliance and the appointment of a supreme commander. The Korean War resulted in the metamorphosis of the North Atlantic alliance into the North Atlantic Treaty Organization. It led to what Charles Bohlen in his memoirs called "the militarization of NATO",[13] and to what Pearson called in July, 1951, "the growing NATO concentration on the military aspects of the alliance." [14]

One of the fascinating might-have-beens of the last quarter of a century is what might have happened if North Korea had not attacked South Korea or if, when the attack did take place, the United States had not decided to send armed forces to the defence of South Korea and if the United Nations had not decided to support the United States. Would there have been a great rearmament of the alliance in the 1950s? Would Greece and Turkey have become members of the alliance? Would West Germany have been rearmed and made a member of the alliance? If these developments had not taken place would the Soviet Union have pushed forward its areas of control in western Europe?

The great increase in the defence expenditures of the alliance after the outbreak of the Korean War provided an opportunity to strengthen not only the military unity of the alliance but also its economic unity. The rearmament should have been accompanied by effective collaboration within the alliance on research and development of armaments, and on their standardization and their production; and by the member countries agreeing that balanced collective armed forces for the alliance meant for most members unbalanced national armed forces.

Even before the outbreak of the Korean War, Emanuel Shinwell, who was then Minister of Defence in the British Labour government, had argued, at a meeting of the North Atlantic alliance in the spring of 1950, that one of the prime military objectives of the alliance should be to achieve some standardization of armaments in the interest both of economy and of efficiency in combat. The Canadian official who reported on this meeting said:

[Mr. Shinwell] said, 'We have to consider the renunciation of at least a part of our industrial sovereignty'. So long as we maintain it, he said, collective security, integration, and co-ordination of our North Atlantic efforts will suffer. We cannot, he added, go on producing where and what and when we like, but must be prepared to make sacrifices in the common interest.[15]

As soon as it became clear by September, 1950, that the North Atlantic countries had embarked on what I then called a "rearmament programme so large as to be unprecedented in peacetime", I urged that under Article 2 of the treaty, the North Atlantic Council should ask a competent group to prepare recommendations to it on what specific steps should be taken in carrying out the collective rearmament programme, first, to minimize the danger that this programme would make more difficult the accomplishment of the long-run task of co-ordinating the economies of the North Atlantic countries, and second, to increase the possibility that the rearmament programme would actually assist in reaching the long-term goal implicit in Article 2.[16]

A year later, D. V. LePan of the Canadian Department of External Affairs put the problem in perspective in a memorandum to Pearson. He said that it was a mistake to think of international economic co-operation in the North Atlantic community in terms of reducing barriers to the movement of goods, capital and people. It should be thought of as similar to national economic policy, which was a mixture of free competition in order to reduce the real costs of production and of deliberate arrangements to protect the welfare of special areas and interests. In a period of heavy rearmament and inflation, planned co-operation within the alliance in defence production and defence finance would ease immediate problems and would hold out hopes of binding the countries in the North Atlantic area permanently together. There should be developed within the North Atlantic alliance techniques for making authoritative recommendations to the member states on what should be produced in the common defence effort, where it should be produced and how it should be financed. In the fullness of time, these decision-making functions might be institutionalized into some virtually supra-national authority. A community, LePan said, could "only be built by meeting successfully (and with as much fairness to all its members as is possible) practical problems as they arise. That conviction lies at the basis of these suggestions." [17]

Little has resulted from the pleas made ever since 1950 that the North Atlantic alliance should co-ordinate defence research and development, standardize defence equipment, and organize joint co-ordinated production. There has been some advance within the European membership of the alliance, little within the alliance as a whole. As a result, North Atlantic armed forces cost much more than they otherwise would; their efficiency in combat is lower; and an opportunity has been lost to strengthen the unity of the Atlantic community.

Similarly, member nations of the alliance have fought shy of unbalancing their own armed forces in order to attain a balanced collective force for the alliance. I remember Prime Minister St. Laurent saying in October, 1948, while the treaty was being negotiated, that once the North Atlantic alliance had been created, what was important was that the alliance as a whole should have a balanced force; it was no longer important that an individual member of the alliance such as Canada should have a balanced force. It was, he suggested, improbable that Canada would be making the most effective contribution to the strengthening of the alliance if it maintained a balanced force; might it not be sensible for Canada to concentrate on two or three of the four aspects of defence – army, navy, air, defence production – and do little or nothing about the other aspects?[18]

In April, 1950, one observer who had attended North Atlantic discussions on defence reported that the North Atlantic alliance had "nearly all the naval forces that it is estimated would be required by 1954, whereas it only [had], in aggregate, about one-third of the air forces and one-fifth of the land forces needed".[19] Presumably, it would have been in the interests of the alliance if countries such as the Netherlands and Canada had replaced their navies by coast guard services and had put the savings into air and land forces. Others of the middle-sized or smaller members of the alliance might have concentrated their defence efforts on certain specialized types of land or air forces.

The North Atlantic allies did not do this. Inertia and the vested interests of each of the branches of the armed forces in each of the capitals fought against it. Countries such as the Netherlands, with a long naval tradition, were reluctant to give up their navies. The opportunity was lost to build a more integrated, less expensive and more efficient allied defence force.

The Korean War resulted not only in the militarization of the North Atlantic alliance, but also in increased apprehension among the allies of the United States that the United States might pursue impatient or provocative policies in its relations with the Soviet Union and China. The United States commander in the Korean War, General Douglas MacArthur, was permitted by the United States government to pursue policies in Korea which resulted in an unnecessary war with China. If Truman had not dismissed him he would have pursued policies which would probably have led to war with the Soviet Union. The administration in Washington had had great difficulty in controlling him, partly because of an anachronistic tradition, probably going back to the wars against the Indians, which granted wide authority to a general in the field, but mainly because of wide-spread public support of MacArthur in the United States. This chilling experience strengthened the belief in Ottawa that the United States must be restrained, and that the most effective means to influence United States policies was to strengthen the procedures for consultation in the North Atlantic alliance.

The European members of the alliance might decide that they could exert more influence on Washington as a western European group rather than as members of a North Atlantic group, and that the more integrated they became the more influence they would possess. But the more integrated they became, the more Canada would be isolated. This provided Canada with a powerful reason for urging the integration of the North Atlantic countries. D. V. LePan put this point starkly in a memorandum to Pearson in September of 1951:

> European economic integration could very easily mean the creation of new trade barriers against Canadian imports; and military cooperation amongst the countries of western Europe could mean a great growth in neutralist sentiment. Both these possibilities would imperil the success of the North Atlantic treaty. They would be particularly dangerous for Canada since we would be left to deal with the United States on our own and almost inevitably would sink into a policy of simple continentalism.

It was therefore, he said, essential for Canada that progress towards the integration of western Europe should be accompanied "by progress more or less *pari passu* towards co-operation in the North Atlantic area".[20]

Pearson believed at this time that in a world which was going to be increasingly dominated by the power of the United States, countries such as Canada could exert more influence on Washington as members of an increasingly more unified North Atlantic community than they could individually. He feared that the proposed extension of the alliance to Greece and Turkey and the increasing militarization of the alliance would make the alliance an unsatisfactory foundation for such a North Atlantic community. Therefore in July, 1951, less than two years after the North Atlantic treaty had come into force, he cast about for a substitute for the North Atlantic alliance as a starting point for the unification of that community. He describes in his memoirs how on a visit to western Europe in July, 1951, he thought aloud about this, and threw out some ideas very tentatively when talking to the British, Dutch and Norwegian governments, and to the United States representative on the North Atlantic Council. Two treaties would be substituted for the North Atlantic

241

treaty. The first would be purely military and would be open to any member of the United Nations prepared to accept the obligations of military collective action. This would mean a return to the idea of an optional protocol to the U.N. Charter, the suggestion which Pearson put in St. Laurent's speech to the U.N. General Assembly on September 18, 1947. The second treaty would promote political, economic, social and cultural co-operation, and would be restricted to countries which were in fact members of the North Atlantic community. Switzerland and Sweden would be included but not Turkey and Greece; possibly, though he did not say so, Portugal would be excluded. This second treaty would replace existing agreements for western European co-operation on non-military matters such as the Organization for European Economic Co-operation and the Council of Europe. The response of Dirk Stikker, Foreign Minister of the Netherlands, and Halvard Lange, Foreign Minister of Norway, was encouraging, but nothing more was heard of the idea.[21]

Pearson instead returned to efforts to improve consultation within the North Atlantic alliance and to strengthen economic and social co-operation between the members of the alliance. He sets forth in his memoirs the efforts which he made, culminating in his work in the Committee of Three appointed by the North Atlantic Council in May of 1956 to advise it "on ways and means to improve and extend NATO co-operation in non-military fields and to develop greater unity within the Atlantic Community". By that time, however, Pearson "was losing hope that NATO would evolve beyond an alliance for defence".[22]

The obstacles to effective consultation within the alliance emerged early in its history and the alliance was not very successful in finding a means to cope with them. The obstacles to effective consultation on issues arising outside the North Atlantic treaty area were particularly great.

An officer of the Department of External Affairs of Canada who had been present at the political discussions at the meeting of the North Atlantic Council in December, 1952, reported that they had been "singularly unproductive."

> The French got a good hearing for their presentation of the Indo-Chinese situation, but there was nothing like an exchange of views. There are several possible explanations for this, but notably the fear that to join issue with the French on this matter might lead to entanglement in a situation in which most NATO countries do not feel they can make any material contribution at the moment. We may, in fact, be getting close to the situation in NATO, where discussions are avoided in order to escape responsibility.[23]

Here we were back again at the doctrine which Prime Minister Mackenzie King of Canada had put forward in the 1930s: avoid giving advice to friendly countries about their foreign policies, because if they take your advice and get into trouble, they will expect you to help them get out of it; consultation involves commitments; therefore avoid consultation in order to escape commitments.

Another obstacle to effective consultation on issues outside the North Atlantic treaty area became apparent whenever Portugal raised in the North Atlantic Council, as if often did in the 1950s, its apprehension of India's ambition to take over the Portuguese territory of Goa. The other members of the alliance would remain silent in the Council after the Portuguese Foreign Minister had made his statement; they did not want, by supporting Portugal, to offend India and other countries which had recently become independent of European rule; they did not want to offend Portugal by stating what most of them must have believed, that the interests of the alliance would be served if Portugal ceded Goa to India, thus removing one of the irritants in the relations between the North Atlantic countries and the Third World. I raised this question in the spring of 1954 in a letter to the Department of External Affairs in Ottawa. I said that the strength of the North Atlantic alliance was "not merely the sum total of the strength of each member" since the strength of the alliance "is also in part made up of the degree of support which the alliance has in the rest of the non-cominform world. It is partly a matter of alliance potential." I went on to say:

> Another obvious consideration is that the strength of an alliance depends not only on the power at the disposal of its members but on the willingness of citizens of member states to use that power. I suggest that support for our obligations under the North Atlantic treaty is not likely to be increased in countries such as Canada if Canadian citizens come to believe that the treaty is being used to hinder the growth of self-government in Portuguese colonies in Africa. If the Portuguese think they can succeed in getting us to support them in Goa they can then try to get us to support them in their controversies about their African colonies. . . .[24]

A third obstacle to effective consultation on matters arising outside the North Atlantic treaty area was, in the mid-1950s, the attitude of John Foster Dulles, the United States Secretary of State. Though Article 4 of the treaty which sets forth the obligation of the allies to consult together made no distinction between threats to the territorial integrity, political independence or security of an ally arising outside the treaty area and those arising inside, Dulles made a sharp distinction. He insisted in June, 1956, that this article imposed no obligation on the United States to consult its North Atlantic allies on questions which did not affect those countries more than other members of the international community; on such questions, the United States would be prepared only to expound United States policies to the North Atlantic Council and to answer questions based on its statements in order, as he put it, to promote "a more sympathetic attitude towards United States policy".[25] This gave little or no opportunity for the other members of the alliance to influence United States policy; rather it gave the United States an opportunity to influence their policies.

Even on threats arising within the North Atlantic treaty area, consultation was sometimes notably absent. I was Canadian Ambassador to Germany from 1958 to 1962, a period of constant crisis in East-West relations over Germany. During those four years, there was no discussion of the substance of the German problem in the North Atlantic Council. This is not surprising since there was no multilateral discussion among the governments of the four North Atlantic allies principally concerned: Germany, the United States, Britain and France. They constantly discussed contingency planning and the tactics and strategy of negotiation with the Soviet government. They did not discuss in a four-power meeting the substance of the problems which would have to be discussed with the Soviet government if real negotiations, real parleying, on the German question were to take place, problems such as the Oder-Neisse line, the status of East Germany and the status of Berlin.

The main obstacle to effective consultation within the alliance in the 1950s and most of the 1960s was the ever increasing preponderance of the United States within the alliance and in the world as a whole. This meant that each member of the alliance always required, or thought it required, the sympathy or support of the United States on a large number of matters of immediate importance to it. A member of the alliance would be apprehensive that its chances of getting United States sympathy or support on these matters would be lessened if at meetings of the North Atlantic alliance it offended the United States government by adversely criticizing its policies. This inhibited discussion in the alliance of such delicate, grave and divisive issues as United States policy in Vietnam, the refusal by the United States to recognize the government in Peking, and its firm opposition to the seating of Peking's representatives in the United Nations. The long-continued adherence of the United States to these unwise policies greatly weakened the alliance.

One example which Alastair Buchan has given of this was the way in which

[President] Johnson brutally used the dependence of sterling on the dollar to exact [Prime Minister] Wilson's support for American policy in Vietnam, except for the bombing of the North. In the end, Wilson failed in both his objectives: to maintain the parity of sterling and to retain any leverage over American policy in Asia. Both countries suffered in the process.[26]

The reluctance of the North Atlantic allies of the United States to discuss issues such as Vietnam and China at meetings of the alliance would have been somewhat less if the alliance had early in its history established appropriate procedures for discussing such issues.

In the negotiations on the North Atlantic treaty the principal negotiators discovered on two occasions that they were unlikely to get very far in composing their differences if they met in the presence of their advisers and of stenographers and if an agreed record were made of their discussions. They therefore met on August 20, 1948, and February 19, 1949, in informal, top-secret meetings with no advisers present, no stenographers, and no agreed minutes. They reduced the number of people at their meetings from about 25 to seven.

I was once present in the early 1960s at a top-secret meeting of the North Atlantic Council in Paris, where Dulles expounded United States policy on Communist China; there must have been at least 200 people in the room. The meeting resembled a press conference, not a consultation between allies. It gave Dulles what he wanted, an opportunity to promote "a more sympathetic attitude towards United States policies". It did not give the allies an opportunity to influence United States policies.

Governments know that multilateral intergovernmental discussions on delicate, grave and divisive issues are more likely to be effective the fewer the number of people present and the more exiguous the record of the discussions. A Cabinet minister is more likely to speak frankly on such issues if he has no one accompanying him in the meeting who can immediately afterwards put down on paper an account of what he said. He likes to be able to decide for himself after the meeting what he wants his colleagues at home to know about what he and others at the meeting said. He is more likely to speak frankly at a meeting with his peers if he can talk to them in a small room across a table seating no more than about 20 people.

The failure of the North Atlantic alliance to hold such meetings of heads of government or of foreign ministers at regular intervals is due no doubt to the reluctance of any government to agree to the establishment of a procedure which would facilitate periodic frank discussion by its allies of issues which it considers of vital importance and on which it is likely to find itself isolated or almost isolated. The more powerful the government, the greater the reluctance.

The militarization of the North Atlantic alliance which resulted from the Korean War and the lack of effective consultation within the alliance on grave issues of foreign policy provide a partial explanation for the failure of the alliance to become a starting point for a North Atlantic federation or even to greatly increased unity within the North Atlantic community. Another and very important reason is that from the beginning of the alliance most of the politically influential people in France and Belgium wanted greater western European unity rather than greater North Atlantic unity and opinion in the other member countries of the alliance was divided. In the 1950s and 1960s increasing doubts about the wisdom of United States' foreign policies, especially in Vietnam, weakened the Atlanticists in western Europe. In the 1960s, France under de Gaulle stood in the way of the development of both the Atlantic community and the European community. In other member countries one of the main reasons for lack of progress was inertia.

Canada was not so active in pressing for the implementation of Article 2 as it had been in pressing for its inclusion in the treaty. Part of the explanation of Canada's half-heartedness was that Pearson was never at his best in dealing with economic issues. He may, indeed, have failed to grasp the implications of the argument which LePan had put to him: that the path of development from alliance to community was for the alliance to meet practical problems, such as defence production and defence finance, successfully, and with as much fairness as possible to all the member states of the alliance. Or perhaps he realized very clearly the domestic political difficulties in the way of this kind of development and he was not prepared to undertake the struggles with the Cabinet, the Liberal party, Parliament and the electorate which would be required to overcome these difficulties.

The kind of development in the alliance proposed by LePan meant the development within the alliance of techniques for making authoritative recommendations to the member states on matters of common concern. In time, as LePan said, these decision-making functions might be institutionalized into some virtually supranational authority. But authoritative recommendations to the Canadian government from the alliance would mean such embarrassing and expensive demands on Canada as that it should increase its expenditures on its own armed forces and give more military supplies to its allies and, probably in due course, that it should admit many more immigrants from Italy, Portugal, Greece and Turkey.

In November of 1948, when I was pressing hard that Canada be very active in the negotiation of the North Atlantic treaty, I received a cautionary note from Arnold Heeney, who was then Secretary of Cabinet and became four months later Under-Secretary for External Affairs. "It may turn out", he wrote me, "that we shall be substantial contributors to the North Atlantic pool because of our position and resources, but we should not take too leading a part in the negotiations until we have more definite indications of what our treaty obligations are to be in men, money and materials. There is, in my view, real danger that we may be open to the charge of speaking loudly but carrying a pretty small twig".[27]

Yet another reason for the failure of the North Atlantic alliance to move towards greater unity is, in my opinion, that it did not make judicious use of its political power to support personal and political freedom within the alliance. If it had done this, it would have strengthened one of the main bonds which united all the original members of the alliance other than Portugal: their common belief in the principles of democracy, individual liberty and the rule of law. The alliance might have been able to do something to weaken the anti-democratic forces in such member countries as Portugal and Greece. Those inside and outside the alliance who were sceptical of its claim to be more than a negative anti-Soviet alliance would have been shaken in their scepticism.

While the inclusion of Portugal as an original member of the alliance made a mockery of the reference in the preamble of the treaty to the freedom of the peoples of the alliance, founded on the principles of democracy, individual liberty and the rule of law, it did not render inoperative Portugal's commitment under Article 2 of the treaty to become more democratic. The Development Assistance Committee of the Organization for Economic Co-operation and Development requires its member nations to report each year on the nature and extent of their development assistance, and each national report is subjected to scrutiny by the other members. The annual report of the Development Assistance Committee discusses what each member country is doing. The members of the North Atlantic alliance could have set up a similar system of annual report, investigation and publicity on what each member state was doing to carry out its treaty obligation to strengthen its free institutions. Other members might have made clear to a recalcitrant Portugal that its failure to carry out this treaty obligation might result in their concluding that Portugal's breach of treaty obligations released them from their treaty obligation to assist it if it were attacked. They would no doubt have couched this message in some such diplomatic language as, "If the government of Portugal is not prepared to carry out its obligation under Article 2 to strengthen its free institutions, many of its fellow members in the alliance would be apt to take this into account in deciding on the nature and extent of the assistance which they would give Portugal if it were attacked." Later they could have given the same sort of warning to the Greek dictatorship.

I regret that it was not until May, 1956, after the treaty had been in force for almost seven years, that I recommended to Pearson that "each Atlantic nation might be required to make an annual report to the [North Atlantic] Council on the steps which it had taken during the previous year to carry out its treaty obligation to strengthen its free institutions." I was then Canadian High Commissioner in New Delhi, and I said that one advantage of doing this would be that "the suspicions in the coloured and colonial world of NATO would be diminished if it could be demonstrated that the inclusion in the Atlantic Community of a country like Portugal results in pressure being put on Portugal to become more democratic." [28]

A further reason for the failure of the North Atlantic alliance to develop in the direction Pearson, Hickerson, Achilles, I and others hoped in 1948 and 1949 that it would, was that from 1952 on, under both Republican and Democratic administrations, and especially from the Kennedy regime on, people who not only rejected the goal of a North Atlantic federation but who never really liked, or even understood, the very idea of an alliance secured a great deal of influence in the White House and the State Department. Some of these people had never wanted an alliance; they had wanted a unilateral declaration by the United States which would extend the Monro Doctrine to Western Europe. They were not anxious to learn the complex and subtle art of how the leader of an alliance conducts its relations with the other members of the alliance. They hankered after unilateral declarations, unilateral decision-making, and unilateral actions. If they were out of step with all their real allies (and in step only with their client states), they were inclined to believe that it was their allies who were out of step with them – in policy towards China and Cuba, and in their war in Vietnam, Laos and Cambodia. This was a weakness not only of Dulles but also of some of the highly-intelligent, but also intellectually-arrogant best and brightest who advised Kennedy and Johnson. In any alliance or quasi-alliance where the leader has a great preponderance of power and bears on his shoulders an Atlantean burden of responsibility, this strain of thinking is likely to be strong. My impression, however, is that this strain of thinking has, from the beginning of the North Atlantic alliance, been particularly strong in Washington.

In 1966 Dirk Stikker, who had been Foreign Minister of the Netherlands and Secretary-General of NATO, wrote, "To really understand Europe and its Atlantic ties, no one should underestimate the feelings which are aroused among Europeans by the all too frequent and undisguised American certainty that the American view is not only the right, but the only possible view." [29]

Two explanations were given in the 1950s and 1960s of why the United States so often gave its North Atlantic allies the impression that it had little or no interest in their views on matters of common concern. One was that until 1949 the United States had had no experience in running an alliance; it did not realize, as had the British as the result of long experience, the importance of giving allies or potential allies, if not a reasonable share in making the policy of the leader of the alliance on issues of common concern, at least the illusion of participating in the decision-making process. The second explanation was the peculiar nature of the process of making decisions on foreign policy in Washington. In other countries which, in the previous hundred years or so, had led alliances or quasi-alliances, decisions on major questions of foreign policy were normally made by the head of government and the foreign minister (acting on the advice of a small group of professional advisers). In Washington, however, in the middle of the twentieth century, such decisions were normally made only as a result of a lengthy, intricate and laborious process of discussion and negotiation within the United States government. This took place first within each of the agencies concerned, whether the State Department, Defence or C.I.A., then between the agencies, and, after that between the administration and Congress. This process took a long time; issues demanded decision; in consequence there might not be much time left for discussion with allies. And the process was exhausting; those who had participated in it were reluctant to get involved in another lengthy negotiation with allies; the agreement reached in Washington was an unstable compromise; if the compromise were changed as the result of consultations with allies, the administration in Washington would have to re-negotiate the compromise with all those who had taken part in framing it.

In 1948 and 1949, when the North Atlantic alliance was created, the partners of the United States supported a broad interpretation of the power of the President of the United States, as Commander-in-Chief of the armed forces, to order the armed forces into action without reference to Congress. This they did first because they wanted instant help if attacked by the Soviet Union; second, because the assurance of instant help would deter the Soviet Union from attacking them; and, third, because they had more confidence in the President than in Congress. At that time Britain, the western European countries and Canada had, so far as I can recall, no qualms about supporting this broad interpretation of presidential powers. This is not surprising; from September, 1939, to December, 1941, they had believed that their hope of survival depended on Roosevelt's ability to push the United States into war by one constitutionally doubtful or improper step after another.

In the mid-1970s, the people of the United States appeared to have decided that the power of the President of the United States to get them involved in war must be curbed; some system of checks and balances on the power of the President must be re-established. There was thus, by the mid-1970s, a partial coincidence of interest between those in the United States who wanted to curb presidential power in foreign affairs, and those in countries allied to the United States who wanted to curb not only presidential power but also the power of the whole United States government – the President combined with Congress and such agencies as the C.I.A. – to create conditions which entailed serious risks of war.

249

The coincidence of interest was, however, only partial. When the North Atlantic treaty was negotiated, Britain, Canada, France and the Benelux countries were afraid that the United States would press the Soviet Union too hard and too fast and not leave it a way out to save its face. They believed that the provisions on consultation in the North Atlantic treaty could be used to restrain the United States from pursuing impatient or provocative policies. At the beginning of the fourth quarter of the twentieth century, some of the governments of the North Atlantic allies of the United States were beginning to fear that the United States might be too reluctant to use its power to restrain the Soviet Union from pursuing expansionist policies.

By 1956 Pearson was "losing hope that NATO would evolve beyond an alliance for defence".[30] By 1960 I was becoming apprehensive that Spaak, as Secretary-General of NATO, was trying, as I put it at the time in a memorandum to Ottawa, [31] "to use the NATO Council as a sort of direc-torate of the free world, a forum for the general deiermination of policies to be carried out by [the members of NATO] through NATO or other agencies as may be deemed expedient but decided nevertheless by the NATO powers in the NATO Council". I had favoured this in the mid-1950s; but by 1960 I had come to the conclusion that though this might have been "an appropriate prescription for the 1950s", it was not appro-priate for the 1960s. The world had changed. NATO had changed. I had changed.

I now argued that many, if not most, of the critical problems of the 1960s were not "in their pith and substance aspects of a contest with Communism or with the Russo-Chinese bloc, [and] that for such prob-lems the NATO Council [was] not the most effective primary organ for consultation and co-ordination of policy." In order to demonstrate this, I examined, one by one, what seemed to me to be the eight most critical problems of the 1960s, and what agency or channel or group of countries was inherently most appropriate in each case for consultation, and for the formulation of agreed policies by the nations of the free world, whether members of NATO or not.

(In this memorandum of September, 1960, I assumed that the Soviet Union and China were firmly united in an alliance, and I therefore referred to the Russo-Chinese bloc. I used the term "free world" to cover the democratic North Atlantic countries and other countries which were not at that time governed by a totalitarian dictatorship, countries such as Japan, India, Pakistan, Egypt, Nigeria, Brazil and Mexico.)

The first of the eight principal problems of the 1960s which I examined was how to minimize the dangers to the free world created by the rise of Communist China to the rank of a first-class power. Since India and

Japan were the two large countries of the free world most directly and immediately concerned, I suggested that it would be appropriate if the problem of China were to be discussed in the first instance by the United States and Britain with India and Japan.

The second problem, the organization of effective help to India to speed up its economic development, should remain with the World Bank and the consortium it had created.

The third problem was how to prevent independent Africa south of the Sahara from degenerating into chaos, and how to facilitate the orderly progress to independence of the remaining dependent territories in Africa. Here, it seemed to me that the agencies of the free world which were most likely to be able to work out a policy on Africa which would carry with it the judgment of the bulk of the free world, both white and coloured, were the Commonwealth, the World Bank and the United Nations in its various aspects, especially the Special Fund, the technical assistance programme and a U.N. police force. "Already the United Nations has demonstrated in the Congo that it can in Africa act as the executive agent of the free world."

The North Atlantic Council was, I contended, obviously an inappropriate body for dealing with the fourth critical world problem of the 1960s, the population explosion. The countries where it might be most difficult to persuade people to use contraceptives were African and Asian, and they would not welcome the intervention of white people in so delicate and intimate a matter.

The fifth of the most critical problems on my list was "how to work out equitable international arrangements under which the western industrialized countries [would] each accept its fair share of a rapidly increasing flow of low-priced manufactured goods from the under-developed countries." I suggested that the countries which were most capable of leading the way to a solution of this problem were the four leading world traders; at that time, they were the United States, Britain, Germany and Canada. Even though these countries were all members of NATO, it seemed to me more appropriate that they should raise the matter in the first instance or primarily in GATT or the World Bank, rather than in the North Atlantic Council.

These five problems were, I said, related – they exacerbated one another. But, I asked, even if communism did not exist, if Russia and China did not exist or if they were liberal democracies, would not these problems be intractable and endanger the peace and welfare of the whole world? Surely these problems had their core and origin in circumstances not directly related to the struggle between the Russo-Chinese bloc and NATO.

The problems had, of course, important implications for NATO's efforts to develop and maintain greater military and economic strength, moral purpose and internal unity, in order that it might continue to deter aggression by the Russo-Chinese bloc and further strengthen the fabric of the North Atlantic community. Exchanges of views on various aspects of problems of this kind should therefore take place in NATO from time to time, and these exchanges might include the examination of possible or proposed courses of action by one or more of the North Atlantic allies. But it was essential, I urged, that when such discussion did take place in the North Atlantic Council, it should not rest on the false assumption that, because these problems had a bearing on the struggle between the Russo-Chinese bloc and NATO, they were in their essence part of that struggle, that the North Atlantic Council should take the lead in working out possible solutions and that, if the lead were taken in some agency other than NATO, the legitimate concerns of NATO were likely to receive less than adequate attention.

So much for five of what I considered in 1960 to be the eight principal world problems of the 1960s. As for the other three on my list, it was, I said, clear that they were of primary concern to NATO: how to work out effective international agreements to reduce the dangers resulting from the development of methods of mass destruction; how to maintain an effective balance of military power with the Russo-Chinese bloc; and how to reduce the dangers created by the division of Europe, particularly the division of Germany and Berlin, into a Soviet zone and a western zone.

My conclusion was that the North Atlantic countries should, in the 1960s, set their sights higher than in the 1950s: they should now strive for the unity of the whole of the free world, rich and poor, white and coloured. The problems of the 1960s would be insoluble without the help of such countries as India, Japan, Pakistan, Egypt, Nigeria, Brazil and Mexico. But, I said, these countries were far more likely to co-operate in implementing a free world policy if they had a sense of having participated fully and as equals in the decision-making process which would finally lead to the formulation of that policy. My conclusion was:

> The free world's chances of survival are increased the more united it becomes, the more prosperous it becomes in all its parts, the more personal and political freedom there is in all its parts. The primary task of the 1960s is to create and maintain within the free world ever greater unity, prosperity and freedom. The pursuit of this objective will at times require sacrificing unity within NATO in order to secure the co-operation in a workable solution of the governments most directly concerned and a wide measure of support throughout the free world. . . . The time is not ripe for trying to build a constitutional or institutional structure for the free world. But the time is ripe for driving down to bedrock the pilings on which a constitutional structure of the free world could eventually be built. Most of the existing international

agencies for free world consultation, co-operation and common action can be made into pilings for such an eventual free world structure.[32]

The North Atlantic treaty was the child of fear and hope. The main fear when it was drafted was that unless the North Atlantic countries united to defend themselves, the Soviet Union would, by all methods short of overt armed attack, steadily expand its power over western Europe until those North Atlantic countries which had not yet been taken over would have to fight the Soviet Union – and fight on most unfavourable terms. The hope was that an alliance of the North Atlantic countries would deter the Soviet government from pursuing expansionist policies, and the governments of the members of the alliance from pursuing impatient or provocative policies, would increase the self confidence of the western world and so establish the basis for its economic recovery and political stability, and that it would increase the unity of the western world and strengthen and enrich the civilization which it had inherited from western Christendom.

In 1976, at the beginning of the last quarter of the twentieth century, the fear persisted that the Soviet Union would by all methods short of overt armed attack, steadily expand its power over western Europe. There was, however, one important difference between 1976 and 1948. It was that the Soviet government could no longer count on using the more important Communist parties of western Europe as its subservient agents.

The conference of European Communist parties in East Berlin in June, 1976, had formally recognized this development when it emphasized the necessity of a strict adherence

> to the principles of equality and sovereign independence of each [Communist] party, non-interference in internal affairs and respect for their free choice of different roads in the struggle for social change of a progressive nature and for socialism.

At this conference and afterwards the leaders of the Communist parties of Italy, France and Spain had committed themselves to defend freedom of thought and of expression, a plurality of political parties and the possibility of democratic alternation of government, meaning that if they came to power by democratic election, they would relinquish power if the voters subsequently turned them out.[33]

How much credence should be attached to these protestations it was in 1976 too early to say. But it appeared likely that the answer would be forthcoming within 10 years or so. If, during the second half of the 1970s, a grand coalition were created in Italy between the Communist party and other parties and the coalition government worked, the French Communists and later perhaps the Spanish Communists might likewise become partners in government. Then the real nature of the Communist parties would, before long, be revealed.

When the North Atlantic treaty was negotiated, the general assumption was that if communists were to become part of the government of a North Atlantic country, that country would either resign from the alliance or be expelled from it. In 1976 this could no longer be assumed. The most that could be assumed was that this event would place great strains on the alliance. It would also result in tension in western Europe between the countries where strong Communist parties had been admitted to a share in the government and the northern countries such as West Germany and Britain where the Communist parties were weak and the social-democratic parties strong. The movement towards western European unity would suffer a setback.

Whether there was more or less ground for hope for the future at the beginning of the last quarter of the twentieth century than there had been in 1948 was a puzzling question.

Ever since the outbreak of the First World War and especially ever since the crash of 1929, the future of the world had seemed to the living generation of mankind to be clouded with uncertainty. At the beginning of the last quarter of the twentieth century the uncertainty was profound. There seemed to be more than the usual number of imponderables, unknowns and unknowables: the coming changes in leaders and possibly in policies in the three greatest powers, the United States, the Soviet Union and China; the ability of the people of the United States to recover their confidence in themselves and in their government and the related ability of the United States to earn the respect and confidence of the peoples and governments of the world; developments in Israel, Yugoslavia and southern Africa; the extent of the changes in the Communist parties of Italy, France and Spain; changes in the balance of military forces; changes in policies on energy, environment and population; changes in climate; the ability of the western world compared with the Soviet Union and China to avoid recessions and depressions, inflation and unemployment; and the results of the pressure from the poorer countries of the world for a new international political and economic order. The most important of all the unknowns was the extent of the resilience, the wisdom, courage, integrity, imagination and creativity of the new generation of leaders. How great would be the ability and determination of the governments of the poor half of the world, communist and noncommunist, to carry out development strategies and projects leading to a high level of employment in productive work and to a high rate of increase in the production of essential goods and services so that adequate food, shelter and clothing would be provided for the mass of the people? How great would be the ability and determination of the governments of the rich countries, communist and non-communist, to assist the governments of the poor half of the world in these endeavours?

By the mid-1950s it was clear that the North Atlantic community could not be an island of stability and well-being in a sea of tempest and misery. By the beginning of the 1960s many, if not most, of the critical problems facing the world were not in their pith and substance aspects of a contest with Communism or with Russia and China and, even if Communism did not exist or if Russia and China did not exist or if they were liberal democracies, these problems would be intractable and would endanger the peace and welfare of the whole world. By 1976, these propositions had become conventional wisdom. But it is discouraging that it took so long for truths so obvious to be accepted. If, in the last quarter of the twentieth century, the governments and peoples of the world continue to be so slow to respond to new problems and challenges, the future of mankind will be bleak.

My generation made the North Atlantic treaty as a partial and imperfect response to some of the challenges which then confronted the western world. Another generation must decide what new ways of thought, what new domestic and foreign policies, new international agreements and institutions are required to make a creative response to the very different challenges which now confront the world.

APPENDICES

Appendix 1

SOURCES AND
LIST OF WORKS CITED

SOURCES

The Department of External Affairs of Canada gave me permission to consult the files of the Department in order that I might refresh my memory of the part which I had played in the making of the North Atlantic treaty. Most of the documents from the files of the Department which I cite are from file 283(s), "North Atlantic Security Pact". This is referred to in the references as NASP. Other files of the Department are referred to by their number: e.g. D.E.A. 277-s. Telegrams from the Canadian embassy in Washington to the Department have the prefix WA. Telegrams from the Department to the embassy in Washington have the prefix EX.

My access to the files of the Department was subject to two conditions. I am not permitted to quote Canadian Cabinet documents after 1946, since they are subject to a strict 30-year rule, or unpublished documents originating from other governments unless they have been officially released. I have sometimes been able to get around this second condition by quoting a message from the British government to the United States government which has been published in place of the corresponding message to the Canadian government which has not been published.

The files of the Department contain few records of the telephone conversations between L. B. Pearson and the Canadian embassy in Washington on the subject of the negotiation of the treaty. Hume Wrong's papers in the Canadian Archives contain memoranda on some of those conversations as well as other documents which are not in the files of the Department. (Wrong papers, Archives Canada, M.G. 30, D. 94, hereafter referred to as Wrong papers.) The Canadian Archives also has a collection of my papers. (Escott Reid papers, Archives Canada, 69/10152/4493, hereafter referred to as Reid papers.)

The only government which has up to the present (1976) published a selection of documents on the making of the North Atlantic treaty is the government of the United States. Canada will probably publish its selection of documents in 1979.

The United States selection is contained in *Foreign Relations of the United States, 1948,* Vol. III, hereafter referred to as *F.R.,* 1948, III, and in *Foreign Relations of the United States, 1949,* Vol. IV, hereafter referred to as *F.R.,* 1949, IV. Most of the documents from the files of the State Department of the United States which are cited in this book have been published in one of these volumes.

The principal United States architect of the treaty was J. D. Hickerson, who worked on the treaty first under Robert A. Lovett and then under Dean Acheson; he gave an interview to the Oral History project of York University, Toronto. Hickerson was assisted by Theodore C. Achilles who wrote a draft of his diplomatic memoirs in 1972 and 1973, but only for private circulation; he has given me permission to include quotations from these memoirs. He also gave an interview to the York University Oral History project. I have had an extensive correspondence with Mr. Hickerson and Mr. Achilles about the making of the treaty and they have kindly given me permission to quote from their letters to me.

The second volume of Lester Pearson's memoirs, *Mike,* contains a chapter on the creation of the alliance ("Atlantic vision") and one on the first eight years of the alliance ("NATO at work"). This is the fullest account yet published by one of the principal architects of the alliance. Pearson also gave an interview to the Oral History project of York University.

Acheson has a chapter on the negotiation of the treaty in his memoirs, *Present at the Creation,* but he was concerned with the 12-month-long negotiations for only the final two months. George Kennan discusses the making of the treaty in his *Memoirs, 1925-1950* and Charles Bohlen in his *Witness to History* but both accounts contain errors which suggest that they were not permitted to refresh their memories by consulting the State Department files.

One of the principal British architects of the treaty was Gladwyn Jebb (later Lord Gladwyn). He deals with the making of the North Atlantic treaty in *The Memoirs of Lord Gladwyn* but he was not allowed to consult the Foreign Office files and he had no papers of his own on the negotiations so that his account is based on memory.

The oral interviews on the making of the treaty have to be treated with caution since few former cabinet ministers or senior officials can, unless they have kept diaries and have consulted them just before being interviewed, recall accurately events which occurred twenty-five years before in long-drawn-out complicated international discussions such as those which resulted in the North Atlantic treaty, especially since they would have been involved at the time in a host of other difficult and pressing problems. Memory is unreliable when it is not refreshed by consulting the documents of the period. Off-the-cuff interviews often confuse events, times, and places. The person interviewed may recollect accurately what he said or wrote; his recollection of when he said or wrote it may be out by a month or more and in diplomatic negotiations this may be important. Pearson made inaccurate statements in the interview he gave in the York University project; indeed he warned the interviewers at the time that "of course, you forget about these things years after. . . ."

Diaries can also contain errors of fact. *The Forrestal Diaries* (of James Forrestal, the United States Secretary of Defense at the time of the opening of the negotiations on the North Atlantic treaty) contain an extract from Forrestal's diary for April 9, 1948, in which Forrestal states that Paul-Henri Spaak, then Prime Minister and Foreign Minister of Belgium, supported most strongly the proposal for an alliance between the United States and the Brussels treaty countries. He did not. Carefully written memoirs, even those like Acheson's which are prepared with the help of scholarly research assistants, contain unintentional errors.

A good deal of diplomatic reporting is in some such terms as: "Mr. Lovett told me [Pearson] today in the strictest confidence that M. Bonnet, the French Ambassador, had called on General Marshall the other day and had told him that the French government believed. . . ." The participants in these talks probably did not take notes at the time. Marshall might therefore have reported Bonnet inaccurately to Lovett. Lovett might have reported Marshall inaccurately to Pearson. Pearson might have reported Lovett inaccurately to Ottawa. These errors could all have been made in good faith. There is also the possibility of tendentious reporting. Lovett might, for example, have succumbed to the temptation to exaggerate Marshall's exasperation at the message Bonnet had given him from the French government in order to make it more likely that Canada would support the United States if it got tough with the French.

Principal documents

1. Tripartite talks, March 22, 1948, to April 1, 1948.

(a) Minutes. No agreed minutes were made of the six meetings of the tripartite talks. Each side kept its own record and did not circulate its record to the other two governments. The minutes prepared by Major-General Alfred M. Gruenther of the United States delegation are contained in *F.R.*, 1948, III, 59-61, 64-66, 66-67, 69-70, 70-71, and 71-72. The Canadian account is in NASP.

(b) Delegation papers, March 23, 1948. As a result of a decision made at the second tripartite meeting on March 23, 1948, *(F.R.* 1948, III, 65) each delegation prepared a paper. These papers have not been printed. They are in NASP. The United States paper was based on a report of March 23, 1948, prepared by the policy planning staff of the State Department concerning Western Union and related problems; this report is printed in *F.R.*,1948, III, 61-64.

(c) Draft report, March 24, 1948. At the third tripartite meeting a drafting committee consisting of Achilles, Jebb and Pearson produced a draft paper. This has not been printed; it is in NASP.

(d) Final report, April 1, 1948. As a result of the tripartite meetings a report was prepared for submission to the three governments. This undated paper, called the Pentagon paper, is in *F.R.*, 1948, III, 72-75.

2. Ambassadors' Committee, July 6, 1943 to March 15, 1949.

(a) Agreed minutes. Agreed minutes were kept of the eighteen formal meetings of the Ambassadors' Committee. A complete set is in D.E.A., file 283-1s. The minutes of sixteen of the meetings are printed in *F.R.,*1948, III and *F.R.,* 1949, IV. The minutes of the thirteenth meeting on February 25, 1949, have not been printed (*F.R.,*1949, IV, 123 fn 3). Only about two-thirds of the minutes of the meeting on March 7, 1949, have been printed (*F.R.,* 1949, IV, 172).

(b) Verbatim transcripts, July 9, 1948 to March 15, 1949. Verbatim transcripts were made of the formal meetings of the Ambassadors' Committee from the fifth meeting on and circulated to the participants. These have not been printed. They are in the Wrong papers.

(c) Informal and unofficial meetings, August 20, 1948, and February 19, 1949. No agreed minutes were made of these meetings. The Canadian account is in NASP. The United States account of the meeting of August 20, 1948, is in *F.R.,* 1948, III, 214-221.

3. Working Group, July 12, 1948 to March 28, 1949.
The Working Group held fifteen meetings between July 12, 1948 and September 9, 1948, five meetings between December 15, 1948 and December 23, 1948, and at least fourteen meetings from January 10, 1949 to March 28, 1949. "Action summaries" of three meetings, (December 15, 16 and 17,) were agreed to *(F.R.* 1948, III, *FN)* but no agreed records were kept of the other meetings. The action summaries of the three meetings in December are in the State Department NATO Research File, Lot 57D 271. *F.R.* 1948, III, contains extracts from the United States record of the first fifteen meetings. Reports from the Canadian embassy in Washington on some of the meetings are in NASP. The Wrong papers contain full minutes of the five meetings in December, 1948, and of the first four meetings in 1949 (January 10, 11, 13 and 18).

4. Washington paper, September 9, 1948.
The Ambassadors' Committee agreed on September 10, 1948, to the "Washington paper" of September 9 summing up the results of the six-power meetings in the summer. This is printed in *F.R.,* 1948, III, 237-248.

5. Canadian commentary, December 6, 1948.
The Canadian government circulated to the Working Group a "Commentary on the Washington Paper of September 9, 1948", dated December 6, 1948. This has not been printed. It is in NASP and in State Department PA/HO Research Files, Lot 57-D271. (*F.R.,* 1948, III, 310, fn 2).

6. London paper.
The Permanent Commission of the Brussels Powers meeting in London in November, 1948, prepared a paper entitled "Notes on paper of September 9, 1948". This consisted of a draft treaty and commentary. This was circulated to the Working Group on December 11. This has not been printed. It is in NASP and in the same State Department file as the preceding paper.

7. December 24, 1948, paper.

The Ambassadors' Committee agreed on December 24, 1948, to a report to their governments which contained a draft treaty and comments on the articles of the treaty. This is printed in *F.R.,* 1948, III, 333-343.

8. Agreed interpretations, March 15, 1949.
The minutes of the meeting of the Ambassadors' Committee of March 15, 1949, include agreed interpretations of certain phrases and articles in the North Atlantic treaty. This is printed in *F.R.,* 1949, IV, 222-223, and in Appendix 4 of this book, pages 269-270. The interpretation was not in fact agreed to at the meeting on March 15 but at subsequent meetings of the Working Group. (WA 749 of March 17, 1949, NASP).

9. Drafts of the treaty.
In addition to the two drafts of the treaty referred to above (December 11 and 24, 1948) officials in Washington, London and Ottawa prepared drafts of the treaty for the guidance of their representatives in the intergovernmental discussions. These were not circulated to the other participating governments. They have not been printed. They consist of:
(a) March 19, 1948. Draft by Escott Reid in NASP. This draft embodied suggestions by Arnold Smith for revision of an earlier draft by Reid. See letter from Smith to Reid of January 10, 1948. (D.E.A. file 211-Js.)
(b) April 1, 1948. Draft by T.C. Achilles of the State Department (Achilles, *Draft Memoirs,* 411G.) This has not yet been found in the Department of State files.
(c) June, 1948. The British prepared a draft treaty before the second stage of discussions. (Letter from United Kingdom High Commissioner in Ottawa to the Department of External Affairs, July 2, 1948, NASP.) This is presumably in the Foreign Office files. I have not seen it.
(d) June 20, 1948. Draft by Escott Reid in NASP.
(e) September, 1948. In September, 1948, T.C. Achilles of the State Department prepared a draft of the treaty. (Achilles to Reid, letter, September 27, 1976). This has not yet been found in the Department of State files.
(f) December 17, 1948. Draft by officers of the Department of External Affairs (D.E.A., file 283-B-s).

10. Conference of foreign ministers, April 2, 1949.
The minutes of the conference of foreign ministers held at Washington on April 2, 1949, have been printed in *F.R.,* 1949, IV, 271-281. The verbatim transcript is in the Wrong papers.

11. Contemporary account.
J.N. Henderson (later Sir Nicholas Henderson), then Second Secretary of the British embassy in Washington, prepared a classified account of the negotiations immediately after they were completed. This will presumably be made available by the British authorities in 1979. I have not seen it.

LIST OF WORKS CITED

Acheson, Dean. *Present at the Creation.* New York, Norton, 1969.

Achilles, Theodore. "Beyond Diplomacy". *Foreign Service Journal,* (April, 1963).

Achilles, Theodore. *Draft Memoirs.* Unpublished.

Armstrong, Hamilton Fish. "Is it Russia vs. U.S. - Or vs. U.N.?" *New York Times Magazine,* (Sept. 14, 1947).

Attlee, C. R. *As It Happened.* London, Heinemann, 1954.

Bohlen, Charles E. *Witness to History, 1929-1969.* New York, Norton, 1973.

Buchan, Alastair. *The End of the Postwar Era.* London, Weidenfeld and Nicolson, 1974.

Buchan, Alastair. "Mother and Daughters (or Greeks and Romans)." *Foreign Affairs,* (July, 1976).

Childs, Marquis. "The Shooting War Comes Closer." *Washington Post,* (March 4, 1948).

Churchill, Randolph S. ed. *The Sinews of Peace: Post-War Speeches by Winston S. Churchill.* London, Cassell, 1961.

Forsey, Eugene, ed. *Canada in a New World.* Toronto, Ryerson Press, 1948.

Francks, Thomas M., Westbank, Edward, ed. *Secrecy and Foreign Policy.* New York, Oxford University Press, 1974.

Freeland, Richard M. *The Truman Doctrine and the Origins of McCarthyism.* New York, Knopf, 1972.

Gladwyn, Lord. *The European Idea.* New York, F. A. Praeger, 1966.

Gladwyn, Lord. *The Memoirs of Lord Gladwyn.* London, Weidenfeld and Nicolson, 1972.

Goodman, Elliot R. *The Fate of the Atlantic Community.* New York, Washington, Praeger Press, 1975.

Kennan, George F. *Memoirs, 1925-1950.* Boston, Little, Brown and Company, 1967.

Kolko, Joyce, Kolko, Gabriel. *The Limits of Power.* New York, Harper and Row, 1972.

Lippmann, Walter. "Half Measures and Generalities." *Washington Post,* (March 30, 1948).

Meade, J. E. *The Atlantic Community and the Dollar Gap.* London, Friends of Atlantic Union, n. d.

Merchant, Livingston T., ed. *Neighbors Taken for Granted.* New York, F. A. Praeger, 1966.

Millis, Walter, ed. *The Forrestal Diaries.* New York, Viking Press, 1951.

New York Times. "Extracts from Statements and Speeches at Communist Meeting in East Berlin." (July 1, 1976).

Pearson, L. B. "H. Hume Wrong." *External Affairs,* Vol. 6, no. 3. Ottawa, Department of External Affairs, (March, 1954).

Pearson, Lester B. *Mike: The Memoirs of the Rt. Hon. Lester B. Pearson. Vol. I and II.* Toronto and Buffalo, University of Toronto Press, 1972 and 1973.

Pickersgill, J. W., Forster, D. F.; *The Mackenzie King Record, Vol. IV, 1947-1948.* Toronto, University of Toronto Press, 1970.

Pickersgill, J. W. *My Years with Louis St. Laurent: A Political Memoir.* Toronto and Buffalo, University of Toronto Press, 1975.

Reid, Escott. "The Revolution in Canadian Foreign Policy, 1947-1951." *India Quarterly,* (April-June, 1958), and *Aussenpolitik,* (July, 1958),

Reston, James. "Basic Decision Facing U.S. in Foreign Policy." *New York Times,* (March 14, 1948).

Statistical Office of the United Nations. *National Income and its Distribution in Underdeveloped Countries.* New York, Department of Economic Affairs, United Nations, 1951.

Stikker, Dirk U. *Men of Responsibility.* London, Harper and Row, 1966.

Strang, Lord. *At Home and Abroad.* London, Deutsch, 1956.

Taylor, A. J. P. *English History 1914-1945.* London, Oxford University Press, 1967.

Toynbee, Arnold. *Civilization on Trial.* New York, Oxford University Press, 1948.

Toynbee, Arnold. *Survey of International Affairs 1949-1950.* Toronto, Oxford University Press, 1953.

Vandenberg, Arthur H. Jr., ed. *The Private Papers of Senator Vandenberg.* Boston, Houghton Mifflin, 1952.

Ward, Barbara. *Britain's Interest in Atlantic Union.* London, Friends of Atlantic Union, n. d.

Williams, Francis. *A Prime Minister Remembers.* London, Heinemann, 1961.

Appendix 2

NORTH ATLANTIC TREATY

The Parties to this Treaty reaffirm their faith in the purposes and principles of the Charter of the United Nations and their desire to live in peace with all peoples and all governments.

They are determined to safeguard the freedom, common heritage and civilization of their peoples, founded on the principles of democracy individual liberty and the rule of law.

They seek to promote stability and well-being in the North Atlantic area.

They are resolved to unite their efforts for collective defense and for the preservation of peace and security.

They therefore agree to this North Atlantic Treaty:

ARTICLE 1

The Parties undertake, as set forth in the Charter of the United Nations, to settle any international disputes in which they may be involved by peaceful means in such a manner that international peace and security, and justice, are not endangered, and to refrain in their international relations from the threat or use of force in any manner inconsistent with the purposes of the United Nations.

ARTICLE 2

The Parties will contribute toward the further development of peaceful and friendly international relations by strengthening their free institutions, by bringing about a better understanding of the principles upon which these institutions are founded, and by promoting conditions of stability and well-being. They will seek to eliminate conflict in their international economic policies and will encourage economic collaboration between any or all of them.

ARTICLE 3

In order more effectively to achieve the objectives of this Treaty, the Parties, separately and jointly, by means of continuous and effective self-help and mutual aid, will maintain and develop their individual and collective capacity to resist armed attack.

ARTICLE 4

The Parties will consult together whenever, in the opinion of any of them, the territorial integrity, political independence or security of any of the Parties is threatened.

ARTICLE 5

The Parties agree that an armed attack against one or more of them in Europe or North America shall be considered an attack against them all; and consequently they agree that, if such an armed attack occurs, each of them, in exercise of the right of individual or collective self-defence recognized by Article 51 of the Charter of the United Nations, will assist the Party or Parties so attacked by taking forthwith, individually and in concert with the other Parties, such action as it deems necessary, including the use of armed force, to restore and maintain the security of the North Atlantic area.

Any such armed attack and all measures taken as a result thereof shall immediately be reported to the Security Council. Such measures shall be terminated when the Security Council has taken the measures necessary to restore and maintain international peace and security.

ARTICLE 6

For the purpose of Article 5 an armed attack on one or more of the Parties is deemed to include an armed attack on the territory of any of the Parties in Europe or North America, on the Algerian departments of France, on the occupation forces of any Party in Europe, on the islands under the jurisdiction of any Party in the North Atlantic area north of the Tropic of Cancer or on the vessels or aircraft in this area of any of the Parties.

ARTICLE 7

This Treaty does not affect, and shall not be interpreted as affecting, in any way the rights and obligations under the Charter of the Parties which are members of the United Nations, or the primary responsibility of the Security Council for the maintenance of international peace and security.

ARTICLE 8

Each Party declares that none of the international engagements now in force between it and any other of the Parties or any third state is in conflict with the provisions of this Treaty, and undertakes not to enter into any international engagement in conflict with this Treaty.

ARTICLE 9

The Parties hereby establish a council, on which each of them shall be represented, to consider matters concerning the implementation of this Treaty. The council shall be so organized as to be able to meet promptly at any time. The council shall set up such subsidiary bodies as may be necessary; in particular it shall establish immediately a defense committee which shall recommend measures for the implementation of Articles 3 and 5.

ARTICLE 10

The Parties may, by unanimous agreement, invite any other European state in a position to further the principles of this Treaty and to contribute to the security of the North Atlantic area to accede to this Treaty. Any state so invited may become a party to the Treaty by depositing its instrument of accession with the Government of the United States of America. The Government of the United States of America will inform each of the Parties of the deposit of each such instrument of accession.

ARTICLE 11

This Treaty shall be ratified and its provisions carried out by the Parties in accordance with their respective constitutional processes. The instruments of ratification shall be deposited as soon as possible with the Government of the United States of America, which will notify all the other signatories of each deposit. The Treaty shall enter into force between the states which have ratified it as soon as the ratifications of the majority of the signatories, including the ratifications of Belgium, Canada, France, Luxembourg, the Netherlands, the United Kingdom and the United States, have been deposited and shall come into effect with respect to other states on the date of the deposit of their ratifications.

ARTICLE 12

After the Treaty has been in force for ten years, or at any time thereafter, the Parties shall, if any of them so requests, consult together for the purpose of reviewing the Treaty, having regard for the factors then affecting peace and security in the North Atlantic area, including the development of universal as well as regional arrangements under the Charter of the United Nations for the maintenance of international peace and security.

ARTICLE 13

After the Treaty has been in force for twenty years, any Party may cease to be a party one year after its notice of denunciation has been given to the Government of the United States of America, which will inform the Governments of the other Parties of the deposit of each notice of denunciation.

ARTICLE 14

This Treaty, of which the English and French texts are equally authentic, shall be deposited in the archives of the Government of the United States of America. Duly certified copies thereof will be transmitted by the Government to the Governments of the other signatories.

In witness whereof, the undersigned plenipotentiaries have signed this Treaty.

Done at Washington, the 4th day of April, 1949.

Appendix 3

AGREED INTERPRETATIONS OF THE TREATY*

During the exploratory talks which resulted in the draft treaty, agreement was reached on the meaning of certain phrases and articles. These agreements were not formal, but constituted the understanding of the representatives participating in the dicussions as to the interpretation of those phrases and articles. The committee reviewed those interpretations and instructed the Secretary to make note of them. They are:

"(1) The participation of Italy in the North Atlantic Treaty has no effect upon the provisions of the Italian Peace Treaty.

"(2) 'Mutual aid' under Article 3 means the contribution by each Party, consistent with its geographic location and resources and with due regard to the requirements of economic recovery, of such mutual aid as it can reasonably be expected to contribute in the form in which it can most effectively furnish it, e.g., facilities, manpower, productive capacity, or military equipment.

"(3) Article 4 is applicable in the event of a threat in any part of the world, to the security of any of the Parties, including a threat to the security of their overseas territories.

"(4) a. For the purposes of Article 6 the British and American forces in the Free Territory of Trieste are understood to be occupation forces.

"b. The words, 'North Atlantic area north of the Tropic of Cancer' in Article 6 mean the general area of the North Atlantic Ocean north of that line, including adjacent sea and air spaces between the territories covered by that Article.

"(5) With reference to Article 8, it is understood that no previous international engagements to which any of the participating states are parties would in any way interfere with the carrying out of their obligations under this Treaty.

"(6) The Council, as Article 9 specifically states, is established 'to consider matters concerning the implementation of the Treaty' and is

*Foreign Relations of the United States, 1949, Volume IV, pages 222-223. Minutes of the Ambassadors' Committee, March 15, 1949.

empowered 'to set up such subsidiary bodies as may be necessary'. This is a broad rather than specific definition of functions and is not intended to exclude the performance at appropriate levels in the organization of such planning for the implementation of Articles 3 and 5 or other functions as the Parties may agree to be necessary.

"(7) It is the common understanding that the primary purpose of this Treaty is to provide for the collective self-defense of the Parties, as countries having common interests in the North Atlantic area, while reaffirming their existing obligations for the maintenance of peace and the settlement of disputes between them.

"It is further understood that the Parties will, in their public statements, stress this primary purpose, recognized and preserved by Article 51, rather than any specific connection with Chapter VIII or other Articles of the United Nations Charter."

Appendix 4

UNITED NATIONS CHARTER, ARTICLES 51 TO 56

Chapter VII. Action with respect to threats to the peace, breaches of the peace, and acts of aggression

Article 51

Nothing in the present Charter shall impair the inherent right of individual or collective self-defence if an armed attack occurs against a Member of the United Nations, until the Security Council has taken the measures necessary to maintain international peace and security. Measures taken by Members in the exercise of this right of self-defence shall be immediately reported to the Security Council and shall not in any way affect the authority and responsibility of the Security Council under the present Charter to take at any time such action as it deems necessary in order to maintain or restore international peace and security.

Chapter VIII. Regional arrangements

Article 52

1. Nothing in the present Charter precludes the existence of regional arrangements or agencies for dealing with such matters relating to the maintenance of international peace and security as are appropriate for regional action, provided that such arrangements or agencies and their activities are consistent with the Purposes and Principles of the United Nations.

2. The Members of the United Nations entering into such arrangements or constituting such agencies shall make every effort to achieve pacific settlement of local disputes through such regional arrangements or by such regional agencies before referring them to the Security Council.

3. The Security Council shall encourage the development of pacific settlement of local disputes through such regional arrangements or by such regional agencies either on the initiative of the states concerned or by reference from the Security Council.

4. This Article in no way impairs the application of Articles 34 and 35.

Article 53

1. The Security Council shall, where appropriate, utilize such regional arrangements or agencies for enforcement action under its authority. But no enforcement action shall be taken under regional arrangements or by

regional agencies without the authorization of the Security Council, with the exception of measures against any enemy state, as defined in paragraph 2 of this Article, provided for pursuant to Article 107 or in regional arrangements directed against renewal of aggressive policy on the part of any such state, until such time as the Organization may, on request of the Governments concerned, be charged with the responsibility for preventing further aggression by such a state.

2. The term enemy state as used in paragraph 1 of this Article applies to any state which during the Second World War has been an enemy of any signatory of the present Charter.

Article 54

The Security Council shall at all times be kept fully informed of activities undertaken or in contemplation under regional arrangements or by regional agencies for the maintenance of international peace and security.

Chapter IX. International economic and social cooperation

Article 55

With a view to the creation of conditions of stability and well-being which are necessary for peaceful and friendly relations among nations based on respect for the principle of equal rights and self-determination of peoples, the United Nations shall promote:

a. higher standards of living, full employment, and conditions of economic and social progress and development;

b. solutions of international economic, social, health, and related problems; and international cultural and educational cooperation; and

c. universal respect for, and observance of, human rights and fundamental freedoms for all without distinction as to race, sex, language, or religion.

Article 56

All Members pledge themselves to take joint and separate action in cooperation with the Organization for the achievement of the purposes set forth in Article 55.

NOTES

CHAPTER ONE: Fear
Page 17
This was the language used in the body of the report but the final paragraph of Appendix B of the report reads as follows, "The Soviet Union will not risk war in the immediate future; however, there is real danger of war within one or two years. The only deterrent at that time would be solid conviction by the Soviet Government that in fact the United States was preponderant in military strength and potential and that war would eventually result in peril to the Communist regime."[1]

CHAPTER FOUR: The Intergovernmental Discussions
Page 45
In the first stage of the negotiations there were six meetings. In the next three stages there were eighteen formal meetings and two informal meetings of the Ambassadors' Committee. The Working Group held over thirty-four meetings: fifteen during the second stage, five during the third and at least fourteen in the fourth. United States and Canadian sources refer to ten meetings of the Working Group in the fourth stage: January 10, 11, 13, 18, 25, 28; February 1; March 10, 16 and 28. There must have been at least four additional meetings.

Page 48
The Consultative Council of the foreign ministers of the Brussels powers in a message of October 29, 1948, said that they "agreed in principle to negotiate a North Atlantic Pact with Canada and the United States".[2] The Canadian government informed the other governments on October 13, 1948, that it had considered the proposals set forth in the Washington paper of September 9, 1948, and was ready to enter into a treaty with the United States, Britain, France and the Benelux countries and such other countries as might be agreed on the general lines of the annex to the Washington paper.[3] The United States stated that it was not able to give a formal acceptance in principle until it had considered the comments of the Brussels powers and had taken soundings of congress and of the Republican high command if the Republicans won the election.[4]

Page 49
Three telegrams to Ottawa sent by Wrong in March, 1949, indicate how quickly the treaty froze once it was published. On March 3, two weeks before it was published, Wrong said that Acheson clearly had in mind some sort of a conference preceding signature. Wrong added, "If you have a conference attended by foreign ministers, it seems evident that the text cannot be considered unalterable when the conference meets."[5] On March 11, he said that the text of the treaty "can therefore now be regarded as almost final, and everyone hopes that no government will ask for any changes, except perhaps on trifling points, before the treaty is

271

signed."[6] On March 25, a week after the treaty was published, he said, "There is a unanimous desire among the negotiators here to make no changes whatever in the published text. The possibility of change between publication and signature was left open only in case comment on the text should reveal important flaws which had previously escaped notice."[7] On March 3, the published treaty could not be considered as unalterable. On March 11, trifling modifications might be possible. On March 25, there should be no change unless important flaws were discovered.

Page 49

The Canadian government put forward its suggestions for the textual improvement of the English and French versions of the North Atlantic treaty in a memorandum sent to the governments of Britain, France and the Benelux countries and to the members of the Ambassadors' Committee.[8] De Margerie of the French Foreign Office said that the alterations Canada had proposed to the French text seemed to him very sensible.[9] The British government accepted the amendments in principle.[10] The Netherlands government accepted the amendments to the English text but could not comment on the amendments to the French text since it had not received the French text.[11] The Belgian government agreed to some of the amendments.[12] But before these governments had informed their representatives in Washington of their views, the Working Group had held a meeting on March 28, 1949, and had rejected all the amendments.[13]

CHAPTER FIVE: The Architects of the Treaty
Page 64

An editorial note in *Foreign Relations of the United States, 1948,* states that Kennan was a regular participant in the fifteen meetings of the Working Group held between July 12 and September 9, 1948.[14] It seems, however, from the United States minutes of these meetings that he may have attended only two of the fifteen meetings, those on September 2 and 7. Bohlen, who is not listed in the editorial note as one of the regular participants, seems to have attended more meetings.

Page 64

Other persons who took part in meetings of the Ambassadors' Committee or the Working Group were: for the United States, George Butler, S. Reber, W. J. Galloway; for Britain, Donald Maclean and J. N. Henderson; for Canada, R. L. Rogers; for France, Arnaud Walper; for Belgium, Roger Taymans and Robert Vaes; and for the Netherlands, Otto Reughlin and Caes Vreede.[15]

Page 64

This group of fifteen consists of foreign ministers or acting foreign ministers of the three countries during the negotiations (Bevin, Lovett, Acheson, St. Laurent, Pearson, Claxton), the ambassadors in Washington (Franks and Wrong), the senior officials concerned in the foreign offices (Jebb, Hickerson and I), the leading representatives on the Working Group (Hoyer Millar, Achilles and Stone), and the chairman of the Senate Foreign Committee during the greater part of the negotiations (Vandenberg).

CHAPTER ELEVEN: More than a Military Alliance
Page 139
I had put this point in a commentary I had prepared in the spring of 1945 on a draft of the U.N. Charter: "Nations do not go to war because of disputes with each other over tariffs, monetary questions, cartels, shipping, aviation and such things but we know from experience that if states are constantly quarreling over questions which involve national prestige, national security and national prosperity, it is much more difficult for them to co-operate in the establishment and maintenance of an effective world security organization to that very high degree which is necessary if world peace is to be preserved."[16]

CHAPTER TWELVE: The Pledge
Page 144
An example of a very strong pledge is that in the quadruple alliance of November, 1815, between Britain, Austria, Prussia and Russia. The allies promised "to employ, in case of need, the whole of their forces, in order to bring the War to a speedy and successful termination. . . ." An example of a weak pledge is that in the abortive Anglo-French and Franco-American treaties of alliance signed in June, 1919. The United Kingdom and the United States "shall be bound to come immediately to [France's] assistance in the event of any unprovoked movement of aggression against her being made by Germany."

Page 146
This message was precipitated by Pearson receiving the March 31 draft of the Pentagon paper which provided that the pledge would be followed by a statement that "each Contracting Party shall determine for itself whether there has occurred an armed attack within the meaning of the agreement".[17] The United States, probably as a result of Pearson's message, withdrew this proposal and substituted the "it considers" phrase, but this still constituted an explicit statement of the right of each party to decide for itself whether an armed attack had occurred.

CHAPTER THIRTEEN: Indirect Aggression
Page 158
The report of March 23, 1948, containing this proposal was transmitted by the Secretary of State to the National Security Council. George Kennan, the Director of the policy planning staff, was away from Washington when this report was submitted. The wording of this section of the report may well, however, have been influenced by his telegram of March 15 to the Secretary of State recommending that the Italian government should outlaw the communist party before the general elections which were to take place on April 18, even though this would presumably mean civil war, a re-occupation by the United States of defence facilities in Italy and probably a military division of the country. Certainly the definition of indirect aggression proposed by Kennan's policy planning staff was so

broad that, if Italy were a member of the North Atlantic alliance, it would cover armed intervention by the United States and other allies of Italy to assist an Italian government to resist an attempted Communist *coup d'*état or to overthrow a Communist government which had taken power as a result of a *coup d'*état or even of an election.

CHAPTER FOURTEEN: Consultation
Page 165
The London Paper presented by the Brussels Powers in December, 1948, proposed that Article 4 should require consultation not only if an ally was of the opinion that the territorial integrity, political independence or security of an ally was threatened but also if it was of the opinion that "there exists any situation which constitutes a threat to the peace." Canada favoured even broader language, "a threat to or breach of the peace."[18]

CHAPTER FIFTEEN: Article 2
Page 170
Two other changes were made in the draft being considered at the beginning of August. The words "between any or all of the parties" were added to the description of the proposed article so that it read "Provision for the encouragement of efforts between any or all of the parties to promote the general welfare through collaboration in the economic, social and cultural fields". The inclusion of this provision would not as in the August draft "provide a basis for the long-range development of practicable cooperation between the North Atlantic nations in other than the military field", it would merely "give substance to the concept of a positive rather than a purely negative treaty".[19]

CHAPTER SEVENTEEN: Membership
Page 198
Hickerson told the Danish embassy in Washington on January 3, 1949, that "the United States would not have arms available for non-members" of the North Atlantic alliance.[20] He told the Norwegian Ambassador on January 13 that he thought that it was "out of the question" that the United States might in a year or so supply arms to countries which were not in a regional association of interest to United States defense.[21] He told the Swedish Ambassador on January 14 that the United States administration had repeatedly pointed out that United States defence materials would be allotted on a priority basis to countries coming within the terms of the Vandenberg resolution and to those to which the United States had previous commitments such as Turkey, Greece and Korea. "Limitations of supply would in the foreseeable future preclude furnishing weapons to countries not so qualified for assistance."[22] President Truman in his inaugural address in Janury, 1949, said that the United States "will provide military advice and equipment to free nations *which will co-operate with us* in the maintenance of peace and security."[23] (Italics added.) The Canadian embassy in Washington reported on January 24, 1949, that the United States had made it clear to the three Scandinavian countries that "no military assistance would be forthcoming if they remained outside

the Atlantic pact." [24] By the beginning of February the talks between the three Scandinavian countries over the possibility of a Scandinavian defence pact had broken down[25] and Acheson had become Secretary of State. The language now used by the United States became milder. Thus Bohlen told Lange, the Foreign Minister of Norway, on February 8 that the United States was anxious to avoid using the question of military supplies as a pressure weapon, that membership in the Atlantic pact would be one factor but not the only one in allotting military supplies and that it did not follow that countries not in the pact would be excluded.[26] Three days later Acheson confirmed this to Lange adding that nevertheless it was clear that demands for military supplies would be much greater than the supplies available and this necessitated a "system of priorities which must be awarded where US has commitments or interests." Countries outside a coordinated military plan "such as an isolated Scandinavian bloc" would be in a less favored position and needs could hardly be considered for some time to come."[27] On March 14, Ernest Gross, an Assistant Secretary of State, told the Danish Foreign Minister that if Denmark was not a member of the North Atlantic alliance, the United States would still have to consider whether to provide Denmark with military supplies but that nevertheless it was always easier to justify aid to those who were part of a collective group and that similar considerations had, of course, applied to economic aid. [28]

Page 210
Kennan in his memoirs states that when Acheson became Secretary of State his influence and the influence of his policy planning staff diminished. It would, he writes, have been strange to Acheson to consult the policy planning staff as an institution and to concede to it as Marshall had, "a margin of confidence within which he was willing to respect its opinion even when that opinion did not fully coincide with his own". In oral discussions with Acheson, Kennan writes that "there were times when I felt like a court jester ... not to be taken fully seriously when it came to the final, responsible decisions of policy."[29]

CHAPTER EIGHTEEN: Algeria
Page 213
On January 16, 1963, the French representative made a statement to the North Atlantic Council on the effects of the independence of Algeria on certain aspects of the North Atlantic treaty. The Council noted that insofar as the former Algerian departments of France were concerned the relevant clauses of the treaty had become inapplicable as from July 3, 1962.[30]

CHAPTER NINETEEN: Disappointments and Frustrations
Page 220
On March 19, 1948, I proposed that the number of representatives from each member state in the Atlantic parliament should range between one and seventy-five and be roughly proportionate to the amount of military, economic and other aid and assistance which the member states had agreed to make immediately available to the North Atlantic Council if an

ally were attacked. Three months later I rejected this attempt to find a formula justifying the allocation of seats in an Atlantic parliament. I said to Pearson that the more I thought about it, the more it seemed to me clear "that in a political matter like this all one can do is to put down on paper what seems to be a reasonable number of votes for each country" and I suggested this allocation of seats.[31]

Page 226
The exception in Article 5 was a mistake. It should have been split into two articles. The advantage of having only one paragraph in an article of a treaty is that it makes it easy to cite provisions of the treaty. It is necessary to say only article such-and-such, not paragraph such-and-such of article such-and-such. An even sloppier type of drafting will make it necessary to say "Section i of Article 5 of Chapter III".

Page 227
The French successfully insisted that the French version should be in the traditional form: "réaffirmant," "determinés", "soucieux" and "résolus".

Page 228
Pearson sent me in September, 1972, his first draft of the two chapters in the second volume of his memoirs which deal with the North Atlantic treaty and asked me for my comments and suggestions for revision. I found that he had referred to me as having striven "so long and with an almost feverish and single-minded intensity to bring into being the perfect North Atlantic treaty". He had, before sending me the chapters, drawn a line through the words "almost feverish" and they do not appear in his memoirs.[32]

Page 229
The passage in my November 6, 1948, draft of the Canadian commentary to which Wrong and Robertson took particular exception were,

> The Canadian Government believes that one of the chief obstacles today to the creation by the Free Nations of an overwhelming preponderance of military, economic and moral force over the Soviet states is the despair, the apathy and the doubt which is so widespread in the Western World. The existence of this despair, apathy and doubt makes it essential that the North Atlantic democracies make a bold and imaginative move sufficient to raise in the hearts and minds and spirits of all those in the world who love freedom that confidence and faith which will restore their vigour. In our opinion this means that the North Atlantic Pact must be more than a mere military alliance or a negative anti-Soviet Pact; it must be the outward and visible sign of a new inward and spiritual unity and purpose in the Western World. The institutions set up by the Treaty should have within them the possibility of growth and adaptation to changing circumstances. They should be given titles symbolic of the ultimate goal of the world order which we have in mind and of which we are building an essential foundation. For this reason we suggest the use of such terms as these in the Pact: (1) "North Atlantic Treaty" instead of "North Atlantic Secu-

rity Pact"; (2) "North Atlantic Community" for the international organization established by the treaty; (3) "North Atlantic Nations" instead of "signatory states" or "contracting parties"; (4) "Council for Collective Self-Defence" instead of "consultative council"; "North Atlantic Assembly" instead of "assembly of the organization".[33]

Page 230
The final draft of this letter to Wrong was dated December 16, 1948. Pearson did not sign it and I believed at the time that he had not given it to Wrong. It was not until 1975 when I was looking through Wrong's papers in the Canadian Archives that I found that, when he saw Wrong in New York on December 29, 1948, he gave him this letter unsigned and "for information". [34]

Page 232
In 1975, the category of foreign service officer included persons who were not called foreign service officers in 1948. The number of foreign service officers serving in the Department of External Affairs in Ottawa in 1975 who would have been classified as foreign service officers in 1948 was 310 (compared with 71 in 1948). Of the 310, 250 had at least three years' experience (compared with 27 in 1948). This information was given me by the Under-Secretary's office in the Department in July, 1976.

CHAPTER TWENTY: Epilogue
Page 237:

NORTH ATLANTIC ALLIANCE — ORIGINAL MEMBERS
DEFENCE EXPENDITURES 1949-1952, AND 1974
(MILLION DOLLARS, U.S.)

	1949	1950	1951	1952	1974
Belgium	$165	$178	$282	$415	$1,558
Canada	337	467	1,199	1,931	2,828
Denmark	52	52	69	98	767
France	1,368	1,597	2,517	3,580	10,637
Italy	520	613	806	792	4,331
Luxembourg	2	3	5	9	19
Netherlands	179	237	279	330	2,522
Norway	52	50	80	116	741
Portugal	49	53	54	59	1,016
United Kingdom	2,181	2,377	3,217	4,372	9,796
United States	13,503	14,307	33,059	47,598	85,906
Total	18,408	19,934	41,567	59,300	120,121
Price Index	99.0	100.0	108.0	110.4	204.8
Total in 1950 Dollars	18,590	19,934	38,490	53,710	58,650
(U.S. only in 1950 Dollars)	13,640	14,307	30,610	43,100	41,940

NATO Facts and Figures, pages 296-7, published by the NATO Information Service in Brussels in January, 1976, gives the statistics of defence expenditures in local currencies; these have been converted into U.S. dollars. The figures for 1974 are a forecast. The price index for 1949 to 1952 comes from the consumer price index, U.S. Dept. of Labor, Bureau of Labor Statistics in Statistical Abstract of the U.S. 1959, Table No. 428, page 333. The index for 1974 is derived from Business Conditions Digest, March, 1976, page 90.

References

PREFACE

1. Hume Wrong, report on the United States-British-Canadian security conversations of March 22 to April 1, 1948, in Wrong to Pearson, April 2, 1948, NASP., file 283(s), part 1.
2. Joyce and Gabriel Kolko, *The Limits of Power,* (New York, 1972), 500.
3. Arnold Toynbee ed., *Survey of International Affairs 1949-1950,* (Oxford, 1953), 1-2.
4. C. R. Attlee, *As It Happened,* (London, 1954), 171, and 204. Lord Strang, Permanent Under-Secretary at the Foreign Office from 1949 to 1951 under Ernest Bevin, confirmed this. He wrote: "No single act during his term of office as Foreign Secretary gave him a more satisfying sense of achievement than the signature of the North Atlantic Treaty." (*Home and Abroad,* [London, 1956,] 289.)
5. Alastair Buchan, *The End of the Postwar Era,* (London, 1974), 18.
6. Dean Acheson, *Present at the Creation,* (New York, 1969), 725.

CHAPTER ONE: FEAR

1. Canadian Ambassador to the Netherlands to Department of External Affairs, Despatch No. 231, July 22, 1948, NASP., file 283(s), part 2.
2. *Foreign Relations of the United States,* (Hereafter listed as *F.R.*), 1948, IV, 858.
3. *F.R.*, 1948, IV, 844.
4. *F.R.*, 1948, III, 142.
5. Canadian Ambassador to France to Department of External Affairs, July 13, 1948, Tel. 397, D.E.A., file 2AE-1s.
6. *F.R.*, 1948, III, 238-40.
7. *F.R.*, 1948, III, 157.
8. George Kennan, talk, Canadian National Defence College, May 31, 1948, transmitted by Arnold Smith to the Department of External Affairs on Aug. 5, 1948, D.E.A., file 2-AEs.
9. *F.R.*, 1948, III, 285.
10. Arthur H. Vandenberg Jr. ed., *The Private Papers of Senator Vandenberg,* (Boston, 1952), 416.
11. U.S. Ambassador to the Soviet Union to the Secretary of State, Despatch No. 315, April 1, 1948, F.R., 1948, I, part 2, 552.
12. Holmes to Pearson, April 9, 1948, D.E.A., file 2AE 1s.
13. *F.R.*, 1948, IV, 843-4.
14. *F.R.*, 1948, III, 206-7.
15. *F.R.*, 1948, III, 848-9.
16. Canadian Ambassador to the Netherlands to Department of External Affairs, Despatch No. 231, July 22, 1948, NASP., file 283(s), part 2.
17. *F.R.*, 1948, I, part 2, 551.
18. Holmes to Pearson, April 9, 1948, D.E.A., file 2AE 1s.
19. Pearson to D.C. Abbott, May 3, 1948, D.E.A., file 277s.
20. J. W. Pickersgill and D. F. Forster, *The Mackenzie King Record,* Vol IV, *1947-1948,* (Toronto, 1970), 169.
21. Pearson, speech, Sept. 21, 1948, Kingston, D.E.A. Statements and Speeches, No. 48/48.
22. *F.R.*, 1948, III, 46.
23. U.S. Ambassador in Denmark to the Secretary of State, March 24, 1948, *F.R.*, 1948, III, 67.
24. *F.R.*, 1948, III, 4-6.
25. *F.R.*, 1948, III, 40-41.
26. *F.R.*, 1948, III, 849.
27. George Kennan, talk, Canadian National Defence College, May 31, 1948, transmitted by Arnold Smith to the Department of External Affairs on Aug. 5, 1948, D.E.A., file 2-AEs.
28. *F.R.*, 1948, III, 46-8.

29. *F.R.*, 1948, III, 775-77.

30. Canadian Embassy in Moscow to Department of External Affairs, April 1, 1948, Tel. 85, D.E.A., file 2-AE(s), Vol. 2.

31. Department of External Affairs to all Canadian diplomatic missions, March 18, 1949, NASP., file 283(s), part 9.

31. For the original in St. Laurent's handwriting see Escott Reid's papers. (Public Archives of Canada, file 13. Hereafter listed as Reid papers.)

32. Interview with J. D. Hickerson, conducted by T. A. Hockin and G. C. V. Wright, Oct. 27, 1969, York University Oral History Project.

33. Marquis Childs, "The Shooting War Comes Closer", *Washington Post*, March 4, 1948.

34. James Reston, "Basic Decision Facing U.S. in Foreign Policy", *New York Times*, March 14, 1948.

35. Walter Lippmann, "Half Measures and Generalities", *Washington Post*, March 30, 1948.

36. Pearson to Abbott, May 3, 1948, D.E.A., file 277s.

37. Richard M. Freeland, *The Truman Doctrine and the Origins of McCarthyism*, (New York, 1972), 264-287.

38. *F.R.*, 1949, IV, 72.

39. *F.R.*, 1948, IV, 943-44, 946. There is a typographical error on page 946, "impending" for "impeding". The phrase "worldwide war scare" came in a telegram of March 14, 1949, from the United States embassy in Moscow. *(F.R.*, 1949, IV, 235.)

40. *F.R.*, 1948, IV, 943, fn. 1.

41. Oliver Franks made the distinction between the two types of Soviet moves at the Ambassadors' Committee on February 8, 1949. The minutes state: "The Swedes had indicated that if Norway were to join the Atlantic Pact, the Russians might take some step such as moving a division up toward Kirkenes, but Sir Oliver thought it difficult to believe that the Russians would go so far as to move a division into Norway. Moves which menace had to be distinguished from moves which matter and he did not think that Norwegian participation in the Pact would be the occasion for an explosion." (*F.R.*, 1949, IV, 78-9.)

CHAPTER TWO: HOPE

1. Acheson, *Creation,* 153.

2. Wrong to Pearson, Feb. 7, 1948, D.E.A., file 277s.

3. Reid to Pearson, April 6, 1949, NASP., file 283(s), part 10.

4. George F. Kennan, *Memoirs, 1925-1950,* (Boston, 1967), 458.

5. Stone to Pearson, Aug. 4, 1948, NASP., file 283(s), part 2.

6. Lord Gladwyn, *The Memoirs of Lord Gladwyn,* (London, 1972), 225.

7. St. Laurent speech at Hamilton, Ontario, March 15, 1948, and at Montreal, April 26, 1948.

8. Pearson to Vanier, Aug. 13, 1948, NASP., file 283(s), part 2.

CHAPTER THREE: THE CONCEPTION OF THE TREATY

1. "The Constitution of the United Nations", Free World Research Bureau, April, 1945, 11.

2. Randolph S. Churchill ed., *The Sinews of Peace: Post-war Speeches by Winston S. Churchill,* (London, 1961), 93-105.

3. Francis Williams, *A Prime Minister Remembers,* (London, 1961), 162.

4. Lester B. Pearson, *Mike: The Memoirs of the Rt. Hon. Lester B. Pearson,* (Toronto, 1973), II, 40.

5. Eugene Forsey ed., *Canada in a New World,* (Toronto, 1948), 29-42.

6. Memorandum, August 30, 1947, "The United States and the Soviet Union", D.E.A., file 52 Fs.

7. St. Laurent, memorandum, Oct. 13, 1947, "Re: Draft 'The United States and the Soviet Union.' " D.E.A., file 52 Fs.

8. Hamilton Fish Armstrong, "Is it Russia vs. U.S. - Or vs. U.N.?" *New York Times Magazine,* Sept. 14, 1947. A revision of this article along with other material was included in Armstrong's book *The Calculated Risk,*

(London, 1947).

9. St. Laurent, speech, Sept 18, 1947, "Canada at the United Nations 1947", Department of External Affairs, Ottawa, 178-80.

10. Vandenberg, ed., *Private Papers*, 400-01.

11. Washington Embassy to Ottawa, Oct. 15, 1947, WA 3249, D.E.A., file 211-J(s).

12. Reid to Wrong, Oct. 20, 1947, D.E.A., file 211-J(s).

13. Wrong to Reid, Oct. 27, 1947, D.E.A., file 211-J(s).

14. Reid to Wrong, Nov. 4, 1947, enclosing draft treaty dated November 4, 1947, D.E.A., file 211-J(s).

15. Wrong to Reid, Oct. 27, 1947, D.E.A., file 211-J(s).

16. Ignatieff to Reid, Tel. ASDEL No. 468, Nov. 22, 1947, D.E.A., file 211-J(s).

17. Riddell to Pearson, Dec. 5, 1947, D.E.A., file 211-J(s).

18. Theodore C. Archilles, *Draft Memoirs*, 412G.

19. Bevin to Marshall, April 29, 1948. *F.R.*, 1948, IV, 843.

20. Interview with J.D. Hickerson, conducted by T.A. Hockin and G.C.V. Wright, Oct. 27, 1969, York University Oral History Project.

21. Ibid.

22. *F.R.*, 1947, II, 815-16.

23. Achilles, *Draft Memoirs*, 413G.

24. *F.R.*, 1948, III, 4-6.

25. Gladwyn, *Memoirs*, 210-211.

26. *F.R.*, 1948, III, 4.

27. *F.R.*, 1948, III, 9-10.

28. *F.R.*, 1948, III, 29.

29. *F.R.*, 1948, III, 20.

30. *F.R.*, 1948, III, 27-9.

31. Memorandum, March 23, 1948, paragraph 12., D.E.A., file 277 (s).

32. *F.R.*, 1948, III, 7-8.

33. *F.R.*, 1948, III, 15.

34. *F.R.*, 1948, III, 9-12.

35. *F.R.*, 1948, III, 13, 15.

36. *F.R.*, 1948, III, 18, 22-23.

37. *F.R.*, 1948, III, 19.

38. *F.R.*, 1948, III, 33.

39. Gladwyn, *Memoirs*, 214.

40. *F.R.*, 1948, III, 46-48.

41. *F.R.*, 1948, III, 48.

42. Documents relating to the North Atlantic Treaty, Senate Foreign Relations Committee, Document No. 48, 1949, 74.

43. Department of External Affairs, Reference paper No. 33, Oct. 29, 1948.

CHAPTER FOUR: THE INTER-GOVERNMENTAL DISCUS-SIONS

1. The text of the Pentagon paper is in *F.R.*, 1948, III, 72-5. A footnote on page 72 gives the paper the title of the "Pentagon Paper."

2. Pearson to Prime Minister, memorandum, March 27, 1948, NASP., file 283(s), part 1.

3. Achilles, *Draft Memoirs*, 417-18G.

4. The text of the Washington paper is in *F.R.*, 1948, III, 237-48. The footnote on page 237 gives the paper the title of the "Washington Paper."

5. The text of the December 24, 1948, "Report of the International Working Group to the Ambassadors' Committee" is in *F.R.*, 1948, III, 333-43. The draft treaty is in *F.R.*, 1948, III, 334-37.

6. *F.R.*, 1949, IV, 222-23.

7. This is the title used by the State Department in its minutes of these meetings. *F.R.*, 1948, III, 59.

8. *F.R.*, 1948, III, 148, and 315, and *F.R.*, 1949, IV, 27.

9. Verbatim transcript of Ambassadors' Committee, Dec. 10, 1948, Wrong Papers, (Public Archives of Canada, file 31. Hereafter listed as Wrong papers.)

10. *F.R.*, 1948, III, 69.

11. Minutes of meeting of Working Group, Dec. 20, 1948, Wrong papers, file 31.

12. Wrong to Reid, Jan. 8, 1949, NASP, file 283(s), part 5.

13. Wrong to Department of External Affairs, Feb. 5, 1949, WA 261, NASP., file 283(s), part 6.

14. *F.R.* 1949, IV, 154, Department of External Affairs to Wrong, March 3,

1949, EX 561, Washington Embassy to Department of External Affairs, March 3, 1949, WA 564, NASP., file 283(s), part 7.

15. Washington Embassy to Department of External Affairs, March 16, 1949, WA 718, NASP., file 283(s), part 8.

16. Acheson, *Creation*, 282.

17. Minutes of a Conference of Foreign Ministers, April 2, 1949, *F.R.*, 1949, IV, 271-81.

18. Pearson to Prime Minister, March 15, 1948, NASP., file 283(s), part 1.

19. Washington Embassy to Department of External Affairs, April 2, 1948, WA 939, NASP., file 283(s), part 1.

20. Wrong to Pearson, May 10, 1948, D.E.A., file 2-AE-1(s).

21. *F.R.*, 1948, IV, 844.

22. *F.R.*, 1948, III, 138.

23. Pearson to Wrong, May 21, 1948, D.E.A., file 2-AE-1(s).

24. *F.R.*, 1948, III, 139.

25. Francis Williams, *A Prime Minister Remembers*, 172.

26. Wrong to Pearson, memorandum, July 12, 1948, NASP, file 283(s), part 2.

27. Wrong to Pearson, memorandum, July 29, 1948, NASP., file 283(s), part 2.

28. Wrong to Pearson, memorandum, May 25, 1948, NASP., file 283(s), part 1.

29. Alastair Buchan, "Mothers and Daughters (or Greeks and Romans)", *Foreign Affairs*, July, 1976, 656.

30. Canadian Ambassador, (France), to Department of External Affairs, May 31, 1948, Despatch 366, D.E.A., file 2AE(s).

31. *F.R.*, 1948, III, 38., Washington Embassy to Department of External Affairs, March 15, 1948, WA 778, NASP., file 283(s), part 1.

32. *F.R.*, 1948, III, 46.

33. *F.R.*, 1948, III, 50.

34. *F.R.*, 1948, III, 55-6.

35. Pearson to St. Laurent and Prime Minister, March 22, 1948, Tel. 345 from Canadian Permanent Delegation to U.N., NASP., file 283(s), part 1.

36. Washington Embassy to Department of External Affairs, March 23, 1948, WA 843, NASP., file 283(s), part 1.

37. Washington Embassy to Department of External Affairs, April 2, 1948, WA 939, NASP., file 283(s), part 1.

38. Wrong to Pearson, May 19, 1948, and Pearson to Wrong, May 25, 1948, NASP., file 283(s), part 1. See also *F.R.*, 1948, III, 132.

39. *F.R.*, 1948, III, 137 and 139.

40. Washington Embassy to Department of External Affairs, June 23, 1948, WA 1832, NASP., file 283(s), part 2.

41. *F.R.*, 1948, III, 143.

42. *F.R.*, 1948, III, 230.

43. Lovett to Jefferson Caffery (United States Ambassador to France) Aug. 24, 1948, NASP., file 283(s), part 2.

44. Stone to Pearson, July 29, 1948, NASP., file 283(s), part 2.

45. *F.R.*, 1948, III, 215.

46. Wrong to Pearson, Feb. 23, 1949, NASP., file 283(s), part 7.

47. *F.R.*, 1948, III, 215.

48. *Ibid.*

49. *F.R.*, 1948, III, 315, fn.

50. Achilles, *Draft Memoirs*, 424G.

51. Washington Embassy to Department of External Affairs, Feb. 23, 1949, WA 464, NASP., file 283(s), part 7.

52. *F.R.,* 1949, IV, 86.

53. *F.R.,* 1949, IV, 157.

54. *F.R.,* 1948, III, 179.

55. *F.R.,* 1948, III, 331.

56. *F.R.,* 1949, IV, 130, and transcript of Ambassadors' Committee of March 1, 1949, Wrong papers, file 34.

57. Vanier to Reid, Jan. 12, 1949, Tel. 24, NASP., file 283(s), part 5.

58. Lovett to Caffery, Aug. 24, 1948, NASP., file 283(s), part 2.

59. Robertson to Reid, Feb. 21, 1949, NASP., file 283(s), part 7.

60. *F.R.,* 1949, IV, 221-22.

CHAPTER FIVE: THE ARCHITECTS OF THE TREATY

1. Speech by Dean Rusk, Apr. 20, 1976. *Topics.* George C. Marshall Research Foundation, Aug., 1976.
2. Interview with J. D. Hickerson, conducted by Ruth C. Smith. Ruth C. Smith to Reid, Sept. 18, 1972.
3. Achilles, *Draft Memoirs,* 423G.
4. Dirk U. Stikker, *Men of Responsibility,* (London, 1966), 284.
5. Pearson to Robertson, March 30, 1948, NASP., file 283(s), part 1.
6. *F.R.,* 1948, III, 226.
7. Charles Ritchie, Canadian Embassy (Paris), memorandum, Nov. 23, 1948, of a conversation with Gladwyn Jebb, NASP., file 283(s), part 4.
8. Lord Gladwyn, *The European Idea,* (London, 1967), 48.

CHAPTER SIX: SECRET DIPLOMACY

1. NATO Information Service, *NATO facts and figures* (Brussels, Jan, 1976) 11-20.
2. Washington Embassy to Department of External Affairs, March 17, 1948, WA 806, NASP., file 283(s), part 1.
3. *F.R.,* 1948, III, 61.
4. Department of External Affairs to Washington Embassy, March 18, 1948, EX 724, NASP., file 283(s), part 1.
5. Wrong, minute, March 18, 1948, Wrong papers, file 25.
6. Wrong to Pearson, March 17, 1948, WA 789, NASP., file 283(s), part 1.
7. Achilles, *Draft Memoirs,* 416-7G.
8. *F.R.,* 1948, III, 72.
9. Lovett had at least four meetings with Vandenberg in April, 1948, one before April 11, and the others on April 11, 18 and 27. On April 18 he showed him a revision of the Working Paper of April 1. He may have showed him the April 1 paper at an earlier meeting. (*F.R.,* 1948, III, 92.)
10. Washington Embassy to Department of External Affairs, March 23, 1948, WA 843, NASP., file 283(s), part 1.
11. Pearson to Prime Minister, March 29, 1948, NASP., file 283(s), part 1.
12. *F.R.,* 1948, III, 79.
13. Department of External Affairs to High Commissioner, (London), July 2, 1948, Tel. 1024, NASP., file 283(s), part 2.
14. *F.R.,* 1948, III, 151.
15. *F.R.,* 1948, III, 182.
16. *F.R.,* 1948, III, 152.
17. Interview with J. D. Hickerson, conducted by T. A. Hockin and G.C.V. Wright, Oct. 27, 1969, York University Oral History Project.
18. Washington Embassy to Department of External Affairs, July 6, 1948, WA 1955, NASP., file 283(s), part 2.
19. Reid to Prime Minister, July 5, 1948, NASP., file 283(s), part 2.
20. Pearson to Prime Minister, March 15, 1948, NASP., file 283(s), part 1.
21. Pearson to Prime Minister, March 27, 1948, NASP., file 283(s), part 1.
22. *F.R.,* 1948, III, 313-14, and transcript of meeting of Dec. 10, 1948, Wrong papers, file 31.
23. Washington Embassy to Department of External Affairs, Dec. 10, 1948, WA 3142, NASP., file 283(s), part 4.
24. Department of External Affairs to Washington Embassy, Feb. 10, 1949, EX 340, NASP., file 283(s), part 6.
25. Wrong to Reid, March 16, 1949, NASP., file 283(s), part 8.
26. Achilles to Reid, memorandum, Jan. 19, 1976, personal communication.
27. Pickersgill and Forster, *Record,* Vol. IV, *1947-1948,* 166-75.
28. St. Laurent's five public speeches were on March 15 in Hamilton, on March 24 in Kitchener, on April 26 in Montreal, on May 26 in Morrisburg, and on June 11 in Toronto. He spoke in the House of Commons on April 29, and June 19. (H. of C Deb., 1948, Vol. IV, VI, 3438-3453, 5551.)
29. Pearson, speech at Kingston, Sept. 21, 1948. (D. of E.A., Statements and Speeches, No. 48/48, 5-7.)

30. Washington Embassy to Department of External Affairs, Feb. 16, 1949, WA 409, NASP., file 283(s), part 7.

31. H. of C. Deb., 1949, Vol. III, 2096.

32. Washington Embassy to Department of External Affairs, Feb. 19, 1949, WA 447, NASP., file 283(s), part 7.

33. Ambassadors' Committee, March 1, 1949, F.R., 1949, IV, 130.

34. Washington Embassy to Department of External Affairs, April 13, 1948, WA 1062, NASP., file 283(s), part 1.

35. Washington Embassy to Department of External Affairs, Feb. 14, 1949, WA 393, NASP., file 283(s), part 6.

36. Thomas M. Franck and Edward Westbank, ed., *Secrecy and Foreign Policy,* (New York, 1974), 209.

37. Ibid, 419.

38. H. of C. Deb., 1949, Vol. III, 2096.

CHAPTER SEVEN: THE ADVICE AND CONSENT OF THE SENATE

1. Theodore Achilles, "Beyond Diplomacy", *Foreign Service Journal,* April, 1963, 54.

2. Washington Embassy to Department of External Affairs, Nov. 1, 1948, WA 2833, NASP., file 283(s), part 3.

3. Vandenberg, ed., *Private Papers,* 405.

4. Stone to Pearson, Aug. 13, 1948, NASP., file 283(s), part 2, See also *F.R.,* 1948, III, 213.

5. The first meeting of which there is a record was on April 11, (*F.R.,* 1948, III, 82-4), but there apparently was a previous meeting, (*F.R.,* 1948, III, 89, fn. 1.) The record of the meetings of April 18 and 27 is in *F.R.,* 1948, III, 92-6, and 104-08. According to the official biography of Vandenberg there were meetings between Lovett and Vandenberg to discuss what became the Vandenberg resolution. "For three or four weeks [during this period] Lovett often stopped at apartment 500G [the Vandenberg suite at the Wardman Park Hotel] for an hour after leaving the Department of State in early evening. Sometimes on Sundays the meetings were prolonged. . . ." (Vandenberg, *Private Papers,* 404.)

6. Achilles to Reid, memorandum, Jan. 19, 1976, personal communication. See also Washington Embassy to Department of External Affairs, April 13, 1948, WA 1062, NASP., file 283(s), part 1.

7. *F.R.,* 1948, III, 83.

8. The United States record suggests that the Rusk-Vandenberg meeting took place on April 16, but the Canadian Embassy in Washington reported on April 15 that the meeting took place on April 13. Possibly there were two meetings between Vandenberg and Rusk. *F.R.,* 1948, III; 92, fn. 2., Washington Embassy to Department of External Affairs, April 15, 1948, WA 1105, NASP., file 283(s), part 1.

9. Washington Embassy to Department of External Affairs, April 15, 1948, WA 1105, NASP., file 283(s), part 1.

10. *F.R.,* 1948, III, 92, fn. 2.

11. *F.R.,* 1948, III, 107.

12. Achilles, *Draft Memoirs,* 420G.

13. The text of the Vandenberg resolution is in "Documents Relating to the North Atlantic Treaty" 81st Congress, 1st Session. Senate Document No. 48, 1949, 84-85.

14. Ibid, 87-88.

15. Stone to Pearson, Aug. 4, 1948, NASP., file 283(s), part 2.

16. Washington Embassy to Department of External Affairs, June 16, 1948, WA 1761, NASP., file 283(s), part 2.

17. Washington Embassy to Department of External Affairs, Oct. 30, 1948, WA 2825, NASP., file 283(s), part 3.

18. Washington Embassy to Department of External Affairs, Nov. 9, 1948, WA 2902, NASP., file 283(s), part 3.

19. Wrong to Reid, Nov. 1, 1948, WA 2833, NASP., file 283(s), part 3.

20. Washington Embassy to Department of External Affairs, Dec. 3, 1948, WA 3071, NASP., file 283(s), part 4.

21. Washington Embassy to Department of External Affairs, Jan. 5, 1949, WA 16, NASP., file 283(s), part 5.

22. Washington Embassy to Department of External Affairs, Jan. 13, 1949, WA 93, NASP., file 283(s), part 5.

23. Washington Embassy to Department of External Affairs, Feb. 9, 1949, WA 337, NASP., file 283(s), part 6.

24. Minutes of Ambassadors' Committee, March 1, 1949, *F.R.*, 1949, IV, 131

25. Washington Embassy to Department of External Affairs, Feb. 5, 1949, WA 307, NASP., file 283(s), part 6 and *F.R.*, 1949, IV, 64-5. Bohlen's account of the conversation with the senators of February 3, 1949, is in Department of State, file 840.-20/2-349. Attached to this are the State Department's recommendations concerning the changes in the draft treaty sought by Connally and Vandenberg. Bohlen's account of the conversation of February 5, 1949 is in the Department of State, file 840.-20/2-549. Both memoranda are signed by Acheson.

26. *F.R.*, 1949, IV, 108-10.

27. *F.R.*, 1949, IV, 117.

28. Washington Embassy to Department of External Affairs, Feb. 19, 1949, WA 446, NASP., file 283(s), part 7.

29. *F.R.*, 1949, IV, 126 and 141.

30. *F.R.*, 1949, IV, 125 and 141.

31. *F.R.*, 1949, IV, 174.

32. Theodore Achilles, "Beyond Diplomacy", 54.

33. Washington Embassy to Department of External Affairs, Feb. 10, 1949, WA 361, NASP., file 283(s), part 6.

34. Vandenberg, ed., *Private Papers*, 472.

35. Ibid, 471.

36. Ibid, 505-06.

37. Reid to Pearson, memorandum, April 6, 1949, NASP., file 283(s), part 10.

38. Vandenberg, ed., *op. cit.*, 506.

39. Acheson, *Creation*, 323.

40. Vandenberg, ed., *op. cit.*, 405, 449, and 453.

41. Charles Ritchie to Department of External Affairs, Feb. 23, 1949, Tel. 130, NASP., file 283(s), part 7.

42. Kennan, *Memoirs*, 413-4.

43. Washington Embassy to Department of External Affairs, Feb. 10, 1949, WA 361, NASP., file 283(s), part 6.

44. Washington Embassy to Department of External Affairs, Feb. 14, 1949, WA 393, NASP., file 283(s), part 6.

CHAPTER EIGHT:
ALTERNATIVES TO A
NORTH ATLANTIC TREATY

1. *F.R.*, 1948, III, 47.

2. *F.R.*, 1948, III, 58-9.

3. *F.R.*, 1948, III, 62-3.

4. Alastair Buchan, *The End of the Postwar Era*, (London, 1974). 19.

5. Reid to Pearson, March 18, 1948, NASP., file 283(s), part 1.

6. *F.R.*, 1948, III, 5.

7. *F.R.*, 1948, III, 64-5.

8. *F.R.*, 1948, III, 67.

9. *F.R.*, 1948, III, 60.

10. *F.R.*, 1948, III, 123.

11. *F.R., 1948, III, 64.*

12. *F.R.*, 1948, III, 80.

13. Memorandum, approved on March 24, 1948, NASP., file 283(s), part 1.

14. Pearson, memorandum, March 27, 1948, NASP., file 283(s), part 1.

15. Pearson to Prime Minister, March 29, 1948, enclosing memorandum of March 27, 1948, NASP., file 283(s), part 1.

16. Washington Embassy to Department of External Affairs, March 23, 1948, WA 843, NASP., file 283(s), part 1.

17. *F.R.*, 1948, III, 64.
18. *F.R.*, 1948, III, 73.
19. *F.R.*, 1948, III, 65.
20. Pearson to Prime Minister, March 29, 1948, NASP., file 283(s), part 1.
21. Pearson, memorandum, March 27, 1948, NASP., file 283(s), part 1.
22. *F.R.*, 1948, III, 64-5.
23. *F.R.*, 1948, III, 66-7.
24. Walter Millis ed. *The Forrestal Diaries,* (New York, 1951), 422-23.
25. Washington Embassy to Department of External Affairs, April 9, 1948, WA 1020, NASP., file 283(s), part 1.
26. *F.R.*, 1948, III, 76-7.
27. *F.R.*, 1948, III, 80.
28. Pearson to Prime Minister, April 12, 1948, NASP., file 283(s), part 1. This was a joint Pearson-Reid memorandum like many others at the time. Pearson wrote paragraphs 1, 2, and 5: Reid wrote paragraphs 3, 4, and 6.
29. Pearson to Prime Minister, April 17, 1948, NASP., file 283(s), part 1.
30. Stone to Pearson, Aug. 4, 1948, NASP., file 283(s), part 2.
31. Wrong to Pearson, April 15, 1948, NASP., file 283(s), part 1.
32. *F.R.*, 1948, III, 92-6.
33. H. of C. Deb., 1948, Vol. IV, 3449-50.
34. Wrong to Pearson, May 8, 1948, NASP., file 283(s), part 1.
35. *F.R.*, 1948, III, 108-09.
36. *F.R.*, 1948, III, 128.
37. Charles E. Bohlen, *Witness to History,* (New York, 1973), 267-68.
38. Kennan, *Memoirs,* 401-03, and 406-07.
39. Wrong to Pearson, May 19, 1948, NASP., file 283(s), part 1.
40. *F.R.*, 1948, III, 122-3.
41. *F.R.*, 1948, III, 128.
42. Wrong to Pearson, May 28, 1948, NASP., file 283(s), part 1.
43. Memorandum of June 1, 1948, "collective defence agreement for the North Atlantic area", NASP., file 283(s), part 2.
44. Reid to Wrong, June 3, 1948, NASP., file 283(s), part 2.
45. Washington Embassy to Department of External Affairs, June 25, 1948, WA 1849, NASP., file 283(s), part 2.
46. *F.R.*, 1948, III, 175.
46. Stone to Pearson, Aug. 4, 1948, NASP., file 283(s), part 1.
48. F. Aandahl, (Acting Director, Historical Office, Bureau of Public Affairs, State Department), to Arthur Blanchette, (Historical Division, D.E.A.), Letter, March 24, 1976.

CHAPTER NINE: HESITATIONS IN FRANCE AND BELGIUM

1. Canadian Ambassador in Paris to Department of External Affairs, May 31, 1948, Despatch No. 366, D.E.A., file 2AE(s).
2. *F.R.*, 1948, I, part 2, 552.
3. C.S.A. Ritchie to Pearson, Aug. 20, 1948, NASP., file 283(s), part 2.
4. *F.R.*, 1948, III, 125-26.
5. *F.R.*, 1948, III, 229-30.
6. Canadian Ambassador in the Hague to Department of External Affairs, July 22, 1948, Despatch No. 231, NASP., file 283(s), part 2.
7. Stone to Pearson, Aug. 4, 1948, NASP., file 283(s), part 2.
8. Pearson to St. Laurent, July 13, 1948, NASP., file 283(s), part 2.
9. Reid to St. Laurent, Aug. 20, 1948, NASP., file 283(s), part 2.
10. Stone to Pearson, July 31, 1948, NASP., file 283(s), part 2.
11. Stone to Pearson, Aug. 10, 1948, NASP., file 283(s), part 2.
12. Pearson, memorandum, Aug. 20, 1948, "North Atlantic Security", NASP., file 283(s), part 2.
13. *F.R.*, 1948, III, 121.
14. *F.R.*, 1948, III, 142.
15. *F.R.*, 1948, III, 121.
16. *F.R.*, 1948, III, 139.
17. Ritchie to Pearson, Aug. 23, 1948, NASP., file 283(s), part 2.
18. Pearson, memorandum, Aug. 20, 1948, NASP., file 283(s), part 2.
19. *F.R.*, 1948, III, 221.
20. Pearson, memorandum, Aug. 20, 1948, NASP., file 283(s), part 2.
21. Pearson to Reid, Aug. 21, 1948,

WA 2315, NASP., file 283(s), part 2.

22. Pearson to Canadian Embassy in Paris, Aug. 25, 1948, Tel. No. 383, NASP., file 283(s), part 2.

23. Department of External Affairs to Canadian Embassy in The Hague, Aug. 4, 1948, Despatch No. 453; Pearson to Vanier, Aug. 13, 1948; Department of External Affairs to Brussels, Aug. 10, 1948, Tel. No. 140; NASP, file 283(s), part 2.

24. Arnold Toynbee, *Civilization on Trial,* (New York, 1948), 137.

25. Washington Embassy to Department of External Affairs, Aug. 26, 1948, WA 2340, NASP., file 283(s), part 2.

26. Lovett to Caffery, Aug. 24, 1948, NASP., file 283(s), part 2.

27. Pearson to Vanier, Aug. 27, 1948, NASP., file 283(s), part 2.

28. *F.R.,* 1948, III, 238.

29. Lovett to Caffery, Aug. 24, 1948, NASP., file 283(s), part 2.

30. Washington Embassy to Department of External Affairs, Oct. 4, 1948, WA 2627, NASP., file 283(s), part 3.

31. Wrong to A.D.P. Heeney, April 7, 1949, NASP., file 283(s), part 10.

32. General Omar N. Bradley, Chief of Staff, United States Army, address, April 5, 1949. (Press release, National Military Establishment, Department of the Army).

33. *F.R.,* 1949, IV, 308.

34. Reid to Pearson, April 6, 1949, NASP., file 283(s), part 10.

35. Hickerson to Reid, January 21, 1976, and Achilles to Reid, memorandum, January 19, 1976, personal communications.

CHAPTER TEN:
THE TWO-PILLAR CONCEPT
OF THE TREATY

1. *F.R.,* 1948, III, 106.

2. *F.R.,* 1948, III, 64.

3. Washington Embassy to Department of External Affairs, Oct. 26, 1949, WA 2975, D.E.A., file 277 (s)

4. Achilles to Reid, memorandum, Jan. 19, 1976, personal communication.

5. H. of C. Deb., 1939, Vol. III, 2419.

6. Washington Embassy to Department of External Affairs, Oct. 15, 1948, WA 2714, D.E.A., file 50149-40.

7. *F.R.,* 1948, III, 151. The second sentence contains a typographical error: "formed" for "favored."

8. *F.R.,* 1948, III, 167-68.

9. *F.R.,* 1948, III, 149.

10. *F.R.,* 1948, III, 177.

11. Wrong to Pearson, Sept. 4, 1948, NASP., file 283(s), part 3.

12. Washington Embassy to Department of External Affairs, July 26, 1948, WA 2135, NASP., file 283(s), part 2.

13. Stone to Pearson, July 29, 1948, NASP., file 283(s), part 2.

14. Wrong to Pearson, Sept. 4, 1948, NASP., file 283(s), part 3.

15. Kennan, *Memoirs,* 458.

16. Wrong to Pearson, Sept. 4, 1948, NASP., file 283(s), part 3.

17. *F.R.,* 1948, III, 234-35.

18. Gladwyn, *Memoirs,* 220-21, and 225.

19. Stone to Pearson, July 29, 1948, NASP., file 283(s), part 2.

20. Department of External Affairs to Washington Embassy, Aug. 10, 1948, EX. 1979, NASP., file 283(s), part 2.

21. Canadian High Commissioner (London), to Department of External Affairs, April 21, 1948, on the increasing continentalization of United Kingdom policy, D.E.A., file 264(s).

22. Gladwyn, *European Idea,* 122-23.

CHAPTER ELEVEN: MORE THAN
A MILITARY ALLIANCE

1. *F.R.,* 1948, III, 159-60.

2. *F.R.,* 1948, III, 175, 178.

3. Achilles to Reid, Feb. 18, 1976, personal communication.

4. Charles Ritchie, Canadian Embassy (Paris), memorandum, Nov. 23, 1948, of a conversation with Gladwyn Jebb, NASP., file 283(s), part 4.

5. Canadian Embassy in Moscow to Department of External Affairs,

April 1, 1948, Tel. 85, D.E.A., file 2-AE(s).

6. Reid, memorandum, March 14, 1948, NASP., file 283(s), part 1.

7. Pearson to King, March 15, 1948, enclosing memorandum of March 14, 1948, NASP., file 283(s), part 1.

8. H. of C. Deb., 1948, Vol. III, 2303. King was quoting from a draft of this article. In the final text the last two words were changed to "or by other means."

9. Reid, memorandum, March 18, 1948, NASP., file 283(s), part 1.

10. Stone to Pearson, memorandum, March 20, 1948, NASP., file 283(s), part 1.

11. St. Laurent, speeches on March 15, Hamilton; on March 24, Kitchener; on April 26, Montreal; on April 29, House of Commons; and on June 11, Toronto.

12. Wrong to Pearson, Feb. 7, 1948, NASP., file 277(s).

13. F.R., 1948, III, 180.

14. F.R., 1948, III, 226.

15. F.R., 1948, III, 285.

16. Canadian commentary, Dec. 6, 1948, NASP., file 283(s), part 4.

17. Pearson to Wrong, Dec. 16, 1948, drafted by Reid, not signed by Pearson, NASP., file 283(s), part 5.

18. F.R., 1948, IX, 407-09.

19. Pickersgill and Forster, Record, Vol. IV, 1947-1948, 264.

20. F.R., 1948, IX, 411-12.

21. Canadian High Commissioner (London) to Department of External Affairs, Feb. 13, 1949, Tel. 350, NASP., file 283(s), part 6.

22. Canadian High Commissioner (London), to Department of External Affairs, Feb. 16, 1949, Tel. 381, NASP., file 283(s), part 7.

23. Canadian High Commissioner, (London), to Department of External Affairs, Feb. 17, 1949, Tel. 387, NASP., file 283(s), part 7.

24. Department of External Affairs to Washington Embassy, Feb. 7, 1949, EX. 300, NASP., file 283(s), part 6.

25. Pearson to Wrong, Dec. 16, 1948, drafted by Reid, not signed by Pearson, NASP., file 283(s), part 5.

26. Washington Embassy to Department of External Affairs, Feb. 9, 1949, WA 337, NASP., file 283 (s), part 6.

27. Transcript of Ambassadors' Committee meeting of Feb. 8, 1949, Wrong papers, file 37.

28. Memorandum from Washington Embassy, Feb. 12, 1949, NASP., file 283(s), part 6.

29. J.W. Pickersgill, My Years with Louis St. Laurent: a Political Memoir, (Toronto and Buffalo, 1975), 86.

CHAPTER TWELVE:
THE PLEDGE

1. F.R., 1949, IV, 77-8.

2. Draft treaty, March 19, 1948, NASP., file 283(s), part 1.

3. Report of drafting committee, March 25, 1948, NASP., file 283(s), part 1.

4. Pearson to Prime Minister, March 28, 1948, NASP., file 283(s), part 1.

5. F.R., 1948, III, 69, 70, 74.

6. Department of External Affairs to Washington Embassy, April 1, 1948, EX 850, NASP., file 283(s), part 1.

7. Department of External Affairs to Washington Embassy, Aug. 10, 1948, EX 1978, NASP., file 283(s), part 2.

8. Department of External Affairs to Washington Embassy, Aug. 16, 1948, EX 2013, NASP., file 283(s), part 2.

9. F.R., 1948, III, 70.

10. Wrong to Pearson, April 7, 1948, NASP., file 283(s), part 1.

11. F.R., 1948, III, 335.

12. Washington Embassy to Department of External Affairs, Feb. 10, 1949, WA 361, NASP., file 283(s), part 6.

13. Memoranda of conversations of February 3 and 5, 1949, signed by Acheson, Department of State, file 840.20/2-349 and file 840.20/2-549.

14. Washington Embassy to Department of External Affairs, Feb. 9, 1949, WA 337, NASP., file 283(s), part 6.

15. F.R., 1949, IV, 74, 85.

16. Washington Embassy to Department of External Affairs, Feb. 10, 1949, WA 361, NASP., file 283(s), part 6.

17. *F.R.*, 1949, IV, 76, 81.

18. Achilles to Reid, memorandum, Jan. 19, 1976, personal communication.

19. *F.R.*, 1948, III, 314.

20. *F.R.*, 1949, IV, 80.

21. Canadian Ambassador (Paris), to Department of External Affairs, Feb. 22, 1949, Tel. 130, NASP., file 283(s), part 7.

22. The debate and the newspaper article which set it off are in Congressional Record, vol. 95, part 1., 81st Congress, 1st Session, Jan. 3, to Feb. 17, 1949, 1163-69. See also Acheson, *Creation*, 280-82.

23. Washington Embassy to Department of External Affairs, Feb. 15, 1949, WA 404, NASP., file 283(s), part 6.

24. Washington Embassy to Department of External Affairs, Feb. 16, 1949, WA 409, NASP., file 283(s), part 7.

25. Canadian Ambassador (Paris), to Department of External Affairs, Feb. 19, 1949, Telegram 117, NASP., file 283(s), part 7.

26. *F.R.*, 1949, IV, 109.

27. *F.R.*, 1949, IV, 113-15, 117.

28. Washington Embassy to Department of External Affairs, Feb. 16, 1949, WA 409, NASP., file 283(s), part 7.

29. Department of External Affairs to Washington Embassy, Feb. 17, 1949, EX 419, and Feb. 18, EX 430, NASP., file 283(s), part 7.

30. Washington Embassy to Department of External Affairs, Feb. 21, 1949, WA 450, NASP., file 283(s), part 7.

31. Washington Embassy to Department of External Affairs, Feb. 25, 1949, WA 5O2, NASP., file 283(s), part 7.

32. Washington Embassy to Department of External Affairs, Feb. 19, 1949, WA 446, NASP., file 283(s), part 7.

33. Minutes of Ambassadors' Committee, Feb. 25, 1949, NASP., file 283(s), part 7.

34. Washington Embassy to Department of External Affairs, Feb. 25, 1949, WA 502, NASP., file 283(s), part 7.

35. Minutes of Ambassadors' Committee, Feb. 25, 1949, NASP., file 283(s), part 7.

CHAPTER THIRTEEN:
INDIRECT AGGRESSION

1. Reid, memorandum, March 18, 1948, NASP., file 283(s), part 1. In my draft of March 19, 1948, I added to my definition of indirect aggression after "economic penetration" the words "or in any other way."

2. Draft treaty, Nov. 19, 1948, D.E.A., file 283-B-s.

3. *F.R.*, 1948, III, 63-4.

4. Pearson, memorandum, March 27, 1948, NASP., file 283(s), part 1. Lord Strang, who represented Britain in the negotiations, stated that, in July, 1939, "The definition of the term [indirect aggression] now proposed by Molotov ... [was] 'an internal *coup d'*état or a reversal of policy in the interests of the aggressor'." (Strang, *At Home and Abroad*, 179.)

5. A.J.P. Taylor, *English History 1914-1945*, (Oxford University Press, 1967), 447.

6. Memorandum, March 24, 1948, NASP., file 283(s), part 1.

7. Pearson, memorandum, March 27, 1948, NASP., file 283(s), part 1.

8. *F.R.*, 1948, III, 66.

9. Drafting Group, report, March 24, 1948, NASP., file 283(s), part 1.

10. *F.R.*, 1948, IV, 74.

11. *F.R.*, 1949, IV, 161.

12. Washington Embassy to Department of External Affairs, Aug. 13, 1948, WA 2253, NASP., file 283(s), part 2.

13. External Affairs to Washington Embassy, Aug. 16, 1948, EX 2013, NASP., file 283(s), part 2.

14. *F.R.*, 1948, III, 246.
15. *F.R.*, 1948, III, 335.
16. Department of External Affairs to Washington Embassy, March 14, 1949, EX 678, NASP., file 283(s), part 8.
17. Department of External Affairs to Washington Embassy, March 15, 1949, EX 695, NASP., file 283(s), part 8.
18. *F.R.*, 1949, IV, 221-22
19. H. of C. Deb., 1949, Vol. III, 2097-98.

CHAPTER FOURTEEN: CONSULTATION
1. Pearson, *Mike, II,* 52-3.
2. Department of External Affairs to NATO delegation (Paris), Jan. 15, 1959, Tel. DL 49, D.E.A., file 50105-E-40.
3. H. of C. Deb., 1938, Vol. III, 3183.
4. Washington Embassy to Department of External Affairs, April 15, 1948, WA 1105, NASP., file 283(s), part 1.
5. *F.R.*, 1949, IV, 161.

CHAPTER FIFTEEN: ARTICLE 2
1. Pearson wrote that Wrong was never "personally convinced that the non-military aspects of the proposed alliance were essential". (Pearson, *Mike, II,* 47.)
2. Reid, draft treaty, March 18, 1948, NASP., file 283(s), part 1.
3. Pearson to King, March 29, 1948, NASP., file 283(s), part 1.
4. Washington Embassy to Department of External Affairs, March 31, 1948, WA 904, NASP., file 283(s), part 1.
5. Undated draft of the Washington paper, NASP., file 283(s). This was an elaboration of a draft prepared in the State Department, dated August 5, 1948, (Stone to Pearson, Aug. 6, 1948, NASP., file 283(s), part 2.)
6. Stone to Pearson, Aug. 4, 1948, NASP., file 283(s), part 2.
7. *F.R.*, 1948, III, 226.
8. Department of External Affairs to Washington Embassy, Dec. 4, 1948,

EX 2788, NASP., file 283(s), part 4.
9. Ritchie to Reid, Nov. 23, 1948, NASP., file 283(s), part 4.
10. *F.R.*, 1948, III, 316-18.
11. *F.R.*, 1948, III, 334-37.
12. Reid to Pearson, Dec. 28, 1948, NASP., file 283(s), part 5.
13. Reid to Pearson, Dec. 28, 1948, and Pearson to St. Laurent, Jan. 4, 1949, NASP., file 283(s), part 5.
14. Washington Embassy to Department of External Affairs, Jan. 5, 1949, WA 16, NASP., file 283(s), part 5.
15. Department of External Affairs to Washington Embassy, Feb. 7, 1949, EX 300, NASP., file 283(s), part 6.
16. Washington Embassy to Department of External Affairs, Feb. 7, 1949, WA 322, NASP., file 283(s), part 6.
17. *F.R.*, 1949, IV, 85-6.
18. Transcript of Ambassadors' Committee, Feb. 8, 1949, Wrong papers, file 37.
19. *F.R.*, 1948, III, 318.
20. Transcript of Ambassadors' Committee, Feb. 8, 1949, Wrong papers, file 37.
21. Washington Embassy to Department of External Affairs, Feb. 9, 1949, WA 342, NASP., file 283(s), part 6.
22. Washington Embassy to Department of External Affairs, Feb. 7, 9, and 19, 1949, WA 322, WA 342, and WA 447, NASP., file 283(s), parts 6 and 7.
23. Washington Embassy to Department of External Affairs, Feb. 19, 1949, WA 447, NASP., file 283(s), part 7.
24. Achilles to Reid, Memorandum, Jan 19, 1976, personal communication.
25. Washington Embassy to Department of External Affairs, Feb. 10, 1949, WA 351, NASP., file 283(s), part 6.
26. Washington Embassy to Department of External Affairs, Feb. 14, 1949, WA 393, NASP., file 283(s),

part 6.

27. Department of External Affairs to High Commissioner (London), Feb. 9 and 15, 1949, Tels. 267 and 307; Department of External Affairs to Canadian Ambassador (Paris), Feb. 17, 1949, Tel. 80; Department of External Affairs to Canadian Ambassador (Brussels), Feb. 17, 1949, Tel. 26; and Department of External Affairs to Canadian Ambassador (The Hague), Feb. 17, 1949, Tel. 31; NASP., file 283(s), parts 6 and 7.

28. Canadian High Commissioner (London), to Department of External Affairs, Feb. 16, 1949, Tel. 381, NASP., file 283(s), part 7.

29. Canadian Ambassador (Paris), to Department of External Affairs, Feb. 19, 1949, Tel. 117, NASP., file 283(s), part 7.

30. Canadian High Commissioner (London), to Department of External Affairs, Feb. 24, 1949, Tel. 431, NASP., file 283(s), part 7.

31. Dirk U. Stikker, *Men of Responsibility,* (London, 1966), 284.

32. Washington Embassy to Department of External Affairs, Feb. 19, 1949, WA 447, NASP., file 283(s), part 7.

33. Department of External Affairs to Washington Embassy, Feb. 21, 1949, EX, 455, NASP., file 283(s), part 7.

34. Washington Embassy to Department of External Affairs, Feb. 21, 1949, WA 450, NASP., file 283(s), part 7.

35. Washington Embassy to Department of External Affairs, Jan. 12, 1949, WA 76, NASP., file 283(s), part 5.

36. Memorandum, Feb. 22, 1949, "Arguments to support the inclusion of a pledge of economic and social collaboration in the North Atlantic treaty", Wrong papers, file 33.

37. Washington Embassy to Department of External Affairs, Feb. 23, 1949, WA 464, NASP., file 283(s), part 7.

38. Wrong, memorandum, Feb. 22, 1949, Wrong papers, file 33.

39. Wrong to Pearson, Feb. 23, 1949, WA 464, NASP., file 283(s), part 7.

40. Interview with J.D. Hickerson, conducted by T.A. Hockin and G.C.V. Wright, Oct. 27, 1969, York University Oral History Project. In the interview Hickerson said that Lovett had accompanied him to the meeting with Acheson. In a letter to Reid of January 21, 1976, he said that this was an error and it was Wrong who had accompanied him.

41. Wrong, note of Feb. 24, 1949, Wrong papers, file 33.

42. Minutes of Ambassadors' Committee, Feb. 25, 1949, NASP., file 283(s), part 7.

43. *F.R.,* 1949, IV, 160.

44. Hickerson, interview, *op. cit.*

45. Minutes of Ambassadors' Committee, Feb. 8, 1949, NASP., file 283(s), part 6.

46. Memorandum of Feb. 3, 1949, written by Bohlen and signed by Acheson, of a conversation between Acheson, Bohlen, Connally and Vandenberg on February 3, 1949, and a list of the State Department's recommendations, Department of State, file No. 840.20/2-349. See reference to these documents in editorial note in *F.R.,* 1949, IV, 64.

47. Acheson, *Creation,* 277.

48. Hickerson, interview, *op. cit.*

49. Washington Embassy to Department of External Affairs, March 25, 1949, WA 847, NASP., file 283(s), part 9.

50. Livingston T. Merchant, ed., *Neighbors Taken for Granted,* (New York, 1966), 141.

51. Acheson, *Creation,* 493. This briefing will probably be published in *United States Foreign Relations* for 1951.

52. Reid, memorandum, "Article 2 of the North Atlantic treaty," July 29, 1954, sent to Pearson with letter, and to Department of External Affairs, with letter, July 31, 1954, D.E.A., file 50105-40.

53. J.E. Meade, *The Atlantic Community and the Dollar Gap,* (Friends of Atlantic Union, London, n.d.)

54. Barbara Ward, *Britain's Interest in Atlantic Union,* (Friends of Atlantic Union, London, n.d.)

CHAPTER SIXTEEN:
THE UNITED NATIONS

1. *F.R.,* 1948, I, 28.
2. *F.R.,* 1948, III, 122-23.
3. Washington Embassy to Department of External Affairs, Jan. 15, 1949, WA 122, NASP., file 283(s), part 6.
4. *F.R.,* 1949, IV, 34.
5. *F.R.,* 1949, IV, 29.
6. Reid to Pearson, memorandum, April 6, 1949, NASP., file 283(s), part 10.
7. Minutes of the Ambassadors' Committee, Feb. 25, 1949, NASP., file 283(s), part 7.
8. Draft treaty, March 19, 1948, NASP., file 283(s), part 1.
9. United Kingdom, United States, and Canada, papers submitted to the tripartite talks, March 23, 1948, NASP., file 283(s), part 1.
10. Washington Embassy to Department of External Affairs, Nov. 25, 1948, WA 3030, NASP., file 283(s), part 4.
11. *F.R.,* 1948, III, 75.
12. Washington Embassy to Department of External Affairs, Nov. 25, 1948, WA 3030, NASP., file 283(s), part 4.
13. Canadian Commentary, Dec. 6, 1948, NASP., file 283(s), part 4.
14. Pearson to Prime Minister, Jan. 4, 1949, NASP., file 283(s), part 5.
15. Wrong to Reid, Jan. 8, 1949, NASP., file 283(s), part 5.
16. Legal Adviser to the D.E.A., memorandum, Jan. 8, 1949, NASP., file 283(s), part 5.
17. *F.R.,* 1949, IV, 33.
18. *F.R.,* 1949, IV, 170 and 172.
19. Department of External Affairs to Washington Embassy, March 14, 1949, EX 677, NASP., file 283(s), part 8.
20. *F.R.,* 1949, IV, 159.
21. Unsigned memorandum, March 1, 1949, NASP., file 283(s), part 7.

CHAPTER SEVENTEEN:
MEMBERSHIP

1. United Nations Statistical Papers, series E, Number 3, *National Income and its Distribution in Underdeveloped Countries,* Statistical Office of the United Nations, Department of Economic Affairs, New York, 1951.
2. Memorandum, approved on March 24, 1948, NASP., file 283(s), part 1.
3. U.S., U.K., and Canadian papers, March 23, 1948, NASP., file 283(s), part 1.
4. *F.R.,* 1948, III, 71.
5. *F.R.,* 1948, III, 179.
6. Hickerson to Reid, letters, Jan. 21, 1976, and July 8, 1976, personal communications.
7. Stone to Pearson, Aug. 10, 1948, NASP., file 283(s), part 2.
8. *F.R.,* 1948, III, 215.
9. *F.R.,* 1948, III, 165, and 175.
10. *F.R.,* 1949, IV, 98-9.
11. Lovett to Caffery, Aug. 24, 1948, NASP., file 283(s), part 2.
12. *F.R.,* 1948, III, 234.
13. *F.R.,* 1948, III, 240.
14. Silvercruys, statement, Ambassadors' Committee, Feb. 25, 1949, NASP., file 283(s), part 7.
15. *F.R.,* 1948, III, 343.
16. Irish Government, Aide-memoire, Feb. 9, 1949, NASP., file 283(s), part 6.
17. *F.R.,* 1949, IV, 78.
18. *F.R.,* 1948, III, 343.
19. *F.R.,* 1949, IV, 79.
20. *F.R.,* 1949, IV, 84.
21. Washington Embassy to Department of External Affairs, Jan. 14, 1949, WA 103, NASP., file 283(s), part 5, and *F.R.,* 1949, IV, 22.
22. Washington Embassy to Department of External Affairs, Jan. 14, 1949, WA 103, NASP., file 283(s), part 5.
23. Canadian Permanent Delegation (U.N.) to the Department of External Affairs, March 22, 1948, Tel. 345,

NASP., file 283(s), part 1.

24. Pearson, memorandum, March 27, 1948, NASP., file 283(s), part 1.

25. *F.R.,* 1948, III, 107.

26. *F.R.,* 1948, III, 179.

27. *F.R.,* 1948, III, 241.

28. *F.R.,* 1948, III, 218.

29. Pearson, marginal comments on Washington paper of Sept. 9, 1948, NASP., file 283(s), part 3.

30. *F.R.,* 1948, III, 332.

31. Reid, memorandum, Oct. 26, 1948, NASP., file 283(s), part 3.

32. Draft treaty, Nov. 19, 1948, D.E.A., file 283-B-s.

33. Wrong, minute, Jan. 4, 1949, on telephone conversation with Pearson, Wrong papers, file 32.

34. Canadian High Commissioner (London), to Department of External Affairs, Jan. 14, 1949, Tel. 121, NASP., file 283(s), part 5.

35. Hickerson to Reid, letter, Jan. 21, 1976, personal communication.

36. *F.R.,* 1948, III, 66.

37. *F.R.,* 1948, III, 107.

38. *F.R.,* 1948, III, 179.

39. *F.R.,* 1948, III, 143.

40. *F.R.,* 1948, III, 234-35.

41. Pearson, memorandum, Aug. 20, 1948, NASP., file 283(s), part 2.

42. Stone to Pearson, Aug. 26, 1948, NASP., file 283(s), part 2, and *F.R.,* 1948, III, 225.

43. *F.R.,* 1948, III, 227-28 and 232, and Wrong, memorandum, Sept. 4, 1948, NASP., file 283(s), part 3.

44. *F.R.,* 1948, III, 282-83.

45. *F.R.,* 1948, III, 267 and 811.

46. Canadian Ambassador (Paris), to Department of External Affairs, Feb. 26, 1949, Tel. 142, NASP., file 283(s), part 7.

47. Silvercruys, statement, Ambassadors' Committee, Feb. 25, 1949, NASP., file 283(s), part 7.

48. *F.R.,* 1948, III, 327.

49. Canadian High Commissioner (London), to Department of External Affairs, Jan. 11, 1949, Tel. 78, NASP., file 283(s), part 5.

50. *F.R.,* 1948, III, 286.

51. *F.R.,* 1948, III, 342.

52. Washington Embassy to Department of External Affairs, Jan. 5, 1949, WA 16, NASP., file 283(s), part 5.

53. Department of External Affairs to Canadian Ambassador, (Paris), Jan. 8, 1949, Tel. 17, NASP., file 283(s), part 5.

54. Canadian Ambassador (Paris), to Department of External Affairs, Jan. 12, 1949, Tel. 24, NASP., file 283(s), part 5.

55. *F.R.,* 1949, IV, 28. Washington Embassy to Department of External Affairs, Jan. 15, 1949, WA 120 and Department of External Affairs, to Washington Embassy, Jan. 18, 1949, EX 132, NASP., file 283(s), part 6.

56. Washington Embassy to Department of External Affairs, Jan. 12, 1949, WA 85, NASP., file 283(s), part 5.

57. Washington Embassy to Department of External Affairs, Jan. 14, 1949, WA 101, NASP., file 283(s), part 5.

58. Reid to G. G. Crean, March 2, 1949, NASP., file 283(s), part 7.

59. Hickerson to Reid, letter, Jan. 21, 1976, personal communication.

60. *F.R.,* 1949, IV, 31.

61. Canadian minutes of Working Group meeting, Jan. 18, 1949, Wrong papers, file 32.

62. *F.R.,* 1949, IV, 40.

63. *F.R.,* 1949, IV 40, fn. 2.

64. *F.R.,* 1949, IV, 43.

65. Washington Embassy to Department of External Affairs, Jan. 24, 1949, WA 189, NASP., file 283(s), part 6.

66. Department of External Affairs to Washington Embassy, Jan. 27, 1949, EX 193, NASP., file 283(s), part 6.

67. Minutes of Ambassadors' Committee, Feb. 25, 1949, NASP., file 283(s), part 7.

68. Ibid.

69. Washington Embassy to Department of External Affairs, Feb. 25, 1949, WA 499, NASP., file 283(s),

part 7.

70. *F.R.*, 1949, IV, 123.

71. Department of External Affairs to Canadian Ambassador (Paris), Feb. 25, 1949, EX 97, and Canadian Ambassador (Paris), to Department of External Affairs, Feb. 26, 1949, Tel. 142, NASP., file 283(s), part 7.

72. *F.R.*, 1949, IV, 129 and 132. "Mr. Acheson understood that the outstanding question of Norway was now settled. . . ." Bonnet, by his silence, assented.

73. *F.R.*, 1949, IV, 125.

74. Memorandum, Feb. 28, 1949, signed by Acheson on "conversation with Senators Connally, George and Vandenberg", Department of State, file No. 840.20/2-2849.

75. Department of External Affairs to Washington Embassy, Feb. 7, 1949, EX. 300, NASP., file 283(s), part 6, and Washington Embassy to Department of External Affairs, March 1 and 2, 1949, WA 534, and 555, NASP., file 283(s), part 7.

76. *F.R.*, 1949, IV, 126-28, 132, and 135.

77. *F.R.*, 1949, IV, 141.

78. *F.R.*, 1949, IV, 142.

79. *F.R.*, 1949, IV, 151.

80. *F.R.*, 1949, IV, 174.

81. Hickerson to Reid, letter, Jan. 21, 1976, personal communication.

82. *F.R.*, 1948, III, 106.

83. *F.R.*, 1948, III, 248.

84. Wrong to Pearson, Sept. 11, 1948, NASP., file 283(s), part 3. The communication reads "The European representatives are not asking . . . ." "Not" is presumably a typographical error.

85. Reid to St. Laurent, Oct. 7, 1948, NASP., file 283(s), part 3.

86. Wrong memorandum, Oct. 23, 1948, NASP., file 283(s), part 3.

87. Canadian commentary, Dec. 6, 1948, NASP., file 283(s), part 4.

88. *F.R.*, 1948, III, 339.

89. Pearson to St. Laurent, Jan. 4, 1949, NASP., file 283(s), part 5.

90. Memorandum of Feb. 3, 1949, written by Bohlen and signed by Acheson. Department of State, file No. 840. 20/2-349.

91. Washington Embassy to Department of External Affairs, Feb. 25, 1949, WA 502, NASP., file 283(s), part 7.

CHAPTER EIGHTEEN:
ALGERIA 586

1. *F.R.*, 1948, III, 39, and 42-4.

2. Washington Embassy to Department of External Affairs, March 31, 1948, WA 904, NASP., file 283(s), part 1.

3. Wrong to Pearson, April 2, 1948, NASP., file 283(s), part 1.

4. *F.R.*, 1948, III, 74.

5. The London paper, draft treaty, Nov. 19, 1948, D.E.A., file 283-B-s.

6. *F.R.*, 1948, III, 326-31.

7. *F.R.*, 1948, III, 314.

8. *F.R.*, 1948, III, 325-26.

9. Pearson to Prime Minister, Jan. 4, 1949, NASP., file 283(s), part 5.

10. Wrong to Pearson, Jan. 4, 1949, NASP., file 283(s), part 5.

11. Washington Embassy to Department of External Affairs, Jan. 5, 1949, WA 16, NASP., file 283(s), part 5.

12. Canadian Embassy (Paris), to Department of External Affairs, Jan. 12, 1949, NASP., file 283(s), part 5.

13. Canadian High Commissioner (London), to Department of External Affairs, Jan. 14, 1949, NASP., file 283(s), part 5.

14. Washington Embassy to Department of External Affairs, Jan. 13, 1949, WA 93, NASP., file 283(s), part 5.

15. Canadian Embassy (Paris), to Department of External Affairs, Jan. 12, 1949, NASP., file 283(s), part 5.

16. *F.R.*, 1949, IV, 32-3.

17. Washington Embassy to Department of External Affairs, Jan. 15, 1949, WA 121, NASP., file 283(s), part 6.

18. Ibid.

19. Department of External Affairs to Washington Embassy, Jan. 18, 1949,.

132, NASP., file 283(s), part 6.

20. Washington Embassy to Department of External Affairs, Jan. 24, 1949, WA 188, NASP., file 283(s), part 6.

21. *F.R.*, 1949, IV, 129-31.

22. Canadian High Commissioner, (London), to Department of External Affairs, Jan. 14, 1949, Tel. 113, NASP., file 283(s), part 5.

CHAPTER NINETEEN: DISAPPOINTMENTS AND FRUSTRATIONS

1. Draft treaty, March 19, 1948, NASP., file 283(s), part 1.

2. Reid to Pearson, June 26, 1948, NASP., file 283(s), part 2.

3. Ibid.

4. Reid to Prime Minister, Nov. 15, 1948, NASP., file 283(s), part 4.

5. Washington Embassy to Department of External Affairs, Nov. 19, 1948, WA 2980, NASP., file 283(s), part 4.

6. Pearson (Canadian Embassy, Paris), to Reid, Nov. 21, 1948, Tel. 441, NASP., file 283(s), part 4.

7. Elliot R. Goodman. *The Fate of the Atlantic Community*, (Praeger, 1975), 538.

8. NATO Information Service, *NATO Facts and Figures* (Brussels, Jan. 1976), 103-4

9. Ambassadors' Committee, March 7, 1949, *F.R.*, 1949, IV, 167-68.

10. Canadian commentary, Dec. 6, 1948, NASP., file 283(s), part 4.

11. Draft commentary, Nov. 13, 1948, footnote to article 42, NASP., file 283(s), part 3.

12. Washington Embassy to Department of External Affairs, Jan. 5, 1949, WA 16, NASP., file 283(s), part 5.

13. Washington Embassy to Department of External Affairs, Jan. 12, 1949, WA 76, NASP., file 283(s), part 5.

14. NATO Information Service, *NATO Facts and Figures* (Brussels, Jan. 1976) 320-1.

15. Reid to Prime Minister, Nov. 15,

1948, NASP., file 283(s), part 4.

16. Canadian commentary, Dec. 6, 1948, NASP., file 283(s), part 4.

17. Draft treaty, Dec. 17, 1948, D.E.A., file 283-B(s).

18. Canadian commentary, Dec. 6, 1948, NASP., file 283(s), part 4,

19. Draft treaty, March 19, 1948, NASP., file 283(s), part 1.

20. Draft treaty, Dec. 17, 1948, NASP., file 283(s), part 5.

21. Department of State *Bulletin*, March 27, 1949, 385.

22. Washington Embassy to Department of External Affairs, Nov. 12, 1948, WA 2911, NASP., file 283(s), part 3.

23. Washington Embassy to Department of External Affairs, Nov. 12, 1948, WA 2912, NASP., file 283(s), part 3.

24. Washington Embassy to Department of External Affairs, Nov. 19, 1948, WA 2980, NASP., file 283(s), part 4.

25. Canadian High Commissioner (London), to Department of External Affairs, Nov. 9, 1948, Tel. 1987, NASP., file 283(s), part 3.

26. Reid to Prime Minister, Nov. 15, 1948, NASP., file 283(s), part 4.

27. Acheson, *Creation*, 702.

28. Claxton to Reid, Dec. 28, 1948, D.E.A., file 283-B(s).

29. Reid to Pearson, memorandum, Dec. 18, 1948, Reid papers, file 11.

30. L.B. Pearson, "H. Hume Wrong", *External Affairs*, (Department of External Affairs, Ottawa), March, 1954, Vol. 6, no. 3, 74.

31. Pearson, *Mike, II, 54, 57, and 70.*

CHAPTER TWENTY: EPILOGUE

1. Reid to Pearson, March 12, 1948, NASP., file 283(s), part 1.

2. Department of National Defence, *Canada's Defence Programme, 1949-1950*, 8.

3. Hickerson to Reid, letter, July 8, 1976, personal communication.

4. *F.R.*, 1949, IV, 54-5.

5. *F.R.*, 1949, IV, 111.

6. *F.R.*, 1948, III, 285.

7. *F.R.*, 1948, III, 281.
8. Reid, memorandum, Oct. 19, 1948, NASP., file 283(s), part 3.
9. James George to Ritchie, April 5, 1950, D.E.A., file 50105-40.
10. Vandenberg, *Private Papers*, 512-13.
11. Reid, memorandum, Dec. 8, 1950, "The defeat in Korea: some suggestions on how the democracies might respond to the challenge", Reid papers, file 10.
12. Reid, "The Revolution in Canadian Foreign Policy, 1947-1951", *India Quarterly*, April-June, 1958, 191-2, and *Aussenpolitik*, July 1958.
13. Bohlen, *Witness*, 304.
14. Pearson, *Mike, II*, 70.
15. James George to Ritchie, April 5, 1950, D.E.A., file 50105-40.
16. Reid to Ritchie, Sept. 7, 1950, D.E.A., file 50105-40.
17. D.V. LePan to Pearson, Sept. 6, 1951, D.E.A., file 50105-40.
18. Reid, memorandum, Oct. 19, 1948, NASP., file 283(s), part 3.
19. James George to Ritchie, April 5, 1950, D.E.A., file 50105-40.
20. LePan to Pearson, memorandum, "The North Atlantic Community", Sept. 6, 1951. D.E.A., file 50105-40.
21. Pearson, *Mike, II*, 70-3
22. Ibid, 92.
23. H.F. Davis memorandum Feb. 4, 1953, "Some recent developments in NATO.", Reid papers, file 13.
24. Reid to R.A. MacKay, April 28, 1954, D.E.A., file 10288-A-46.
25. Pearson, memorandum, June 15, 1956, Reid papers, file 13.
26. Alastair Buchan, "Mothers and Daughters (or Greeks and Romans)," *Foreign Affairs*, July, 1976, 666-7.
27. A.D.P. Heeney to Reid. Nov. 20, 1948, NASP., file 283(s) part 4.
28. Reid to Department of External Affairs, May 31, 1956, Despatch 896, Reid papers, file 10.
29. Dirk Stikker, *Responsibility*, 118.
30. Pearson, *Mike, II*, 92.
31. Reid to Department of External Affairs, "NATO Long-term planning", Sept. 12, 1960, Reid papers, file 11.
32. Ibid.
33. "Extracts from Statements and Speeches at Communist meeting in East Berlin", *New York Times*, July 1, 1976.

NOTES
1. *F.R.*, 1948, I, part 2, 557.
2. Consultative Council of the Foreign Ministers of the Brussels Powers to the Department of External Affairs, Oct. 29, 1948, NASP., file 283(s), part 3.
3. Department of External Affairs to Consultative Council of the Foreign Ministers of the Brussels Powers, Oct. 13, 1948, NASP., file 283(s), part 3.
4. Washington Embassy to Department of External Affairs, Nov. 1, 1948, WA 2833, NASP., File 283(s), part 3.
5. Washington Embassy to Department of External Affairs, March 3, 1949, WA 564, NASP., file 283(s), part 7.
6. Washington Embassy to Department of External Affairs, March 11, 1949, WA 667, NASP., File 283(s), part 8.
7. Washington Embassy to Department of External Affairs, March 25, 1949, WA 856, NASP., File 283(s), part 9.
8. Department of External Affairs to Britain, France, Benelux Countries, and Ambassadors' Committee, letter, March 28, 1949, Wrong papers, file 35.
9. Canadian Embassy (Paris), to Department of External Affairs, March 29, 1949, Tel. 220, NASP., file 283(s), part 9.
10. Canadian High Commissioner (London), to Department of External Affairs, March 28, 1949, Tel 644, NASP., file 283(s), part 9.
11. Canadian Embassy (The Hague), to Department of External Affairs, March 29, 1949, Tel. 86, NASP., File 283(s), part 9.
12. Canadian Embassy (Brussels), to

Department of External Affairs, March 29, 1949, Tel. 43, NASP., File 283(s), part 9.

13. Reid to Wrong, letter, March 23, 1949; Department of External Affairs to Canadian High Commissioner (London), March 23, 1949, Tel. 539; Department of External Affairs to Washington Embassy, March 26, 1949, EX 805; Washington Embassy to Department of External Affairs, March 29, 1949, WA 883; and Department of External Affairs to Washington Embassy, March 30, 1949, EX 866; NASP, file 283(s), part 9.

14. F.R., 1948, III, 182.

15. *F.R.,* 1948, III, 148-9, 182.

16. *The Constitution of the United Nations,* (Free World Research Bureau, April, 1945), 12.

17. Pentagon paper, March 31, 1948, NASP., file 283(s), part 1.

18. Department of External Affairs to Washington Embassy, Feb. 7, 1949, EX 300, and Feb. 27, 1949, EX 510,

NASP., File 283(s), parts 6 and 7.

19. *F.R.*, 1948, III, 246, 248.

20. *F.R.*, 1949, IV, 3.

21. *F.R.*, 1949, IV, 25.

22. *F.R.*, 1949, IV, 27.

23. *F.R.*, 1949, IV, 61, fn. 4

24. Washington Embassy to Department of External Affairs, Jan. 24, 1949, WA 188, NASP., file 283(s), part 6.

25. *F.R.*, 1949, IV, 63, and 66.

26. *F.R.*, 1949, IV, 71.

27. *F.R.*, 1949, IV, 103-04.

28. *F.R.*, 1949, IV, 208.

29. Kennan, *Memoirs*, 426-27.

30. NATO Information Service, *NATO Facts and Figures,* (Brussels, Jan., 1976), 301, fn. 2.

31. Reid to Pearson, June 26, 1948, NASP., file 283(s), part 2.

32. Pearson, *Mike, II*, 59.

33. Draft of Canadian commentary, Nov. 6, 1948, NASP., file 283(s), part 3.

34. Pearson to Wrong, letter, unsigned, Dec. 16, 1948, Wrong papers, file 31.

Index